CATHOLIC HIGH SCHOOL ENTRANCE EXAMS COOP/ HSPT/ TACHS

Fifth Edition

LEARNINGEXPRESS®

NEW YORK

Library of Congress Cataloging-in-Publication Data
Catholic high school entrance exams : COOP/HSP/TACHS.—Fifth edition.
   pages   cm
  ISBN 978-1-57685-933-9
  1. Catholic high schools—United States—Entrance examinations—Study guides—Juvenile literature.
I. LearningExpress (Organization) II. Title: COOP/HSPT.
  LB3060.24.C28 2013
  373.126'2—dc23

                             2013026868

Printed in the United States of America

9 8 7 6 5 4 3 2 1

Fifth Edition

For more information or to place an order, contact LearningExpress at:
  80 Broad Street
  Suite 400
  New York, NY 10004

Or visit us at:
  www.learningexpressllc.com

CONTENTS ▶

CONTENTS

ABOUT THE HSPT

LESSON SUMMARY

This lesson introduces you to the High School Placement Test (HSPT). You'll find out all about the HSPT—its purpose, where it is used, its scoring criteria, how to find out about the exam in your area, and a summary of the exam content. This lesson is also the key to the study lessons in this book—it tells you exactly which lessons you need to study to get a high score.

I f you are an eighth-grade student who plans to attend a private, parish, or diocesan high school, this book is for you. Entry into one of these schools is competitive—that is, more students want to enter the freshman class of a given high school than there are openings in that class. Your edge will come from knowing as much as you can about the entrance exam for the school you've chosen and from careful preparation for taking that exam. This book is designed to give you that edge.

Purpose and Content of the HSPT

Many schools in the United States require applicants to take the High School Placement Test (HSPT), which is the subject of this lesson. (If you live in the Archdiocese of New York, the Archdiocese of Newark, New Jersey, or the Diocese of Brooklyn or Rockland County, however, you will be asked to take the Cooperative Admissions Examination, or COOP, which is the subject of Lesson 2.) The HSPT is a two-and-a-half hour exam whose purpose is to see whether you, as an eighth-grade student, are ready for high school. Your readiness is tested using 298 consecutively numbered questions over five skill areas.

SUBTESTS	NUMBER OF QUESTIONS	TIME ALLOTTED
1. Verbal Skills	60	16 minutes
2. Quantitative Skills	52	30 minutes
3. Reading	62	25 minutes
4. Mathematics	64	45 minutes
5. Language Skills	60	25 minutes

The HSPT also offers optional tests in science, mechanical aptitude, and Catholic religion. The school to which you are applying decides whether you need to take one of these tests. Since these optional areas are not part of the regular HSPT, they are not covered in this book.

Each part of the exam includes several different kinds of questions. You can see examples of all these types of questions in Lesson 4, Practice HSPT Exam 1.

Part 1: Verbal Skills

Verbal Analogies (10 questions): These questions test your ability to see relationships between words and concepts. You'll be given a sentence that contains a set of two words that are related, followed by a third word and four choices. Of the four choices, you will be asked to choose the word that best completes the second set so that the second set expresses the same relationship as the first. For examples and help with answering analogy questions, see Lesson 10, Verbal Reasoning.

Synonyms (15 questions): These questions test your word knowledge. You'll be given a word and asked to pick the word that most nearly means the *same* as the given word. For examples and tips, see Lesson 8, Vocabulary.

Logic (10 questions): These questions test your ability to reason and think logically. You'll be asked whether, based on two statements, a third statement is true, false, or uncertain. See Lesson 10, Verbal Reasoning, for examples of logic questions and advice on how to answer them.

Verbal Classification (16 questions): These questions test both your word knowledge and your verbal reasoning ability. You'll be given four words and asked to pick the one that does not belong with the others. Verbal classification questions are also covered in Lesson 10.

Antonyms (9 questions): Like the synonym questions, these questions test your word knowledge, only this time, you will be asked to pick the word that most nearly means the *opposite* of the given word. For examples and help with antonym questions, see Lesson 8, Vocabulary.

Part 2: Quantitative Skills

Number Series (18 questions): These questions test your ability to reason nonverbally. You'll be given a series of numbers arranged in a set pattern and asked to pick the number that would logically come next in the series. For examples and help in answering number series questions, see Lesson 11, Nonverbal Reasoning.

Geometric Comparison (9 questions): These questions also test your ability to reason nonverbally. You will be shown three geometric figures and asked quantitative questions about the figures—for example, which has more than, which has less than, or which is equal to one of four choices. Geometric comparison questions are covered in Lesson 11, Nonverbal Reasoning.

Non-Geometric Comparison (8 questions): Again, your nonverbal reasoning skills will be tested. You'll be given three number statements and asked quantitative questions about the statements—for example, which is greater than, which is less than, or which is equal to one of four choices. These questions, too, are discussed in Lesson 11, Nonverbal Reasoning.

Number Manipulation (17 questions): These questions test basic math ability. You'll be asked to perform mathematical operations in order to decide which of four choices is the correct answer. For examples and discussion, see Lesson 12, Math Skills.

Part 3: Reading

Comprehension (40 questions): These questions test your ability to understand what you read. You will be asked to read a passage and then answer questions about it. Some questions will test your ability to identify facts in the passage, some will ask you to draw conclusions from what you read, and some will ask you to say what the author intended in writing the passage. For examples and tips on answering reading questions, see Lesson 7, Reading Comprehension.

Vocabulary (22 questions): These questions will ask you to read a short phrase in which one of the words is underlined. From four possible choices, you will choose the word that means the *same* or about the same as the underlined word. Lesson 8, Vocabulary, will help you prepare for this part of the exam.

Part 4: Mathematics

Concepts (24 questions): These questions test your general knowledge of principles underlying math problems. You will be given a math problem and asked to select the general principle or rule behind it. Examples and a review of the math concepts you need are found in Lesson 12, Math Skills.

Problem Solving (40 questions): These questions test your practical math knowledge by asking you to solve mathematical problems. The math you need for these questions is also found in Lesson 12.

Part 5: Language Skills

Punctuation and Capitalization (12 questions): These questions test your knowledge of punctuation and capitalization in the context of a sentence. You will be presented with three sentences from which you are to pick the one with a mistake in capitalization or punctuation. If you do not find an error, you will choose a fourth option, "No mistakes." For examples of and help with the punctuation and capitalization questions, see Lesson 9, Language Skills.

Usage (28 questions): These questions test your knowledge of English word usage. You'll be presented with three sentences from which you are asked to pick the one with a mistake—that is, grammar, word choice, subject-verb agreement, pronoun agreement, and other kinds of mistakes in English usage. If you do not find an error, you may choose a fourth option, "No mistakes." Usage questions are covered in Lesson 9, Language Skills.

Spelling (10 questions): These questions test your knowledge of how to spell particular words. You'll be presented with three sentences from which you are to pick the one with a mistake in spelling. If you do not find an error, you may choose a fourth option, "No mistakes." Lesson 9 is where you should go to get help with spelling questions.

Composition (10 questions): These questions test your ability to recognize effective writing. Some of the questions will ask you to fill in the blank by picking the best word or words to join two thoughts together. Other questions will ask you to choose the sentence that best expresses an idea. Still other questions will ask you to choose which sentence does not belong in a paragraph. Composition questions are also covered in Lesson 9, Language Skills.

Where to Take the Exam

To find out where and when you'll take the HSPT, simply call one of the schools on your list of choices.

Scoring

Scholastic Testing Service, the makers of the test, will determine your HSPT score on the basis of the number of questions you answer right. Wrong answers don't count, so you should respond to as many questions as you can, even by guessing if necessary.

The Scholastic Testing Service will then convert your raw scores to standard scores using a scale of 200 to 800. Included in the HSPT score report are your standard scores, national and local percentile rank, grade equivalent, and Cognitive Skills Quotient. For now, don't worry about what all those things are. Basically, the school to which you are applying will decide what constitutes a passing score.

Your record will be used by Scholastic Testing Service to compare your performance with that of other students in your area, and a report will be sent to the high schools you've listed as ones you'd like to attend. After that, it's up to the individual schools to decide whether your scores qualify you for entrance.

How to Prepare

You've taken your first step in preparing for the HSPT by reading this lesson. You're already starting to get an idea of what to expect.

Take the first practice HSPT exam in Lesson 4. You'll be familiarizing yourself with the test while you find out what your strengths and weaknesses are. After you take the test, you'll know which instructional lessons you need to concentrate on. When you've spent some serious time studying, take the second practice exam in Lesson 13 to see how much you've improved.

Neither this nor any other test-prep book can make up for things you should have learned in grammar school. But you've come to the right place if you need to brush up on some concepts, if you need practice in answering questions in HSPT format, or if you need a good boost in your self-confidence.

2 ▶ ABOUT THE COOP

LESSON SUMMARY

This lesson introduces you to the Cooperative Admissions Examination (COOP). It gives a brief overview of the exam—its purpose, where it is used, its scoring criteria, how to find out about the exam in your area, and a summary of the exam content. Find out how to use this book to prepare for your exam by reading this lesson.

Y ou will have to take the Cooperative Admissions Examination (COOP) if you are an eighth-grade student wishing to make the transition to one of the 36 participating Catholic high schools in the Archdiocese of New York, the Archdiocese of Newark, New Jersey, or the Diocese of Brooklyn or Rockland County. Far more students apply to Catholic high schools in these areas than can be admitted, so the high schools use COOP exam scores to help them decide whether you will be able to do the work required at the given school. This book will give you an important advantage by providing you with information about the exam—and the more information you have, the better off you'll be—as well as by helping you carefully prepare for the exam.

The Application Process

Application forms are distributed through Catholic elementary schools and participating high schools, usually early in September. However, the dates can change from year to year, so *it is important that you call one of the participating schools well before the time of the exam to find out exact deadline dates.* You will return your application form promptly either to your Catholic elementary school or to the testing agency along with a non-refundable fee. (Currently, the fee is $33.00, but you should verify the amount before sending it in.) This fee will entitle you to have a report of your scores sent to three schools of your choice. All admission decisions are made by the schools themselves.

Purpose and Content of the COOP

The COOP exam tests your ability to handle high-school level work. It lasts a little over two-and-a-half hours (plus one 15-minute break).

> The format of the COOP changes slightly from year to year, but you should see approximately seven subtests on the exam.

Read on for a more detailed description of each test on the COOP and a pointer toward the chapters that will help you with each question type.

Test 1: Sequences

This test is designed to measure your ability to reason sequentially. You will be given a sequence of shapes, numbers, or letters in a set pattern and asked to select the shape, number, or letter that would continue the pattern. For examples and help with the sequences test, see Lesson 11, Nonverbal Reasoning.

Test 2: Analogies

This test measures your ability to see and understand relationships. You'll be given a set of two pictures that are somehow related, plus a third picture. You will be asked to select a picture that causes the second set to be related in the same way as the first set. For example, the first two pictures might be a shoe and a foot. If the third picture is a ring, then you should choose a finger, because a ring fits on a finger just as a shoe fits on a foot. See Lesson 11 for examples and help with this kind of analogy question.

SUBTESTS	NUMBER OF QUESTIONS (APPROXIMATE)	TIME ALLOTTED (APPROXIMATE)
1. Sequences	20	15 minutes
2. Analogies	20	7 minutes
3. Quantitative Reasoning	20	15 minutes
4. Verbal Reasoning—Words	20	15 minutes
5. Verbal Reasoning—Context	20	15 minutes
15-MINUTE BREAK		
6. Reading and Language Arts	40	40 minutes
7. Mathematics	40	35 minutes

Test 3: Quantitative Reasoning

Quantitative reasoning questions measure your aptitude for thinking with numbers. Rather than focusing on learned skills, these questions test your reasoning ability. There are three types of quantitative reasoning questions: number relationships, visual problems, and symbol relationships. For examples and practice for this test, see Lesson 11, Nonverbal Reasoning.

Test 4: Verbal Reasoning—Words

Verbal reasoning questions measure your ability to solve verbal problems by reasoning deductively, analyzing category attributes, and discerning relationships and patterns. This test uses a variety of question types. Some questions require you to identify essential elements of objects or concepts, and others require you to classify the choices according to common attributes. Another question type requires you to infer relationships between separate but related sets of words. Lesson 10, Verbal Reasoning, gives you tips and hints on how to tackle these questions.

Test 5: Verbal Reasoning—Context

The verbal reasoning questions (also known as logic questions) measure your ability to solve verbal problems by reasoning deductively. You are required to identify essential elements of ideas presented in short passages and draw logical conclusions. Turn to the Logic Questions section of Lesson 10 for examples and practice with these question types.

Test 6: Reading and Language Arts

This test measures your understanding of reading comprehension and vocabulary. Reading comprehension questions focus on the central meaning of a passage and its specific details. Language questions assess your ability to understand:

- the structure of words
- how words work together to form sentences
- how sentences and paragraphs come together to convey ideas
- how language conventions, such as punctuation and capitalization, combine with the other structures to convey meaning

Aspects of the writing process, such as topic selection, editing, and proofreading, may also be included. See Lessons 7, 8, and 9 for practice in these areas.

Test 7: Mathematics

This test measures your grasp of the principles and rules of mathematics and your ability to solve math problems. Some problems are word problems, and some are not. Your ability to solve the problems depends on your general knowledge of mathematical rules and common sense. Lesson 12, Math Skills, will help you review the math you need for this test.

Scoring

Your raw score on the COOP is determined by allotting one point for each correct answer. There is no penalty for wrong answers, so it is to your advantage to guess if you do not know the answer. Each test on the COOP contains a different number of questions, so test administrators have created a formula by which to convert your raw score to a scaled score, making it possible for them to compare your score to that of other students, as well as to compare your score on one version of the COOP to your score on another. The three schools of your choice will receive a percentile rank for you, for each part of the test.

No one fails and no one passes the COOP. Each student simply receives a score and ranking, and each school has its own standards of admission. These standards include the COOP scores and ranking, and also school grades, recommendations, and other factors.

How to Prepare

You've taken your first step in preparing for the COOP by reading this lesson. You're already starting to get an idea of what to expect.

Take the first practice COOP exam in Lesson 5. You'll be familiarizing yourself with the test while you discover your strengths and weaknesses. After you take the test, you'll know which instructional chapters you need to concentrate on. When you've spent some serious time studying, take the second practice exam in Lesson 14 to see how much you've improved.

Neither this nor any other test-prep book can make up for things you should have learned in elementary school. But you've come to the right place if you need to brush up on some concepts, if you need practice in answering questions in COOP format, or if you need a good boost in your self-confidence.

3 ▶ ABOUT THE TACHS

LESSON SUMMARY
In this lesson, you will learn everything you need to know about the Test for Admission into Catholic High Schools (TACHS). After reading it you will know how to apply for the TACHS, the topics it tests, how you'll receive your scores, and where to find testing centers in your area.

Taking the TACHS is necessary for eighth-grade students interested in attending a Catholic high school. With their smaller classes, advanced courses, and excellent tutoring programs, Catholic high schools have a 95% to 98% graduation rate. So, a lot of students are trying to get into them and the entry process is competitive. The TACHS is an important part of that process. This book will give you a leg up when applying to a Catholic school.

The Registration Process

It is best to register for the TACHS in advance since there may not be enough seats available for test takers who just show up on the day of the exam. Before registering, you'll need school codes for your three preferred schools. These codes can be found in the TACHS handbook on www.tachsinfo.com. Your principal, teacher, or counselor will also have to complete and submit your TACHS Applicant Record to your preferred schools. The Applicant Record form is also on www.tachsinfo.com.

Registering is easy and can be done on the Internet, by telephone, or on paper. The Internet method is the quickest and easiest. Visit www.tachsinfo.com to fill out an online registration form available at certain times of the year. You may also register over the phone by calling 1-866-61TACHS (1-866-618-2247). Multilingual operators are on call Monday to Friday from 8:00 A.M. to 7:00 P.M. and Saturday to Sunday from 10:00 A.M. to 2:00 P.M. Finally, you can register with a mail-in paper registration form. If you choose the paper method you must submit the required $52 examination fee by certified check or money order. Internet and telephone applicants pay by credit card.

Purpose and Content of the TACHS

Catholic schools in the United States require applicants to take the Test for Admission into Catholic High Schools (TACHS) to measure the academic skills of potential students. The TACHS takes about two hours. Its multiple-choice questions test your abilities in four areas: reading, language, math, and abstract reasoning. Don't panic—the questions are designed for average eighth-grade students.

Part 1: Reading

The TACHS opens with a Reading section divided into two parts. First up is the vocabulary test. Here you will be expected to define a word based on how it is used in a sentence or short phrase. You will then select the single-word answer choice with the most similar meaning.

The second part of the Reading portion is the reading comprehension test. This will require a bit more concentration. You will have to read several passages and answer questions about their details and meanings. There is quite a bit of variation in the passages. Some are as short as a few paragraphs; others may be as long as a page. The topics range from fic-tion, including stories, poems, and plays, to nonfiction, including science articles, biographies, and histories.

Part 2: Language

The Language section of the TACHS is broken down into five subsections. The first subsection is the spelling test. This test involves examining four words and deciding which one is misspelled. However, there's a little curve ball in this test. The spelling test is the only section of the TACHS with a fifth answer choice. No need to worry, though. This fifth choice is always the same: "No mistakes." Choose that one when the other four answer choices are all spelled correctly.

The capitalization subsection also features a "no mistakes" option, but there are only four answer choices here. You will have to figure out whether there are any mistakes in the capitalization of names, titles, dates, holidays, places, and organizations in this test.

In the punctuation test, you'll be looking for—you guessed it!—punctuation errors. Select the answer choices in which all punctuation—apostrophes, colons, semicolons, commas, and quotation marks—are used correctly. If they're used correctly in each answer choice, choose—you guessed it again!—"No mistakes."

"No mistakes" is also an option on the usage test. This time you'll read one or two sentences and decide whether there are mistakes in the use of pronouns, verbs, modifiers, and wording.

The final subsection is the expression test. Here you will exercise your editing skills to decide whether a sentence or paragraph is written as clearly as possible. The expression test requires you to evaluate matters of appropriateness, clarity, conciseness, expression, and organization.

Part 3: Math

Unlike the previous two parts, the Math section is not chopped up into subsections. This test is one big bundle of estimation, problem solving, and data interpretation questions. Some questions will require you to interpret information in graphs, tables, and stories.

Part 4: Ability

This last part of the TACHS tests your ability to use your basic abstract reasoning skills. These abilities include memorizing, recognizing patterns, making inferences, and problem solving. The TACHS presents a variety of tasks to measure these abilities, which may require you to use reasoning skills you might not have learned in school.

Where to Take the Exam and What to Take

On the fourth page of the registration form you will find a list of test site choices. There you will select your three preferred sites. After registering you will receive an Admit Card with confirmation of your test site.

On the day of the test, it is wise to arrive at 8:15 A.M. Be sure to have your Admit Card and a valid ID, such as a library card. Food, drinks, calculators, cell phones, and other electronic devices are not allowed in the test site.

Scores

After your TACHS exam has been scored, the results will be sent to your three preferred schools. You can find the latest delivery dates on www.tachsinfo.com. Admission will be based on both your TACHS score and your Applicant Record.

How to Prepare

Okay, so now you know the basics of the TACHS. That means it's time to get specific. In the following chapter you will learn the ins and outs of the TACHS: tips on how to study and perform well on the exam. After that you'll take your first practice TACHS exam. Taking the practice test will give you a good idea of what to expect on the day of the test. It will also give you an idea of your strengths and the weaknesses you need to work on. The lessons that follow won't teach you anything you haven't learned in school, but they will help you improve your weak spots and sharpen your strong ones. The practice test at the end of the book will show you how your skills have improved.

L E S S O N

4 PRACTICE HSPT EXAM 1

LESSON SUMMARY

This is the first of the two practice tests in this book based on the High School Placement Test (HSPT) used by many Catholic high schools as an admissions test. Use this practice exam to see how you would do if you were to take the exam today.

This practice exam is similar to the real High School Placement Test you will be taking. Like the real exam, it is divided into five parts, covering five general skill areas, subdivided and timed as shown on the next page.

SUBTESTS	NUMBER OF QUESTIONS
1. Verbal Skills (16 minutes)	**60 questions**
Verbal Analogies	10
Synonyms	15
Logic	10
Verbal Classification	16
Antonyms	9
2. Quantitative Skills (30 minutes)	**52 questions**
Number Series	18
Geometric Comparison	9
Non-Geometric Comparison	8
Number Manipulation	17
3. Reading (25 minutes)	**62 questions**
Comprehension	40
Vocabulary	22
4. Mathematics (45 minutes)	**64 questions**
Concepts	24
Problem Solving	40
5. Language Skills (25 minutes)	**60 questions**
Punctuation and Capitalization	12
Usage	28
Spelling	10
Composition	10

In the real exam, each part is timed, but for now, don't worry too much about timing. Just find a quiet place and some sharpened number 2 pencils. Then take this practice test to find out in which areas you are skilled and which ones will need extra work. You can follow the time limits when you take the second exam.

The answer sheets are on pages 15–17. Then comes the exam itself, followed by the answer key. In the key, the correct answers are explained in detail. Be sure to read these explanations in order to find out why the correct answers are right and the incorrect answers are wrong. The answer key is followed by a section on how to score your exam.

Part 1: Verbal Skills

1. ⓐ	ⓑ	ⓒ	ⓓ
2. ⓐ	ⓑ	ⓒ	ⓓ
3. ⓐ	ⓑ	ⓒ	ⓓ
4. ⓐ	ⓑ	ⓒ	ⓓ
5. ⓐ	ⓑ	ⓒ	ⓓ
6. ⓐ	ⓑ	ⓒ	ⓓ
7. ⓐ	ⓑ	ⓒ	ⓓ
8. ⓐ	ⓑ	ⓒ	ⓓ
9. ⓐ	ⓑ	ⓒ	ⓓ
10. ⓐ	ⓑ	ⓒ	ⓓ
11. ⓐ	ⓑ	ⓒ	ⓓ
12. ⓐ	ⓑ	ⓒ	ⓓ
13. ⓐ	ⓑ	ⓒ	ⓓ
14. ⓐ	ⓑ	ⓒ	ⓓ
15. ⓐ	ⓑ	ⓒ	ⓓ
16. ⓐ	ⓑ	ⓒ	ⓓ
17. ⓐ	ⓑ	ⓒ	ⓓ
18. ⓐ	ⓑ	ⓒ	ⓓ
19. ⓐ	ⓑ	ⓒ	ⓓ
20. ⓐ	ⓑ	ⓒ	ⓓ
21. ⓐ	ⓑ	ⓒ	ⓓ
22. ⓐ	ⓑ	ⓒ	ⓓ
23. ⓐ	ⓑ	ⓒ	ⓓ
24. ⓐ	ⓑ	ⓒ	ⓓ
25. ⓐ	ⓑ	ⓒ	ⓓ
26. ⓐ	ⓑ	ⓒ	ⓓ
27. ⓐ	ⓑ	ⓒ	ⓓ
28. ⓐ	ⓑ	ⓒ	ⓓ
29. ⓐ	ⓑ	ⓒ	ⓓ
30. ⓐ	ⓑ	ⓒ	ⓓ
31. ⓐ	ⓑ	ⓒ	ⓓ
32. ⓐ	ⓑ	ⓒ	ⓓ
33. ⓐ	ⓑ	ⓒ	ⓓ
34. ⓐ	ⓑ	ⓒ	ⓓ
35. ⓐ	ⓑ	ⓒ	ⓓ
36. ⓐ	ⓑ	ⓒ	ⓓ
37. ⓐ	ⓑ	ⓒ	ⓓ
38. ⓐ	ⓑ	ⓒ	ⓓ
39. ⓐ	ⓑ	ⓒ	ⓓ
40. ⓐ	ⓑ	ⓒ	ⓓ
41. ⓐ	ⓑ	ⓒ	ⓓ
42. ⓐ	ⓑ	ⓒ	ⓓ
43. ⓐ	ⓑ	ⓒ	ⓓ
44. ⓐ	ⓑ	ⓒ	ⓓ
45. ⓐ	ⓑ	ⓒ	ⓓ
46. ⓐ	ⓑ	ⓒ	ⓓ
47. ⓐ	ⓑ	ⓒ	ⓓ
48. ⓐ	ⓑ	ⓒ	ⓓ
49. ⓐ	ⓑ	ⓒ	ⓓ
50. ⓐ	ⓑ	ⓒ	ⓓ
51. ⓐ	ⓑ	ⓒ	ⓓ
52. ⓐ	ⓑ	ⓒ	ⓓ
53. ⓐ	ⓑ	ⓒ	ⓓ
54. ⓐ	ⓑ	ⓒ	ⓓ
55. ⓐ	ⓑ	ⓒ	ⓓ
56. ⓐ	ⓑ	ⓒ	ⓓ
57. ⓐ	ⓑ	ⓒ	ⓓ
58. ⓐ	ⓑ	ⓒ	ⓓ
59. ⓐ	ⓑ	ⓒ	ⓓ
60. ⓐ	ⓑ	ⓒ	ⓓ

Part 2: Quantitative Skills

61. ⓐ	ⓑ	ⓒ	ⓓ
62. ⓐ	ⓑ	ⓒ	ⓓ
63. ⓐ	ⓑ	ⓒ	ⓓ
64. ⓐ	ⓑ	ⓒ	ⓓ
65. ⓐ	ⓑ	ⓒ	ⓓ
66. ⓐ	ⓑ	ⓒ	ⓓ
67. ⓐ	ⓑ	ⓒ	ⓓ
68. ⓐ	ⓑ	ⓒ	ⓓ
69. ⓐ	ⓑ	ⓒ	ⓓ
70. ⓐ	ⓑ	ⓒ	ⓓ
71. ⓐ	ⓑ	ⓒ	ⓓ
72. ⓐ	ⓑ	ⓒ	ⓓ
73. ⓐ	ⓑ	ⓒ	ⓓ
74. ⓐ	ⓑ	ⓒ	ⓓ
75. ⓐ	ⓑ	ⓒ	ⓓ
76. ⓐ	ⓑ	ⓒ	ⓓ
77. ⓐ	ⓑ	ⓒ	ⓓ
78. ⓐ	ⓑ	ⓒ	ⓓ
79. ⓐ	ⓑ	ⓒ	ⓓ
80. ⓐ	ⓑ	ⓒ	ⓓ
81. ⓐ	ⓑ	ⓒ	ⓓ
82. ⓐ	ⓑ	ⓒ	ⓓ
83. ⓐ	ⓑ	ⓒ	ⓓ
84. ⓐ	ⓑ	ⓒ	ⓓ
85. ⓐ	ⓑ	ⓒ	ⓓ
86. ⓐ	ⓑ	ⓒ	ⓓ
87. ⓐ	ⓑ	ⓒ	ⓓ
88. ⓐ	ⓑ	ⓒ	ⓓ
89. ⓐ	ⓑ	ⓒ	ⓓ
90. ⓐ	ⓑ	ⓒ	ⓓ
91. ⓐ	ⓑ	ⓒ	ⓓ
92. ⓐ	ⓑ	ⓒ	ⓓ
93. ⓐ	ⓑ	ⓒ	ⓓ
94. ⓐ	ⓑ	ⓒ	ⓓ
95. ⓐ	ⓑ	ⓒ	ⓓ
96. ⓐ	ⓑ	ⓒ	ⓓ
97. ⓐ	ⓑ	ⓒ	ⓓ
98. ⓐ	ⓑ	ⓒ	ⓓ
99. ⓐ	ⓑ	ⓒ	ⓓ
100. ⓐ	ⓑ	ⓒ	ⓓ
101. ⓐ	ⓑ	ⓒ	ⓓ
102. ⓐ	ⓑ	ⓒ	ⓓ
103. ⓐ	ⓑ	ⓒ	ⓓ
104. ⓐ	ⓑ	ⓒ	ⓓ
105. ⓐ	ⓑ	ⓒ	ⓓ
106. ⓐ	ⓑ	ⓒ	ⓓ
107. ⓐ	ⓑ	ⓒ	ⓓ
108. ⓐ	ⓑ	ⓒ	ⓓ
109. ⓐ	ⓑ	ⓒ	ⓓ
110. ⓐ	ⓑ	ⓒ	ⓓ
111. ⓐ	ⓑ	ⓒ	ⓓ
112. ⓐ	ⓑ	ⓒ	ⓓ

Part 3: Reading

113.	ⓐ ⓑ ⓒ ⓓ	134.	ⓐ ⓑ ⓒ ⓓ	154.	ⓐ ⓑ ⓒ ⓓ
114.	ⓐ ⓑ ⓒ ⓓ	135.	ⓐ ⓑ ⓒ ⓓ	155.	ⓐ ⓑ ⓒ ⓓ
115.	ⓐ ⓑ ⓒ ⓓ	136.	ⓐ ⓑ ⓒ ⓓ	156.	ⓐ ⓑ ⓒ ⓓ
116.	ⓐ ⓑ ⓒ ⓓ	136.	ⓐ ⓑ ⓒ ⓓ	157.	ⓐ ⓑ ⓒ ⓓ
117.	ⓐ ⓑ ⓒ ⓓ	137.	ⓐ ⓑ ⓒ ⓓ	158.	ⓐ ⓑ ⓒ ⓓ
118.	ⓐ ⓑ ⓒ ⓓ	138.	ⓐ ⓑ ⓒ ⓓ	159.	ⓐ ⓑ ⓒ ⓓ
119.	ⓐ ⓑ ⓒ ⓓ	139.	ⓐ ⓑ ⓒ ⓓ	160.	ⓐ ⓑ ⓒ ⓓ
120.	ⓐ ⓑ ⓒ ⓓ	140.	ⓐ ⓑ ⓒ ⓓ	161.	ⓐ ⓑ ⓒ ⓓ
121.	ⓐ ⓑ ⓒ ⓓ	141.	ⓐ ⓑ ⓒ ⓓ	162.	ⓐ ⓑ ⓒ ⓓ
122.	ⓐ ⓑ ⓒ ⓓ	142.	ⓐ ⓑ ⓒ ⓓ	163.	ⓐ ⓑ ⓒ ⓓ
123.	ⓐ ⓑ ⓒ ⓓ	143.	ⓐ ⓑ ⓒ ⓓ	164.	ⓐ ⓑ ⓒ ⓓ
124.	ⓐ ⓑ ⓒ ⓓ	144.	ⓐ ⓑ ⓒ ⓓ	165.	ⓐ ⓑ ⓒ ⓓ
125.	ⓐ ⓑ ⓒ ⓓ	145.	ⓐ ⓑ ⓒ ⓓ	166.	ⓐ ⓑ ⓒ ⓓ
126.	ⓐ ⓑ ⓒ ⓓ	146.	ⓐ ⓑ ⓒ ⓓ	167.	ⓐ ⓑ ⓒ ⓓ
127.	ⓐ ⓑ ⓒ ⓓ	147.	ⓐ ⓑ ⓒ ⓓ	168.	ⓐ ⓑ ⓒ ⓓ
128.	ⓐ ⓑ ⓒ ⓓ	148.	ⓐ ⓑ ⓒ ⓓ	169.	ⓐ ⓑ ⓒ ⓓ
129.	ⓐ ⓑ ⓒ ⓓ	149.	ⓐ ⓑ ⓒ ⓓ	170.	ⓐ ⓑ ⓒ ⓓ
130.	ⓐ ⓑ ⓒ ⓓ	150.	ⓐ ⓑ ⓒ ⓓ	171.	ⓐ ⓑ ⓒ ⓓ
131.	ⓐ ⓑ ⓒ ⓓ	151.	ⓐ ⓑ ⓒ ⓓ	172.	ⓐ ⓑ ⓒ ⓓ
132.	ⓐ ⓑ ⓒ ⓓ	152.	ⓐ ⓑ ⓒ ⓓ	173.	ⓐ ⓑ ⓒ ⓓ
133.	ⓐ ⓑ ⓒ ⓓ	153.	ⓐ ⓑ ⓒ ⓓ	174.	ⓐ ⓑ ⓒ ⓓ

Part 4: Mathematics

175.	ⓐ ⓑ ⓒ ⓓ	197.	ⓐ ⓑ ⓒ ⓓ	218.	ⓐ ⓑ ⓒ ⓓ
176.	ⓐ ⓑ ⓒ ⓓ	198.	ⓐ ⓑ ⓒ ⓓ	219.	ⓐ ⓑ ⓒ ⓓ
177.	ⓐ ⓑ ⓒ ⓓ	199.	ⓐ ⓑ ⓒ ⓓ	220.	ⓐ ⓑ ⓒ ⓓ
178.	ⓐ ⓑ ⓒ ⓓ	200.	ⓐ ⓑ ⓒ ⓓ	221.	ⓐ ⓑ ⓒ ⓓ
179.	ⓐ ⓑ ⓒ ⓓ	201.	ⓐ ⓑ ⓒ ⓓ	222.	ⓐ ⓑ ⓒ ⓓ
180.	ⓐ ⓑ ⓒ ⓓ	202.	ⓐ ⓑ ⓒ ⓓ	223.	ⓐ ⓑ ⓒ ⓓ
181.	ⓐ ⓑ ⓒ ⓓ	203.	ⓐ ⓑ ⓒ ⓓ	224.	ⓐ ⓑ ⓒ ⓓ
182.	ⓐ ⓑ ⓒ ⓓ	204.	ⓐ ⓑ ⓒ ⓓ	225.	ⓐ ⓑ ⓒ ⓓ
183.	ⓐ ⓑ ⓒ ⓓ	205.	ⓐ ⓑ ⓒ ⓓ	226.	ⓐ ⓑ ⓒ ⓓ
184.	ⓐ ⓑ ⓒ ⓓ	206.	ⓐ ⓑ ⓒ ⓓ	227.	ⓐ ⓑ ⓒ ⓓ
185.	ⓐ ⓑ ⓒ ⓓ	207.	ⓐ ⓑ ⓒ ⓓ	228.	ⓐ ⓑ ⓒ ⓓ
186.	ⓐ ⓑ ⓒ ⓓ	208.	ⓐ ⓑ ⓒ ⓓ	229.	ⓐ ⓑ ⓒ ⓓ
187.	ⓐ ⓑ ⓒ ⓓ	209.	ⓐ ⓑ ⓒ ⓓ	230.	ⓐ ⓑ ⓒ ⓓ
188.	ⓐ ⓑ ⓒ ⓓ	210.	ⓐ ⓑ ⓒ ⓓ	231.	ⓐ ⓑ ⓒ ⓓ
189.	ⓐ ⓑ ⓒ ⓓ	211.	ⓐ ⓑ ⓒ ⓓ	232.	ⓐ ⓑ ⓒ ⓓ
190.	ⓐ ⓑ ⓒ ⓓ	212.	ⓐ ⓑ ⓒ ⓓ	233.	ⓐ ⓑ ⓒ ⓓ
191.	ⓐ ⓑ ⓒ ⓓ	213.	ⓐ ⓑ ⓒ ⓓ	234.	ⓐ ⓑ ⓒ ⓓ
192.	ⓐ ⓑ ⓒ ⓓ	214.	ⓐ ⓑ ⓒ ⓓ	235.	ⓐ ⓑ ⓒ ⓓ
193.	ⓐ ⓑ ⓒ ⓓ	215.	ⓐ ⓑ ⓒ ⓓ	236.	ⓐ ⓑ ⓒ ⓓ
194.	ⓐ ⓑ ⓒ ⓓ	216.	ⓐ ⓑ ⓒ ⓓ	237.	ⓐ ⓑ ⓒ ⓓ
195.	ⓐ ⓑ ⓒ ⓓ	217.	ⓐ ⓑ ⓒ ⓓ	238.	ⓐ ⓑ ⓒ ⓓ
196.	ⓐ ⓑ ⓒ ⓓ				

Part 5: Language Skills

239.	ⓐ	ⓑ	ⓒ	ⓓ
240.	ⓐ	ⓑ	ⓒ	ⓓ
241.	ⓐ	ⓑ	ⓒ	ⓓ
242.	ⓐ	ⓑ	ⓒ	ⓓ
243.	ⓐ	ⓑ	ⓒ	ⓓ
244.	ⓐ	ⓑ	ⓒ	ⓓ
245.	ⓐ	ⓑ	ⓒ	ⓓ
246.	ⓐ	ⓑ	ⓒ	ⓓ
247.	ⓐ	ⓑ	ⓒ	ⓓ
248.	ⓐ	ⓑ	ⓒ	ⓓ
249.	ⓐ	ⓑ	ⓒ	ⓓ
250.	ⓐ	ⓑ	ⓒ	ⓓ
251.	ⓐ	ⓑ	ⓒ	ⓓ
252.	ⓐ	ⓑ	ⓒ	ⓓ
253.	ⓐ	ⓑ	ⓒ	ⓓ
254.	ⓐ	ⓑ	ⓒ	ⓓ
255.	ⓐ	ⓑ	ⓒ	ⓓ
256.	ⓐ	ⓑ	ⓒ	ⓓ
257.	ⓐ	ⓑ	ⓒ	ⓓ
258.	ⓐ	ⓑ	ⓒ	ⓓ

259.	ⓐ	ⓑ	ⓒ	ⓓ
260.	ⓐ	ⓑ	ⓒ	ⓓ
261.	ⓐ	ⓑ	ⓒ	ⓓ
262.	ⓐ	ⓑ	ⓒ	ⓓ
263.	ⓐ	ⓑ	ⓒ	ⓓ
264.	ⓐ	ⓑ	ⓒ	ⓓ
265.	ⓐ	ⓑ	ⓒ	ⓓ
266.	ⓐ	ⓑ	ⓒ	ⓓ
267.	ⓐ	ⓑ	ⓒ	ⓓ
268.	ⓐ	ⓑ	ⓒ	ⓓ
269.	ⓐ	ⓑ	ⓒ	ⓓ
270.	ⓐ	ⓑ	ⓒ	ⓓ
271.	ⓐ	ⓑ	ⓒ	ⓓ
272.	ⓐ	ⓑ	ⓒ	ⓓ
273.	ⓐ	ⓑ	ⓒ	ⓓ
274.	ⓐ	ⓑ	ⓒ	ⓓ
275.	ⓐ	ⓑ	ⓒ	ⓓ
276.	ⓐ	ⓑ	ⓒ	ⓓ
277.	ⓐ	ⓑ	ⓒ	ⓓ
278.	ⓐ	ⓑ	ⓒ	ⓓ

279.	ⓐ	ⓑ	ⓒ	ⓓ
280.	ⓐ	ⓑ	ⓒ	ⓓ
281.	ⓐ	ⓑ	ⓒ	ⓓ
282.	ⓐ	ⓑ	ⓒ	ⓓ
283.	ⓐ	ⓑ	ⓒ	ⓓ
284.	ⓐ	ⓑ	ⓒ	ⓓ
285.	ⓐ	ⓑ	ⓒ	ⓓ
286.	ⓐ	ⓑ	ⓒ	ⓓ
287.	ⓐ	ⓑ	ⓒ	ⓓ
288.	ⓐ	ⓑ	ⓒ	ⓓ
289.	ⓐ	ⓑ	ⓒ	ⓓ
290.	ⓐ	ⓑ	ⓒ	ⓓ
291.	ⓐ	ⓑ	ⓒ	ⓓ
292.	ⓐ	ⓑ	ⓒ	ⓓ
293.	ⓐ	ⓑ	ⓒ	ⓓ
294.	ⓐ	ⓑ	ⓒ	ⓓ
295.	ⓐ	ⓑ	ⓒ	ⓓ
296.	ⓐ	ⓑ	ⓒ	ⓓ
297.	ⓐ	ⓑ	ⓒ	ⓓ
298.	ⓐ	ⓑ	ⓒ	ⓓ

Part 1: Verbal Skills

Time: 16 minutes

1. Which word does NOT belong with the others?
   a. fire
   b. log
   c. stone
   d. spark

2. Which word does NOT belong with the others?
   a. sincere
   b. honest
   c. genuine
   d. deceitful

3. Betty is older than Megan. Polly is older than Betty. Megan is older than Polly. If the first two statements are true, the third is
   a. true.
   b. false.
   c. uncertain.
   d. repetitive.

4. Saturate most nearly means
   a. deprive.
   b. construe.
   c. soak.
   d. verify.

5. A cheerful person is
   a. industrious.
   b. ebullient.
   c. tired.
   d. shy.

6. Door is to hinge as jet is to
   a. passenger.
   b. wing.
   c. ticket.
   d. airport.

7. Marathon is to race as hibernation is to
   a. winter.
   b. bear.
   c. nap.
   d. sleep.

8. Which word does NOT belong with the others?
   a. apple
   b. cherry
   c. tomato
   d. red

9. Punctual means the opposite of
   a. random.
   b. smooth.
   c. intermittent.
   d. tardy.

10. Communication is to telephone as transportation is to
   a. aviation.
   b. travel.
   c. information.
   d. bus.

11. Tactful is to diplomatic as bashful is to
   a. timid.
   b. confident.
   c. uncomfortable.
   d. bold.

12. Impassive most nearly means
   a. active.
   b. apathetic.
   c. blatant.
   d. abundant.

13. A dormant plant is
   a. dead.
   b. resting.
   c. expanding.
   d. green.

14. During the past year, Zoe read more books than Jenna. Jenna read fewer books than Heather. Heather read more books than Zoe. If the first two statements are true, the third is
 a. true.
 b. false.
 c. uncertain.
 d. repetitive.

15. Scarcely is to mostly as quietly is to
 a. secretly.
 b. rudely.
 c. loudly.
 d. silently.

16. Passive means the opposite of
 a. active.
 b. hideous.
 c. exit.
 d. left.

17. Which word does NOT belong with the others?
 a. radio
 b. magazine
 c. newspaper
 d. book

18. Which word does NOT belong with the others?
 a. milk
 b. water
 c. juice
 d. cereal

19. All the houses on Reynolds Road have roofs made of shingles. No shingles are purple. None of the houses on Reynolds Road have purple roofs. If the first two statements are true, the third is
 a. true.
 b. false.
 c. uncertain.
 d. repetitive.

20. Zipper is to button as oak is to
 a. jacket.
 b. elm.
 c. banana.
 d. run.

21. Timid most nearly means
 a. frightened.
 b. angry.
 c. apologetic.
 d. hungry.

22. Replica most nearly means
 a. snakelike.
 b. lackluster.
 c. metamorphosis.
 d. duplicate.

23. Lake Mead is colder than Walden Pond. Brown River is warmer than Red Swamp. Red Swamp is colder than Lake Mead. If the first two statements are true, the third is
 a. true.
 b. false.
 c. uncertain.
 d. repetitive.

24. Battery X lasts longer than Battery Y. Battery Y doesn't last as long as Battery Z. Battery Z lasts longer than Battery X. If the first two statements are true, the third is
 a. true.
 b. false.
 c. uncertain.
 d. repetitive.

25. Which word does NOT belong with the others?
 a. speedy
 b. quickly
 c. hurried
 d. late

26. Which word does NOT belong with the others?
　　a. book
　　b. index
　　c. glossary
　　d. lesson

27. Amateur means the opposite of
　　a. reality.
　　b. professional.
　　c. corrupt.
　　d. precise.

28. Tacit means the opposite of
　　a. exit.
　　b. explicit.
　　c. reverse.
　　d. expend.

29. Which word does NOT belong with the others?
　　a. noun
　　b. preposition
　　c. punctuation
　　d. adverb

30. If a person is called a sage, he or she is
　　a. wise.
　　b. obnoxious.
　　c. conceited.
　　d. heartless.

31. Unite most nearly means
　　a. engineer.
　　b. enhance.
　　c. sunder.
　　d. amalgamate.

32. Play is to actor as concert is to
　　a. symphony.
　　b. musician.
　　c. piano.
　　d. percussion.

33. All spotted Gangles have long tails. Short-haired Gangles always have short tails. Long-tailed Gangles never have short hair. If the first two statements are true, the third statement is
　　a. true.
　　b. false.
　　c. uncertain.
　　d. repetitive.

34. Requirement means the opposite of
　　a. plan.
　　b. consequence.
　　c. option.
　　d. accident.

35. Pacify means the opposite of
　　a. complicate.
　　b. dismiss.
　　c. excite.
　　d. liberate.

36. Which word does NOT belong with the others?
　　a. pillow
　　b. cushion
　　c. pad
　　d. pitch

37. The temperature on Monday was lower than on Tuesday. The temperature on Wednesday was lower than on Tuesday. The temperature on Monday was higher than on Wednesday. If the first two statements are true, the third statement is
　　a. true.
　　b. false.
　　c. uncertain.
　　d. repetitive.

38. Rectify most nearly means
　　a. correct.
　　b. add.
　　c. bonus.
　　d. historical.

39. Antagonist most nearly means
   a. comrade.
   b. opponent.
   c. master.
   d. perfectionist.

40. Which word does NOT belong with the others?
   a. ski
   b. sled
   c. toboggan
   d. snow

41. Pride is to lion as school is to
   a. teacher.
   b. student.
   c. self-respect.
   d. fish.

42. Control is to dominate as magnify is to
   a. enlarge.
   b. preserve.
   c. decrease.
   d. divide.

43. Enumerate most nearly means
   a. pronounce.
   b. count.
   c. explain.
   d. plead.

44. An impartial jury is
   a. complete.
   b. prejudiced.
   c. fair.
   d. emotional.

45. Airfare at Eastern Airlines costs less than airfare at Northern Airlines. Airfare at Western Airlines costs more than airfare at Northern Airlines. Of the three, Western Airlines costs the most. If the first two statements are true, the third is
   a. true.
   b. false.
   c. uncertain.
   d. repetitive.

46. Which word does NOT belong with the others?
   a. inch
   b. ounce
   c. centimeter
   d. yard

47. Equine most nearly means
   a. elegant.
   b. tardy.
   c. horse.
   d. domesticated.

48. Faltering means the opposite of
   a. steady.
   b. adoring.
   c. explanatory.
   d. reluctant.

49. Which word does NOT belong with the others?
   a. street
   b. freeway
   c. interstate
   d. expressway

50. Fruit is to lemon as store is to
   a. yellow.
   b. cat.
   c. grocery.
   d. credit.

51. Humidify most nearly means
  a. moisten.
  b. warm.
  c. gather.
  d. spray.

52. Which word does NOT belong with the others?
  a. sunshine
  b. rain
  c. umbrella
  d. snow

53. The opposite of ventilate is
  a. caterpillar.
  b. radiate.
  c. smother.
  d. crawl.

54. Which word does NOT belong with the others?
  a. dodge
  b. flee
  c. duck
  d. avoid

55. Girl Scout Troop 101 sells more cookies than Troop 102. Troop 103 sells fewer cookies than Troop 102. Troop 101 sold more cookies than Troop 103. If the first two statements are true, the third statement is
  a. true.
  b. false.
  c. uncertain.
  d. repetitive.

56. Andre jumps higher than Rodney. James jumps higher than Andre. Rodney jumps higher than James. If the first two statements are true, the third statement is
  a. true.
  b. false.
  c. uncertain.
  d. repetitive.

57. A studious person is
  a. reticent.
  b. tardy.
  c. thin.
  d. scholarly.

58. Which word does NOT belong with the others?
  a. heading
  b. body
  c. closing
  d. letter

59. Which word does NOT belong with the others?
  a. toe
  b. heel
  c. arch
  d. walk

60. Levitate means the opposite of
  a. plod.
  b. undulate.
  c. whisper.
  d. sink.

Part 2: Quantitative Skills

Time: 30 minutes

61. Look at this series: $1, 4, 7, 8, 7, \ldots$
What number should come next?
a. 6
b. 9
c. 12
d. 15

62. Examine (A), (B), and (C) and find the best answer.

   (A)   (B)   (C)

a. (A) is more shaded than (B).
b. (B) is less shaded than (C).
c. (A) and (B) are equally shaded.
d. (B) and (C) are equally shaded.

63. What number is $\frac{1}{2}$ of 40% of 10?
a. 1
b. 2
c. 3
d. 4

64. Examine (A), (B), and (C) and find the best answer.
   (A) $3 + (2 \times 1)$
   (B) $8 - (2 \times 2)$
   (C) 10 divided by $(1 + 1)$
a. (A) and (B) are equal.
b. (C) is greater than (B).
c. (A) is greater than (B) but less than (C).
d. (C) is greater than (B) but less than (A).

65. Look at this series: $567, 542, 517, 492, \ldots$
What number should come next?
a. 499
b. 483
c. 477
d. 467

66. Look at this series: $9, 12, 11, 14, 13, 16, 15, \ldots$
What two numbers should come next?
a. 14, 13
b. 8, 21
c. 14, 17
d. 18, 17

67. Examine (A), (B), and (C) and find the best answer.

   (A)   (B)   (C)

a. The number of lines in (A) and (C) together equals the number of lines in (B).
b. The number of lines in (B) is five more than the number of lines in (C).
c. The number of lines in (A) is two more than the number of lines in (B).
d. The number of lines in (B) and (C) together is five more than the number of lines in (A).

68. What number is 7 less than $\frac{3}{4}$ of 20?
a. -2
b. 8
c. 10
d. 13

69. Examine (A), (B), and (C) and find the best answer.

    (A) $\frac{1}{3}$ of 12

    (B) 4% of 100

    (C) $\frac{1}{5}$ of 10

  a. (A) is less than (C).

  b. (A) and (B) are equal.

  c. (A) plus (B) is equal to (C).

  d. (C) is greater than (B).

70. What number is 2 less than 3% of 200?

  a. 1

  b. 4

  c. 22

  d. 58

71. What number divided by 6 is $\frac{1}{2}$ of 18?

  a. 9

  b. 24

  c. 36

  d. 54

72. Look at this series: $1, \frac{7}{8}, \frac{3}{4}, \frac{5}{8}, \ldots$
What number should come next?

  a. $\frac{2}{3}$

  b. $\frac{1}{2}$

  c. $\frac{3}{8}$

  d. $\frac{1}{4}$

73. Examine the triangle and find the best answer.

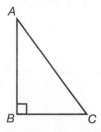

  a. *AB* is equal to *AC*.

  b. *AB* is less than *AC*.

  c. *BC* is greater than *AC*.

  d. *AB* is equal to *BC*.

74. What is 12 more than 30% of 90?

  a. 15

  b. 39

  c. 42

  d. 52

75. Examine (A), (B), and (C) and find the best answer.

    (A) $\frac{1}{2} \times \frac{1}{4}$

    (B) $\frac{1}{8} \times \frac{1}{2}$

    (C) $\frac{1}{4} \times \frac{1}{8}$

  a. (A) is greater than (B) or (C).

  b. (A) is greater than (B) but less than (C).

  c. (C) is greater than (A) or (B).

  d. (B) is greater than (C) or (A).

76. What number is 20% of 10 times 16?

  a. 11

  b. 22

  c. 32

  d. 36

77. What number divided by 3 equals $\frac{1}{3}$ of 9?

  a. 3

  b. 5

  c. 7

  d. 9

78. Look at this series: XX, XVI, XII, VIII, . . .
What number should come next?

  a. IV

  b. V

  c. VI

  d. III

79. Examine the graph and find the best answer.

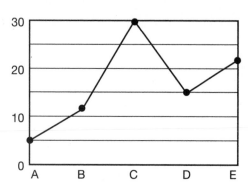

    a. (B) is greater than (E).
    b. (C) minus (A) is equal to (B).
    c. (C) minus (E) is equal to (D).
    d. (D) plus (E) is greater than (C).

80. Examine (A), (B), and (C) and find the best answer where a is a positive number.
    (A) $3a$
    (B) $2(a + a)$
    (C) $2a + a$
    a. (A) and (B) are equal.
    b. (A) and (C) are equal.
    c. (C) is greater than (B).
    d. (A) and (C) are equal to (B).

81. What number is 7 times 3 divided by $\frac{1}{3}$?
    a. $2\frac{1}{3}$
    b. 7
    c. 63
    d. 84

82. Look at this series: $2, 1, \frac{1}{2}, \frac{1}{4}, \ldots$
What number should come next?
    a. $\frac{1}{3}$
    b. $\frac{1}{8}$
    c. $\frac{2}{8}$
    d. $\frac{1}{16}$

83. Look at this series: 21, 24, 30, 21, 36, 42, . . .
What number should come next?
    a. 21
    b. 27
    c. 42
    d. 46

84. What number subtracted from 50 leaves 13 more than $\frac{1}{4}$ of 8?
    a. 15
    b. 25
    c. 27
    d. 35

85. Examine (A), (B), and (C) and find the best answer.

(A) 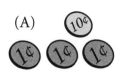   (B)

(C)

    a. (A) plus (C) is greater than (B).
    b. (A) plus (C) is less than (B).
    c. (C) minus (B) equals (A).
    d. (B) minus (C) equals (A).

86. Look at this series: 90, 30, _____, 20, 40, . . .
What number should fill in the blank?
    a. 36
    b. 45
    c. 60
    d. 80

87. Examine (A), (B), and (C) and find the best answer.

(A) $\frac{1}{3} \times 9$

(B) $\frac{1}{4} \times 16$

(C) $\frac{1}{3} \times 15$

a. (A) and (C) are equal.

b. (B) is less than (A).

c. (A) and (B) are equal to (C).

d. (B) is greater than (A) but less than (C).

88. What number is 17 less than 140% of 5?

a. −10

b. −7

c. 7

d. 53

89. Look at this series: 20, 10, 12, 6, 8, . . . What number should come next?

a. 2

b. 3

c. 4

d. 6

90. Look at this series: 5.6, 6.4, 7.2, 8.0, . . . What number should come next?

a. 8.4

b. 10.6

c. 8.8

d. 9.4

91. Examine (A), (B), and (C) and find the best answer.

(A) 2^3

(B) 3^2

(C) 7

a. (A) is greater than (B) or (C).

b. (A) is less than (B) or (C).

c. (B) is greater than (A) or (C).

d. (A) and (B) are equal to (C).

92. Examine (A), (B), and (C) and find the best answer.

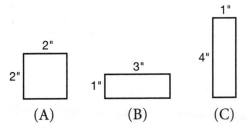

(A)   (B)   (C)

a. The area of (A) is equal to the area of (B).

b. The area of (A) is equal to the area of (C).

c. The area of (B) is equal to the area of (C).

d. The area of (A) is less than the area of (B).

93. What number added to 16 more than the same number equals 136?

a. 152

b. 120

c. 72

d. 60

94. Look at this series: 10, 34, 12, 31, __, 28, 16, . . . What number should fill the blank?

a. 14

b. 18

c. 30

d. 34

95. What number times 8 less than 20% of 60 equals 24?

a. −6

b. 6

c. 18

d. 34

96. Examine (A), (B), and (C) and find the best answer.

(A)   (B)   (C)

    a. (A) is more shaded than (C).
    b. (A) and (C) are equally shaded.
    c. (B) and (C) are equally shaded.
    d. (B) is less shaded than (A).

97. What number is half as large as $\frac{1}{3}$ of 75?
    a. 8.75
    b. 12.5
    c. 15
    d. 16.25

98. What number divided by 3 is $\frac{3}{5}$ of 50?
    a. 150
    b. 130
    c. 90
    d. 10

99. Examine (A), (B), and (C) and find the best answer.
    (A) $(1 + 5)^2$
    (B) $3(13 - 2)$
    (C) $(4 + 2) + (12 + 12)$
    a. (A) is greater than (C) but less than (B).
    b. (B) and (C) are equal.
    c. (C) is less than (A) or (B).
    d. (B) is less than (C).

100. Look at this series: 6, 9, 13.5, 20.25, . . . What number should come next?
    a. 18.675
    b. 22
    c. 28.5
    d. 30.375

101. What number times 7 is $\frac{1}{2}$ of 28?
    a. 2
    b. 4
    c. 21
    d. 56

102. Examine (A), (B), and (C) and find the best answer.

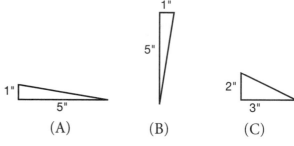

(A)   (B)   (C)

    a. The area of (A), the area of (B), and the area of (C) are all equal.
    b. The area of (A) is equal to the area of (B).
    c. The area of (C) is less than the area of (B).
    d. The area of (A) is greater than the area of (C).

103. Look at this series: K12, J16, I20, H24, . . . What number should come next?
    a. I28
    b. G22
    c. G28
    d. F32

104. Look at this series: 31, 29, 24, 22, 17, . . . What number should come next?
    a. 15
    b. 14
    c. 13
    d. 12

105. Examine (A), (B), (C), and (D) and find the best answer.

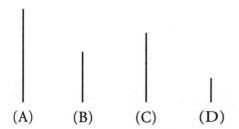

(A)   (B)   (C)   (D)

    a. (A) is longer than (B) but shorter than (C).
    b. (C) is longer than (B) but shorter than (A).
    c. (B) and (C) are equal to (A).
    d. (D) minus (B) is equal to (C).

106. What number times 4 is equal to 72 minus 20?
    a. 208
    b. 48
    c. 13
    d. 7.5

107. Look at this series: VI, 10, V, 11, IV, 12, . . .
What number should come next?
    a. VII
    b. III
    c. IX
    d. 13

108. Three times what number plus 50 equals 74?
    a. 8
    b. 24
    c. 41.3
    d. 48

109. Look at this series: 14, 28, 20, 40, 32, 64, . . .
What number should come next?
    a. 52
    b. 56
    c. 96
    d. 128

110. Look at this series: $0.2, \frac{1}{5}, 0.4, \frac{2}{5}, 0.8, \frac{4}{5}, \ldots$
What number should come next?
    a. $\frac{8}{10}$
    b. $1\frac{3}{5}$
    c. 1.6
    d. 0.16

111. What number is 16 times $\frac{1}{2}$ of 10% of 40?
    a. 3.2
    b. 12
    c. 28
    d. 32

112. Examine (A), (B), and (C) and find the best answer.
    (A) $\frac{9}{5}$
    (B) 1.6
    (C) $1\frac{3}{10}$
    a. (B) is greater than (C) but less than (A).
    b. (A) is less than (B).
    c. (A) and (C) are equal to (B).
    d. (B) minus (A) is equal to (C).

Part 3: Reading

Time: 25 minutes

For questions 113 through 152, read each passage carefully. Answer the questions that follow only on the basis of their preceding passage.

Greyhounds

Greyhound racing is the sixth most popular spectator sport in the United States. Over the last decade, a growing number of greyhounds have been adopted to live out their retirement as household pets, once their racing career is over.

    Many people hesitate to adopt a retired racing greyhound because they think only very old dogs are available. Actually, even champion racers only work until they are about three-and-a-half years old. Since greyhounds usually live to between 12 and 15 years old, their retirement is much longer than their racing careers.

People worry that a greyhound will be more nervous and active than other breeds and will need large space to run. These are false <u>impressions</u>. Greyhounds have naturally <u>sweet, mild dispositions</u>, and while they love to run, they are sprinters rather than distance runners. With a few laps around a fenced-in backyard every day, they are sufficiently exercised.

Greyhounds do not make good watchdogs, but they are very good with children, get along well with other dogs (and usually cats as well), and are affectionate and loyal. They are intelligent, well-behaved dogs, usually housebroken in only a few days. A retired racing greyhound is a wonderful pet for almost anyone.

113. Based on the tone of the passage, the author's main purpose is to
   a. teach prospective owners how to transform their racing greyhound into a good pet.
   b. encourage people in the dog-racing business to stop racing greyhounds.
   c. encourage people to adopt retired racing greyhounds as pets.
   d. objectively present the pros and cons of adopting a racing greyhound.

114. The passage promotes the idea that a greyhound is a good pet, particularly for people who
   a. do not have children.
   b. live in apartments.
   c. do not usually like dogs.
   d. already have another dog or cat.

115. Which of the following is implied by the passage?
   a. The public is more aware of greyhounds than it used to be.
   b. Greyhounds are more competitive than other dogs.
   c. Greyhound racing should not be allowed.
   d. People who own pet rabbits should not adopt greyhounds.

116. The word <u>impressions</u>, as used in the passage, most nearly means
   a. beliefs.
   b. questions.
   c. fictions.
   d. troubles.

117. The phrase <u>sweet, mild dispositions</u>, as used in the passage, most nearly means
   a. appetites for sugary foods.
   b. pleasing faces.
   c. happy but unintelligent natures.
   d. easygoing temperaments.

118. The passage suggests that more people would adopt retired racing greyhounds if they realized that the dogs
   a. were housebroken.
   b. were long-distance runners.
   c. were only about three-and-a-half years old.
   d. loved to be in groups of other dogs.

119. According to the author, greyhounds could best be described as
   a. loving and devoted.
   b. shy and retiring.
   c. nervous but passive.
   d. watchful and independent.

120. Families who adopt a greyhound might expect their dog to live
  a. about three or four years.
  b. to about the age of five.
  c. to about the age of ten.
  d. up to the age of 15.

121. One drawback of adopting a greyhound is that
  a. greyhounds are not good with children.
  b. greyhounds are old when they retire from racing.
  c. the greyhound's sensitivity makes it temperamental.
  d. greyhounds are not good watchdogs.

122. A retired racing greyhound available for adoption will most likely be
  a. happy to be retiring.
  b. easily housebroken.
  c. a champion.
  d. high-strung.

Mark Twain is one of America's most beloved authors. His early novel *The Adventures of Tom Sawyer* has been enjoyed by young and old for more than 100 years. His later novel *The Adventures of Huckleberry Finn* is one of the greatest pieces of American literature.

Mark Twain, however, was a <u>pseudonym</u>; his real name was Samuel L. Clemens. He was born in 1835; Halley's Comet also appeared that year. The comet appears every 75 years, and Twain used to say, "I came in with Halley's Comet and I expect to go out with it." True to his word, Samuel Clemens died in 1910, the year of the comet's next appearance. He was joking that the comet had been a <u>portent</u> of his life.

123. This passage is primarily about
  a. Mark Twain.
  b. Tom Sawyer.
  c. Huck Finn.
  d. American literature.

124. According to this passage, Mark Twain lived to be about
  a. 100 years old.
  b. 89 years old.
  c. 75 years old.
  d. 35 years old.

125. Halley's Comet is important to this passage because
  a. it appeared in the years of Twain's birth and death.
  b. it appears only once every 75 years.
  c. it was named by Mark Twain.
  d. it appeared again in 1986.

126. Based on this passage, which of the following is NOT true of Mark Twain?
  a. He wrote *The Adventures of Huckleberry Finn.*
  b. He lived to be 100 years old.
  c. He died in 1910.
  d. He was a great American writer.

127. As it is used in the passage, the word <u>pseudonym</u> most nearly means
  a. celebrity.
  b. writer.
  c. criminal.
  d. false name.

128. When Mark Twain said, "I came in with Halley's Comet," he meant
  a. the comet appeared the year he was born.
  b. he was from another planet.
  c. his life depended on the comet's appearance.
  d. the comet would never come back.

129. As it is used in the passage, the word <u>portent</u> most nearly means
a. wall.
b. importance.
c. announcement.
d. tragedy.

130. The author of this passage probably
a. respects Mark Twain's writing.
b. wrote *The Adventures of Tom Sawyer*.
c. hates reading Mark Twain.
d. grew up in the South.

131. Samuel L. Clemens is
a. the author of this passage.
b. Mark Twain.
c. the man who named Halley's Comet.
d. a famous astronomer.

132. A good title for this passage would be
a. "The Real Tom Sawyer."
b. "Halley's Comet, Past and Present."
c. "Great American Authors."
d. "Mark Twain and Halley's Comet."

The Olympics
Today's Olympic Games differ greatly from the original Olympics of nearly 3,000 years ago. The first recorded Olympic Games were held in 776 B.C., and consisted of one event: a great foot race of about 200 yards held just outside the little town of Olympia in Greece. As the years went by, more events were added. However, it was from that date the Greeks began to keep their calendar by "Olympiads," the four-year spans between the celebrations of the famous games.

Greek women, <u>forbidden</u> not only to participate in but also to watch the Olympic games, held games of their own, called the Heraea. The women's games were also held every four years but had fewer events than the Olympics. Winning was of prime importance in both male and female festivals. The winners of the Olympics and of the Heraea were crowned with chaplets of wild olive, and in their home city-states, male champions were also awarded numerous honors, valuable gifts, and privileges.

The modern Olympic Games, which started in Athens in 1896, are the result of the <u>devotion</u> of French educator Baron Pierre de Coubertin. He believed that because young people and athletics have gone together through the ages, education and athletics might go hand-in-hand toward a better international understanding. Since then, the games have been held in cities throughout the world, with the goal of fostering world cooperation and athletic excellence. What started in a small town in Greece has become one of the most well-known and honored events in the world.

133. Which of the following titles best expresses the topic of this passage?
a. "Greece: Where the Olympics Began"
b. "Training for the Olympics"
c. "The Olympics: Then and Now"
d. "World Cooperation and Athletic Excellence at the Olympics"

134. Another word for <u>forbidden</u>, as used in the passage, is
a. encouraged.
b. allowed.
c. refused.
d. banned.

135. Today's Olympics are similar to the games of 3,000 years ago because
a. women participate.
b. there is more than one event.
c. more than one country competes.
d. they have foot races.

136. Another word for <u>devotion</u>, as used in the passage, is
   a. actions.
   b. prayer.
   c. enthusiasm.
   d. worship.

137. Which is NOT mentioned as a goal of today's Olympics?
   a. world cooperation
   b. athletic excellence
   c. international understanding
   d. winning awards

138. How many years is an Olympiad?
   a. two
   b. four
   c. six
   d. one

139. In the original Olympics, Greek women were not allowed to participate or watch. They responded by
   a. watching from afar.
   b. winning prizes.
   c. conducting their own games.
   d. staying home.

140. The author's purpose in writing this selection was most likely to
   a. encourage readers to train for the Olympics.
   b. show how the Olympics are different for men and women.
   c. describe how the Olympics came to be.
   d. share the goals of the Olympics.

141. In the early days of the Olympics, male champions
   a. won all the awards.
   b. were the strongest in the country.
   c. stayed away from the female champions.
   d. were awarded valuable gifts.

142. The third paragraph describes
   a. how the modern-day Olympics came to exist.
   b. the goals of ancient Greece's Olympics.
   c. what the winners of the Olympics receive.
   d. why athletic excellence is important.

Genius

The word *genius* conjures up many definitions. It is looked on by some as supernatural, something that an ordinary human being could not achieve. Others might describe a genius as <u>eccentric</u> or abnormal, but in a good way. As examples of genius, one has to look only at Mozart or Einstein. After all, Mozart's symphonies and Einstein's theory of relativity are outstanding but unusual human accomplishments. It is also thought that genius is a completely unpredictable abnormality.

Until recently, psychologists regarded the quirks of a genius as too inconsistent to describe intelligibly. However, a groundbreaking study by Anna Findley has uncovered <u>predictable</u> patterns in the biographies of geniuses. These patterns, however, do not <u>dispel</u> the common belief that there is a kind of supernatural intervention in the lives of unusually talented men and women, even though these patterns occur with regularity. For example, Findley's study shows that all geniuses experience three intensely productive periods in their lives. One of these periods always occurs shortly before the genius's death; this is true whether the genius lives to nineteen or ninety.

143. According to the information presented in the passage, which of the following best sums up the general populace's opinion of a genius?
   a. It is predictable and uncommon.
   b. It is scornful and abnormal.
   c. It is unpredictable and erratic.
   d. It is extraordinary and erratic.

144. Which of the following would be the best title for the passage?
   a. "Understanding Mozarts and Einsteins"
   b. "Predicting the Life of a Genius"
   c. "The Patterns in the Lives of Geniuses"
   d. "Pattern and Disorder in the Lives of Geniuses"

145. The word <u>eccentric</u>, as it is used in the passage, most nearly means
   a. honored.
   b. unusual.
   c. intelligent.
   d. enthusiastic.

146. In which of the following would you expect to find this passage?
   a. a newspaper or magazine article
   b. an advertisement in a magazine
   c. a book on various kinds of mental illness
   d. a novel or short story

147. The word <u>predictable</u>, as it is used in the passage, most nearly means
   a. undependable.
   b. foreseeable.
   c. reasonable.
   d. careful.

148. Given the information in the passage, which of the following statements is true?
   a. Anna Findley is a biographer.
   b. The lives of geniuses are eccentric and unpredictable.
   c. A genius has three very productive times in his or her life.
   d. Mozart discovered relativity.

149. The word <u>dispel</u>, as used in the passage, most nearly means
   a. blot out.
   b. allow in.
   c. applaud.
   d. indicate.

150. Findley's study is described as "groundbreaking" most likely because
   a. it was written in an intelligent way.
   b. it was conducted by a genius.
   c. other psychologists agreed with Findley.
   d. it provides information that was not known earlier.

151. The tone of this passage could best be described as
   a. gloomy.
   b. informative.
   c. humorous.
   d. joyful.

152. The passage gives all of the following pieces of information EXCEPT
   a. what Anna Findley's study discovered.
   b. what Mozart did exceptionally well.
   c. how many people define genius.
   d. why geniuses have three productive periods.

For questions 153 through 174, choose the word or phrase that most nearly means the same as the underlined word.

153. an <u>ingenious</u> solution
   a. clever
   b. remarkable
   c. sincere
   d. unsophisticated

154. to lie <u>prostrate</u>
   a. strongly
   b. glandular
   c. helpless
   d. vigorously

155. to <u>defraud</u> investors
   a. announce
   b. defray
   c. defy
   d. cheat

156. a <u>malevolent</u> wish
   a. evil
   b. ill-formed
   c. grand
   d. perfect

157. the governor's <u>oration</u>
   a. election
   b. independence
   c. speech
   d. candidacy

158. the <u>eccentric</u> old man
   a. frail
   b. stingy
   c. peculiar
   d. elective

159. a <u>taciturn</u> person
   a. quiet
   b. overweight
   c. intelligent
   d. boisterous

160. a <u>rational</u> decision
   a. deliberate
   b. invalid
   c. prompt
   d. reasonable

161. <u>expedite</u> the process
   a. accelerate
   b. evaluate
   c. reverse
   d. justify

162. the <u>obsolete</u> machine
   a. complicated
   b. simple
   c. unnecessary
   d. outmoded

163. a <u>diligent</u> student
   a. successful
   b. tardy
   c. hardworking
   d. happy

164. an <u>ambiguous</u> statement
   a. left-handed
   b. uncertain
   c. snakelike
   d. rude

165. its <u>inferior</u> quality
   a. absurd
   b. distinguished
   c. lower
   d. personal

166. the <u>proponent</u> of new laws
   a. advocate
   b. delinquent
   c. idealist
   d. critic

167. your <u>disparaging</u> remark
   a. encouraging
   b. final
   c. restricting
   d. belittling

168. to <u>scrutinize</u> the document
  a. vanish
  b. examine
  c. neglect
  d. weaken

169. a <u>colossal</u> structure
  a. Greek
  b. ancient
  c. sports
  d. huge

170. our teacher's <u>rigidity</u>
  a. misery
  b. viewpoint
  c. inflexibility
  d. disagreement

171. to <u>coerce</u> the participants
  a. force
  b. permit
  c. promote
  d. deny

172. to <u>collaborate</u> on a project
  a. cooperate
  b. collect
  c. entice
  d. elaborate

173. the <u>erroneous</u> explanation
  a. accurate
  b. incorrect
  c. previous
  d. confusing

174. a <u>malignant</u> cancer
  a. widespread
  b. temporary
  c. harmful
  d. harmless

Part 4: Mathematics

Time: 45 minutes

175. 56.73647 rounded to the nearest hundredth is equal to
  a. 100.
  b. 57.
  c. 56.7.
  d. 56.74.

176. Which of the following decimals has the least value?
  a. 0.0012
  b. 0.0102
  c. 0.012
  d. 0.12

177. Which of the following is the equivalent of $\frac{13}{25}$?
  a. 0.38
  b. 0.4
  c. 0.48
  d. 0.52

178. Which of the following has the greatest value?
  a. $\frac{7}{8}$
  b. $\frac{3}{4}$
  c. $\frac{2}{3}$
  d. $\frac{5}{6}$

179. Which of the following does NOT have two pairs of parallel line segments?
  a. a rhombus
  b. a square
  c. a trapezoid
  d. a rectangle

180. 184 is evenly divisible by
   a. 46.
   b. 43.
   c. 41.
   d. 40.

181. Write ten million forty-three thousand seven hundred three in numerals.
   a. 143,703
   b. 1,043,703
   c. 10,043,703
   d. 10,430,703

182. A polygon is a plane figure composed of connected lines. How many connected lines must there be to make a polygon?
   a. 3 or more
   b. 4 or more
   c. 5 or more
   d. 6 or more

183. $(-12)^2 =$
   a. 144
   b. −144
   c. −24
   d. 24

184. The greatest common factor of 8 and 24 is
   a. 2.
   b. 4.
   c. 6.
   d. 8.

185. Bonnie is planting a garden that is 6 feet wide and 8 feet long. How many feet of fencing will she need to surround the garden's perimeter?
   a. 12
   b. 18
   c. 24
   d. 28

186. Which is the longest side? (Note: not drawn to scale.)

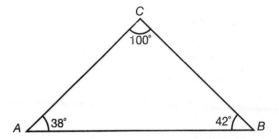

   a. AB
   b. AC
   c. BC
   d. AC and BC

187. If $n = 3$, which of the following statements is true?
   a. $9 - n > 6$
   b. $3n < 8$
   c. $2n > n^2$
   d. $3n < n^3$

188. What is the reciprocal of $3\frac{7}{8}$?
   a. $\frac{31}{8}$
   b. $\frac{8}{31}$
   c. $\frac{8}{21}$
   d. $-\frac{31}{8}$

189. What is the ratio of one inch to one foot?
   a. 1:1
   b. 1:3
   c. 1:12
   d. 1:36

190. 2 hours 10 minutes − 45 minutes =
   a. 1 hour 25 minutes
   b. 1 hour 45 minutes
   c. 2 hours
   d. 2 hours 15 minutes

191. Jane wants to cover one solid wall with wall-paper. The wall is 8 feet high and 12 feet long with no windows. How many square feet of wallpaper does she need?
  a. 72 square feet
  b. 85 square feet
  c. 96 square feet
  d. 108 square feet

192. Which of the following numbers is evenly divisible by 3?
  a. 235
  b. 236
  c. 237
  d. 238

193. What lines are parallel in the following diagram?

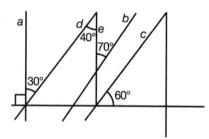

  a. *d* and *b*
  b. *a* and *e*
  c. *e* and *d*
  d. *d* and *c*

194. Simplify the following: Richard has three times the number of tennis trophies Aaron has.
  a. $R = A + 3$
  b. $A = R - 3$
  c. $R = 3A$
  d. $A = 3R$

195. Which of the following has the same value as $\frac{5}{8}$?
  a. 5.8
  b. 0.16
  c. 0.625
  d. 0.375

196. Which is the shortest time?
  a. $\frac{1}{3}$ day
  b. 9 hours
  c. 540 minutes
  d. 32,400 seconds

197. What number belongs in the box?
  $7 - 12 + \square = 1$
  a. -6
  b. 6
  c. -10
  d. 18

198. Which is greatest?
  a. 0.23
  b. 0.09
  c. 0.18
  d. 0.3

199. The Neighborhood Association organized a playgroup for cats. Fifteen people joined, and each brought three cats. How many cats were brought to the playgroup?
  a. 60 cats
  b. 45 cats
  c. 30 cats
  d. 25 cats

200. While driving, Ben averaged 60 miles per hour for 45 minutes, and then slowed to 45 miles per hour for the next 30 minutes. How far did Ben drive?
  a. 67.5 miles
  b. 72 miles
  c. 75.75 miles
  d. 82.75 miles

201. Last week, Felicity had $67.98 saved from baby-sitting. She made another $15.75 babysitting this week and spent $27.58 on CDs. How much money does she have now?
   a. $71.55
   b. $24.65
   c. $111.31
   d. $56.15

202. 7.25 − 3.6 =
   a. 3.65
   b. 3.8
   c. 4.3
   d. 4.85

203. Four hundred pounds of cod are shipped to Jerry's Fish Market packed into 20-pound crates. How many crates are needed for the shipment?
   a. 80 crates
   b. 40 crates
   c. 20 crates
   d. 10 crates

204. 3 hours 20 minutes − 1 hour 48 minutes =
   a. 5 hours 8 minutes
   b. 4 hours 8 minutes
   c. 2 hours 28 minutes
   d. 1 hour 32 minutes

205. Which is least?
   a. 0.8101
   b. 0.0801
   c. 0.0018
   d. 0.1018

206. $\frac{7}{8} \times \frac{1}{4} =$
   a. $4\frac{1}{2}$
   b. $\frac{7}{32}$
   c. $3\frac{1}{8}$
   d. $\frac{2}{7}$

207. 3.6 − 1.89 =
   a. 1.47
   b. 1.53
   c. 1.71
   d. 2.42

208. 60% of 390 =
   a. 234
   b. 190
   c. 180
   d. 134

209. What is the perimeter of the following rectangle?

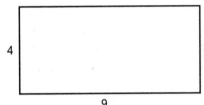

   a. 13
   b. 22
   c. 26
   d. 36

210. Reva earns $10 an hour for walking the neighbor's dog. Today, she can walk the dog for only 45 minutes. How much will Reva make today?
   a. $6.25
   b. $7.50
   c. $7.75
   d. $8.00

211. 7 hours 12 minutes + 2 hours 14 minutes =
   a. 9 hours 26 minutes
   b. 12 hours 19 minutes
   c. 10 hours 22 minutes
   d. 18 hours 18 minutes

212. Nathan saves $5\frac{1}{4}$% of his weekly salary. If Nathan earns $380.00 per week, how much does he save each week?
  a. $19.95
  b. $20.52
  c. $21.95
  d. $25.20

213. Change $\frac{160}{40}$ to a whole number.
  a. 16
  b. 10
  c. 8
  d. 4

214. If $8n + 25 = 65$, then n is
  a. 5.
  b. 10.
  c. 40.
  d. 90.

215. $1.18 + 6.03 =$
  a. 5.19
  b. 6.85
  c. 7.12
  d. 7.21

216. What is the area of the following triangle?

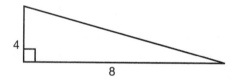

  a. 6
  b. 12
  c. 16
  d. 32

217. Dave is paid $8 per hour to paint the fence. If it takes him $4\frac{1}{2}$ hours to complete, how much will he be paid?
  a. $32.50
  b. $36.00
  c. $40.00
  d. $48.75

218. At the city park, 32% of the trees are oaks. If there are 400 trees in the park, how many trees are NOT oaks?
  a. 128
  b. 272
  c. 278
  d. 312

219. What is the perimeter of the following right triangle?

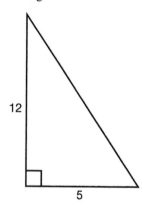

  a. 17
  b. 20
  c. 30
  d. 40

220. Edward purchased a house for $70,000. Five years later, he sold it for an 18% profit. What was his selling price?
  a. $82,600
  b. $83,600
  c. $85,500
  d. $88,000

221. The price of gasoline drops from $1.00 per gallon to 95¢ per gallon. What is the percent of decrease?
a. 2%
b. 3%
c. 4%
d. 5%

222. Meda arrived at work at 8:14 A.M., and Kirstin arrived at 9:12 A.M. How long had Meda been at work when Kirstin got there?
a. 1 hour 8 minutes
b. 1 hour 2 minutes
c. 58 minutes
d. 30 minutes

223. $4.5 \div 2.5 =$
a. 20.0
b. 2.0
c. 1.8
d. 0.2

224. George earns $418 each week, 15% of which goes to the government for taxes. How much of his paycheck does George get to keep?
a. $283.63
b. $300.75
c. $328.00
d. $355.30

225. $(6 \times 2) \div 3 =$
a. 3
b. 4
c. 5
d. 6

226. $x = 12 + y^2(10 - 8)$
$y = 2$
$x = ?$
a. 14
b. 20
c. 46
d. 120

227. What is the measure of angle B in the following diagram?

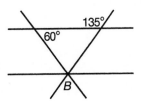

a. 45°
b. 60°
c. 75°
d. 130°

228. If a population of yeast cells grows from 10 to 320 in a period of five hours, what is the rate of growth?
a. It doubles its numbers every hour.
b. It triples its numbers every hour.
c. It doubles its numbers every two hours.
d. It triples its numbers every two hours.

229. $3^3 =$
a. 9
b. 18
c. 27
d. 32

230. Pluto is estimated at a mean distance of 3,666 million miles from the sun. The planet Mars is estimated at a mean distance of 36 million miles from the sun. How much closer to the sun is Mars than Pluto?
a. 36,300,000 million miles
b. 36,300 million miles
c. 3,630 million miles
d. 363 million miles

231. Three coolers of water per game are needed for a baseball team of 25 players. If the roster is expanded to 40 players, how many coolers are needed?
  a. 4
  b. 5
  c. 6
  d. 7

232. D'Andre rides the first half of a bike race in two hours. If his partner, Adam, rides the return trip five miles per hour less, and it takes him three hours, how fast was D'Andre traveling?
  a. 10 mph
  b. 15 mph
  c. 20 mph
  d. 25 mph

233. $7.25 \times 3.5 =$
  a. 15.675
  b. 18.75
  c. 21.5
  d. 25.375

234. If $ab - 16 = 14$, and $b = 5$, $a =$
  a. 2
  b. 3
  c. 6
  d. 30

235. $(8 - 4)^3 =$
  a. 12
  b. 16
  c. 36
  d. 64

236. The length of a rectangle is equal to 4 inches more than twice the width. Three times the length plus two times the width is equal to 28 inches. What is the area of the rectangle?
  a. 8 square inches
  b. 16 square inches
  c. 24 square inches
  d. 28 square inches

237. A certain number when added to 50% of itself is 27. What is the number?
  a. 7
  b. 9
  c. 11
  d. 18

238. What percentage of 18,000 is 234?
  a. 1,300%
  b. 130%
  c. 13%
  d. 1.3%

Part 5: Language Skills

Time: 25 minutes

*For questions 239 through 278, find the sentence that has a mistake in capitalization, punctuation, or usage. If you find no mistakes, mark choice **d**.*

239. a. A women in red was driving the car.
  b. Two books fell on the floor.
  c. Paula's on the way to school.
  d. No mistakes.

240. a. I like coffee, tea, and milk for breakfast.
  b. Whenever it rains, it pours.
  c. I missed, the ball in the game.
  d. No mistakes.

241. a. We visited New York City.
    b. My favorite class is English.
    c. David wore a purple shirt.
    d. No mistakes.

242. a. No, it's false.
    b. The temperature fell, and the pond frozen.
    c. My father is a store manager.
    d. No mistakes.

243. a. She asked me, to show her how to make an apple pie.
    b. He shouted from the window, but we couldn't hear him.
    c. Occasionally, someone will stop and ask for directions.
    d. No mistakes.

244. a. Of the four of us, I am the tallest.
    b. Wilson's brother is a chemical engineer.
    c. That fine circus elephant now belongs to my sister and I.
    d. No mistakes.

245. a. His family has lived in this town for 35 years.
    b. You're the only one who can remember that song.
    c. That's the quickest way to get to Sylvia's house.
    d. No mistakes.

246. a. We searched every inch of the room.
    b. The words in this document does not make sense.
    c. We always have chicken for Sunday dinner.
    d. No mistakes.

247. a. Please send them my love.
    b. You gave me to much food!
    c. Carl is a very funny man!
    d. No mistakes.

248. a. This would be a good time for a break.
    b. What church do you attend?
    c. Well, that was certainly a surprise!
    d. No mistakes.

249. a. Whenever you get around to it.
    b. Who was that masked man?
    c. Look up at the sky!
    d. No mistakes.

250. a. When you come to the end of Newton Road, turn left onto Wilson Boulevard.
    b. A small river runs alongside the highway.
    c. We learned that cape Cod was formed 20,000 years ago.
    d. No mistakes.

251. a. "Meet me at six o'clock," she said.
    b. Tired of running, she slowed her pace to a fast walk.
    c. Gabriel and me will attend the geography bee.
    d. No mistakes.

252. a. He wore two different shoes to class.
    b. Rhonda's sister bought a new Pontiac.
    c. Lake Superior is the largest of the Great Lakes.
    d. No mistakes.

253. a. Mark liked the movie alot.
    b. The chicken lived in a coop.
    c. Today is the first day of spring.
    d. No mistakes.

254. a. His desk is near the wall.
    b. I been there before.
    c. George threw the baseball very fast.
    d. No mistakes.

255. a. Me and Jamie went to the store.
　　b. When will you meet me there?
　　c. Go down to the bottom of the hill.
　　d. No mistakes.

256. a. She and I have been friends for more than
　　　ten years.
　　b. Is that one of the O'Farrell children?
　　c. They took too much time to answer.
　　d. No mistakes.

257. a. Did you read that article in *Newsweek?*
　　b. My Uncle took us to Yankee Stadium.
　　c. Christina has a Persian cat named Snowball.
　　d. No mistakes.

258. a. Reena took little Sean to kindergarten.
　　b. Gregory is learning to be a chef.
　　c. Paul drunk four bottles of grape soda.
　　d. No mistakes.

259. a. "Mike, come outside as soon as possible."
　　b. When is Christmas this year?
　　c. The people are demanding there rights.
　　d. No mistakes.

260. a. When was this book due at the library.
　　b. You should see her new haircut!
　　c. Call me if it's postponed.
　　d. No mistakes.

261. a. Do you know where the dog is?
　　b. Please put a log on the fire.
　　c. That lunch was very filling.
　　d. No mistakes.

262. a. I always have a hard time getting up in the
　　　morning.
　　b. We took: a tent, a cooler, and a sleeping bag.
　　c. The fog was as thick as potato soup.
　　d. No mistakes.

263. a. This is someone elses coat.
　　b. Which of these songs was recorded by Bruce
　　　Springsteen?
　　c. That book must be yours.
　　d. No mistakes.

264. a. They're planning to drive to Vermont today.
　　b. When will you teach me to play the guitar?
　　c. There's no reason to stay up so late.
　　d. No mistakes.

265. a. Make sure your seat belt is fastened.
　　b. I'm afraid of spiders George is too.
　　c. Yes, I will bring the dessert.
　　d. No mistakes.

266. a. Don't stand in my way.
　　b. Cecilia and I fought our way through the
　　　crowd.
　　c. The vegetables were old rubbery and
　　　tasteless.
　　d. No mistakes.

267. a. After you left, I took the dog for a walk.
　　b. For the first time, I understood what he was
　　　talking about.
　　c. We visited the house where George
　　　Washington lived last fall.
　　d. No mistakes.

268. a. Sandra Day O'Connor was the first woman
　　　to serve on the U.S. Supreme Court.
　　b. The judge met with both attorneys in his
　　　chambers.
　　c. Which of the Beatles' songs do you like best?
　　d. No mistakes.

269. a. The steam rose up from the hot pavement.
　　b. She put the kitten down carefully beside
　　　its mom.
　　c. Neither of us is going to the party.
　　d. No mistakes.

270. a. Here are four different varieties of the same species.
  b. The oldest one of these books are not for sale.
  c. This is the most exciting vacation I have ever had.
  d. No mistakes.

271. a. Remember to walk the dog.
  b. "Don't run"! Mr. Ellington shouted.
  c. It's supposed to snow today and tomorrow.
  d. No mistakes.

272. a. When I go to the mall, I took Harrison with me.
  b. There are two buildings on this property.
  c. I was invited, but I declined the invitation.
  d. No mistakes.

273. a. Charleen's parents worried whenever she drove the car.
  b. Who designed the Brooklyn Bridge?
  c. Diseases like Smallpox and Polio have been eradicated.
  d. No mistakes.

274. a. They traveled south and hiked in the desert.
  b. "Don't shout at me," she yelled back.
  c. Joshua enters lots of contests, until he knows he can't win.
  d. No mistakes.

275. a. The students' backpacks were all put away.
  b. Do you want to go to Yellowstone National Park?
  c. Keep off the grass!
  d. No mistakes.

276. a. I love Italian food.
  b. The people in the office, including all the assistants.
  c. George likes to play basketball better than football.
  d. No mistakes.

277. a. Who's that person in the red hat?
  b. The letter arrived addressed to Emily and me.
  c. After running, it's important to stretch.
  d. No mistakes.

278. a. When I heard the siren, I run to the door.
  b. Ms. Smith is the treasurer of the bank.
  c. In the morning, I woke up.
  d. No mistakes.

For questions 279 through 288, find the sentence that has a mistake in spelling. If you find no mistakes, mark choice d.

279. a. Bert will probibly stay home tonight.
  b. The coach praised the team for last night's game.
  c. It was a relief to learn that Brett had arrived safely.
  d. No mistakes.

280. a. The movie was immensely popular.
  b. Joshua made a commitment to practice the piano each day.
  c. We did not know the correct pronounciation.
  d. No mistakes.

281. a. The speaker presented an idea that was foreign to us.
  b. Marcus spoke directly to the governor.
  c. The boys and girls in the chorus gave a stunning performance.
  d. No mistakes.

282.
a. The winners received their prizes several days ago.
b. The principle met with the members of the student council.
c. How many passengers traveled by train?
d. No mistakes.

283.
a. English is the principle language of the United States.
b. Andrew addressed the audience.
c. She broached the subject gently.
d. No mistakes.

284.
a. What time is dinner?
b. The elektric power came back on temporarily.
c. I forgot to bring my house keys.
d. No mistakes.

285.
a. Bobby thought the team did not play aggressively.
b. The mayor and the city manager were not in agreement.
c. The basement of the building seemed more like a dungeon.
d. No mistakes.

286.
a. The scizzors were not sharp enough.
b. The intense heat scorched my houseplants.
c. The Milky Way is only one of many galaxies.
d. No mistakes.

287.
a. We knew that Ellen was embarassed.
b. I am teaching my brother to read mathematical symbols.
c. Neither Joe nor Gary has done the research for his report.
d. No mistakes.

288.
a. Which of the following countries is not a democracy?
b. Occasionally, our dog Skippy will dig under the fence.
c. This weather is terribly depressing.
d. No mistakes.

For questions 289 through 298, follow the directions for each question.

289. Choose the word that best joins the thoughts.
The water threatened to engulf the boat, ____ the man ran to help the drowning woman.
a. although
b. that
c. yet
d. which

290. Choose the word that best joins the thoughts.
The policeman thought he had caught the thief; ___ he had an innocent person in custody.
a. finally
b. unless
c. thus
d. instead

291. Which of these expresses the idea most clearly?
a. Martin phoned his friend every day when he was in the hospital.
b. When his friend was in the hospital, Martin phoned him every day.
c. When in the hospital, a phone call was made every day by Martin to his friend.
d. His friend received a phone call from Martin every day while he was in the hospital.

292. Which of these expresses the idea most clearly?

   a. Some of the reports I have to type for school are very long, but that doesn't bother one if they are interesting.

   b. Some of the reports I have to type for school are very long, but that doesn't bother you if they are interesting.

   c. Some of the reports I have to type for school are very long, but it doesn't bother a person if the reports are interesting.

   d. Some of the reports I have to type for school are very long, but that doesn't bother me if they are interesting.

293. Which of these expresses the idea most clearly?

   a. In search of the missing teenagers, who still had not been found through snake-ridden underbrush all day, the exhausted volunteers had struggled.

   b. All day, the exhausted volunteers had struggled through snake-ridden underbrush in search of the missing teenagers, who still had not been found.

   c. All day, the exhausted volunteers had struggled through snake-ridden underbrush who still had not been found, in searching for the missing teenagers.

   d. The exhausted volunteers who still had not found in search of the missing teenagers when they had struggled through snake-ridden underbrush.

294. Choose the group of words that best completes this sentence.

As soon as she realized that the hurricane was going to strike, _____.

   a. the mayor told the residents to evacuate the city.

   b. the city residents were told to evacuate by the mayor.

   c. the mayor tells the city residents of her decision to evacuate.

   d. the residents of the city were told to evacuate by the mayor.

295. Which of the following topics is best for a one-page essay?

   a. Why I Have a Vegetable Garden in My Backyard

   b. How Pesticides Are Contributing to Various Diseases

   c. Why Agribusiness Is Not Good for the U.S. Economy

   d. Iowa, Nebraska, and Kansas: America's Bread Basket

296. Which of these best fits under the topic, "Help for the Nearsighted"?

   a. Eye surgeons perform delicate operations with the use of magnifying lenses.

   b. The pupil is the round aperture in the iris of the eye; it contracts and expands in relation to the amount of light.

   c. Tiny, transparent rings that are implanted into the cornea might correct mild to moderate nearsightedness.

   d. Most children in the United States have their eyes tested by the time they are in the third or fourth grade.

297. Which sentence does NOT belong in the paragraph?
1) The 1990s will go down as the hottest decade on record. 2) The average temperature was 1.2 degrees higher than normal. 3) Scientists are trying to figure out the cause. 4) When temperatures are high, people use more air conditioning.

  a. sentence 1
  b. sentence 2
  c. sentence 3
  d. sentence 4

298. Where should the sentence, "Between the sketch and the photo, artists have just about all they will need to begin the painting" be placed in the following paragraph?
1) Today, painters often use their photographs to document the scenes they later will paint. 2) Photographs function most effectively when they are used along with the artist's sketch of the same scene. 3) A sketch records the composition exactly as the artist viewed it and responded to it. 4) The camera records the details and fills in whatever the sketch may have missed.

  a. before sentence 1
  b. between sentences 1 and 2
  c. between sentences 3 and 4
  d. after sentence 4

Answers

Part 1: Verbal Skills

1. c. A *fire*, a *log*, and a *spark* are all part of a campfire. A *stone* is not related.

2. d. *Sincere*, *honest*, and *genuine* are all synonyms. *Deceitful* is an antonym.

3. b. The first two statements are true, so Megan is the youngest of the three. The third statement, therefore, is false.

4. c. *Saturate* means to fill to capacity, to *soak*, or to penetrate.

5. b. *Cheerful* and *ebullient* both mean happy. The other choices are incorrect because cheerful people are not necessarily industrious, tired, or shy.

6. b. A *door* moves on a *hinge*, just as a *jet* moves on a *wing*. The other choices may have some connection to a jet, but only choice **b** has the same relationship.

7. d. A *marathon* is a long race and *hibernation* is a lengthy period of *sleep*. The answer is not choice **a** or **b** because even though bear and winter have a relationship with the word *hibernation*, neither of these completes the analogy. Choice **c** is incorrect because a nap is a short period of sleep.

8. d. An *apple*, a *cherry*, and a *tomato* are all foods, while *red* is a color.

9. d. To be *punctual* means to be on time; to be *tardy* means to be late.

10. d. The *telephone* is a means of *communication*. The *bus* is a means of *transportation*. Aviation, choice **a**, is not the answer because it is a type of transportation, not a means. The answer is not choice **b** or **c** because neither of these represents a means of transportation.

11. **a.** *Tactful* and *diplomatic* are synonyms (they mean about the same thing). *Bashful* and *timid* are also synonyms. The answer is not choice **b** or **c** because neither of these means the same as bashful. Bold, choice **d**, is incorrect because it means the opposite of bashful.

12. **b.** *Impassive* means not feeling or showing emotion; *apathetic* means showing or feeling no interest, enthusiasm, or concern.

13. **b.** A *dormant* plant is *resting* or *hibernating*.

14. **c.** The first two statements are true, both Zoe and Heather read more books than Jenna, but it is uncertain as to whether Heather read more than Zoe.

15. **c.** *Scarcely* is the opposite of *mostly*, and *quietly* is the opposite of *loudly*. Choices **a** and **b** are clearly not opposites of quietly. Choice **d** means the same as quietly.

16. **a.** *Passive* means that a person does not take any action, so the opposite would be *active*.

17. **a.** The *magazine*, *newspaper*, and *book* all convey information via reading. Radio uses sound.

18. **d.** *Milk*, *water*, and *juice* are all beverages. Cereal is a food.

19. **a.** If no shingles are purple and all the houses have roofs with shingles, none of the houses has a purple roof.

20. **b.** A *zipper* is a fastener, as is a *button*. An *oak* is a tree, and so is an *elm*. Jackets might use buttons and zippers, but they have no relationship to an oak. Choices **c** and **d** also have no relation to an oak tree.

21. **a.** A *timid* person approaches a challenge with fear; a *frightened* person does the same.

22. **d.** *Replica* is an exact copy; *duplicate* means exactly like something else.

23. **c.** Lake Mead is compared to Walden Pond in the first statement, and Red Swamp is compared to Brown River in the second, but no comparison is made between Red Swamp and Lake Mead. Therefore, the third statement is uncertain.

24. **c.** The first two statements indicate that Battery Y lasts the least amount of time, but it cannot be determined whether Battery Z lasts longer than Battery X.

25. **d.** The first three choices are all synonyms. Choice **d** has a different meaning altogether.

26. **a.** The *index*, the *glossary*, and the *lesson* are all parts of a *book*. Choice **a** is incorrect because the book is the whole, not a part.

27. **b.** *Amateur* means engaging in a pursuit, especially a sport, without getting paid; *professional* describes a person skilled in a particular activity who receives payment for it.

28. **b.** *Tacit* means unspoken or generally understood. *Explicit* means openly stated or addressed.

29. **c.** The *noun*, the *preposition*, and the *adverb* are classes of words that make up a sentence. Punctuation belongs in a sentence, but punctuation is not a word class.

30. **a.** *Sage* and *wise* both mean intelligent, perceptive.

31. **d.** *Unite* and *amalgamate* both mean combine.

32. **b.** An *actor* performs in a *play*. A *musician* performs at a *concert*. Choices **a**, **c**, and **d** are incorrect because none are people who perform.

33. **c.** We know only that long-tailed Gangles have spots. We cannot know for certain whether long-tailed Gangles also have short hair.

34. **c.** *Requirement* means something obligatory; *option* means something chosen.

35. **c.** To *pacify* means to calm; to *excite* means to stir up.

36. d. *Pillow, cushion,* and *pad* are all items found on furniture, but pitch is not.

37. c. We know from the first two statements that Tuesday had the highest temperature, but we cannot know whether Monday's temperature was higher than Wednesday's.

38. a. To *rectify* something is to *correct* it or make it right.

39. b. To have an *antagonist* is to have an *opponent*, or one who opposes you.

40. d. A *ski, sled,* and *toboggan* are all sports equipment, but snow is the place where they're used.

41. d. A group of *lions* is called a *pride.* A group of *fish* swim in a *school.* Teacher, choice **a,** and student, choice **b,** refer to another meaning of the word school. The answer is not choice **c** because self-respect has no obvious relationship to this particular meaning of *school.*

42. a. *Control* and *dominate* are synonyms, and *magnify* and *enlarge* are synonyms. The answer is not choice **b** or **d** because neither of these means the same as enlarge. Choice **c** is incorrect because decrease is the opposite of enlarge.

43. b. To *enumerate* means to ascertain the number of; to *count.*

44. c. *Impartial* means unbiased, unprejudiced, or fair-minded.

45. a. Since Northern Airlines costs more than Eastern Airlines, and Western Airlines costs more than Northern Airlines, it is true that Western Airlines costs the most.

46. b. An *ounce* measures weight; the other choices measure length.

47. c. *Equine* refers to horses.

48. a. *Faltering* means stumbling; *steady* means unfaltering.

49. a. *Freeway, interstate,* and *expressway* are all high-speed highways; a street is for low-speed traffic.

50. c. A *lemon* is a type of *fruit,* just as a *grocery* is a type of *store.*

51. a. To *humidify* and to *moisten* both mean to make damp.

52. c. *Sunshine, rain,* and *snow* are all types of weather conditions.

53. c. *Ventilate* means to let the air in; the opposite is to *smother.*

54. b. *Dodge, duck,* and *avoid* are all synonyms meaning evade. Flee means to run away from.

55. a. From the first two statements, you know that Troup 101 sold the most cookies, so Troop 101 would have sold more than Troop 103.

56. b. We know from the first two statements that James jumps highest. Therefore, the third statement must be false.

57. d. A *studious* person studies and is *scholarly.*

58. d. *Heading, body,* and *closing* are all parts of a letter.

59. d. The *toe, heel,* and *arch* are all parts of a foot, while walking is what is done with the feet.

60. d. To *levitate* means to rise and float; to *sink* means to go under the surface.

Part 2: Quantitative Skills

61. a. This is an alternating series. In the first sequence, 3 is added (1, 4, 7). In the second sequence, 1 is subtracted (8, 7, 6).

62. c. Determine how each figure is shaded by counting the number of blocks.

63. b. 40% of 10 is 4; half of 4 is 2.

64. b. First, solve for (A), (B), and (C): $3 + (2 \times 1) = 5$; $8 - (2 \times 2) = 4$; $10 \div (1 + 1) = 5$. Then find out which choice is true.

65. d. This is a simple subtraction series; each number is 25 less than the previous number.

66. d. This is a simple alternating addition and subtraction series. First, 3 is added, then 1 is subtracted; then 3 is added, 1 subtracted, and so on.

67. a. Count the number of individual lines in (A), (B), and (C) and then test each choice to find out whether it is true: (A) = 4, (B) = 7, (C) = 3.

68. b. $\frac{3}{4}$ of 20 = 15; 15 − 7 = 8.

69. b. First, solve for (A), (B), and (C): $\frac{1}{3}$ of 12 is 4; 4% of 100 is 4; $\frac{1}{5}$ of 10 is 2. Then find out which choice is true.

70. b. 3% of 200 = 6; 6 − 2 = 4.

71. d. First, set up the equation: $\frac{n}{6} = \frac{1}{2}(18)$. Then solve: $\frac{n}{6} = 9$; $n = 54$.

72. b. This is a simple subtraction series. Each number decreases by $\frac{1}{8}$.

73. b. AC is the hypotenuse of this right triangle, so AC must be greater than AB.

74. b. 30% of 90 = 27; 27 + 12 = 39.

75. a. First, solve for (A), (B), and (C): (A) = $\frac{1}{8}$, (B) = $\frac{1}{16}$, (C) = $\frac{1}{32}$. Then find out which choice is true.

76. c. $10 \times 16 = 160$; 20% of 100 is 20, and 20% of 60 is 12; 12 + 20 = 32.

77. d. First, set up the equation: $n \div 3 = \frac{1}{3} \times 9$. Then solve: $n \div 3 = 3$; $n = 9$.

78. a. This is a simple subtraction series; each number is 4 less than the previous number.

79. d. First, determine the value of each letter: A = 5, B = 12, C = 30, D = 15, E = 22. Then test each choice to find out whether it is true.

80. b. First, solve for (A), (B), and (C): (A) = 3a, (B) = 4a, (C) = 3a. Then find out which choice is true.

81. c. $7 \times 3 = 21$; $21 \div \frac{1}{3} = 63$.

82. b. This is a simple division series; each number is one-half the previous number.

83. a. This is a simple addition series with a random number, 21, interpolated as every third number. In the series, 6 is added to each number except 21, to arrive at the next number.

84. d. First, set up the equation: $50 - n = 13 + \frac{1}{4} \times 8$. Then solve: $50 - n = 13 + 2$; $50 - n = 15$; $n = 50 - 15$; $n = 35$.

85. d. First, determine the amounts shown in (A), (B), and (C), and then test each statement to find out whether it is true.

86. c. In this series, the first number is divided by 3, and the next number is multiplied by 2.

87. d. First, solve for (A), (B), and (C): (A) = 3, (B) = 4, and (C) = 5. Then find out which choice is true.

88. a. 140% of 5 = 7; 7 − 17 = −10.

89. c. In this simple addition series, each number increases by 0.8.

90. c. The first number in this series is divided by 2, then 2 is added, then divided by 2, and so forth.

91. c. First, solve for (A), (B), and (C): (A) = 8, (B) = 9, (C) = 7. Then find out which choice is true.

92. b. The formula is: *area = length × width*. Using this formula, determine the area of each rectangle: (A) is 4 square inches, (B) is 3 square inches, and (C) is 4 square inches. Then test each choice to find out which answer is true.

93. d. First, set up the equation: $n + (16 + n) = 136$. Then solve: $16 + 2n = 136$; $2n = 120$; $n = 60$.

94. a. This is a simple alternating addition and subtraction series. The first series begins with 10 and adds 2; the second begins with 34 and subtracts 3.

95. b. First, set up the equation: $n[(0.2 \times 60) - 8] = 24$. Then solve: $n(12 - 8) = 24$; $4n = 24$; $n = 6$.

96. a. Determine how each figure is shaded by counting the number of blocks.

97. b. First, set up the equation: $n = (\frac{1}{3} \times 75) \div 2$. Then solve: $n = 12.5$.

98. c. First, set up the equation: $\frac{n}{3} = \frac{3}{5}(50)$. Then solve: $\frac{n}{3} = 30$; $n = 90$.

99. c. First, solve for (A), (B), and (C): (A) = 36, (B) = 33, (C) = 30. Then find out which choice is true.

100. d. Each number in this series is $1\frac{1}{2}$ times the preceding number.

101. a. First, set up the equation: $7n = \frac{1}{2}(28)$. Then solve: $7n = 14$; $n = 2$.

102. b. Use this formula to determine the area of a triangle: area = $\frac{1}{2}$ of base × height. The area of (A) is $2\frac{1}{2}$ inches, (B) is $2\frac{1}{2}$ inches, and (C) is 3 inches. Test each choice to find out which answer is true.

103. c. In this series, the letters are working backward while the numbers increase by 4.

104. a. This is a simple alternating subtraction series, which subtracts 2, then 5.

105. b. Note the length of each line and test each statement.

106. c. First, set up the equation: $4n = 72 - 20$. Then solve: $4n = 52$; $n = 13$.

107. b. This is an alternating addition and subtraction series. Roman numbers alternate with Arabic numbers. In the Roman numeral pattern, each number decreases by 1. In the Arabic numeral pattern, each number increases by 1.

108. a. First, set up the equation: $3n + 50 = 74$. Then solve: $3n = 24$; $n = 8$.

109. b. This is an alternating multiplication and subtracting series. First, multiply by 2, and then subtract 8.

110. c. This is a multiplication series with repetition. The decimal is repeated by a fraction with the same value and is then multiplied by 2.

111. d. First, set up the equation: $n = 16(\frac{1}{2} \times 4)$. Then solve: $n = 16 \times 2$; $n = 32$.

112. a. First, change (A) and (C) to decimals: (A) = 1.8 and (C) = 1.3. Then find out which choice is true.

Part 3: Reading

113. c. The tone of the passage is enthusiastic in its recommendation of the greyhound as a pet and thereby encourages people to adopt one. It does not give advice on transforming a greyhound (choice **a**). The passage does not address the dog-racing audience (choice **b**). The author's tone is not objective (choice **d**), but rather enthusiastic.

114. d. See the last paragraph. The passage does not mention choices **b** or **c**. Choice **a** is clearly wrong; the passage states the opposite.

115. a. This is implied by the first paragraph. Choices **b, c,** and **d** are not touched on in the passage.

116. a. In the context of the passage, the word *impressions* means a person's ideas or beliefs about something.

117. d. In the context of the passage, the phrase *sweet, mild dispositions* refers back to the greyhound's temperament, which is mild or easygoing.

118. c. The first two sentences in the second paragraph support this answer. Choice **a** is incorrect because the passage states that greyhounds are easily housebroken, not that they are already housebroken. Choice **b** is contradicted in the passage. There is no support for choice **d**.

119. a. In the last paragraph, greyhounds are described as *affectionate and loyal,* which is the same as *loving and devoted.* The other choices are incorrect, according to the information given.

120. d. This detail is stated directly in the second paragraph.

121. d. See the last paragraph. Choices **a, b,** and **c** are contradicted in the passage.

122. b. See the end of the next-to-last sentence in the passage. Choices **a, c,** and **d** are not to be found in the passage.

123. a. The passage mentions all the choices listed, but Mark Twain is the central topic from start to finish.

124. c. The passage states that Twain lived between 1835 and 1910, or roughly 75 years. Do not be distracted by other numbers that appear in the article.

125. a. The passage states that the comet appeared on the years of Twain's birth and death. None of the other choices is stated in the passage.

126. b. The article states that *The Adventures of Tom Sawyer* has been read for 100 years, not that Twain lived for 100 years.

127. d. In the context of the passage, *pseudonym* means a *false name* or a pen name.

128. a. Twain was saying that he'd been born when the comet appeared once, and he would die when it next appeared.

129. c. In the context of the passage, the word *portent* means an *announcement* or sign.

130. a. The opening sentence in the passage calls Mark Twain "one of America's most beloved authors." This suggests that the writer of the passage admires Twain.

131. b. The passage states that Samuel L. Clemens was Mark Twain's real name.

132. d. "Mark Twain and Halley's Comet" is the best choice. Choice **c** is too broad, since only one author is discussed. Choices **a** and **b** are not addressed in the passage.

133. c. "The Olympics: Then and Now" is the best choice. Choices **a** and **d** are too limited. Choice **b** is not covered in the text.

134. d. A synonym for *forbidden* is *banned*, as it is used in this passage.

135. d. Choices **a**, **b**, and **c** are ways in which today's Olympic games differ from the old Olympic games.

136. c. A synonym for *devotion* is *enthusiasm*, as it is used in this passage.

137. d. *Winning awards* was mentioned as a goal of the Olympics in the past.

138. b. An Olympiad is four years.

139. c. Women participated in their own games called the Heraea.

140. c. The tone of the passage is informative. The author gives some basic history of the Olympics and describes how it became the games we are familiar with today.

141. d. Male champions were awarded numerous honors, valuable gifts, and privileges.

142. a. The best answer is how the modern-day Olympics came to exist.

143. d. The passage says that people in general consider a genius *supernatural, but also . . . eccentric*; the pairing of *extraordinary* and *erratic* in choice **d** includes both meanings given in the passage. Choices **a** and **c** cover only one side of the passage's meaning. Choice **b** contains definitions that the passage does not ascribe to the common view of a genius.

144. c. This title covers the main point of the passage that, while there are predictable patterns in the life of a genius, the pattern increases the sense of something supernatural touching his or her life. Choices **a** and **b** are too general. Choice **d** is inaccurate because the passage does not talk about disorder in the life of a genius.

145. b. The passage indicates that geniuses have "a good abnormality"; this helps define the use of the word *eccentric* as meaning abnormal or *unusual*.

146. a. You can arrive at this as the best choice by ruling out the other choices. Choice **b** is wrong because the piece is not like an advertisement in either content or tone. Choice **c** can be ruled out because, although the passage states that people regard geniuses as abnormal, it does not say they are mentally ill. Choice **d** is not a good choice because this passage is nonfiction.

147. b. The passage states that the "patterns occur with regularity," so the patterns are *predictable* or *foreseeable*.

148. c. The answer is found in the second-to-last sentence. Choices **a** and **d** are clearly false. The statement in choice **b** is wrong because Findley's study found some predictable patterns in the lives of geniuses.

149. a. In the context of this passage, this is the only choice that makes sense.

150. d. This answer is arrived at through the context of the passage. Findley's study uncovered some new information about geniuses. Choice **a** may be true, but it is not stated in the passage. There is no support for choice **b** or choice **c**.

151. b. The main purpose of this passage is clearly to provide information.

152. d. Notice that this question asks for something that is NOT in the passage. Choice **d** is correct because the passage states that there are three very productive times in a genius's life, but it does not say why. Choice **a** is not stated in the passage; choices **b** and **c** appear in the second paragraph.

153. a. clever
154. c. helpless
155. d. cheat
156. a. evil
157. c. An *oration* is a formal speech.
158. c. *Eccentric* means deviating from accepted conduct; *peculiar*.
159. a. *Taciturn* means *quiet*.
160. d. *Rational* means based on reason.
161. a. *Expedite* means to *accelerate* the process; to speed up.
162. d. *Obsolete* and *outmoded* both mean no longer in use.
163. c. *Diligent* means *hardworking*.
164. b. An *ambiguous* statement is *uncertain* or unclear.

165. c. *Inferior* is *lower* in rank, quality, or importance.

166. a. A *proponent* is an *advocate* or supporter; someone who argues in favor of something.

167. d. To *disparage* is to talk about something or someone in a negative manner; to belittle.

168. b. To *scrutinize* is to *examine* carefully.

169. d. *Colossal* means *huge* or immense.

170. c. *Rigidity* is uncompromising *inflexibility*.

171. a. *Coerce* means to bring about by *force* or threat.

172. a. *Collaborate* means to work jointly; to *cooperate*.

173. b. *Erroneous* means characterized by error; *incorrect*.

174. c. Something *malignant* causes harm.

Part 4: Mathematics

175. d. The hundredth is the second digit to the right of the decimal point. Because the third decimal is 6, the second is rounded up to 4.

176. a. Because there are zeros in both the tenths and hundredths places, the other choices are all greater than choice **a**.

177. d. Divide the numerator of the fraction, or top number, by the denominator of the fraction, or bottom number: So $\frac{13}{25}$ becomes $13 \div 25$, or 0.52, or $\frac{52}{100}$.

178. a. To solve this problem, you must first convert all the fractions to the lowest common denominator, 24. $\frac{7}{8} = \frac{21}{24}$; $\frac{3}{4} = \frac{18}{24}$; $\frac{2}{3} = \frac{16}{24}$; $\frac{5}{6} = \frac{20}{24}$.

179. c. A trapezoid is the only one that does not have two pairs of parallel lines by definition.

180. a. 46 goes into 184 four times. The other choices cannot be divided evenly into 184.

181. c. 10,043,703 is the correct answer. The millions place is the third group of numbers from the right. (If any group of digits *except the first* has less than 3 digits, you must add a zero at the beginning of that group.)

182. a. A polygon is a plane figure composed of three or more lines.

183. a. The square is: $-(12) \times (-12) = 144$. Because the signs of the numbers are the same, the answer is positive.

184. d. The greatest common factor is 8 itself; 2 and 4 are common factors, but they are smaller.

185. d. To determine the perimeter, simply add the four sides of the figure: $6 + 6 + 8 + 8 = 28$.

186. a. The side opposite the largest angle is the longest side. In this case, it is side AB.

187. d. This is the only true statement: $3n$ is less than n^3, because $n^3 = 27$, and $3n = 9$.

188. b. Convert the mixed number $3\frac{7}{8}$ to the improper fraction $\frac{31}{8}$ and then invert.

189. c. There are 12 inches in a foot, so the ratio is 1 to 12.

190. a. 1 hour = 60 (minutes) $\times 2 = 120$; $(120 + 10) - 45 = 85 = 1$ hour 25 minutes.

191. c. To find square footage, multiply one side by the other side: $8 \times 12 = 96$.

192. c. 79 goes into 237 three times.

193. d. The angle between a and d and the angle adjacent to it are complementary, so the adjacent angle is 60°. The angle between c and the bottom line is also 60°, so d and c must be parallel.

194. c. Take the words in order and substitute the letters and numbers: Richard has (=) **3** times (×) the number of tennis trophies Aaron has translates to R = 3A.

195. c. $\frac{5}{8} = 5$ divided by 8, or 0.625.

196. a. $\frac{1}{3}$ day = 8 hours; the other choices equal 9 hours.

197. b. $7 - 12 = -5$; $-5 + 6 = 1$.

198. d. The 3 in the tenths position makes this number the greatest.

199. b. This is a problem in multiplication: 15 (number of people who brought cats) × 3 (number of cats) = 45 (cats).

200. a. 60 miles per hour = 1 mile per minute, so 45 minutes = 45 miles. 45 miles per hour for 1 hour = 45 miles, but he drove for half an hour, so $45 \div 2 = 22.5$. $45 + 22.5 = 67.5$.

201. d. Add $15.75 to $67.98 and then subtract $27.58. The answer is $56.15.

202. a. This is a simple subtraction problem; just be sure to line up the decimals.

203. c. Divide the amount of cod by the number of crates: $400 \div 20 = 20$.

204. d. You must "borrow" 60 minutes from the 3 hours to be able to subtract.

205. c. The zeros in the tenths and hundredths places make this the smallest number.

206. b. The correct answer is $\frac{7}{32}$.

207. c. This is a simple subtraction problem, as long as the decimals are lined up correctly.

208. a. Change the percent to a decimal to get 0.60, then multiply: $390(0.60) = 234$.

209. c. The perimeter is equal to $(2 \times 4) + (2 \times 9) = 26$.

210. b. 45 minutes is equal to $\frac{3}{4}$ of an hour, so Reva will make only $\frac{3}{4}$ her usual fee. Change $\frac{3}{4}$ to a decimal: 0.75. Now multiply: $10 \times 0.75 = 7.5$. Reva will make $7.50 today.

211. a. The minutes add up to 26 minutes (12 + 14), less than an hour, so simply add the hours: $7 + 2 = 9$.

212. a. To solve this problem, change the percent to a decimal and multiply: $0.0525 \times 380 = 19.95$.

213. d. Divide the top number by the bottom number: $160 \div 40 = 4$.

214. a. The problem is solved by first determining that $8n = 40$, then dividing 40 by 8 to get the answer, which is 5.

215. d. If you line up the decimal points, simple addition yields the correct answer.

216. c. The area is $\frac{1}{2}$ base × height. This gives $\frac{1}{2} \times 4 \times 8 = 16$.

217. b. $8 \times 4.5 = 36$.

218. b. This is a two-step problem. First, determine what percent of the trees are NOT oaks by subtracting: $100\% - 32\% = 68\%$. Change 68% to a decimal and multiply: $0.68 \times 400 = 272$.

219. c. In order to find the perimeter, the hypotenuse of the triangle must be found. This comes from recognizing that the triangle is a 5–12–13 triangle, or by using the Pythagorean theorem. Therefore, $5 + 12 + 13 = 30$.

220. a. This is a two-step problem. First, find the amount of profit. Convert the percent to a decimal and multiply: $70,000 \times 0.18 = 12,600$. Next, add the result to the original price: $70,000 + 12,600 = 82,600$.

221. d. To find the percent of decrease, first calculate the amount of the decrease: $1.00 - 0.95 = 0.05$. Set up the formula to solve for percent. Since $x\% = \frac{x}{100}$, the equation is $\frac{x}{100} = \frac{0.05}{1.00}$. Cross multiply: $(1.00)(x) = (0.05)(100)$. Simplify: $x = 5$. There is a 5% decrease.

222. c. Between 8:14 and 9:00, 46 minutes elapse, and between 9:00 and 9:12, 12 minutes elapse, so this is a simple addition problem: $46 + 12 = 58$.

223. c. The correct answer is 1.8.

224. d. To solve this problem, change the percent to a decimal and multiply: $0.15 \times 418 = 62.7$; $418 - 62.7 = 355.30$.

225. b. Solve for the parentheses first: $6 \times 2 = 12$. Divide 12 by $3 = 4$.

226. b. $x = 12 + (4 \times 2)$; $x = 12 + 8$; $x = 20$.

227. c. 135° and its adjacent angle within the triangle are supplementary, so $180° - 135° = 45°$. Angle B and the remaining unknown angle inside the triangle are vertical, so the angle within the triangle's measure is needed: $180° - 60° - 45° = 75°$, so angle B is also 75°.

228. a. It is easiest to use trial and error to arrive at the solution to this problem. Begin with choice **a**: After the first hour, the number would be 20, after the second hour, 40, after the third hour, 80, after the fourth hour, 160, and after the fifth hour, 320. Fortunately, in this case, you need go no further. The other answer choices do not have the same outcome.

229. c. $3^3 = 3 \times 3 \times 3 = 27$.

230. c. This is a subtraction problem. First, simplify the problem by dropping the word *million*. The problem then becomes $P = 3,666$, $M = 36$. So $P - M = 3,666 - 36 = 3,630$. Now add the word *million* back, and the answer becomes 3,630 million.

231. b. To solve this problem, set up the proportion 3 is to 25 as x is to 40: $\frac{3}{25} = \frac{x}{40}$. Cross multiplying: $(3)(40) = 25(x)$. Solving for x gives 4.8, but since coolers must be whole numbers, this number is rounded up to 5.

232. b. Let D'Andre's rate $= x$. D'Andre's rate multiplied by his travel time equals the distance he travels; this equals Adam's rate multiplied by his travel time; $2x = D = 3(x - 5)$. Therefore, $2x = 3x - 15$ or $x = 15$ mph.

233. d. Line up the decimal points, then perform simple multiplication.

234. c. $5a - 16 = 14$; $5a = 30$; $a = 6$.

235. d. $(8 - 4)^3 = 4^3$; $4^3 = 4 \times 4 \times 4$.

236. b. This must be solved with algebraic equations. $l = 2w + 4$ and $3l + 2w = 28$. Together: $6w + 12 + 2w = 28$, so $8w = 16$; $w = 2$. Thus, $l = 8$ and the area is $2 \times 8 = 16$ square inches.

237. d. Let $x =$ the unknown number. We have $x + 0.50x = 27$ or $1.50x = 27$. Therefore, $x = 18$.

238. d. A percentage is a portion of 100 where $x\% = \frac{x}{100}$. So the equation is $\frac{x}{100} = \frac{234}{18,000}$. Cross multiply: $18,000x = 234 \times 100$. Simplify: $x = \frac{23,400}{18,000}$. Thus, $x = 1.3$.

Part 5: Language Skills

239. a. The word *women* is plural; it should be *woman*.

240. c. There should not be a comma after *missed*.

241. d. All the answer choices are correct.

242. b. The correct verb form is *froze*.

243. a. The comma is unnecessary and should be deleted.

244. c. The subjective pronoun *I* should be replaced with the objective pronoun *me*, because the pronoun is the object, not the subject.

245. d. All the answer choices are correct.

246. b. There is no subject–verb agreement. The verb should be plural (*do not make*), because the subject is words, which is a plural noun.

247. b. The word *to* is misspelled—it should be *too*.

248. d. All the answer choices are correct.

249. a. Choice **a** is an incomplete sentence.

250. c. *Cape Cod* is a proper noun, so both words should be capitalized.

251. c. The correct pronoun is *I*, not *me*.

252. d. All the answer choices are correct.

253. a. There is no such word as *alot*. It should be *a lot*.

254. b. The sentence should read: *I have been there before.*

255. a. Remove *Jamie* from the sentence, and you will quickly see that you would not say *Me went to the store*. It should be *Jamie and I went to the store*.

256. d. All the answer choices are correct.

257. b. *Uncle* is not used as a proper noun and should not be capitalized.

258. c. The verb in this sentence has been incorrectly formed; it should be *drank*, not *drunk*.

259. c. The word *there* should be *their*.

260. a. This sentence is a question and should end in a question mark rather than a period.

261. d. All the answer choices are correct.

262. b. A colon should not be used between a verb and its objects.

263. a. There should be an apostrophe in the word *else's*, which is possessive.

264. d. All the answer choices are correct.

265. b. This is a run-on sentence.

266. c. The commas are missing from this series of adjectives.

267. c. This sentence has a misplaced modifier, which makes the statement illogical. The sentence should read: *Last fall, we visited the house where George Washington lived.*

268. d. All the answer choices are correct.

269. d. All the answer choices are correct.

270. b. There is no subject–verb agreement. *Oldest one* is the subject of this sentence and is used as a singular noun; therefore, it requires the singular verb *is*.

271. b. The quotation mark should appear on the outside of the exclamation point: *"Don't run!"*

272. a. This sentence makes an illogical shift in tense—from present to past tense.

273. c. *Polio* and *smallpox* should not be capitalized. Diseases are not capitalized unless a proper noun is part of the name.

274. c. The connecting word between the two clauses creates an illogical statement. The word *unless* should be changed to the word *but*.

275. d. All the answer choices are correct.

276. b. This is a sentence fragment.

277. d. All the answer choices are correct.

278. a. This sentence makes an illogical shift in tense, from the past to the present tense.

279. a. probably

280. c. pronunciation

281. d. All the words are spelled correctly.

282. b. principal

283. a. principal

284. b. electric

285. d. All the words are spelled correctly.

286. a. scissors

287. a. embarrassed

288. d. All the words are spelled correctly.

289. c. This is the only choice that results in a logical statement. The other choices can be ruled out because they do not show that the man's action is the opposite of what you would expect.

290. d. This is the only choice that contradicts the first half of the sentence.

291. b. In the other choices, the pronoun reference is ambiguous—who's in the hospital? Choice **c** also contains a misplaced modifier, *When in the hospital*, which seems to refer to *a phone call.*

292. d. The other answers contain unnecessary shifts in person from *I* to *one, you,* and *a person.*

293. b. This is the only choice that is clear and unambiguous. All the other choices contain misplaced modifiers, resulting in unclear and illogical statements.

294. a. This choice is clear, has no misplaced modifiers, and has no shifts in verb tense. Choices **b** and **d** have misplaced modifiers and result in unclear sentences; Choice **c** has an unnecessary shift from past to present tense.

295. a. The other choices are much too broad to be adequately covered in a short essay.

296. c. This is the only choice that directly mentions the topic of *nearsightedness.*

297. d. This sentence shifts the topic away from the *hottest decade on record.*

298. d. This sentence sums up the information already given and is best used as this paragraph's concluding sentence.

Scoring

Your raw score on the HSPT will be converted by the Scholastic Testing Service into a standard score to be reported on a scale of 200–800, but for the purpose of seeing how you do on this practice test, just consider simple percentages.

First, find the number of questions you got right in each section. Questions you skipped or answered incorrectly don't count; just add up how many questions you got right in each section. Then, divide the number of questions you got right by the number of questions in each section:

Part 1: Verbal Skills

_____ correct divided by 60 = _____ %

Part 2: Quantitative Skills

_____ correct divided by 52 = _____%

Part 3: Reading

_____ correct divided by 62 = _____%

Part 4: Mathematics

_____ correct divided by 64 = _____%

Part 5: Language Skills

_____ correct divided by 60 = _____%

It is up to the individual high schools to decide what is an acceptable score for admission as a high school freshman. You want to try for the best possible score you can reach to ensure you get into the school you choose. You can use the percentage scores to show you your strong and weak areas. You should study all the lessons of this book that relate to the HSPT exam, but spend more time on the lessons that relate to the parts of the exam that troubled you most. Later, when you take the second HSPT exam in this book, you can compare your percentages on that exam with this first exam to see how much you've improved.

The table that follows shows you which parts of the practice HSPT you just took correspond with which lessons of this book. That way, you'll know where to concentrate your study time.

HSPT PART	LESSON(S)
1: Verbal Skills	8: Vocabulary 10: Verbal Reasoning
2: Quantitative Skills	11: Nonverbal Reasoning 12: Math Skills
3: Reading	7: Reading Comprehension
4: Mathematics	12: Math Skills
5: Language Skills	9: Language Skills

LESSON

5 ▶ PRACTICE COOP EXAM 1

LESSON SUMMARY

This is the first of the two practice tests in this book based on the Cooperative Entrance Exam (COOP). Use this test to see how you would do if you were to take the exam today.

Like the actual COOP that you will be taking, this practice exam is divided into seven separate tests, covering seven different skills. The test itself will be subdivided and timed as follows:

SUBTESTS	NUMBER OF QUESTIONS (APPROXIMATE)	TIME ALLOTTED (APPROXIMATE)
1. Sequences	20	15 minutes
2. Analogies	20	7 minutes
3. Quantitative Reasoning	20	15 minutes
4. Verbal Reasoning—Words	20	15 minutes
5. Verbal Reasoning—Context	20	15 minutes
15-MINUTE BREAK		
6. Reading and Language Arts	40	40 minutes
7. Mathematics	40	35 minutes

The exam is timed, but it will probably be best not to be concerned about that on this first practice exam. Just get some sharpened number 2 pencils, find a place where you won't be disturbed, and take this practice test in as low-key a way as possible, so that you can find out which areas you are best at and which ones will need extra effort.

The answer sheets you should use for the multiple-choice questions are on the following pages. After that comes the exam itself and then the answer key. Many, though not all, of the answers in the key are accompanied by detailed explanations. Read these carefully, as they will tell you why your correct answers are right and your incorrect ones wrong. The answer key is followed by a scoring section so you can see how well you did on the exam.

Test 1: Sequences

1.	ⓐ ⓑ ⓒ ⓓ	8.	ⓐ ⓑ ⓒ ⓓ	15.	ⓐ ⓑ ⓒ ⓓ
2.	ⓐ ⓑ ⓒ ⓓ	9.	ⓐ ⓑ ⓒ ⓓ	16.	ⓐ ⓑ ⓒ ⓓ
3.	ⓐ ⓑ ⓒ ⓓ	10.	ⓐ ⓑ ⓒ ⓓ	17.	ⓐ ⓑ ⓒ ⓓ
4.	ⓐ ⓑ ⓒ ⓓ	11.	ⓐ ⓑ ⓒ ⓓ	19.	ⓐ ⓑ ⓒ ⓓ
5.	ⓐ ⓑ ⓒ ⓓ	12.	ⓐ ⓑ ⓒ ⓓ	20.	ⓐ ⓑ ⓒ ⓓ
6.	ⓐ ⓑ ⓒ ⓓ	13.	ⓐ ⓑ ⓒ ⓓ		
7.	ⓐ ⓑ ⓒ ⓓ	14.	ⓐ ⓑ ⓒ ⓓ		

Test 2: Analogies

1.	ⓐ ⓑ ⓒ ⓓ	8.	ⓐ ⓑ ⓒ ⓓ	15.	ⓐ ⓑ ⓒ ⓓ
2.	ⓐ ⓑ ⓒ ⓓ	9.	ⓐ ⓑ ⓒ ⓓ	16.	ⓐ ⓑ ⓒ ⓓ
3.	ⓐ ⓑ ⓒ ⓓ	10.	ⓐ ⓑ ⓒ ⓓ	17.	ⓐ ⓑ ⓒ ⓓ
4.	ⓐ ⓑ ⓒ ⓓ	11.	ⓐ ⓑ ⓒ ⓓ	19.	ⓐ ⓑ ⓒ ⓓ
5.	ⓐ ⓑ ⓒ ⓓ	12.	ⓐ ⓑ ⓒ ⓓ	20.	ⓐ ⓑ ⓒ ⓓ
6.	ⓐ ⓑ ⓒ ⓓ	13.	ⓐ ⓑ ⓒ ⓓ		
7.	ⓐ ⓑ ⓒ ⓓ	14.	ⓐ ⓑ ⓒ ⓓ		

Test 3: Quantitative Reasoning

1.	ⓐ ⓑ ⓒ ⓓ	8.	ⓐ ⓑ ⓒ ⓓ	15.	ⓐ ⓑ ⓒ ⓓ
2.	ⓐ ⓑ ⓒ ⓓ	9.	ⓐ ⓑ ⓒ ⓓ	16.	ⓐ ⓑ ⓒ ⓓ
3.	ⓐ ⓑ ⓒ ⓓ	10.	ⓐ ⓑ ⓒ ⓓ	17.	ⓐ ⓑ ⓒ ⓓ
4.	ⓐ ⓑ ⓒ ⓓ	11.	ⓐ ⓑ ⓒ ⓓ	19.	ⓐ ⓑ ⓒ ⓓ
5.	ⓐ ⓑ ⓒ ⓓ	12.	ⓐ ⓑ ⓒ ⓓ	20.	ⓐ ⓑ ⓒ ⓓ
6.	ⓐ ⓑ ⓒ ⓓ	13.	ⓐ ⓑ ⓒ ⓓ		
7.	ⓐ ⓑ ⓒ ⓓ	14.	ⓐ ⓑ ⓒ ⓓ		

Test 4: Verbal Reasoning—Words

1.	ⓐ ⓑ ⓒ ⓓ	8.	ⓐ ⓑ ⓒ ⓓ	15.	ⓐ ⓑ ⓒ ⓓ
2.	ⓐ ⓑ ⓒ ⓓ	9.	ⓐ ⓑ ⓒ ⓓ	16.	ⓐ ⓑ ⓒ ⓓ
3.	ⓐ ⓑ ⓒ ⓓ	10.	ⓐ ⓑ ⓒ ⓓ	17.	ⓐ ⓑ ⓒ ⓓ
4.	ⓐ ⓑ ⓒ ⓓ	11.	ⓐ ⓑ ⓒ ⓓ	19.	ⓐ ⓑ ⓒ ⓓ
5.	ⓐ ⓑ ⓒ ⓓ	12.	ⓐ ⓑ ⓒ ⓓ	20.	ⓐ ⓑ ⓒ ⓓ
6.	ⓐ ⓑ ⓒ ⓓ	13.	ⓐ ⓑ ⓒ ⓓ		
7.	ⓐ ⓑ ⓒ ⓓ	14.	ⓐ ⓑ ⓒ ⓓ		

Test 5: Verbal Reasoning—Context

1. ⓐ ⓑ ⓒ ⓓ
2. ⓐ ⓑ ⓒ ⓓ
3. ⓐ ⓑ ⓒ ⓓ
4. ⓐ ⓑ ⓒ ⓓ
5. ⓐ ⓑ ⓒ ⓓ
6. ⓐ ⓑ ⓒ ⓓ
7. ⓐ ⓑ ⓒ ⓓ

8. ⓐ ⓑ ⓒ ⓓ
9. ⓐ ⓑ ⓒ ⓓ
10. ⓐ ⓑ ⓒ ⓓ
11. ⓐ ⓑ ⓒ ⓓ
12. ⓐ ⓑ ⓒ ⓓ
13. ⓐ ⓑ ⓒ ⓓ
14. ⓐ ⓑ ⓒ ⓓ

15. ⓐ ⓑ ⓒ ⓓ
16. ⓐ ⓑ ⓒ ⓓ
17. ⓐ ⓑ ⓒ ⓓ
19. ⓐ ⓑ ⓒ ⓓ
20. ⓐ ⓑ ⓒ ⓓ

Test 6: Reading and Language Arts

1. ⓐ ⓑ ⓒ ⓓ
2. ⓐ ⓑ ⓒ ⓓ
3. ⓐ ⓑ ⓒ ⓓ
4. ⓐ ⓑ ⓒ ⓓ
5. ⓐ ⓑ ⓒ ⓓ
6. ⓐ ⓑ ⓒ ⓓ
7. ⓐ ⓑ ⓒ ⓓ
8. ⓐ ⓑ ⓒ ⓓ
9. ⓐ ⓑ ⓒ ⓓ
10. ⓐ ⓑ ⓒ ⓓ
11. ⓐ ⓑ ⓒ ⓓ
12. ⓐ ⓑ ⓒ ⓓ
13. ⓐ ⓑ ⓒ ⓓ
14. ⓐ ⓑ ⓒ ⓓ

15. ⓐ ⓑ ⓒ ⓓ
16. ⓐ ⓑ ⓒ ⓓ
17. ⓐ ⓑ ⓒ ⓓ
18. ⓐ ⓑ ⓒ ⓓ
19. ⓐ ⓑ ⓒ ⓓ
20. ⓐ ⓑ ⓒ ⓓ
21. ⓐ ⓑ ⓒ ⓓ
22. ⓐ ⓑ ⓒ ⓓ
23. ⓐ ⓑ ⓒ ⓓ
24. ⓐ ⓑ ⓒ ⓓ
25. ⓐ ⓑ ⓒ ⓓ
26. ⓐ ⓑ ⓒ ⓓ
27. ⓐ ⓑ ⓒ ⓓ
28. ⓐ ⓑ ⓒ ⓓ

29. ⓐ ⓑ ⓒ ⓓ
30. ⓐ ⓑ ⓒ ⓓ
31. ⓐ ⓑ ⓒ ⓓ
32. ⓐ ⓑ ⓒ ⓓ
33. ⓐ ⓑ ⓒ ⓓ
34. ⓐ ⓑ ⓒ ⓓ
35. ⓐ ⓑ ⓒ ⓓ
36. ⓐ ⓑ ⓒ ⓓ
37. ⓐ ⓑ ⓒ ⓓ
38. ⓐ ⓑ ⓒ ⓓ
39. ⓐ ⓑ ⓒ ⓓ
40. ⓐ ⓑ ⓒ ⓓ

Test 7: Mathematics

1. ⓐ ⓑ ⓒ ⓓ
2. ⓐ ⓑ ⓒ ⓓ
3. ⓐ ⓑ ⓒ ⓓ
4. ⓐ ⓑ ⓒ ⓓ
5. ⓐ ⓑ ⓒ ⓓ
6. ⓐ ⓑ ⓒ ⓓ
7. ⓐ ⓑ ⓒ ⓓ
8. ⓐ ⓑ ⓒ ⓓ
9. ⓐ ⓑ ⓒ ⓓ
10. ⓐ ⓑ ⓒ ⓓ
11. ⓐ ⓑ ⓒ ⓓ
12. ⓐ ⓑ ⓒ ⓓ
13. ⓐ ⓑ ⓒ ⓓ
14. ⓐ ⓑ ⓒ ⓓ

15. ⓐ ⓑ ⓒ ⓓ
16. ⓐ ⓑ ⓒ ⓓ
17. ⓐ ⓑ ⓒ ⓓ
18. ⓐ ⓑ ⓒ ⓓ
19. ⓐ ⓑ ⓒ ⓓ
20. ⓐ ⓑ ⓒ ⓓ
21. ⓐ ⓑ ⓒ ⓓ
22. ⓐ ⓑ ⓒ ⓓ
23. ⓐ ⓑ ⓒ ⓓ
24. ⓐ ⓑ ⓒ ⓓ
25. ⓐ ⓑ ⓒ ⓓ
26. ⓐ ⓑ ⓒ ⓓ
27. ⓐ ⓑ ⓒ ⓓ
28. ⓐ ⓑ ⓒ ⓓ

29. ⓐ ⓑ ⓒ ⓓ
30. ⓐ ⓑ ⓒ ⓓ
31. ⓐ ⓑ ⓒ ⓓ
32. ⓐ ⓑ ⓒ ⓓ
33. ⓐ ⓑ ⓒ ⓓ
34. ⓐ ⓑ ⓒ ⓓ
35. ⓐ ⓑ ⓒ ⓓ
36. ⓐ ⓑ ⓒ ⓓ
37. ⓐ ⓑ ⓒ ⓓ
38. ⓐ ⓑ ⓒ ⓓ
39. ⓐ ⓑ ⓒ ⓓ
40. ⓐ ⓑ ⓒ ⓓ

Test 1: Sequences

You have 15 minutes for this section. Select the answer choice that best completes the sequence given.

1.

2.

3.

4.

5.

6.

7.

8. 75 67 59 | 43 35 27 | 16 8 __
   a. 7
   b. 9
   c. 3
   d. 0

9. 8 12 16 | 33 37 41 | 57 61 __
   a. 62
   b. 65
   c. 73
   d. 57

10. 10 | 15 | 13 | 22 | 27 | 25 | 38 | 43 ____
   a. 39
   b. 40
   c. 41
   d. 48

11. $\frac{1}{2}$ 1 $\frac{1}{4}$ | 2 4 1 | 1 __ $\frac{1}{2}$
   a. $\frac{1}{4}$
   b. 2
   c. 3
   d. 6

12. 24 48 8 | 36 72 12 | 15 30 __
   a. 5
   b. 9
   c. 7
   d. 13

13. 8 | 22 | 9 | 12 | 26 | 13 | 15 | 29 ____
   a. 15
   b. 16
   c. 28
   d. 36

14. 12 6 3 | 16 8 4 | 36 __ 9
   a. 4.5
   b. 6
   c. 18
   d. 27

15. VUT SRQ PON _____
   a. MLK
   b. PDQ
   c. JHI
   d. ABC

16. AZB YCX DWE ____
   a. JKL
   b. VFU
   c. ZPI
   d. FVG

17. $ABCD_4$ ABC_3D _____ A_1BCD
   a. AB_3CD
   b. AB_2CD
   c. DEF_3G
   d. AC_2BC

18. ELFA GLHA ILJA ____ MLNA
   a. OLPA
   b. KLMA
   c. LLMA
   d. KLLA

19. P_5QR P_4QS P_3QT ____ PQV
   a. PQW
   b. PQV_2
   c. P_2QU
   d. PQ_3U

20. CMM EOO GQQ __ KUU
   a. GRR
   b. GSS
   c. ISS
   d. ITT

Test 2: Analogies

You have seven minutes for this section. For questions 1 through 20, choose the picture that would go in the empty box so that the two bottom pictures are related in the same way as the top two are related.

1.

a.   b.   c.   d.

2.

a.   b.   c.   d.

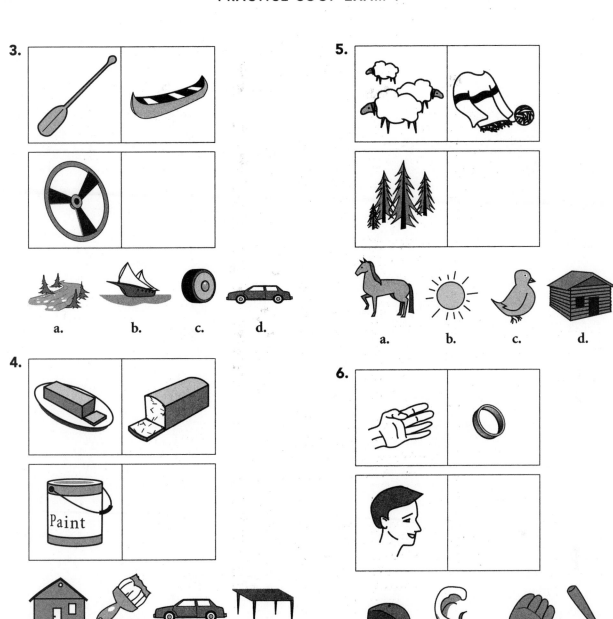

3.

a.　b.　c.　d.

4.

a.　b.　c.　d.

5.

a.　b.　c.　d.

6.

a.　b.　c.　d.

7.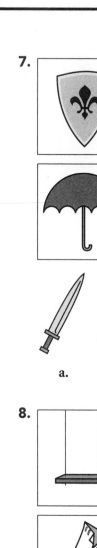

a. b. c. d.

8.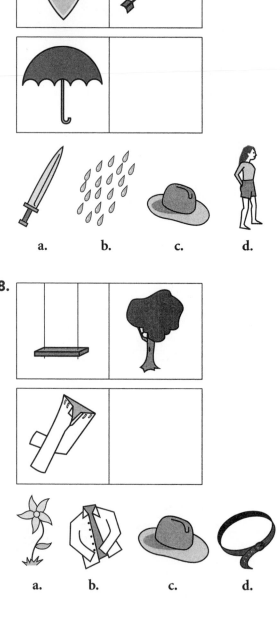

a. b. c. d.

9.

a. b. c. d.

10.

a. b. c. d.

11.

a.　　　b.　　　c.　　　d.

13.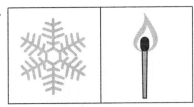

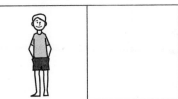

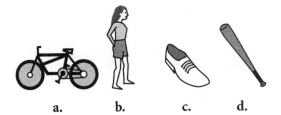

a.　　　b.　　　c.　　　d.

12.

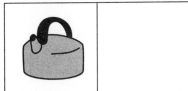

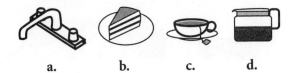

a.　　　b.　　　c.　　　d.

14.

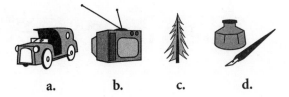

a.　　　b.　　　c.　　　d.

15.

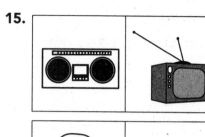

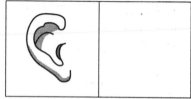

a.   b.   c.   d.

17.

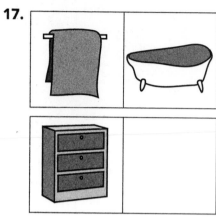

a.   b.   c.   d.

16.

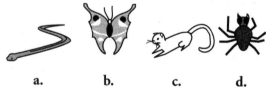

a.   b.   c.   d.

18.

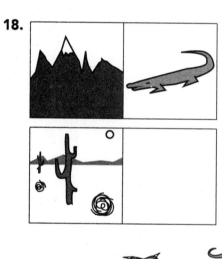

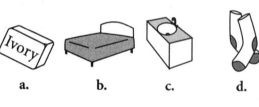

a.   b.   c.   d.

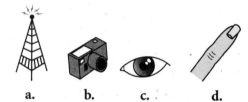

19.

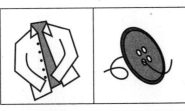

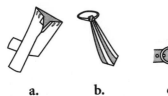

   a.   b.   c.   d.

20.

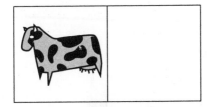

   a.   b.   c.   d.

Test 3:
Quantitative Reasoning

For questions 1 through 7, find the relationship of the numbers in one column to the numbers in the other column. Then find the missing number.

1. 10 → ▌→ 2
   20 → ▌→ 4
   5 → ▌→ 1
   100 → ▌→
   a. 5
   b. 20
   c. 8
   d. 4

2. 13 → ▌→ 7
   24 → ▌→ 18
   8 → ▌→ 2
   12 → ▌→
   a. 16
   b. 14
   c. 8
   d. 6

3. 0.3 → ▌→ 3
   0.021 → ▌→ 0.21
   0.01 → ▌→ 0.1
   10 → ▌→
   a. 100
   b. 10
   c. 0.1
   d. 0.01

4. 6 → ▌→ −3
   13 → ▌→ 4
   21 → ▌→ 12
   8 → ▌→
   a. −1
   b. −9
   c. 3
   d. −3

5. 4 → ▌ → 12
    15 → ▌ → 45
    6 → ▌ → 18
    3 → ▌ →
    a. 6
    b. 9
    c. 11
    d. 17

6. 5 → ▌ → 11
    13 → ▌ → 19
    −6 → ▌ → 0
    8 → ▌ →
    a. 4
    b. 11
    c. 14
    d. 8

7. 12 → ▌ → 3
    24 → ▌ → 6
    36 → ▌ → 9
    44 → ▌ →
    a. 8
    b. 11
    c. 12
    d. 15

For questions 8 through 14, find the shaded fraction of the grid.

8.

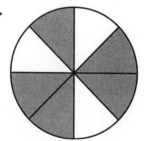

    a. $\frac{8}{5}$
    b. $\frac{5}{8}$
    c. $\frac{3}{8}$
    d. $\frac{1}{5}$

9.

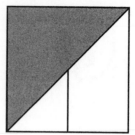

    a. $\frac{1}{2}$
    b. $\frac{1}{8}$
    c. $\frac{4}{8}$
    d. $\frac{3}{4}$

10.

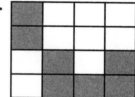

    a. $\frac{16}{7}$
    b. $\frac{8}{7}$
    c. $\frac{4}{16}$
    d. $\frac{7}{16}$

11.

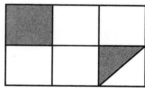

    a. $\frac{4}{3}$
    b. $\frac{5}{6}$
    c. $\frac{1}{4}$
    d. $\frac{3}{4}$

12.

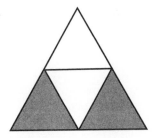

a. $\frac{3}{4}$

b. $\frac{1}{2}$

c. $\frac{2}{4}$

d. $\frac{3}{2}$

13.

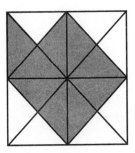

a. $\frac{9}{16}$

b. $\frac{7}{9}$

c. $\frac{6}{9}$

d. $\frac{3}{16}$

14.

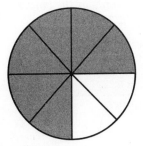

a. $\frac{3}{4}$

b. $\frac{2}{3}$

c. $\frac{8}{6}$

d. $\frac{3}{4}$

For questions 15 through 20, look at the scale showing sets of shapes of equal weight. Find an equivalent pair of sets that would also balance the scale.

15.

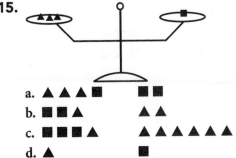

a. ▲▲▲■   ■■

b. ■■▲   ▲▲

c. ■■▲   ▲▲▲▲▲▲

d. ▲   ■

16.

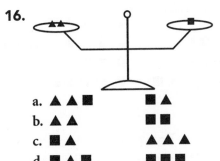

a. ▲▲■   ■▲

b. ▲▲   ■■

c. ■▲   ▲▲▲

d. ■▲■   ■■■

17.

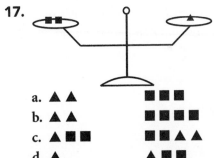

a. ▲▲   ■■■

b. ▲▲   ■■■■

c. ▲■■   ■■▲▲

d. ▲   ▲■■

18.

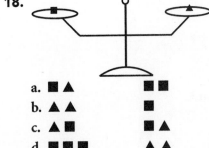

a. ■▲   ■■

b. ▲▲   ■

c. ▲■   ■▲

d. ■■■   ▲▲

19.

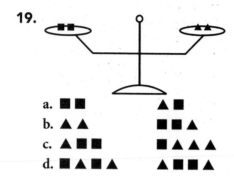

a. ■■ ▲■
b. ▲ ▲ ■■ ▲
c. ▲ ■■ ■ ▲ ▲ ▲
d. ■ ▲ ■ ▲ ▲ ■ ■ ▲

20.

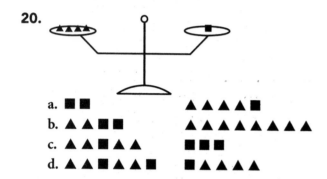

a. ■■ ▲ ▲ ▲ ▲ ■
b. ▲ ▲ ■■ ▲ ▲ ▲ ▲ ▲ ▲ ▲
c. ▲ ▲ ■ ▲ ▲ ▲ ■ ■ ■
d. ▲ ▲ ■ ▲ ▲ ■ ■ ▲ ▲ ▲ ▲

Test 4:
Verbal Reasoning—Words

You have 15 minutes for this section. For questions 1 through 6, find the word that names a necessary part of the underlined word.

1. book
   a. fiction
   b. pages
   c. pictures
   d. learning

2. piano
   a. orchestra
   b. notes
   c. teacher
   d. keyboard

3. tree
   a. trunk
   b. forest
   c. fruit
   d. acorn

4. bed
   a. sheets
   b. mattress
   c. pillows
   d. sleep

5. dishwasher
   a. kitchen
   b. water
   c. spoon
   d. plate

6. hurricane
   a. wind
   b. rain
   c. clouds
   d. weather

For questions 7 through 12, the words in the top row are related in some way. The words in the bottom row are related in the same way. For each item, find the word that completes the bottom row of words.

7. fork   knife   spoon
   wrench   hammer   _____
   a. wood
   b. pencil
   c. saw
   d. plate

8. snow   mountain   ski
   warmth   lake   _____
   a. sand
   b. swim
   c. sunburn
   d. vacation

9. candle   lamp   floodlight

    hut   cottage   _____

    a. tent

    b. city

    c. dwelling

    d. house

10. aspirin   medicine   pharmacy

    lettuce   vegetable   _____

    a. grocery

    b. carrots

    c. fruit

    d. shopping

11. bedroom   basement   kitchen

    tires   engine   _____

    a. attic

    b. wheelbarrow

    c. garden

    d. headlight

12. walk   skip   run

    toss   pitch   _____

    a. swerve

    b. hurl

    c. jump

    d. dance

For questions 13 through 17, three of the words in the group belong together. Find the word that does NOT belong.

13. Which word does NOT belong with the others?

    a. leopard

    b. cougar

    c. elephant

    d. lion

14. Which word does NOT belong with the others?

    a. couch

    b. rug

    c. table

    d. chair

15. Which word does NOT belong with the others?

    a. tape

    b. twine

    c. cord

    d. yarn

16. Which word does NOT belong with the others?

    a. calendar

    b. time

    c. watch

    d. clock

17. Which word does NOT belong with the others?

    a. book

    b. magazine

    c. periodical

    d. library

For questions 18 through 20, find the word that is most like the underlined words.

18. clean   spotless   neat

    a. efficient

    b. careful

    c. tidy

    d. hazardous

19. unimportant   insignificant   irrelevant

    a. trivial

    b. familiar

    c. restless

    d. boring

20. index   glossary   lesson

    a. appendix

    b. book

    c. imprint

    d. manuscript

Test 5:
Verbal Reasoning—Context

For questions 1 through 20, find the statement that is true according to the given information.

1. Mary uses four cups of flour when she bakes brownies, but only three cups when she bakes cookies. She likes brownies, but saves money by making cookies.
   a. Cookies require less flour than brownies.
   b. The price of flour has gone up.
   c. Mary does not like cookies.
   d. The recipes make more cookies than brownies.

2. Last week, Lia celebrated her birthday. She received many presents, flowers, and a large box of Godiva chocolates, which she has not yet opened.
   a. Lia has not yet opened the chocolates because she plans to share them with her friends.
   b. Lia received a box of Godiva chocolates for her birthday.
   c. Lia does not like Godiva chocolate.
   d. Lia loves her birthday.

3. The Bolshoi Theater is one of Moscow's oldest and most esteemed theaters. Last summer, Max visited the Bolshoi Theater and saw a brilliant ballet performance of *Swan Lake*.
   a. The Bolshoi Theater is the center of Moscow's cultural life.
   b. Many tourists visit the Bolshoi Theater every season.
   c. Some of the most incredible performers of our time have been on the stage of the Bolshoi Theater.
   d. Max had been to Moscow last summer.

4. To enter a creative writing program, all students must submit a 50-page portfolio of original work. Veronika is in a creative writing program.
   a. Veronika submitted a 50-page portfolio of original work.
   b. Veronika is an excellent student.
   c. Veronika does not enjoy her program.
   d. Veronika is a better writer than most students in her program.

5. Oscar Wilde said: "I always pass on good advice. It is the only thing to do with it. It is never of any use to oneself." Oscar Wilde was a great Irish writer best known for his sophisticated plays and witty remarks.
   a. Oscar Wilde felt that a sophisticated play must always include good advice.
   b. Oscar Wilde believed that good advice must always be witty.
   c. Oscar Wilde didn't believe that taking good advice can be useful to oneself.
   d. Oscar Wilde listened to good advice whenever possible.

6. Mike makes paperweights out of empty soda cans that he collects on the beach. He sells them at several stores in town and also on the Internet. He is saving the proceeds to buy a new computer.
   a. Mike is a good environmentalist.
   b. The beach is covered with litter.
   c. Paperweights sell better in stores than on the Internet.
   d. Mike is saving his money rather than spending it.

7. Francesca and Mario shared an art space for a photography exhibition in New Orleans. Mario sold four of his works and Francesca sold six.
   a. Mario and Francesca are the best photographers in New Orleans.
   b. Mario sold fewer works than Francesca.
   c. Francesca is a better photographer than Mario.
   d. Mario bought one of Francesca's works.

8. There are about 200 calories in a cup of cappuccino at a local coffee shop. A cup of espresso at the same coffee shop has about 100 calories.
   a. People prefer to drink espresso because it is less fattening.
   b. Cappuccino tastes better than an espresso.
   c. There are more calories in a cup of cappuccino than in a cup of espresso.
   d. People generally do not care about their caloric intake.

9. Dave listens to classical music when he relaxes, but he likes Irish music when he exercises. He does not play any music when he does his homework so that he can concentrate better.
   a. Music distracts Dave from concentrating.
   b. Dave listens to more classical than Irish music.
   c. Irish music is good for exercise.
   d. Dave likes Irish music more than jazz.

10. Michael has a 6-pound puppy named Lucy, and Ilsa has a 35-pound puppy named Thurber. Michael and Ilsa are both very fond of their dogs.
   a. Michael loves his puppy more than Ilsa loves hers.
   b. Lucy is smaller than Thurber.
   c. Thurber is older than Lucy.
   d. Thurber is smarter than Lucy.

11. Mr. Brown, a popular local baker, offers a loaf of bread free of charge to every one of his customers who believes the bread they bought at Mr. Brown's bakery was stale. Mr. Brown's bread is Gabriela's favorite.
   a. Gabriela is a customer of Mr. Brown.
   b. Gabriela is the only customer of Mr. Brown.
   c. Gabriela is Mr. Brown's favorite customer.
   d. Gabriela buys bread only at Mr. Brown's bakery.

12. For his drawings, Christopher uses only his special black-ink pen. Tonight, Christopher has forgotten his pen at a friend's apartment.
   a. Christopher is usually very forgetful.
   b. Christopher does not have too many friends.
   c. Christopher will probably not draw tonight.
   d. Christopher draws every night.

13. When it is cold and rainy outside, Dan does not like to go out. When the weather is nice, Dan never stays in. Yesterday, Dan spent an entire day at home.
   a. Dan likes to stay at home and read.
   b. Dan does very little work at home.
   c. Yesterday, the weather was nice.
   d. Yesterday was a cold and rainy day.

14. Mary is taking a bus ride from New York to Boston. The bus ride from New York to Boston takes approximately 4.5 hours.
   a. Mary does not enjoy her bus ride.
   b. It takes approximately 4.5 hours by bus to get from New York to Boston.
   c. Mary will be in Boston in 4.5 hours.
   d. Mary has never taken a bus ride to Boston before.

15. The Smiths own a small house with a large garden, two cars, and a small garage. Mr. and Mrs. Smith drive a blue Jeep Cherokee, which they park in their garage every night. Their son, Josh, has a black Nissan, which he keeps in the driveway.

   a. The Smiths own more than two cars.

   b. The Smiths have a one-car garage.

   c. Josh uses his car more often than his parents.

   d. The Smiths like their car more than Josh likes his.

16. Alex and Jim are brothers. Alex is older than Jim. Jim is almost as tall as his father.

   a. Jim is younger than Alex.

   b. Alex is taller than his father.

   c. Alex is taller than Jim.

   d. Alex and Jim's father looks very young for his age.

17. Mark was 12 when he began to learn about photography. He started by playing with his father's camera, but he began to progress when he read some books on photography. He picked up his father's camera the day that his father died, and it changed his life.

   a. Mark is a famous photographer.

   b. Reading books is the best way to learn.

   c. Photography is hard to learn.

   d. Mark was 12 when his father died.

18. The only convenience store near Kevin's house is 20 minutes away and closes at midnight. At 11:50 P.M., Kevin remembered that he forgot to pick up a bottle of juice. He went to the store as soon as he remembered, but returned shortly empty-handed.

   a. Kevin does not like going to the convenience store.

   b. The convenience store was probably already closed.

   c. Kevin did not go to the store.

   d. Kevin is usually very lazy.

19. May keeps her spare change in a bowl on her desk. A dollar is missing from her bowl. May's brother Andy is always borrowing change from her.

   a. Andy does not have an income.

   b. Andy took a dollar from May's bowl.

   c. May always has a lot of spare change.

   d. May keeps her spare change in a bowl on her desk.

20. Betty writes letters to friends using fountain pens, but when she writes to Bill, she uses a special calligraphy pen. The calligraphy pen has not been used in three weeks.

   a. Bill is not out of town at present.

   b. Betty has not written to Bill in three weeks.

   c. Betty's friends have continued to receive letters.

   d. Betty is in love with Bill.

Test 6: Reading and Language Arts

You have 40 minutes for this section. For questions 1 and 2, read the passage carefully. Then read each item and choose the correct answer.

The Frankish Empire

Emperor Charlemagne of the Franks was crowned in 800 A.D. The Frankish Empire at that time extended over what is now Germany, Italy, and France. Charlemagne died in 814, but his brief reign marked the dawn of a distinctly European culture. The artists and thinkers who helped create this European civilization drew on the ancient texts of the Germanic, Celtic, Greek, Roman, Hebrew, and Christian worlds. Many of the traditions of these cultures remained active in Frankish society for centuries. These ways of life, in turn, laid the groundwork for the laws, customs, and even attitudes of today's Europeans.

1. According to the passage, for how many years was Charlemagne Emperor of the Franks?
   a. 14 years
   b. 15 years
   c. 13 years
   d. 16 years

2. What does the passage imply about modern European culture?
   a. It began well after the death of Charlemagne.
   b. Charlemagne forced his ideas about culture on the Europeans.
   c. It is narrower than other cultures.
   d. It is made up of several different cultures.

For questions 3 through 7, read the passage carefully. Then read each item and choose the correct answer.

Hearing Loss

Before you turn up your boom box or buy front-row seats to a rock concert, you might want to consider how excessive noise affects your hearing. According to Nancy Hadler, director of the League for the Hard of Hearing's Noise Center, dance clubs, over-amped stereos, noisy vehicles, and even movie soundtracks can contribute to hearing loss.

Hearing loss is sly, slow, and irreversible. There are 30,000 tiny fibers inside each cochlea, which is the spiral-shaped cavity of the inner ear. These hair cells bend in response to sound and create a charge that stimulates the nerve endings at the bottom of each cell. With repeated noise bombardment, these nerve cells can burn out. Hadler compares the nerve fibers to a shag carpet. A good vacuuming will restore the fluffy nap, but if you walk across the same spot too many times, all the vacuuming in the world won't bring the dead fibers back.

Protect yourself from excessive, loud noise. If you are <u>routinely</u> exposed, wear earplugs. And turn down the sound on all your machines.

3. This passage is mainly about how
   a. to protect yourself from loud noise.
   b. the inner ear works.
   c. loud noise affects hearing.
   d. a person's nerve cells are destroyed.

4. According to the passage, the cochlea is
   a. a tiny nerve fiber.
   b. part of the inner ear.
   c. part of the outer ear.
   d. a synonym for the term *hearing loss.*

5. The passage includes a metaphor (comparison) that compares a shag carpet to
   a. loud music.
   b. earplugs.
   c. hearing loss.
   d. tiny fibers in the ear.

6. Which of the following most likely states the opinion of the author?
   a. Wear earplugs when you operate any loud machinery.
   b. Give up going to the movie theater.
   c. Have your hearing tested every six months.
   d. Don't listen to music on a boom box.

7. A synonym for the word <u>routinely</u>, as it is used in the last paragraph, is
   a. sometimes.
   b. regularly.
   c. carelessly.
   d. periodically.

For questions 8 through 11, read the passage carefully. Then read each item and choose the correct answer.

Amelia Earhart is the most celebrated aviatrix in history and was one of the most famous women of her time. As America's <u>charismatic</u> "Lady of the Air," she set many aviation records, including becoming the first woman to fly across the Atlantic in 1928 as a passenger, the first woman (and second person after Lindbergh) to fly solo across the Atlantic in 1932, and the first person to fly alone across the Pacific, from Honolulu, Hawaii, to Oakland, California, in 1935. In an era when men dominated aviation, she was truly a pioneer.

   In 1937, Earhart attempted to become the first person ever to fly around the world at its longest point—the equator—a challenging trip of 29,000 miles. She intended this feat to be the last record-setting flight of her legendary career. On July 2, 1937, after successfully completing 22,000 miles of the journey in her silver twin-engine Electra, she took off from Lae, New Guinea, on the longest and most dangerous leg of her flight. She was to fly some 18 hours and 2,556 miles across the vast ocean to Howland Island where she could get supplies. Somewhere along this part of the route, Earhart vanished along with her navigator, Frederick Noonan. A great naval, air, and land search failed to locate the two aviators or the aircraft, and it was assumed they were lost at sea. To this day, their fate is the subject of unending speculation.

8. Which of the following would be the best title for this passage?
   a. "Amelia Earhart: Lady of the Air"
   b. "Finding Amelia Earhart"
   c. "Around the World with Amelia Earhart"
   d. "Amelia Earhart: Lost at Sea"

9. What is the best definition for the word <u>charismatic</u> as it is used in the first paragraph of the passage?
   a. having feelings of great charity for others
   b. giving serious attention to the health, welfare, and protection of someone or something
   c. a power or talent that is divinely conferred
   d. exercising a compelling charm that inspires devotion in others

10. According to the passage, Amelia Earhart vanished closest to what location?
   a. Howland Island
   b. Lae, New Guinea
   c. Honolulu, Hawaii
   d. Oakland, California

11. With which of the following statements about Amelia Earhart would the author of the passage most likely agree?

    a. She was foolish to fly so far.

    b. She was a great aviatrix.

    c. She is probably still alive.

    d. Her navigator caused the crash.

For questions 12 through 17, read the passage carefully. Then read each item and choose the correct answer.

Mt. Desert Island

The coast of the state of Maine is one of the most irregular in the world. A straight line running from the southernmost city in Maine, Kittery, to the northernmost coastal city, Eastport, would measure about 225 miles. If you followed the coastline between the same two cities, you would travel more than ten times as far. This irregularity is the result of what is called a *drowned coastline*. The term comes from the glacial activity of the ice age. At that time, the whole area that is now Maine was part of a mountain range that towered above the sea. As the glacier descended, however, it expended enormous force on those mountains and they sank into the sea.

As the mountains sank, ocean water charged over the lowest parts of the remaining land, forming a series of twisting inlets and lagoons of contorted grottos and nooks. The highest parts of the former mountain range, nearest the shore, remained as islands. Mt. Desert Island was one of the most famous of all the islands left behind by the glacier. Marine fossils found here were 225 feet above sea level, indicating the level of the shoreline prior to the glacier.

The long, rocky, and jagged coastline of Maine keeps watch over nearly 2,000 islands. Many of these islands are tiny and uninhabited, but many are home to thriving communities. Mt. Desert Island is one of the largest, most beautiful of the Maine coast islands. Measuring 16 miles by 12 miles, Mt. Desert was very nearly formed at two distinct islands. It is split in half by Somes Sound, a very deep and very narrow stretch of water seven miles long.

For years, Mt. Desert Island, particularly its major settlement, Bar Harbor, afforded summer homes for the wealthy. Recently, Bar Harbor has become a burgeoning arts community as well. But the best part of the island is the unspoiled forest land known as Acadia National Park. Since the island sits on the boundary line between the temperate and subarctic zones, the island supports the flora and fauna of both zones as well as beach, inland, and alpine plants. It also lies in a major bird migration land and is a resting spot for many birds. The establishment of Acadia National Park in 1916 means that this natural monument will be preserved and that it will be available to all people, not just the wealthy. Visitors to Acadia may receive nature instructions from the park naturalists as well as enjoy camping, hiking, cycling, and boating. Or they may choose to spend time at the archeological museum learning about the Stone Age inhabitants of the island.

The best view on Mt. Desert Island is from the top of Cadillac Mountain. This mountain rises 1,532 feet, making it the highest mountain on the Atlantic seaboard. From the summit, you can gaze back toward the mainland or out over the Atlantic Ocean and contemplate the beauty created by a retreating glacier.

12. Which of the following lists of topics best outlines the information in the selection?
   a. —Ice-age glacial activity
       —Maine's mountain ranges
       —Summer residents of Mt. Desert Island
   b. —Formation of a drowned coastline
       —Formation of coastal islands
       —The environment of Mt. Desert Island
   c. —Mapping the Maine coastline
       —The arts community at Bar Harbor
       —History of the National Park system
   d. —The effect of glaciers on small islands
       —The importance of biodiversity
       —Acadia National Park

13. Which of the following statements best expresses the main idea of the second to last paragraph?
   a. The wealthy residents of Mt. Desert Island selfishly kept it to themselves.
   b. Acadia National Park is most likely one of the smallest of the national parks.
   c. On Mt. Desert Island, there is tension between the year-round residents and the summer tourists.
   d. Mt. Desert Island supports an incredibly diverse animal and plant life.

14. According to the passage, the large number of small islands along the coast of Maine are the result of
   a. glaciers forcing a mountain range into the sea.
   b. Maine's location between the temperate and subarctic zones.
   c. the irregularity of the Maine coast.
   d. the need for summer communities for wealthy tourists and artists.

15. According to the passage, the coast of Maine is
   a. 2,500 miles long.
   b. 3,500 miles long.
   c. 225 miles long.
   d. 235 miles long.

16. According to the passage, when the glacier moved over what is now the state of Maine, it helped to create all the following EXCEPT
   a. an irregular coastline.
   b. coastal islands.
   c. a mountain range.
   d. inlets and lagoons.

17. One of the main reasons that Mt. Desert Island has so many different plants and animals is that
   a. there are so many wealthy people who live there.
   b. Bar Harbor is a national park.
   c. it is all forest land.
   d. it sits between two climate zones.

For questions 18 through 22, read the passage carefully. Then read each item and choose the correct answer.

The Blizzard of 1978 was one of the worst snowstorms in memory for the Northeast. The weather reports had predicted snow flurries for that day in February, and public transportation and highway departments had taken no special precautions. But those "flurries" quickly changed to blinding snow, driven by strong winds, and within hours all roads were closed.

For several days after the storm had cleared, major highways remained legally closed—even the most <u>intrepid</u> motorists were not venturing out of their driveways.

Businesses, schools, public transportation—all of New England was brought to a standstill, yet the storm's effects could have been <u>ameliorated</u> with better preparations.

18. According to the passage, when did the Northeast experience a bad snowstorm?
  a. January 1978
  b. February 1978
  c. March 1977
  d. December 1872

19. As used in the passage, the word <u>intrepid</u> most nearly means
  a. fearless.
  b. stupid.
  c. clumsy.
  d. native.

20. According to the passage, the storm might have done less damage if
  a. it had gone out to sea sooner.
  b. the federal government had sent help.
  c. the highways had remained open.
  d. people had been better prepared.

21. Which of the following would be the best title for this passage?
  a. "Fun in the Snow"
  b. "The Conspiracy Behind the Storm"
  c. "The Dangers of Global Warming"
  d. "The Blizzard That Caught Us Off Guard"

22. As it is used in the passage, the word <u>ameliorated</u> most nearly means
  a. increased.
  b. past due.
  c. made less.
  d. slippery.

For questions 23 through 26, read the passage carefully. Then read each item and choose the correct answer.

Cowboy

The meaning of the term *cowboy* has changed dramatically through the years. *Cowboy* was first applied during the Revolutionary War to pro-British gangs, who roamed the <u>neutral</u> ground just north of New York City. Their enemies, who favored the Revolutionary cause and who operated in the same territory at the same period, were called *skinners*.

By the 1870s, however, the word cowboy was used to describe the mounted outdoorsmen who herded cattle on the Great Plains. These cowboys rounded up cattle and branded them, drove them to pasture and water, protected them from wild animals and thieves, and ultimately drove them to their shipping point.

The life of a cowboy changed again with the introduction of barbed wire. These prickly fences rapidly encroached on the open ranges, and by 1895, railway expansion had made trail-driving uneconomical. These trail herders settled down to work on cattle ranches, becoming the cowboys with whom we are familiar today.

23. Which of the following is NOT correct according to the information given in the passage?
  a. Cowboys are responsible for branding cattle.
  b. Barbed wire changed the life of a cowboy.
  c. *Cowboy* originated on the ranches out West.
  d. The meaning of *cowboy* has changed through the years.

24. The people who favored the Revolutionary War were called
  a. cowboys.
  b. thieves.
  c. skinners.
  d. outdoorsmen.

25. The author's purpose in writing this passage was probably to
  a. inform readers about the life of a cowboy.
  b. encourage young people to become cowboys.
  c. tell some interesting facts about the history of the word *cowboy*.
  d. dispel myths about the duties of cowboys.

26. Which of the following best defines the word <u>neutral</u> as used in the first paragraph?
  a. a mass without an electric charge
  b. discovered recently or for the first time
  c. neither masculine or feminine
  d. not helping or supporting either opposing side

For questions 27 through 32, read the passage carefully. Then read each item and choose the correct answer.

The Hershey Chocolate Company
Milton Hershey was born near the small village of Derry Church, Pennsylvania, in 1857. It was a modest beginning; Milton attended school through only the fourth grade, at which point he was apprenticed to a printer in a nearby town. Fortunately for all chocolate lovers, Milton did not excel as a printer. After a while, he left the printing business and was apprenticed to a Lancaster, Pennsylvania, candymaker. It was apparent he had found his calling in life, and at the age of 18, he opened his own candy store in Philadelphia. In spite of his talents as a candymaker, however, the shop failed after six years.

After the failure of his store, Milton headed for Denver, where he learned the art of making caramels. There, he saw that using fresh milk made the caramels especially tasty. After a time in Denver, Milton once again made several attempts to open his own candymaking businesses. Finally, in 1886, he went to Lancaster, Pennsylvania, where he raised enough money to open the Lancaster Caramel Company.

In 1893, Milton attended the Chicago International Exposition, where he saw a display of German chocolate-making implements. Captivated by the equipment, he purchased it for his candy factory and began producing chocolate, which he used for coating his caramels. By the next year, production had grown to include cocoa, sweet chocolate, and baking chocolate. The Hershey Chocolate Company was born in 1894 as a <u>subsidiary</u> of the Lancaster Caramel Company.

Milton returned to the village where he had been born. He opened his chocolate manufacturing plant and began producing the finest milk chocolate. The plant that opened in 1905, in a small Pennsylvania village now known as Hershey, Pennsylvania, is today the largest chocolate factory in the world.

27. Based on the passage, which of the following statements is accurate?
  a. Chocolate is popular in every country in the world.
  b. The Hershey Chocolate Company's factory is near Derry Church, Pennsylvania.
  c. Chocolate had never been manufactured in the United States before Milton Hershey did it.
  d. The Hershey Chocolate Company is run by Milton Hershey's children.

28. The writer's main purpose in this passage is to
   a. recount the founding of the Hershey Chocolate Company.
   b. describe the process of manufacturing chocolate.
   c. compare the popularity of chocolate to other candies.
   d. explain how apprenticeships work.

29. Which of the following words best describes Milton Hershey's character, as he is presented in the passage?
   a. defective
   b. determined
   c. carefree
   d. cautious

30. According to the passage, Milton Hershey first began to produce chocolate in order to
   a. make cocoa and baking chocolate.
   b. save his caramel company from bankruptcy.
   c. make chocolate-covered caramels.
   d. attend the Chicago International Exposition.

31. Which of the following best defines the word subsidiary, as used in the third paragraph?
   a. a company owned entirely by one person
   b. a company founded to support another company
   c. a company that is not incorporated
   d. a company controlled by another company

32. The passage implies that Hershey opened his first chocolate company in
   a. Chicago.
   b. Denver.
   c. Philadelphia.
   d. Lancaster.

For questions 33 through 38, read the passage carefully. Then read each item and choose the correct answer.

Sylvia

For perhaps the fourth time since the clock struck two, Sylvia crosses to the front-facing window of her apartment, pulls back the curtain, and looks down at the street. Although people hurry along the sidewalk, she sees no one enter her building.

She walks back to the center of the living room, where she stands twisting a silver bracelet around and around on her wrist. She is an attractive young woman with a narrow and delicate face, but she is restless now, because she is being kept waiting. It is nearly two-thirty; a woman named Lola Parrish was to come at two o'clock to look at the apartment.

She considers leaving a note and going out. The woman is late, after all, and besides, Sylvia is certain that Lola Parrish will not be a suitable person with whom to share the apartment. On the phone, she had sounded too old, for one thing, and her voice was oddly flat. However, the moment for saying the apartment was no longer available slipped past, and Sylvia found herself agreeing to the two o'clock appointment. If she leaves now, as she has a perfect right to do, she can avoid the awkwardness of turning the woman away.

She walks back to the center of the room, aware now that the idea of sharing the apartment, never appealing, was born of necessity. She knows she will have to become accustomed to the notion, because her savings are nearly gone. She has a job, but it does not pay well. Once the roommate situation is resolved, however, she will consider taking another job, perhaps something connected with music. In her childhood, she had loved to play the flute, and people had said she was gifted.

33. Which of the following adjectives best describes Sylvia's mood as depicted in the first three paragraphs?
   a. anxious
   b. angry
   c. meditative
   d. serene

34. Based on the passage, which of the following is the most likely reason Sylvia is looking for someone to share her apartment?
   a. She is lonely and wants company.
   b. She is bored with her job.
   c. She needs someone to help pay the rent.
   d. She is hoping to find someone who will share her interest in music.

35. The passage suggests that when Sylvia looks out her window, she is
   a. concerned that someone will see her.
   b. worried about the weather.
   c. looking at a clock across the street.
   d. looking for Lola to enter the building.

36. The passage suggests that Sylvia has skill and talent as
   a. a musician.
   b. an apartment manger.
   c. an office manager.
   d. a decorator.

37. The details in the third paragraph illustrate that Sylvia is
   a. excited about meeting and interviewing Lola.
   b. having trouble deciding whether she should leave the apartment or wait longer.
   c. upset that she did not set the appointment with Lola for a later time.
   d. thinking about moving out of her present apartment.

38. The last two sentences mark a change in the tone of this passage from
   a. cheerful to peaceful.
   b. sentimental to realistic.
   c. stressful to hopeful.
   d. magical to charming.

For questions 39 and 40, read the passage carefully. Then read each item and choose the correct answer.

Light Pollution
Light pollution is a growing problem worldwide. Like other forms of pollution, light pollution degrades the quality of the environment. Where once it was possible to look up at the night sky and see thousands of twinkling stars in the inky blackness, one now sees little more than the yellow glare of urban sky-glow. When we lose the ability to connect visually with the vastness of the universe by looking up at the night sky, we lose our connection with something profoundly important to the human spirit, our sense of wonder.

39. The author's main purpose in writing this passage is most likely to
   a. give reasons why light pollution is occurring worldwide.
   b. persuade readers that light pollution may change the quality of their lives.
   c. persuade readers to try stargazing.
   d. persuade readers to leave urban areas.

40. The passage implies that the most serious damage done by light pollution is to our
   a. artistic appreciation.
   b. sense of physical well-being.
   c. cultural advancement.
   d. spiritual selves.

Test 7: Mathematics

You have 35 minutes for this section. For questions 1 through 40, read each problem and find the answer.

1. Which input-output equation was used to create this table?

Input	Output
3	11
4	15
5	19

   a. Output = Input + 8
   b. Output = 3 × Input + 2
   c. Output = 3 × Input + 4
   d. Output = 4 × Input − 1

2. The kinds of socks and pants that students in Mrs. Scott's class were wearing on Monday are given in the following diagram.

   S = Set of all students in Mrs. Scott's class
   J = Set of students wearing jeans
   C = Set of students wearing colored socks

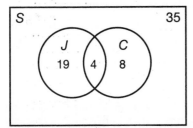

   How many students were wearing either jeans or colored socks, but not both jeans and colored socks?
   a. 4
   b. 19
   c. 27
   d. 31

3. Which of the following means $5n + 7 = 17$?
   a. 7 more than 5 times a number is 17.
   b. 5 more than 7 times a number is 17.
   c. 7 less than 5 times a number is 17.
   d. 12 times a number is 17.

4. Which answer choice is equivalent to the following expression?
   $$\frac{18 \div 2}{3(19 + 8)}$$
   a. 3^{-2}
   b. 3^{-3}
   c. 3^2
   d. 3^3

5. Dan rented two movies to watch last night. The first was 1 hour 40 minutes long, the second 1 hour 50 minutes long. How much time did it take for Dan to watch the two videos?
   a. 4.5 hours
   b. 3.5 hours
   c. 2.5 hours
   d. 1.5 hours

6. $(4\sqrt{7})^2 = ?$
   a. $8\sqrt{7}$
   b. 28
   c. $16\sqrt{7}$
   d. 112

7. The following chart shows how many seventh-, eighth-, and ninth-grade parents came to the teacher conference nights throughout all four quarters of the school year. During the fourth quarter, what fraction of the parents who attended were parents of eighth graders?

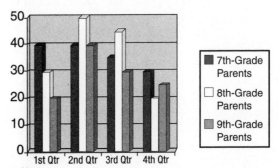

   a. $\frac{30}{90}$
   b. $\frac{20}{75}$
   c. $\frac{30}{75}$
   d. $\frac{50}{130}$

8. As part of his science project, Edwin measures the height of a plant every other day and marks it on a graph. This is Edwin's graph:

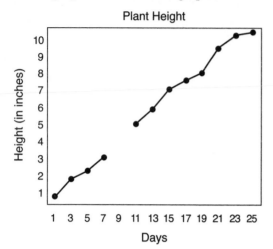

Plant Height

What was *most likely* the height of the plant on the day he forgot to measure it?

a. 3 inches

b. 3.75 inches

c. 4.75 inches

d. 5.25 inches

9. The Tigers and the Cobras were playing each other in a basketball game. After the Tigers scored eight points and the Cobras scored 13 points, the Tigers were still ahead. Which inequality describes the relationship between T, the number of points the Tigers had, and C, the number of points the Cobras had in the basketball game?

a. $T + C < 8 + 13$

b. $T - 8 > C + 13$

c. $T + 8 > C + 13$

d. $T \times 8 < C \times 13$

10. Which expression shows two million, thirty-seven thousand, eight hundred four in expanded notation?

a. $(2 \times 10,000) + (3 \times 1,000) + (7 \times 100) + (8 \times 10) + (4 \times 1)$

b. $(2 \times 100,000) + (3 \times 10,000) + (7 \times 1,000) + (8 \times 100) + (0 \times 10) + (4 \times 1)$

c. $(2 \times 1,000,000) + (3 \times 100,000) + (7 \times 10,000) + (0 \times 1,000) + (8 \times 100) + (0 \times 10) + (4 \times 1)$

d. $(2 \times 1,000,000) + (0 \times 100,000) + (3 \times 10,000) + (7 \times 1,000) + (8 \times 100) + (0 \times 10) + (4 \times 1)$

11. One inch equals 2.54 centimeters. What operation would you perform to calculate the number of centimeters in a foot?

a. divide 2.54 by 12

b. multiply 2.54 by 12

c. divide 12 by 2.54

d. multiply 2.54 by $\frac{1}{12}$

12. A grain elevator operator wants to mix two batches of corn with a resultant mix of 54 pounds per bushel. If he uses 20 bushels of 56 pounds per bushel corn, which of the following expressions gives the amount of 50 pounds per bushel corn needed?

a. x times $56 + x$ times $50 = 2x$ times 54

b. 20 times $56 + x$ times $50 = (x + 20)$ times 54

c. 20 times $56 + x$ times $50 = 2x$ times 54

d. x times $56 + x$ times $50 = (x + 20)$ times 54

13. The following chart gives the times that four swimmers had in their race. Which swimmer had the fastest time?

Swimmer	Time (sec.)
Molly	38.51
Jeff	39.23
Asta	37.95
Risa	37.89

  a. Molly
  b. Jeff
  c. Asta
  d. Risa

14. The heights of eight students were measured in feet and then ordered from least to greatest on a number line. Their heights were as follows: $5\frac{1}{2}$ ft., 5.25 ft., $5\frac{1}{6}$ ft., 5.8 ft., $5\frac{3}{4}$ ft., 5.4 ft., 5.2 ft., and $5\frac{7}{8}$ ft. Which number was third on the number line?

  a. $5\frac{1}{2}$ feet
  b. 5.25 feet
  c. $5\frac{3}{4}$ feet
  d. 5.4 feet

15. The perimeter of a rectangle is 148 feet. Its two longest sides add up to 86 feet. Which equation can be used to solve for the length of each of its two shortest sides, w?

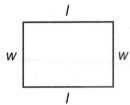

  a. $148 - 86 = w$
  b. $w + l + 86 = 148$
  c. $2l + 2w = 148 + 86$
  d. $86 + 2w = 148$

16. Which value of x will make this number sentence true?
$$x + 25 \leq 13$$
  a. -12
  b. -11
  c. 12
  d. 38

17. Which of the following is equivalent to $x^2 + 3x$?
  a. $x(x + 3)$
  b. $2(x + 3)$
  c. $(x + 3)^2$
  d. $(x + 1)(x + 3)$

18. What number is added to 10 to reach 25% of 52?
  a. 1
  b. 3
  c. 5
  d. 7

19. A triangle has sides that are consecutive even integers. The perimeter of the triangle is 24 inches. What is the length of the shortest side?

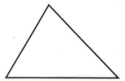

    a. 10 inches
    b. 8 inches
    c. 6 inches
    d. 4 inches

20. The dimensions of the floor of Joe's rectangular tent are 7 feet by 5 feet. If Joe buys a tent with twice the length and width of his original tent, what will be the change in the area of the tent's floor?

5 ft.

7 ft.

    a. 4 times as large
    b. 2 times as large
    c. $\frac{1}{2}$ as large
    d. $\frac{1}{4}$ as large

21. If a bus weighs 2.5 tons, how many pounds does it weigh? (1 ton = 2,000 pounds)
    a. 800 pounds
    b. 4,500 pounds
    c. 5,000 pounds
    d. 5,500 pounds

22. Bridget wants to hang a garland of silk flowers all around the ceiling of a square room. Each side of the room is 9 feet long; the garlands are only available in 15-foot lengths. How many garlands will she need to buy?

side = 9 feet

    a. 2 garlands
    b. 3 garlands
    c. 4 garlands
    d. 5 garlands

For questions 23 and 24, use the following graph. Then read each item and choose the correct answer.

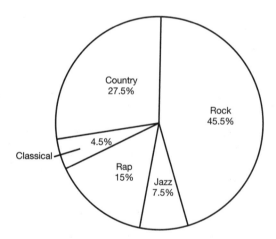

23. If 400 compact discs were sold altogether, which expression can be used to calculate the number of country music compact discs sold?
    a. $45.5 \times \frac{400}{100}$
    b. $0.275 \times \frac{400}{100}$
    c. $\frac{400}{45.5} \times 100$
    d. $\frac{27.5}{100} \times 400$

24. Based on the graph, which types of music represent exactly half of the compact discs sold?
   a. rock and jazz
   b. classical and rock
   c. rap, classical, and country
   d. jazz, classical, and rap

25. Which mathematical expression best describes the quotient of two numbers added to a third number?
   a. $(x)(y) \div z$
   b. $(x \div y)(z)$
   c. $x \div y + z$
   d. $(x + y) \div z$

26. What is the area of the following shaded triangle?

   a. 20 square units
   b. 25 square units
   c. 44 square units
   d. 46 square units

27. Molly needs $\frac{5}{8}$ of a cup of diced onion for a recipe. After chopping all the onions she has, Molly has $\frac{3}{5}$ of a cup of chopped onion. How much more chopped onion does she need?
   a. $\frac{1}{8}$ cup
   b. $\frac{1}{5}$ cup
   c. $\frac{1}{40}$ cup
   d. $\frac{1}{60}$ cup

28. White stones cost $3.59 for 25 pounds. Which proportion can be used to solve for the cost, c, of 100 pounds?
   a. $\frac{25}{100} = \frac{c}{3.59}$
   b. $\frac{3.59}{100} = \frac{25}{c}$
   c. $\frac{3.59}{25} = \frac{c}{100}$
   d. $\frac{c}{3.59} = \frac{25}{100}$

29. Which expression best describes the sum of three numbers multiplied by the sum of their reciprocals?
   a. $(a + b + c)(\frac{1}{a} + \frac{1}{b} + \frac{1}{c})$
   b. $(a)(\frac{1}{a}) + (b)(\frac{1}{b}) + (c)(\frac{1}{c})$
   c. $(a + b + c) \div (\frac{1}{a})(\frac{1}{b})(\frac{1}{c})$
   d. $(a)(b)(c) + (\frac{1}{a})(\frac{1}{b})(\frac{1}{c})$

30. Line A is parallel to line B in the following figure. What is the value of x?

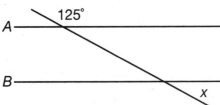

   a. 45°
   b. 55°
   c. 65°
   d. 76°

31. Which point best represents $-\frac{1}{3}$ on the number line?

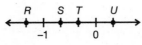

   a. R
   b. S
   c. T
   d. U

32. A circular pool with a 30-foot diameter is surrounded by a 4-foot-wide walk, as shown in the following figure. What is the area, in square feet, of the walk?

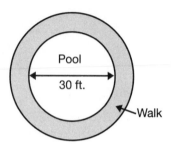

a. 16π
b. 136π
c. 169π
d. 676π

33. What is the area in square units of the shaded region of the diagram?

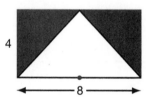

a. 2π
b. 4
c. $4\pi + 2$
d. 16

34. What percentage of 600 is 750?
a. 80%
b. 85%
c. 110%
d. 125%

35. What is the perimeter of the following polygon?

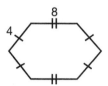

a. 12
b. 16
c. 24
d. 32

36. $(7x^3y^2)^2 =$
a. $49x^3y^2$
b. $49x^5y^4$
c. $49x^6y^4$
d. $7x^5y^4$

37. The following chart lists the number of students present at the monthly meetings for the Environment Protection Club. What was the average monthly attendance over the course of all the months listed?

Environment Protection Club Attendance	
Month	# of Students
September	54
October	61
November	70
December	75

a. 71
b. 65
c. 61
d. 56

38. 5.133 multiplied by 10^{-6} is equal to
a. 0.0005133.
b. 0.00005133.
c. 0.000005133.
d. 0.0000005133.

39. What are the coordinates for the endpoints of line segment *AB?*

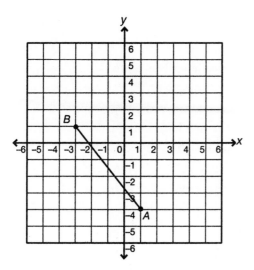

a. $(-3,1)$ and $(1,-4)$
b. $(1,-3)$ and $(-4,-1)$
c. $(-1,-3)$ and $(4,1)$
d. $(-3,-1)$ and $(1,4)$

40. What is the perimeter of the following triangle?

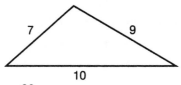

a. 90
b. 70
c. 26
d. 19

Answers

Test 1: Sequences

1. b. Look at each segment. In the first segment, the arrows are both pointing to the right. In the second segment, the first arrow is up and the second is down. The third segment repeats the first segment. In the fourth segment, the arrows are up and then down. Because this is an alternating series, the two arrows pointing right will be repeated, so choice **b** is the only possible answer.

2. b. Notice that in each segment, the figures are all the same shape, but the one in the middle is larger than the two on either side. Also, notice that one of the figures is shaded and that this shading alternates first right and then left. To continue this pattern in the third segment, you will look for a square, which narrows your choices to either choice **a** or **b**. Choice **b** is correct because this choice will put the large square between the two smaller squares.

3. c. This is an alternating series. In the first segment, the letter "E" faces right, then down, then right. In the second segment, the letters all face down. To follow this pattern, in the fourth segment, the letters must all face up.

4. c. In this series, the shaded part inside the circle gets larger and then smaller.

5. d. Look for opposites in this series of figures. The first and second segments are opposites of each other. The same is true for the third and fourth segments.

6. a. Look carefully at the number of dots in each dominolike figure. The first segment goes from five to three to one. The second segment goes from one to three to five. The third segment repeats the first segment.

7. c. All four segments use the same figures: two squares, one circle, and one triangle. In the first segment, the squares are on the outside of the circle and triangle. In the second segment, the squares are below the other two. In the third segment, the squares are on the inside. In the fourth segment, the squares are above the triangle and circle.

8. d. In this simple subtraction series, each number in each set of three segments is 8 less than the previous number.

9. b. In this simple addition series, each number in each set of three segments is 4 more than the previous number.

10. c. This is an alternating addition and subtraction series. In each set of three numbers, 5 is added to the first number and 2 is subtracted from the second number.

11. b. This is an alternating multiplication and division series. In each segment, the first number is multiplied by 2, and then the second number is divided by 4.

12. a. This is an alternating multiplication and division series. In each segment, the first number is multiplied by 2, and then the second number is divided by 6.

13. b. This is an alternating addition series. Add 14 to the first number to get the second number. Add 1 to the first number to get the third number.

14. c. This is a simple division series. Each number is half of the previous number.

15. a. This series consists of letters in a reverse alphabetical order.

16. b. There are two alternating series in these letters. The odd letters (1st, 3rd, etc.) are in normal alphabetical order, while the even letters are in reverse alphabetical order.

17. b. The letters remain the same in this series, so we know that choices **c** and **d** are wrong. The number moves left and decreases each time.

18. d. The second and fourth letters in this series, *L* and *A,* are static. The first and third letters consist of an alphabetical order beginning with the letter *E.*

19. c. The first two letters, *PQ,* are static. The third letter is in alphabetical order, beginning with *R.* The number series is in descending order beginning with 5.

20. c. The first letters are in alphabetical order with a letter skipped in between each segment: *C, E, G, I, K.* The second and third letters are repeated; they are also in order with a skipped letter: *M, O, Q, S, U.*

Test 2: Analogies

1. d. A can of paint is to a paintbrush as a spool of thread is to a sewing needle. This is a relationship of function. Both show the tool needed to perform a task.

2. a. A car is powered by gasoline, just as a bicycle is powered by feet.

3. d. An oar is to a canoe as a steering wheel is to a car. This is a functional relationship. The oar helps to steer the canoe in the way that the steering wheel steers the car.

4. a. Butter is to bread as paint is to a house. The butter is spread over the bread, just as paint is spread on the house.

5. d. Sheep is to sweater as pine trees are to log cabin. Wool comes from the sheep to make a sweater; wood comes from the trees to make the log cabin.

6. a. Hand is to ring as head is to cap. A ring is worn on a person's hand; a cap is worn on a person's head.

7. b. A shield protects a person from arrows, just as an umbrella protects a person from raindrops.

8. d. A swing is to a tree as pants are to a belt. The belt holds up the pants just as the tree holds up the swing.

9. d. A fish is to a dragonfly as a chicken is to corn. Fish eat insects; chickens eat corn.

10. a. A telephone is to a stamped letter as an airplane is to a bus. A telephone and letter are both forms of communication. An airplane and bus are both forms of transportation.

11. c. A trapeze performer is to a clown as swings are to a sliding board. This relationship shows a classification. Trapeze performers and clowns are found at circuses; swings and sliding boards are found on play-grounds.

12. c. Camera is to photograph as teakettle is to a cup of tea. The camera is used to make the photo; the teakettle is used to make the tea.

13. b. A snowflake is cold, while a match is hot—they are opposites, just as a boy and a girl are opposites.

14. d. Car is to horse and buggy as computer is to pen and ink. This relationship shows the difference between modern times and times past.

15. c. Radio is to television as ear is to eye. A person listens to the radio and watches TV.

16. b. A toddler is to an adult as a caterpillar is to a butterfly. This relationship shows the young and the adult. The caterpillar is an early stage of the adult butterfly.

17. b. Towel is to bathtub as chest of drawers is to bed. The towel and bathtub are both found in a bathroom; the chest and the bed are both found in a bedroom.

18. a. A snowcapped mountain is to a crocodile as a cactus is to a starfish. This relationship shows an opposition. The crocodile does NOT belong on the mountain; the starfish does NOT belong in the desert.

19. c. A shirt is to a button as a belt is to a belt buckle. A button is used to close a shirt; a belt buckle is used to close a belt.

20. c. Chicken is to egg as cow is to milk. The chicken produces eggs just as the cow produces milk.

Test 3: Quantitative Reasoning

1. b. What is done to 10 to make 2? It is divided by 5. What is done to 20 to make 4? It is divided by 5. What is done to 5 to make 1? It is divided by 5. Thus, 100 divided by 5 makes 20.

2. d. In this set, 6 is subtracted from each first number. Thus, $12 - 6 = 6$.

3. a. What is done to 0.3 to make it 3? It is multiplied by 10. Multiplying 0.021 by 10 gives 0.21, and 0.01 multiplied by 10 gives 0.1. Thus, 10 multiplied by 10 gives 100.

4. a. First, figure out what action is being performed. What is done to 6 to make it –3? Nine is subtracted from 6 to make –3. Similarly, $13 - 9 = 4$, and $21 - 9 = 12$. Thus, $8 - 9 = -1$.

5. b. 4 becomes 12 when multiplied by 3. Each number is multiplied by 3, so $3 \times 3 = 9$.

6. c. In this set, 6 is being added to all first numbers. To make 11, 6 is added to 5. To make 19, 6 is added to 13. Six is added to –6 to make zero. So, $8 + 6$ gives us 14.

7. b. In this set, each number is divided by 4. $12 \div 4 = 3$; $24 \div 4 = 6$. Thus, $44 \div 4 = 11$.

8. b. There are 8 parts total, of which 5 are shaded. That is 5 parts out of 8, or $\frac{5}{8}$.

9. a. There are 8 parts total, of which 4 are shaded. That is 4 parts out of 8, or $\frac{4}{8}$, which reduces to $\frac{1}{2}$.

10. d. There are 16 parts total, of which 7 are shaded. That is 7 parts out of 16, or $\frac{7}{16}$.

11. c. There are 12 parts total, of which 3 are shaded. That is 3 parts out of 12, or $\frac{3}{12}$, which reduces to $\frac{1}{4}$.

12. b. There are 4 parts total, of which 2 are shaded. That is 2 parts out of 4, or $\frac{2}{4}$, which reduces to $\frac{1}{2}$.

13. a. There are 16 parts total, of which 9 are shaded. That is 9 parts out of 16, or $\frac{9}{16}$.

14. a. There are 8 parts total, of which 6 are shaded. That is 6 parts out of 8, or $\frac{6}{8}$, which reduces to $\frac{3}{4}$.

15. a. The scales indicate that 1 cube = 3 cones. To make it easier for you to see the answers, convert all shapes to cones as follows:
   a. 3 cones (1 cube) + 1 cube = 2 cubes. That's the correct answer.
   b. 3 cones (1 cube) + 3 cones (1 cube) + 1 cone $\uparrow$ 2 cones
   c. 3 cones (1 cube) + 3 cones (1 cube) + 3 cones (1 cube) + 1 cone $\uparrow$ 6 cones
   d. 1 cone $\uparrow$ 3 cones (1 cube)

16. c. The scales indicate that 1 cube = 2 cones. Convert all shapes to cones as follows:
   a. 2 cones + 2 cones (1 cube) $\uparrow$ 2 cones (1 cone) + 1 cone
   b. 2 cones $\uparrow$ 4 cones (2 cubes)
   c. 2 cones (1 cube) + 1 cone = 3 cones. That's the correct answer.
   d. 4 cones (2 cubes) + 1 cone $\uparrow$ 6 cones (3 cubes)

17. b. The scale indicates that 2 cubes = 1 cone. Convert all shapes to cones, and count the results:
   a. 2 cones $\uparrow$ 1.5 cones (3 cubes)
   b. 2 cones = 2 cones (4 cubes). That's the correct answer.
   c. 1 cone + 1 cone (2 cubes) $\uparrow$ 1 cone (2 cubes) + 2 cones
   d. 1 cone $\uparrow$ 1 cone + 1 cone (2 cubes)

18. c. The scale shows that 1 cube = 1 cone. Therefore:
   a. 1 cube + 1 cone $\uparrow$ 2 cubes
   b. 2 cones $\uparrow$ 1 cube
   c. 1 cone + 1 cube = 1 cube + 1 cone. That's the correct answer.
   d. 3 cubes $\uparrow$ 2 cones

19. d. The scale shows that 2 cubes = 2 cones. Therefore:
   a. 2 cubes $\uparrow$ 1 cube + 1 cone
   b. 2 cones $\uparrow$ 2 cubes + 1 cone
   c. 1 cone 2 cubes $\uparrow$ 1 cube + 3 cones
   d. 1 cube + 1 cone + 1 cube + 1 cone (2 cones + 2 cubes) = 1 cone + 2 cubes + 1 cone (2 cones + 2 cubes). That's the correct answer.

20. a. The scales indicate that 4 cones = 1 cube. Convert all shapes to cubes as follows:
   a. 2 cubes = 1 cube (4 cones) + 1 cube. That's the correct answer.
   b. $\frac{1}{2}$ cubes (2 cones) + 2 cubes $\uparrow$ 2 cubes (8 cones)
   c. $\frac{1}{2}$ cubes + 1 cubes + $\frac{1}{2}$ cubes (2 cubes) $\uparrow$ 3 cubes
   d. $\frac{1}{2}$ cubes + 1 cube + $\frac{1}{2}$ cubes + 1 cube (3 cubes) $\uparrow$ 1 cube + 1 cube (4 cones)

Test 4: Verbal Reasoning—Words

1. b. Some books are fiction, and some books have pictures. Learning may or may not take place with a book. The necessary part of a book is its pages.

2. d. A keyboard is an essential part of a piano. Notes are byproducts. Pianos are not essential to an orchestra. Piano playing can be learned without a teacher.

3. a. All trees have trunks. Not all trees are in a forest or bear fruit and acorns.

4. b. All beds have a mattress. Not all beds have sheets or pillows. Sleep is not essential to a bed.

5. b. All dishwashers need water. The kitchen, spoon, and plate are not essential to a dishwasher.

6. a. All hurricanes require wind. There may be rain and clouds, but they are not essential. Weather is not a part of a hurricane.

7. c. The tools above the line are used for eating. The tools below are used for carpentry.

8. b. The relationship above the line is that snow on a mountain creates conditions for skiing. Below the line, the relationship is that warmth at a lake creates conditions for swimming.

9. d. Above the line, the relationship shows a progression of sources of light. The relationship below the line shows a progression of types of housing, from smallest to largest. Choice **a** is incorrect because a tent is smaller than a house. Choice **c** is wrong because it is not part of the progression.

10. a. The relationship above the line is as follows: Aspirin is a medicine; medicine is sold in a pharmacy. Below the line, the relationship is: Lettuce is a vegetable; vegetables are bought in a grocery.

11. d. The items on the top row are parts of a house. The items on the bottom row are parts of a car.

12. b. Walk, skip, and run represents a continuum of movement: Skipping is faster than walking; running is faster than skipping. Below the line, the continuum is about throwing. Pitch is faster than toss; hurl is faster than pitch.

13. c. A leopard, cougar, and lion all belong to the cat family, while an elephant does not.

14. b. The couch, table, and chair are pieces of furniture, while the rug is not.

15. a. The yarn, twine, and cord are all used for tying. The tape is not used in the same way.

16. b. A calendar, clock, and watch all keep track of time, so choice **b** is out of place.

17. d. Books, magazines, and periodicals are all reading materials, but a library collects reading materials.

18. c. Think about what the three words have in common. All three are adjectives with the same meaning—clean. Now evaluate your answer choices. Is efficient clean? No, it is not. (Efficient means competent.) Does careful mean clean? No, it does not. (Careful means alert, cautious.) Is *tidy* clean? Yes, it is. But, always be sure to check all the other choices to make sure you picked the best one. Does hazardous mean clean? No, it does not. (Hazardous means dangerous.)

19. a. Think about what the three adjectives have in common. All three mean inconsequential, unimportant. Now, look at your answer choices for a word that is most similar to inconsequential, unimportant. The most similar word is *trivial* (choice **a**).

20. a. Again, think about what the three nouns have in common. Index, glossary, and lesson are all sections of a book. Now, look at your answer choices for a word that is also a book section. Your best answer is an *appendix* (choice **a**). All other choices are not sections of a book.

Test 5: Verbal Reasoning—Context

1. a. Choices **b**, **c**, and **d** may or may not be true—we cannot know because we don't have enough information. We do know, however, that cookies use three cups of flour, while brownies use four.

2. b. The first statement says that Lia celebrated her birthday; and the second statement says that she received many presents, including a box of Godiva chocolates. From this, we can conclude that Lia received a box of chocolates for her birthday (choice **b**). She may love her birthday (choice **d**); or she may not have opened the chocolates because she does not like them (choice **c**), or because she plans to share them with her friends (choice **a**). However, we cannot conclude for certain that these other statements are true.

3. d. Although choices **a**, **b**, and **c** may be true, there is nothing in the information provided to support these conclusions. The only thing known for certain is that Max visited Moscow last summer, since he had been to the Bolshoi Theater.

4. a. Since the first statement claims that all students in a creative writing program must submit a 50-page portfolio of original work, and we know that Veronika is in a creative writing program, we can conclude that Veronika submitted a 50-page portfolio of original work (choice **a**). We cannot conclude for certain that the other statements are true.

5. c. The only thing that can be concluded from Oscar Wilde's quote, for certain, is that he did not believe that taking good advice can be useful to oneself. Although choices **a** and **b** may be true, based only on the information given we do not know what Oscar Wilde felt should be included in a play (choice **a**) or what constitutes good advice (choice **b**). Choice **d** is an opinion unsupported by the facts stated.

6. d. Mike is saving his money for a computer, rather than spending it. The other statements may or may not be true—we don't have enough information to know.

7. b. The only thing we know for sure is that Francesca sold more works than Mario. We do not know from the statements given to us whether or not Mario bought one of Francesca's works (choice **d**), and which one of them is a better photographer (choice **c**). The fact that they shared space for the exhibition means neither that they are the best photographers in New Orleans, nor that they necessarily live in New Orleans (choice **a**). The only certain thing is that Mario sold fewer works than Francesca (choice **b**).

8. c. Based on the information provided, the only thing we know for a fact is that there are more calories in a cup of cappuccino than in a cup of espresso (100 calories more). We can judge neither that the people prefer to drink espresso (choice **a**), nor that a cappuccino tastes better (choice **b**). The fact that people do not generally care about their caloric intake (choice **d**) is merely an opinion unsupported by the facts.

9. a. The reason Dave does not listen to music while doing homework is clearly stated: He concentrates better without it. The other statements are not addressed in the passage.

10. b. Based on the two statements, the only answer choice that we can conclude is correct is that Lucy is smaller than Thurber (choice **b**), because we are told Lucy is a 6-pound puppy, and Thurber is a 35-pound puppy. There is no point of comparison to measure the love of Michael and Ilsa for their puppies (choice **a**). Choices **c** and **d** could be true, but these are statements unsupported by the facts.

11. a. The one fact we know for certain from the two statements is that Gabriela is a customer of Mr. Brown (choice **a**)—since his bread is her favorite. We know for a fact that Gabriela is not the only customer of Mr. Brown's (choice **b**) because we are told in the first statement that he is a popular local baker. Choices **c** and **d** could be true, but they are unsupported by the facts.

12. c. Based only on the information given, we do not know whether Christopher is usually forgetful (choice **a**) or how many friends he has (choice **b**). We can conclude that Christopher will probably not draw tonight (choice **c**) since we are told that for his drawings, he uses his special pen only, which he has forgotten at a friend's apartment. It is possible that Christopher draws every night (choice **d**), but it is a statement unsupported by the facts.

13. d. Based on the statements given, we can conclude that yesterday was a cold and rainy day (choice **d**), since we are told that Dan spent an entire day at home, and we know that Dan never stays in when the weather is nice. We are not told what Dan does when he stays at home (choices **a** and **b**). We can also assume that if the weather was nice yesterday (choice **c**), Dan would not have stayed in.

14. b. The only information we have is where Mary is and where she is going. We do not know how Mary feels about her bus ride (choice **a**). We also do not know whether she has taken a bus ride to Boston before (choice **d**). Since we do not know how long Mary has been on the bus, we cannot assume when Mary will get to Boston (choice **c**). The only information we know for certain from the two statements is that it takes approximately 4.5 hours by bus to get from New York to Boston.

15. b. The assumption that the Smiths own more than two cars (choice **a**) is incorrect because we are told in the first statement that the Smiths own two cars. Choices **c** and **d** could be true, but they are unsupported by the facts. Therefore, the only choice we can be certain of is that the Smiths have a one-car garage (choice **b**), since they park only one of their cars there, and we do not have any other information available to us.

16. a. Based on the information available to us, the only answer choice we can conclude is correct is that Jim is younger than Alex (choice **a**) since we are told that Alex is older than Jim. Since there is no mention of how tall Alex and Jim's father is or what he looks like, we cannot make any assumptions about choices **b**, **c**, and **d**.

17. d. Mark was 12 when he started photography, and he began photography by picking up his father's camera—all of which is stated in the first two sentences. The last sentence tells us that he picked up the camera on the day his father died, so we can infer that he was 12.

18. b. The only information we can safely assume is that the store was probably already closed by the time Kevin got there (choice **b**), since we know it is 20 minutes away from his house, and he remembered that he needed to pick up a bottle of juice at 11:50 P.M. We cannot assume that Kevin did not go to the store (choice **c**), because we are told in the third statement that he did go. Choices **a** and **d** could be true, but there is nothing in the information given that supports these facts.

19. d. All we know is that a dollar is missing from May's bowl. Although Andy is always borrowing change from May, there is no evidence that Andy took this money from May's bowl (choice **b**). We do not know whether Andy does not have an income (choice **a**) or whether May always has a lot of spare change (choice **c**). The only information we have based on the statements is that May keeps her spare change in a bowl on her desk (choice **d**).

20. b. We are not told what Betty's feelings are for Bill, nor whether she has continued writing to friends. We are told, however, that she uses a calligraphy pen when she writes to Bill. The fact that the calligraphy pen has not been used for three weeks means that she has not used it to write to Bill for that amount of time.

Test 6: Reading and Language Arts

1. a. The passage explicitly states that Charlemagne was crowned emperor in 800 and died in 814—a period of 14 years. Therefore, choices **b**, **c**, and **d** are mathematically incorrect.

2. d. The passage states that *this European civilization drew on the ancient texts of the Germanic, Celtic, Greek, Roman, Hebrew, and Christian worlds,* which supports this choice. Choice **a** is contradicted in the passage. There is no support for choice **b** or choice **c**.

3. c. The main focus of this passage is how loud noises can cause hearing loss. Although choices **a** and **b** are mentioned, these are not the main focus of the passage. The passage also mentions the destruction of nerve cells (choice **d**), but the passage discusses only those cells in the inner ear, not nerve cells in general.

4. b. The second paragraph clearly states that the cochlea is *the spiral-shaped cavity of the inner ear.*

5. d. The second paragraph compares the fibers in a shag carpet to the fibers in the inner ear.

6. a. This is the only choice that can reasonably be inferred from the information in the passage; the basis for this inference is the last paragraph. There is no support that the author believes either choice **b** or choice **c**. As for choice **d**, the author suggests turning down the boom box, not giving up listening.

7. b. This is the only choice that is in keeping with the context of the passage. Choices **a** and **d** both mean on occasion, not steadily. Choice **c** can be ruled out because there is no context to support this answer.

8. a. "Amelia Earhart: Lady of the Air" is the most appropriate title. Choices **b** and **c** are off-subject. Choice **d** insinuates that Amelia Earhart was on a boat lost at sea. Plus, the passage says they don't know what happened to her.

9. d. Choices **a** and **b** are not definitions of charismatic. Choice **c** is not correct because there is no mention of divinity in the description.

10. a. Howland Island; this is a detail question. The answer is clearly stated in the second paragraph.

11. b. She was a great aviatrix. The author does not seem to think Amelia Earhart was foolish to fly so far. Although there is not a definitive answer about Amelia Earhart's death, the author never actually says she is probably still alive. There is no mention about who caused the crash.

12. b. This choice includes the main points of the passage and is not too broad. Choices **a** and **c** include minor points in the passage. Choice **d** includes points not discussed in the passage.

13. d. This choice expresses the main focus of the paragraph. Choices **a**, **b**, and **c** express opinions, but these opinions are not supported by the details given.

14. a. This choice is correct according to the second sentence in the second paragraph. Choices **b** and **c** are mentioned in the passage but not as causing the islands. There is no support for choice **d**.

15. a. This is a detail in the passage, and arriving at the correct answer requires a careful reading of the first three sentences. The coast of Maine, according to the passage, is ten times longer than 225 miles, which is equal to 2,500 miles.

16. c. Note that this question asked you to find the answer that is NOT included in the passage. Choices **a**, **b**, and **d** can all be found in the first two paragraphs. Choice **c** is the best answer because the passage states that after the glacier, *the mountain ranges were never to return.*

17. d. This detail is clearly stated in the fourth paragraph. The passage makes no connection between wealth and plant and animal life (choice **a**). Choices **b** and **c** are inaccurate, according to the passage.

18. b. The passage opens by referring to the storm as the Blizzard of 1978. The next sentence mentions that it was a day in February.

19. a. The word *intrepid* means courageous or fearless.

20. d. The passage concludes with the observation that the effects of the storm would have been less if the northeast had been prepared. The other ideas are not addressed.

21. d. Choice **d** summarizes the main idea of the passage, that the blizzard caught people by surprise. No conspiracy is suggested, and the other choices are not addressed.

22. c. The word *ameliorate* means to lessen the effect of something. In the passage, the author suggests that the effects of the storm might have been made less damaging.

23. c. The passage clearly states in the first paragraph that the word *cowboy* originated in New York State.

24. c. Skinners; this is a detail question from the first paragraph.

25. c. Choices **a** and **d** are not correct because although some of the passage is about the life and duties of cowboys, the main point is not. Choice **b** is not correct because there is nothing about how to become a cowboy in the passage.

26. d. Both the British and the Revolutionary forces were present, so choice **d** is the best choice.

27. b. Because the passage states that Hershey *returned to the village where he had been born* to open his plant, and the passage also states that he was born near Derry Church, this statement must be accurate. The other choices cannot be supported. Although the author mentions the popularity of chocolate internationally, you cannot assume that it is popular in every country (choice **a**), nor is there any indication that Milton Hershey was the first person to manufacture chocolate in the United States (choice **c**). Choice **d** is not discussed in the passage at all.

28. a. Choice **a** is the best choice because it is the most complete statement of the material. Choices **c** and **d** focus on small details of the passage; choice **b** is not discussed in the passage.

29. b. This is the best choice because the passage clearly shows Hershey's determination to be successful in the candy business. Although he had some failures, he could not be described as defective (choice **a**). There is nothing to indicate that he was either carefree (choice **c**) or cautious (choice **d**).

30. c. The third paragraph states that Hershey first used chocolate for *coating his caramels.* Choice **a** can be ruled out because he didn't make cocoa or baking chocolate until a year after he began producing chocolate. Choice **b** is not in the passage. Choice **d** is incorrect because he purchased the chocolate-making equipment at the exposition.

31. d. This question tests your ability to use context clues to determine the intended meaning of a word. In paragraph 3, the passage says, *The Hershey Chocolate Company was born in 1894 as a subsidiary of the Lancaster Caramel Company.* This indicates that a subsidiary company is one controlled by another company, choice **d**. While it may be true that Milton Hershey owned each company in its entirety (choice **a**), that is not clear from the material. There is also no indication that the chocolate company was created to support the caramel company (choice **b**). Finally, the passage contains no discussion of whether any of Hershey's companies were incorporated (choice **c**).

32. d. This is an inference taken from the third and fourth paragraphs. The third paragraph indicates that Hershey's caramel company was in Lancaster, and the chocolate company was a subsidiary. The fourth paragraph states that Hershey moved his plant in 1905, 11 years after he first got into the chocolate business. From these two facts, it is reasonable to conclude that the first chocolate business was in Lancaster.

33. a. In paragraph 2, Sylvia is described as *restless*; she keeps looking out the window and playing with her bracelet. These are all clues that her mood is most likely anxious. Choice **b** is wrong because there are no details that would indicate anger. There is no support for choices **c** and **d**.

34. c. This is an inference question. The last paragraph indicates that Sylvia has a financial need: Her job doesn't pay well, and she has no savings. It is reasonable to conclude, therefore, that she needs help with the rent.

35. d. The details of the story show that Lola was supposed to arrive a half hour earlier, so it is reasonable to conclude that she is looking to see whether Lola is entering the building. There are no details that would support the other choices.

36. a. This choice is confirmed by the last two sentences in the passage. There are no details to support any of the other choices.

37. b. The entire paragraph gives details that show Sylvia is wavering between leaving the apartment and waiting longer for Lola to arrive. There is no indication that she is excited about meeting Lola (choice **a**); in fact, the opposite may be true. There are no clues to support choice **c** or choice **d**.

38. c. All through the passage, Sylvia is anxious and stressed, but the last two sentences give Sylvia hope that she will resolve her situation and find a job in music, where she has talent. Choice **a** can be ruled out because the passage is never cheerful; choices **b** and **d** are equally poor choices because the tone of the passage is in no way sentimental or magical.

39. b. This is the main focus of the passage. The other choices can be ruled out. The author does not say why light pollution is occurring (choice **a**). Although it is reasonable to conclude that the author enjoys stargazing, this is not the purpose of the passage (choice **c**). There is no support in the passage for choice **d**.

40. d. This detail can be found in the final sentence of the passage.

Test 7: Mathematics

1. d. One way to find which equation was used to create this table is to place the numbers from the table into the given equations. Both the input and output numbers follow the equation, Output = 4 × Input − 1: 11 = 4 × 3 − 1; 15 = 4 × 4 − 1; and 19 = 4 × 5 − 1.

2. c. The number of students who were wearing either jeans or colored socks can be found by looking at the numbers in the circles labeled *J* and *C*. There were 19 students wearing jeans and eight students wearing colored socks. When combined, there were 27 students wearing either jeans or colored socks; choice **a** is incorrect because it is the number of students who were wearing both jeans and colored socks; choice **b** is incorrect because it is the number of students who were wearing jeans but not colored socks; choice **d** is incorrect because it is the number of students wearing jeans, colored socks, or both jeans and colored socks.

3. a. The expression 5*n* means 5 times *n*. The addition sign before the 7 indicates the phrase *more than*.

4. a. First, simplify the expression. Remember to use the correct order of operations. The simplified expression is: $\frac{9}{3(27)} \rightarrow \frac{9}{81} \rightarrow \frac{1}{9}$. When using exponential notation, you can remove a number from the denominator of a fraction by representing it using a negative exponent: $\frac{1}{9}$ becomes $(\frac{1}{3})^2$, which can be represented as 3^{-2}.

5. b. Change the hours to minutes: 1 hour 40 minutes = 100 minutes; 1 hour 50 minutes = 110 minutes. Now add: 100 minutes + 110 minutes = 210 minutes. Now change back to hours and minutes: 210 minutes ÷ 60 = 3.5 hours.

6. d. $(4\sqrt{7})^2 = (4\sqrt{7})(4\sqrt{7}) = 16\sqrt{49} = 16 \times 7 = 112$.

7. b. First, note that this is a plot with *numbers of parents* versus *quarters,* and you are interested only in the fourth quarter. The three bars all the way on the right of the graph represent all the parents who were there for the fourth quarter conference night. In looking at the height of each of these three bars, you know that the total number of parents attending that night would be 20 + 30 + 25, or 75. Next, use the code to the right of the diagram to see that the white bars represent the eighth-grade parents. If you look at the white bar for the fourth quarter, you see that it goes up to a value of 20. So the fraction of eighth-grade parents present that night would be eighth-grade parents/total parents = $\frac{20}{75}$.

8. b. On the graph, 3.75 inches is approximately in the middle between the heights measured on the days on either side of the forgotten day (day 9). Although choice **a** (3 inches) and choice **c** (4.75 inches) are possible, they do not fit the graph as well as 3.75 inches. Choice **d** is clearly incorrect.

9. c. Even after scoring only eight points compared to the Cobras' 13 points, the Tigers were still in the lead. The Tigers' original score plus eight points is larger than the Cobras' original score plus 13 points. Therefore, $T + 8 > C + 13$.

10. d. This expression shows 2,037,804 in expanded notation.

11. b. You are given that 1 inch = 2.54 centimeters and asked to find the number of centimeters in one foot, or 12 inches. So, if each inch is 2.54 centimeters, and you have 12 inches, you should multiply 2.54 by 12.

12. b. Solve this problem by finding the weight of each portion. The sum of the weights of the initial corn is equal to the weight of the final mixture. Therefore, (20 bushels) + (x bushels) = (20 + x bushels). Thus, 20 times 56 + x times 50 = (x + 20) times 54.

13. d. Risa's time of 37.89 is less than the next fastest time (Asta's) of 37.95.

14. b. Arrange the numbers in order from least to greatest. Changing the mixed numbers to decimal numbers will make the comparison easier. The correct order for the numbers is as follows: $5\frac{1}{6}$ (5.17), 5.2, 5.25, 5.4, $5\frac{1}{2}$ (5.5), $5\frac{3}{4}$ (5.75), 5.8, $5\frac{7}{8}$ (5.875). The third number is 5.25.

15. d. The perimeter of the rectangle is the distance around the rectangle, or $l + l + w + w$. We know that the perimeter is 148, so $l + l + w + w = 148$. You also know that the two longest sides (the sides labeled l) add up to 86. This means that you can replace "$l + l$" in our formula with 86. The formula becomes $86 + w + w = 148$, or $86 + 2w = 148$.

16. a. Since the solution to the problem $x + 25 \leq 13$ is -12, choices **b**, **c**, and **d** are all too large to be correct.

17. a. $x(x + 3) = x(x) + 3x = x^2 + 3x$.

18. b. Let x = the number that we're looking for. $x + 10$ = 25% of 52. Half of 52 is 26; half of 26 is 13. Thus, 25% of 52 = 13. Now, $x + 10 = 13$, so $x = 3$.

19. c. An algebraic equation must be used to solve this problem. The shortest side can be denoted s. Therefore, $s + (s + 2) + (s + 4) = 24$. So, $3s + 6 = 24$, and $s = 6$.

20. a. Doubling the length and width of Joe's original tent floor gives new dimensions of 14 feet by 10 feet. The area of the new tent is 140 square feet. The original tent floor had an area of 35 square feet (140 divided by 35 equals 4). The new tent has four times the area of the original tent floor. Choice **b** is incorrect because the new tent floor has an area 4 times the original tent, not 2 times. Choice **c** is incorrect because the new tent floor's area is larger than the original tent's, not smaller. Choice **d** is incorrect because the new tent floor's area is larger than the original tent's, not smaller.

21. c. This is a multiplication problem with decimals ($2.5 \times 2,000 = 5,000$).

22. b. The perimeter of the room is 36 feet (9×4); $36 \div 15$ (the length of each garland) = 2.4. So Bridget will need three garlands.

23. d. First, look at the pie chart to see that "Country" represents 27.5% of sales. We were told that the total sale was 400 discs, so we need to find 27.5% of 400. Another way to express 27.5% is to write $\frac{27.5}{100}$, and "of" means *times*, so we have: $\frac{27.5}{100} \times 400$.

24. b. Rock is 45.5%; when we add 4.5% for classical, we arrive at 50%.

25. c. The quotient of two numbers is $x \div y$. When a third number, z, is added, the result is: $x \div y + z$.

26. a. To get the height (h) of the triangle, use the Pythagorean theorem: $6^2 + h^2 = 10^2$. The height equals 8. Then 5 is plugged in for the base and 8 for the height in the area equation, $A = \frac{bh}{2}$, which yields 20 square units.

27. c. To subtract fractions, first convert to a common denominator, in this case, $\frac{25}{40} - \frac{24}{40} = \frac{1}{40}$.

28. c. When you set up a proportion, you need to be careful with units. This question deals with two different units: dollars and pounds. You will set up a proportion with *dollars* over *pounds*: this many dollars – this many pounds = that many dollars – that many pounds. Using the numbers in the question, you have $\frac{3.59 \text{ dollars}}{25 \text{ pounds}} = \frac{c \text{ dollars}}{100 \text{ pounds}}$.

29. a. The sum of three numbers means: $(a + b + c)$. The sum of their reciprocals means: $(\frac{1}{a} + \frac{1}{b} + \frac{1}{c})$. Combining terms: $(a + b + c)(\frac{1}{a} + \frac{1}{b} + \frac{1}{c})$.

30. b. Since line A is parallel to line B, angles in corresponding positions are equal to each other. Therefore, the angle directly above x° is also 125°. Since these two angles form a straight line, their sum must be 180°. Thus, $x = 180° - 125° = 55°$.

31. c. Point T is $\frac{1}{3}$ of the way between 0 and -1. Choice **a** is incorrect because point R represents $-1\frac{1}{3}$. Choice **b** is incorrect because point S represents $-\frac{2}{3}$. Choice **d** is incorrect because point U represents $\frac{1}{3}$.

32. b. The diameter of the outer circle (the pool plus the walk) = 30 + 4 + 4 = 38 feet. Therefore, the radius of the outer circle is 19 feet, and its area = $\pi \times r^2 = \pi \times (19)^2 = 361\pi$ square feet. The diameter of the inner circle (just the pool) = 30 feet, and its radius is 15 feet. Thus, the area of the inner circle = $\pi \times r^2 = \pi \times (15)^2 = 225\pi$ square feet. Therefore, the area of the walk = $361\pi - 225\pi = 136\pi$ square feet.

33. d. The shaded area is simply the area of the rectangle minus the area of the triangle. The width of the rectangle and the height of the triangle are both 4, because the radius of the circle is 4. You get:

$A_{rect} - A_{triangle}$

$(lw) - (\frac{1}{2}bh)$

$(8)(4) - \frac{1}{2}(8)(4)$

$32 - 16$

16

34. d. Since a percentage is a portion of 100 where $x\% = \frac{x}{100}$, the equation is $\frac{x}{100} = \frac{750}{600}$. Cross multiply: $600x = 750(100)$. Simplify: $x = \frac{75,000}{600}$ or $x = 125$.

35. d. There are four sides of 4 and two sides of 8. Therefore, the perimeter is $(4 \times 4) + (2 \times 8) = 32$.

36. c. First, square 7 to get 49. Then square each of the variables; this means multiplying each exponent by 2.

37. b. To calculate the average, use this formula: Average $= \frac{\text{sum of all values}}{\text{\# of values}}$ The sum of all the values is: 54 + 61 + 70 + 75 = 260. Divide 260 by 4 to get 65.

38. c. $5.133 \times 10^{-6} = 5.133 \times 0.000001 = 0.000005133$. This is the same as simply moving the decimal point to the left six places.

39. a. The x-axis is always listed first.

40. c. The sum of the side lengths is 7 + 9 + 10 = 26.

Scoring

For the real exam, your raw score on the COOP will be converted to a scaled score so that your score can be compared with that of other students. For this practice exam, however, simply determine a percentage for each part. This will enable you to get an idea of how well you did on each section, so that you'll know which tests you need to study for. When you take the second COOP test in this book, you can compare your percentage score on this test with your score on the second test to see how you improved. (Figuring out your percentage score will also be good math practice!)

First, find the number of questions you got right in each test in the COOP. There is no penalty for skipping questions, and wrong answers don't count against your score. Just add up the number of correct answers on each of the tests. Divide the number of questions you got right by the number of questions in that particular test. That's your percentage score. The following tables will help you check your math by giving you percentage equivalents for some possible scores on each of the COOP tests. (There is a table for the 20-question tests and a table for the 40-question tests.)

Did you pass? Each school sets its own standards, so there's really no such thing as a "passing score." The point, for now, isn't your total score, anyway. Instead, concentrate on how you did on each of the skills tested by the exam. Diagnose your strengths and weaknesses so that you can concentrate more on the weaker areas as you prepare for the exam.

Use your scores to help you devise a study plan. Then turn to the instructional lessons, spending more of your time on the areas that correspond to the questions you found hardest and less time on the areas in which you did well. The following key shows you which lessons correspond to which tests.

SEQUENCES, ANALOGIES, QUANTITATIVE REASONING, VERBAL REASONING—WORDS, VERBAL REASONING—CONTEXT (20 QUESTIONS EACH)

NUMBER OF QUESTIONS RIGHT	APPROXIMATE PERCENTAGE
20	100%
18	90%
16	80%
15	75%
14	70%
13	65%
11	57%
10	50%

TEST	LESSON
1: Sequences	11: Nonverbal Reasoning
2: Analogies	11: Nonverbal Reasoning
3: Quantitative Reasoning	11: Nonverbal Reasoning
4 & 5: Verbal Reasoning	10: Verbal Reasoning
6: Reading and Language Arts	9: Language Skills
7: Mathematics	12: Math Skills

READING AND LANGUAGE ARTS, MATHEMATICS (40 QUESTIONS EACH)

NUMBER OF QUESTIONS RIGHT	APPROXIMATE PERCENTAGE
40	100%
36	90%
32	80%
30	75%
28	70%
26	65%
23	57%
20	50%

PRACTICE TACHS EXAM 1

LESSON SUMMARY

This is the first of the two practice tests in this book based on the Test for Admission into Catholic High Schools (TACHS). Use this test to see how you would do if you were to take the exam today.

L ike the actual TACHS exam, this practice exam is divided into four separate sections. The test itself will be subdivided as follows.

SUBTESTS	NUMBER OF QUESTIONS
READING	50
Vocabulary	20
Reading Comprehension	30
LANGUAGE	50
MATH	50
ABILITY	50

The answer sheets are on pages 109–110. Then comes the exam itself, followed by the answer key. In the key, the correct answers are explained in detail. Be sure to read these explanations in order to find out why the correct answers are right and why the incorrect answers are wrong. Then use the scoring section at the end of the exam to see your progress and judge how you did overall.

Reading: Part 1

1.	ⓐ	ⓑ	ⓒ	ⓓ
2.	ⓐ	ⓑ	ⓒ	ⓓ
3.	ⓐ	ⓑ	ⓒ	ⓓ
4.	ⓐ	ⓑ	ⓒ	ⓓ
5.	ⓐ	ⓑ	ⓒ	ⓓ
6.	ⓐ	ⓑ	ⓒ	ⓓ
7.	ⓐ	ⓑ	ⓒ	ⓓ

8.	ⓐ	ⓑ	ⓒ	ⓓ
9.	ⓐ	ⓑ	ⓒ	ⓓ
10.	ⓐ	ⓑ	ⓒ	ⓓ
11.	ⓐ	ⓑ	ⓒ	ⓓ
12.	ⓐ	ⓑ	ⓒ	ⓓ
13.	ⓐ	ⓑ	ⓒ	ⓓ
14.	ⓐ	ⓑ	ⓒ	ⓓ

15.	ⓐ	ⓑ	ⓒ	ⓓ
16.	ⓐ	ⓑ	ⓒ	ⓓ
17.	ⓐ	ⓑ	ⓒ	ⓓ
19.	ⓐ	ⓑ	ⓒ	ⓓ
20.	ⓐ	ⓑ	ⓒ	ⓓ

Reading: Part 2

1.	ⓐ	ⓑ	ⓒ	ⓓ
2.	ⓐ	ⓑ	ⓒ	ⓓ
3.	ⓐ	ⓑ	ⓒ	ⓓ
4.	ⓐ	ⓑ	ⓒ	ⓓ
5.	ⓐ	ⓑ	ⓒ	ⓓ
6.	ⓐ	ⓑ	ⓒ	ⓓ
7.	ⓐ	ⓑ	ⓒ	ⓓ
8.	ⓐ	ⓑ	ⓒ	ⓓ
9.	ⓐ	ⓑ	ⓒ	ⓓ
10.	ⓐ	ⓑ	ⓒ	ⓓ

11.	ⓐ	ⓑ	ⓒ	ⓓ
12.	ⓐ	ⓑ	ⓒ	ⓓ
13.	ⓐ	ⓑ	ⓒ	ⓓ
14.	ⓐ	ⓑ	ⓒ	ⓓ
15.	ⓐ	ⓑ	ⓒ	ⓓ
16.	ⓐ	ⓑ	ⓒ	ⓓ
17.	ⓐ	ⓑ	ⓒ	ⓓ
18.	ⓐ	ⓑ	ⓒ	ⓓ
19.	ⓐ	ⓑ	ⓒ	ⓓ
20.	ⓐ	ⓑ	ⓒ	ⓓ

21.	ⓐ	ⓑ	ⓒ	ⓓ
22.	ⓐ	ⓑ	ⓒ	ⓓ
23.	ⓐ	ⓑ	ⓒ	ⓓ
24.	ⓐ	ⓑ	ⓒ	ⓓ
25.	ⓐ	ⓑ	ⓒ	ⓓ
26.	ⓐ	ⓑ	ⓒ	ⓓ
27.	ⓐ	ⓑ	ⓒ	ⓓ
28.	ⓐ	ⓑ	ⓒ	ⓓ
29.	ⓐ	ⓑ	ⓒ	ⓓ
30.	ⓐ	ⓑ	ⓒ	ⓓ

Language

1.	ⓐ	ⓑ	ⓒ	ⓓ
2.	ⓐ	ⓑ	ⓒ	ⓓ
3.	ⓐ	ⓑ	ⓒ	ⓓ
4.	ⓐ	ⓑ	ⓒ	ⓓ
5.	ⓐ	ⓑ	ⓒ	ⓓ
6.	ⓐ	ⓑ	ⓒ	ⓓ
7.	ⓐ	ⓑ	ⓒ	ⓓ
8.	ⓐ	ⓑ	ⓒ	ⓓ
9.	ⓐ	ⓑ	ⓒ	ⓓ
10.	ⓐ	ⓑ	ⓒ	ⓓ
11.	ⓐ	ⓑ	ⓒ	ⓓ
12.	ⓐ	ⓑ	ⓒ	ⓓ
13.	ⓐ	ⓑ	ⓒ	ⓓ
14.	ⓐ	ⓑ	ⓒ	ⓓ
15.	ⓐ	ⓑ	ⓒ	ⓓ
16.	ⓐ	ⓑ	ⓒ	ⓓ
17.	ⓐ	ⓑ	ⓒ	ⓓ

18.	ⓐ	ⓑ	ⓒ	ⓓ
19.	ⓐ	ⓑ	ⓒ	ⓓ
20.	ⓐ	ⓑ	ⓒ	ⓓ
21.	ⓐ	ⓑ	ⓒ	ⓓ
22.	ⓐ	ⓑ	ⓒ	ⓓ
23.	ⓐ	ⓑ	ⓒ	ⓓ
24.	ⓐ	ⓑ	ⓒ	ⓓ
25.	ⓐ	ⓑ	ⓒ	ⓓ
26.	ⓐ	ⓑ	ⓒ	ⓓ
27.	ⓐ	ⓑ	ⓒ	ⓓ
28.	ⓐ	ⓑ	ⓒ	ⓓ
29.	ⓐ	ⓑ	ⓒ	ⓓ
30.	ⓐ	ⓑ	ⓒ	ⓓ
31.	ⓐ	ⓑ	ⓒ	ⓓ
32.	ⓐ	ⓑ	ⓒ	ⓓ
33.	ⓐ	ⓑ	ⓒ	ⓓ
34.	ⓐ	ⓑ	ⓒ	ⓓ

35.	ⓐ	ⓑ	ⓒ	ⓓ
36.	ⓐ	ⓑ	ⓒ	ⓓ
37.	ⓐ	ⓑ	ⓒ	ⓓ
38.	ⓐ	ⓑ	ⓒ	ⓓ
39.	ⓐ	ⓑ	ⓒ	ⓓ
40.	ⓐ	ⓑ	ⓒ	ⓓ
41.	ⓐ	ⓑ	ⓒ	ⓓ
42.	ⓐ	ⓑ	ⓒ	ⓓ
43.	ⓐ	ⓑ	ⓒ	ⓓ
44.	ⓐ	ⓑ	ⓒ	ⓓ
45.	ⓐ	ⓑ	ⓒ	ⓓ
46.	ⓐ	ⓑ	ⓒ	ⓓ
47.	ⓐ	ⓑ	ⓒ	ⓓ
48.	ⓐ	ⓑ	ⓒ	ⓓ
49.	ⓐ	ⓑ	ⓒ	ⓓ
50.	ⓐ	ⓑ	ⓒ	ⓓ

Math

1.	ⓐ	ⓑ	ⓒ	ⓓ
2.	ⓐ	ⓑ	ⓒ	ⓓ
3.	ⓐ	ⓑ	ⓒ	ⓓ
4.	ⓐ	ⓑ	ⓒ	ⓓ
5.	ⓐ	ⓑ	ⓒ	ⓓ
6.	ⓐ	ⓑ	ⓒ	ⓓ
7.	ⓐ	ⓑ	ⓒ	ⓓ
8.	ⓐ	ⓑ	ⓒ	ⓓ
9.	ⓐ	ⓑ	ⓒ	ⓓ
10.	ⓐ	ⓑ	ⓒ	ⓓ
11.	ⓐ	ⓑ	ⓒ	ⓓ
12.	ⓐ	ⓑ	ⓒ	ⓓ
13.	ⓐ	ⓑ	ⓒ	ⓓ
14.	ⓐ	ⓑ	ⓒ	ⓓ
15.	ⓐ	ⓑ	ⓒ	ⓓ
16.	ⓐ	ⓑ	ⓒ	ⓓ
17.	ⓐ	ⓑ	ⓒ	ⓓ
18.	ⓐ	ⓑ	ⓒ	ⓓ
19.	ⓐ	ⓑ	ⓒ	ⓓ
20.	ⓐ	ⓑ	ⓒ	ⓓ
21.	ⓐ	ⓑ	ⓒ	ⓓ
22.	ⓐ	ⓑ	ⓒ	ⓓ
23.	ⓐ	ⓑ	ⓒ	ⓓ
24.	ⓐ	ⓑ	ⓒ	ⓓ
25.	ⓐ	ⓑ	ⓒ	ⓓ
26.	ⓐ	ⓑ	ⓒ	ⓓ
27.	ⓐ	ⓑ	ⓒ	ⓓ
28.	ⓐ	ⓑ	ⓒ	ⓓ
29.	ⓐ	ⓑ	ⓒ	ⓓ
30.	ⓐ	ⓑ	ⓒ	ⓓ
31.	ⓐ	ⓑ	ⓒ	ⓓ
32.	ⓐ	ⓑ	ⓒ	ⓓ
33.	ⓐ	ⓑ	ⓒ	ⓓ
34.	ⓐ	ⓑ	ⓒ	ⓓ
35.	ⓐ	ⓑ	ⓒ	ⓓ
36.	ⓐ	ⓑ	ⓒ	ⓓ
37.	ⓐ	ⓑ	ⓒ	ⓓ
38.	ⓐ	ⓑ	ⓒ	ⓓ
39.	ⓐ	ⓑ	ⓒ	ⓓ
40.	ⓐ	ⓑ	ⓒ	ⓓ
41.	ⓐ	ⓑ	ⓒ	ⓓ
42.	ⓐ	ⓑ	ⓒ	ⓓ
43.	ⓐ	ⓑ	ⓒ	ⓓ
44.	ⓐ	ⓑ	ⓒ	ⓓ
45.	ⓐ	ⓑ	ⓒ	ⓓ
46.	ⓐ	ⓑ	ⓒ	ⓓ
47.	ⓐ	ⓑ	ⓒ	ⓓ
48.	ⓐ	ⓑ	ⓒ	ⓓ
49.	ⓐ	ⓑ	ⓒ	ⓓ
50.	ⓐ	ⓑ	ⓒ	ⓓ

Ability

1.	ⓐ	ⓑ	ⓒ	ⓓ
2.	ⓐ	ⓑ	ⓒ	ⓓ
3.	ⓐ	ⓑ	ⓒ	ⓓ
4.	ⓐ	ⓑ	ⓒ	ⓓ
5.	ⓐ	ⓑ	ⓒ	ⓓ
6.	ⓐ	ⓑ	ⓒ	ⓓ
7.	ⓐ	ⓑ	ⓒ	ⓓ
8.	ⓐ	ⓑ	ⓒ	ⓓ
9.	ⓐ	ⓑ	ⓒ	ⓓ
10.	ⓐ	ⓑ	ⓒ	ⓓ
11.	ⓐ	ⓑ	ⓒ	ⓓ
12.	ⓐ	ⓑ	ⓒ	ⓓ
13.	ⓐ	ⓑ	ⓒ	ⓓ
14.	ⓐ	ⓑ	ⓒ	ⓓ
15.	ⓐ	ⓑ	ⓒ	ⓓ
16.	ⓐ	ⓑ	ⓒ	ⓓ
17.	ⓐ	ⓑ	ⓒ	ⓓ
18.	ⓐ	ⓑ	ⓒ	ⓓ
19.	ⓐ	ⓑ	ⓒ	ⓓ
20.	ⓐ	ⓑ	ⓒ	ⓓ
21.	ⓐ	ⓑ	ⓒ	ⓓ
22.	ⓐ	ⓑ	ⓒ	ⓓ
23.	ⓐ	ⓑ	ⓒ	ⓓ
24.	ⓐ	ⓑ	ⓒ	ⓓ
25.	ⓐ	ⓑ	ⓒ	ⓓ
26.	ⓐ	ⓑ	ⓒ	ⓓ
27.	ⓐ	ⓑ	ⓒ	ⓓ
28.	ⓐ	ⓑ	ⓒ	ⓓ
29.	ⓐ	ⓑ	ⓒ	ⓓ
30.	ⓐ	ⓑ	ⓒ	ⓓ
31.	ⓐ	ⓑ	ⓒ	ⓓ
32.	ⓐ	ⓑ	ⓒ	ⓓ
33.	ⓐ	ⓑ	ⓒ	ⓓ
34.	ⓐ	ⓑ	ⓒ	ⓓ
35.	ⓐ	ⓑ	ⓒ	ⓓ
36.	ⓐ	ⓑ	ⓒ	ⓓ
37.	ⓐ	ⓑ	ⓒ	ⓓ
38.	ⓐ	ⓑ	ⓒ	ⓓ
39.	ⓐ	ⓑ	ⓒ	ⓓ
40.	ⓐ	ⓑ	ⓒ	ⓓ
41.	ⓐ	ⓑ	ⓒ	ⓓ
42.	ⓐ	ⓑ	ⓒ	ⓓ
43.	ⓐ	ⓑ	ⓒ	ⓓ
44.	ⓐ	ⓑ	ⓒ	ⓓ
45.	ⓐ	ⓑ	ⓒ	ⓓ
46.	ⓐ	ⓑ	ⓒ	ⓓ
47.	ⓐ	ⓑ	ⓒ	ⓓ
48.	ⓐ	ⓑ	ⓒ	ⓓ
49.	ⓐ	ⓑ	ⓒ	ⓓ
50.	ⓐ	ⓑ	ⓒ	ⓓ

Reading: Part 1

For questions 1 through 5, choose the word or phrase that most nearly means the same as the underlined word.

1. a necessary <u>function</u>
   a. sense
   b. appearance
   c. purpose
   d. feeling

2. a sudden <u>uproar</u>
   a. calm
   b. chaos
   c. idea
   d. meal

3. a <u>subordinate</u> position
   a. special
   b. lesser
   c. firm
   d. curious

4. a <u>distasteful</u> chore
   a. delicious
   b. daily
   c. unpleasant
   d. important

5. a <u>wily</u> plan
   a. flimsy
   b. short
   c. weird
   d. cunning

For questions 6 through 10, choose the word or phrase that most nearly means the OPPOSITE of the underlined word.

6. an <u>attentive</u> student
   a. neglectful
   b. superior
   c. careful
   d. entertaining

7. <u>eliminate</u> a mistake
   a. copy
   b. add
   c. stop
   d. remove

8. an <u>obsolete</u> method
   a. extinct
   b. preferred
   c. smooth
   d. current

9. an <u>ingenious</u> invention
   a. stupid
   b. huge
   c. fine
   d. shiny

10. a <u>genial</u> host
    a. hilarious
    b. friendly
    c. rude
    d. athletic

*For questions 11 through 15, choose the word or **phrase** that most nearly means the same as the underlined word.*

11. The squirrels love to <u>frolic</u> in the trees on **a** sunny summer day.
    a. play
    b. work
    c. watch
    d. dance

12. The swimmers <u>immerse</u> themselves in the warm pool.
    a. hover
    b. cool
    c. swim
    d. plunge

13. Our firewood supply will <u>diminish</u> by the **end** of the winter.
    a. expand
    b. shrink
    c. replenish
    d. fall

14. The birdhouse is a <u>sanctuary</u> for the larks **when** the cat is on the hunt.
    a. safe place
    b. dangerous room
    c. holy building
    d. distant area

15. Because she was so busy at work, Andrea decided to <u>terminate</u> her gym membership.
    a. extend
    b. study
    c. pay
    d. end

For questions 16 through 20, choose the word that best completes the sentence.

16. Because his antique car was always breaking down, Rudolph decided to replace it with a more _____ one.
    a. ancient
    b. luxurious
    c. contemporary
    d. expensive

17. The storm could really _____ our picnic.
    a. disrupt
    b. improve
    c. pass
    d. create

18. If you assemble the go-cart in a _____ way, it might fall apart when you try to drive it.
    a. careful
    b. haphazard
    c. speedy
    d. thorough

19. If you turn the music to the _____ volume, the neighbors will probably complain.
    a. lowest
    b. reasonable
    c. clearest
    d. maximum

20. The baby was talking _____ in its crib.
    a. distinctly
    b. intelligently
    c. nonsense
    d. pleasantly

Reading: Part 2

For questions 1 through 30, read each passage carefully. Answer the questions that follow only on the basis of the preceding passage.

Tracing Genealogy

In a day and age when storytelling is beginning to be considered one of the lost arts, and keeping records means booting up instead of writing down, families may find themselves wondering how to create and preserve their genealogy. Perhaps they want to just save the family stories or trace the most recent generations. Others might want to explore their families' role in history or just put something together to commemorate an anniversary or other important event. Putting together a family tree may sound like a great idea, but how do you even begin to make the first step, and how can it be a total family project?

Investigating the many different people who came before you is a multilayered task that involves asking questions, doing research, combing through real and virtual archives, and even taking a field trip or two to places like cemeteries. After all, a graveyard is really like a museum without walls since it contains fascinating historical artifacts that are hundreds of years old, all in the form of gravestones.

Another great source is the census records that can be found on the Internet. Often, you find more than birth and death records. Resources for information include national archives, as well as local family records. Your local library can connect you with basic genealogy guidebooks and reference books as well.

Make sure not to overlook one of the best resources of all—your family. Grandparents, uncles, aunts, and cousins are often wonderful sources of stories, traditions, facts, and other helpful information. Taking the time to talk to them about family stories can bring all of you closer—another side benefit from a project like this one.

1. What is the main idea of this passage?
   a. Tracing genealogy can be a rewarding project, but it is important to know how to go about it.
   b. Tracing genealogy involves taking a trip to a cemetery, which contains fascinating historical artifacts.
   c. Tracing genealogy has become rare now that people prefer to spend their time using computers.
   d. Tracing genealogy can be as much fun as any other project you are likely to undertake.

2. Which word would be most similar to the word commemorate in the third sentence?
   a. dismiss
   b. honor
   c. prove
   d. describe

3. Which statement is NOT true?
   a. Investigating genealogy involves research.
   b. Family records are resources for information.
   c. Saving family stories is one reason to trace genealogy.
   d. Libraries are the best sources for genealogy information.

4. Information in the passage leads you to believe:

  a. Tracing genealogy is best left to older people.

  b. Tracing genealogy involves reading newspapers.

  c. Tracing genealogy is usually an easy project.

  d. Tracing genealogy can be time-consuming.

5. Which word in the passage describes the process of tracing genealogy?

  a. multilayered

  b. lost

  c. great

  d. wonderful

6. As it is used in the passage, the word <u>benefit</u> most nearly means

  a. consideration.

  b. suggestion.

  c. advantage.

  d. fundamental.

The Chunnel

The incredible notion of connecting England and France, two powerful countries that had been separated for more than 12,000 years, had been tossed around for more than two centuries. Everyone from engineers to architects to politicians had come up with a plan or a blueprint. The Chunnel, or underwater tunnel, is considered to be one of the true wonders of the modern world for its size and complexity and for the fact that it succeeded even though it was full of structural dilemmas, budget catastrophes, and safety nightmares.

The idea for a connection between France and England was first mentioned at the end of the eighteenth century. Although frequently ignored, squashed, and thrown out, the idea would not die. It continued to pop up again and again for over 200 years. Both European countries were gaining in power, and trade between them was on the rise. A century ago, the 20-plus miles that separated them made trade not only slow, but also quite dangerous. Under the best weather conditions, the trip from one coastline to the other took six to eight hours, and frequently, vicious storms delayed ships for days—even weeks. Frustration on both ends grew as shipments fell behind schedule and workers arrived at the docks too seasick to load or unload their cargo. Even later, when ferries and airplanes came along to make the trip faster and safer, passengers still had to put up with paying high transportation fees, standing in crowded airports, and other inconveniences.

For decades, the debate had raged over the best way to link these two countries. Ideas ranged from sunken tubes to iron bridges. Which could be easiest and safest—a bridge, a tunnel, or some combination of the two? Every single plan posed some kind of unique problems. A bridge over 20 miles long would be a nightmare to support. Experts argued that it would cause problems with the many ships that needed to pass through the Channel. Even the best lighthouses, foghorns, and other precautions were not enough to warn a ship that the bridge was ahead. That was asking for a real disaster. However, the plan to use sunken tubes succeeded, and construction on the Chunnel began in 1988. It opened in 1994, and runs underneath the English Channel between England and France. It is one of the most remarkable feats of architecture ever created.

7. Which statement would the author probably agree with?

  a. Creating the Chunnel was a waste of time.

  b. It is good that England and France did not give up on the Chunnel.

  c. The Chunnel may be a wonder of modern architecture, but it is dangerous.

  d. Ferries and airplanes are more practical means of trade than the Chunnel.

8. According to the passage, how was the Chunnel different from traveling by airplane?

    a. It is not as expensive as air travel.

    b. It is the only way to go from England to France.

    c. It is not as unsafe as air travel.

    d. It eliminates the inconvenience of seasickness.

9. When was a connection between France and England first mentioned?

    a. 12,000 years ago

    b. 1988

    c. the eighteenth century

    d. 1994

10. Because the connection needed to be 20 miles long, people thought it might

    a. take too long to build.

    b. be too long to travel.

    c. be too expensive to build.

    d. be difficult to support.

11. The concluding paragraph of this passage implies which of the following?

    a. There was little discussion about the construction of the Chunnel.

    b. The Chunnel is now an important trade route.

    c. The Chunnel was a good idea, but in the end, it just wasn't practical.

    d. England and France are now planning a bigger and better Chunnel.

12. Which would be another title for this passage?

    a. "Traveling by Sea"

    b. "A Storm at Sea"

    c. "A Direct Link from England to France"

    d. "The Failures of Lighthouses and Foghorns"

Voting

Voting is a <u>privilege</u> for which wars have been fought, protests have been organized, and editorials have been written. "No taxation without representation" was a battle cry of the American Revolution. Women struggled for suffrage, as did all minorities. Eighteen-year-olds clamored for the right to vote, saying that if they were old enough to go to war, they should be allowed to vote. Yet Americans have a deplorable voting history. Interviewing people about their voting habits is revealing. There are individuals who state that they have never voted. Often, they claim that their individual vote doesn't matter. Some people blame their absence from the voting booth on the fact that they do not know enough about the issues. In a democracy, we can express our opinions to our elected leaders, but more than half of us avoid choosing the people who make the policies that affect our lives.

13. The best title for this passage might be

    a. "Voting: An American Institution"

    b. "No Taxation without Representation"

    c. "Voting in the 2012 Election"

    d. "Wasting a Valuable Right"

14. As it is used in the passage, the word <u>privilege</u> most nearly means

    a. right.

    b. award.

    c. object.

    d. privacy.

15. According to the passage, what happens when people do not vote?

    a. They prove that voting does not matter.

    b. They show that they are not afraid to express their opinions.

    c. They fail to get involved in making policies.

    d. They make future wars more likely.

16. Which statement is NOT true?
   a. Some people have never voted.
   b. Some people do not know much about the issues.
   c. Individual votes do not matter.
   d. People can express their opinions in a democracy.

17. Why did eighteen-year-olds believe they had the right to vote?
   a. because they were old enough to go to war
   b. because they had driver's licenses
   c. because they fought a war to win the right to vote
   d. because they had the right to express their opinions

18. How were the statistics in the passage gathered?
   a. by studying voting booths
   b. by interviewing people
   c. by counting votes
   d. by asking elected leaders

Cuttlefish

Cuttlefish are intriguing little animals. The cuttlefish resembles a rather large squid and is, like the octopus, a member of the order of cephalopods. Although cuttlefish are not considered the most highly evolved of the cephalopods, they are extremely intelligent. While observing them, it is hard to tell who is doing the observing, you or the cuttlefish, especially since the eye of the cuttlefish is similar in structure to the human eye.

Cuttlefish are also highly mobile and fast creatures. They come equipped with a small <u>jet</u> located just below the tentacles that can expel water to help them move. Ribbons of flexible fins on each side of the body allow cuttlefish to hover, move, stop, and start.

The cuttlefish is sometimes referred to as the "chameleon of the sea" because it can change its skin color and pattern instantaneously. Masters of camouflage, cuttlefish can blend into any environment for protection, but they are also capable of the most imaginative displays of iridescent, brilliant color and intricate designs, which scientists believe they use for communication and mating displays. However, judging from the riot of ornaments and hues cuttlefish produce, it is hard not to believe they paint themselves so beautifully just for the sheer joy of it. At the very least, cuttlefish conversation must be the most sparkling in all the sea.

19. What is the main idea of the passage?
   a. Cuttlefish can change their skin color.
   b. Cuttlefish are highly mobile.
   c. Cuttlefish are named for their "cuttle" shells.
   d. Cuttlefish are interesting animals.

20. Which of the following is the best definition of the word <u>jet</u> in the second paragraph?
   a. stream
   b. spout
   c. airplane
   d. coal

21. Which of the following is NOT a fact?
   a. Ribbons of flexible fins on each side of the cuttlefish allow it to move.
   b. The cuttlefish is sometimes referred to as the "chameleon of the sea."
   c. The cuttlefish's eye is similar in structure to the human eye.
   d. The cuttlefish's most intriguing characteristic is its ability to change color.

22. How is the cuttlefish like an octopus?
  a. They are both cephalopods.
  b. They are both compared to chameleons.
  c. They both produce ornaments.
  d. They are both land animals.

23. The passage implies that
  a. cuttlefish do not communicate.
  b. cuttlefish live dull lives.
  c. cuttlefish can feel joy.
  d. cuttlefish are nothing like squids.

24. Of the following, which would be the best title for this passage?
  a. "Moving with Tentacles"
  b. "A Fascinating Cephalopod"
  c. "Changing Colors"
  d. "The Human Eye"

Learning with a Laptop
The vast majority of schools entered the high-tech age years ago by installing computers throughout their libraries and classrooms or in special computer labs. All administrative offices were equipped with computer systems as well. The new <u>trend</u>, however, is taking this one step further at an innovative school in Arizona, which is providing an all-new way for students to do their homework. They provide them with their own laptops!

Instead of using money to buy all new textbooks for Empire High School, the administration bought laptop computers with its funds. This helps students stay on top of the latest computer technology. The teachers commonly select educational <u>materials</u> on the Internet for students to consult to complete homework assignments. To make the laptops feel more personal, students are allowed to store their own music collections on them.

Instead of handing in reports and homework on paper, these Arizona students just e-mail it to their individual teachers. New Web programs ensure the assignment has not been copied from any Internet sources. So much for that old excuse that your dog ate your homework!

25. As it is used in the passage, the word <u>trend</u> most nearly means
  a. development.
  b. hobby.
  c. chore.
  d. construction.

26. Why did Empire High School provide students with laptop computers?
  a. The school could not afford textbooks.
  b. To give students a place to store their music.
  c. To make students familiar with the latest technology.
  d. The school wanted to use its computer lab for other purposes.

27. As it is used in the passage, the word <u>materials</u> most nearly means
  a. cloths.
  b. fabrics.
  c. substances.
  d. notes.

28. A good title for this passage might be
  a. "No Cheating at Empire High School"
  b. "Buying Your Own Laptop"
  c. "An Education Innovation"
  d. "A History of Empire High School"

29. Which use of laptop computers is NOT discussed in the passage?
  a. storing music
  b. chatting with friends
  c. preventing copying
  d. submitting homework

30. How do students at Empire High School send homework to their teachers?

    a. through a file system

    b. by sending e-mail

    c. by handing in papers

    d. by handing in their laptops

Language

For questions 1 through 30, find the sentence that has a mistake in capitalization, punctuation, or usage. If you find no mistakes, mark choice **d.**

1. a. Whose coming to the party?

    b. Where is the library?

    c. We've run out of paper.

    d. No mistakes.

2. a. The book is in my knapsack.

    b. The gum is losing it's flavor.

    c. We visited Mt. Rushmore.

    d. No mistakes.

3. a. I prefer cream cheese to butter on my bagel.

    b. How do you get to St. Marks Street?

    c. Will you ask uncle Ira for his opinion?

    d. No mistakes.

4. a. Please take off your shoes I don't want the carpet to get dirty.

    b. Let's go to the museum and check out the new exhibit.

    c. I'm finally getting the hang of this computer program.

    d. No mistakes.

5. a. That's not the way to my house; it's a dead end.

    b. I packed my clothes, books, and toothbrush in the bag.

    c. If you don't have anything nice to say, don't say anything.

    d. No mistakes.

6. a. There's a lot of traffic on the Golden Gate Bridge.

    b. Please don't bother me while I'm studying!

    c. Can't we reach an agreement on this matter?

    d. No mistakes.

7. a. My friend Peter is in my English class.

    b. Will you take a walk with me!

    c. These are not my shoes.

    d. No mistakes.

8. a. We are not running; we are sitting.

    b. When does the movie begin?

    c. Those woman live in my neighborhood.

    d. No mistakes.

9. a. We saw that movie at the paddington theater.

    b. Greg doesn't want to go to the supermarket.

    c. Whenever I get sleepy, I take a little nap.

    d. No mistakes.

10. a. There's a strange sound coming from the yard.

    b. Ingrid and me went to the beach.

    c. I've got a secret I can't wait to tell you!

    d. No mistakes.

11. a. Whenever you're feeling lonely, don't hesitate to call me!
 b. If Josette is correct, then this is where everyone is meeting.
 c. The time has come to make some tough decisions.
 d. No mistakes.

12. a. My son is learning to crawl.
 b. Dip your feet into the sand.
 c. The sun are shining in my eyes.
 d. No mistakes.

13. a. "Hold on," Ruiz said. "Are you telling me what I think you're telling me?"
 b. The teacher said "Please hand in your homework."
 c. "Where is the gas station?" Mom asked.
 d. No mistakes.

14. a. We saw some seagulls in Bodega bay.
 b. The ship set sail on the sea.
 c. When the wind started blowing, we lowered the sails.
 d. No mistakes.

15. a. What is Mr. Sanchez doing this weekend?
 b. I am busy on Saturday, Monday, and Tuesday.
 c. I hope this summer isn't too hot!
 d. No mistakes.

16. a. The assignment is taking longer than I thought it would.
 b. Will you be taking guitar lessons, or are you going to study the piano?
 c. The magazine was not very interesting, so I read a book instead.
 d. No mistakes.

17. a. Grace, wants to know when we will be arriving.
 b. The basketball game may go into overtime.
 c. May I have a piece of that pie?
 d. No mistakes.

18. a. There was little damage because the earth quake was not very strong.
 b. All the students filed into the schoolhouse.
 c. "Samantha," Mr. Reynolds began. "Please write your answer on the blackboard."
 d. No mistakes.

19. a. He chose the wrong answer.
 b. She flung the ball right into the hoop.
 c. The sled slided down the hill.
 d. No mistakes.

20. a. My dog Pickles is sleeping in the sun.
 b. Scotty is loyal honest and brave.
 c. We are putting on a play called *Our Town*.
 d. No mistakes.

21. a. I'm making lemonade for everyone.
 b. Those girls play on the soccer team.
 c. Is that the boys lost cat?
 d. No mistakes.

22. a. That shirt comes in blue, green, and red.
 b. Some people like to go out at night; some people prefer to stay at home.
 c. If there is nothing worth watching on television, why don't you just turn it off?
 d. No mistakes.

23. a. When the school bell rang.
 b. The bird chirped.
 c. Close the door.
 d. No mistakes.

24. a. I don't have any homework, so I'm going to the park.
   b. I am going to the theater to watched the show.
   c. That book you are reading is one of my favorites.
   d. No mistakes.

25. a. This is my old elementary school.
   b. I'm trying to get into a good college.
   c. She went to Monterey high school.
   d. No mistakes.

26. a. When is the bus going to arrive?
   b. I can't wait to see you again!
   c. The kids in the back row—Todd, Patty, and Li—started whispering.
   d. No mistakes.

27. a. The basket contained many delicious things, apples, cheese, fruit punch, and granola bars.
   b. From here I can see the moon, the Orion constellation, and many, many stars.
   c. Please take the plates, glasses, bowls, spoons, and knives out of the dishwasher.
   d. No mistakes.

28. a. Shel Silverstein wrote the poem "Where the Sidewalk Ends."
   b. *Citizen Kane* is often called "the best movie ever made."
   c. Have you read the novel *The Catcher in The Rye*?
   d. No mistakes.

29. a. Helena parked her car on Grant Park Road.
   b. The computer froze, so I had to restart it.
   c. My desk is getting so dusty!
   d. No mistakes.

30. a. Is this going to be another exciting day?
   b. Hand that book to me, please?
   c. Why do bears like honey?
   d. No mistakes.

For questions 31 through 40, find the sentence that has a mistake in spelling. If you find no mistakes, mark choice **d.**

31. a. What is that weird sound?
   b. The writer has a great imagination.
   c. I had to make an amendmant to my homework.
   d. No mistakes.

32. a. Are you finaly going to visit me this summer?
   b. How many passengers are on that boat?
   c. The note was written on very old parchment.
   d. No mistakes.

33. a. I have to fill out this questionaire.
   b. Our baseball team was victorious!
   c. The temperature is too high in this room!
   d. No mistakes.

34. a. I have a subscription to that magazine.
   b. Can you help me find a suitabel outfit to wear?
   c. This spaghetti is delicious!
   d. No mistakes.

35. a. Close your eyes and don't peek!
   b. Meanwhile, the joggers were running down the street.
   c. There has been a real increase in productivaty lately.
   d. No mistakes.

36. a. Please hand me that handkerchief.
   b. The tree is completely hollow.
   c. Are you familiar with this song?
   d. No mistakes.

37. a. Yosef has a really nice disposition.
   b. Do not disregard the rules.
   c. The bowl is made of fine crystel.
   d. No mistakes.

38. a. Ms. Curtis will supervize the project.
   b. We all live in a society.
   c. The dog will retrieve that ball.
   d. No mistakes.

39. a. Sandra has citizenship in two countries.
   b. I'm putting this story into my portfoleo.
   c. The villain in that movie was really cruel.
   d. No mistakes.

40. a. The man wrinkled his brow.
   b. Place your bags underneath your seats.
   c. Anthony put on his swayde jacket.
   d. No mistakes.

For questions 41 through 50, follow the directions for each question.

41. Choose the word that best joins the sentences.
   I was expecting Felicia to come over for dinner.
   _____, she called at the last minute to say she had to work late.
   a. Thus
   b. Consequently
   c. While
   d. However

42. Choose the word that best joins the thoughts together.
   I want to do well on tomorrow's test,
   _____ I'm going to study hard to achieve that goal.
   a. nevertheless
   b. and
   c. but
   d. because

43. Which of these expresses the idea most clearly?
   a. When the summer comes, Meredith and Lashawn are going to take a bike ride to the beach; then they will go for a swim in the ocean.
   b. When the summer comes, going to take a bike ride to the beach; then they will go for a swim in the ocean.
   c. Meredith and Lashawn are going to take a bike ride, when the summer comes, to the beach; then they will go for a swim in the ocean.
   d. When the summer comes, Meredith and Lashawn are going to take a bike ride to the beach they will go for a swim in the ocean.

44. Which of these expresses the idea most clearly?
   a. Why anyone would think that movie is funny, there is no reason.
   b. There is no reason why anyone would think that movie is funny?
   c. There is no reason why anyone would think that movie is funny.
   d. There is no reason, that movie is funny, why anyone would think.

45. Which of these expresses the idea most clearly?

   a. There just isn't enough room on the shelf for all of your books I'm sorry to say.

   b. There just isn't enough room on the shelf for all of your books, I'm sorry to say.

   c. There just isn't, I'm sorry to say, enough room on the shelf for all of your books,.

   d. There just isn't enough room on the shelf for all of your book, I'm sorry to say.

46. Choose the group of words that best completes this sentence

My friend Malika is such a great student that

   a. for four years in a row she has made the honor roll.

   b. she, for four years, has made the honor roll in a row.

   c. in a row she has made the honor roll for four years.

   d. she has made the honor roll for four years in a row.

47. Which of the following topics is best for a one-page essay?

   a. your favorite work of art

   b. a history of the arts in America

   c. a comparison of all the major art forms

   d. major artworks created by Europeans

48. Which of these best fits under the topic "Why Recycling is Important"?

   a. Always find out whether a particular plastic item can be recycled, because recycling centers do not accept certain items.

   b. About 500,000 trees must be cut down just to provide enough pulp to make enough Sunday newspapers for a single week!

   c. Among the items that can be recycled are newspapers, certain plastic containers, glass jars, boxes, and bottles.

   d. Different areas have recycling pickups on different days, so always check with your local recycling facility to find out when you should put out your recyclables.

49. Which sentence does NOT belong in the paragraph?

1) Red foxes may look cute, but they are considered an invasive species in many urban areas. 2) An animal that does not belong in a certain environment, and can be very damaging to that area, is considered an invasive species. 3) Red foxes have been known to make messes by overturning garbage cans, destroying gardens, and stealing chickens from farms. 4) Red foxes also have exceptional hearing; they are able to hear a mouse squeak from more than 300 feet away.

   a. sentence 1

   b. sentence 2

   c. sentence 3

   d. sentence 4

50. Where should the sentence "Then you should learn where these notes are on the guitar strings." be placed in the following paragraph?

1) Learning to play the guitar is a step-by-step process. 2) Before even picking up the instrument, you should become familiar with the different notes. 3) Before attempting to play chords, get comfortable picking individual notes. 4) Then you will be ready to put them together to make chords.

- **a.** before sentence 1
- **b.** between sentences 1 and 2
- **c.** between sentences 2 and 3
- **d.** between sentences 3 and 4

Math

1. Compute $821 - 619$.
- **a.** 202
- **b.** 112
- **c.** 202
- **d.** 212

2. Compute $6,327 \div 9$.
- **a.** 703
- **b.** 73
- **c.** 730
- **d.** 683

3. Compute 333×4.
- **a.** 1,222
- **b.** 1,232
- **c.** 1,322
- **d.** 1,332

4. Compute $55 + 85 + 300$.
- **a.** 340
- **b.** 440
- **c.** 430
- **d.** 330

5. Compute $(1.1)^2$.
- **a.** 12.1
- **b.** 2.2
- **c.** 1.21
- **d.** 1.44

6. Compute $3 \div 0.15$.
- **a.** 0.20
- **b.** 20
- **c.** 0.45
- **d.** 0.05

7. Compute $2(5.3 - 2.2) + 4(1.9 - 1.7)$.
- **a.** 6.2
- **b.** 7.0
- **c.** 6.88
- **d.** 6.8

8. Compute $2\frac{1}{3} + 4\frac{7}{9}$.
- **a.** $6\frac{2}{3}$
- **b.** $6\frac{8}{9}$
- **c.** $7\frac{1}{9}$
- **d.** $\frac{34}{9}$

9. Compute 0.06×0.009.
- **a.** 54
- **b.** 0.54
- **c.** 0.0054
- **d.** 0.00054

10. Compute $15 - \frac{11}{6}$.

    a. $11\frac{1}{3}$

    b. $13\frac{1}{6}$

    c. $12\frac{5}{6}$

    d. $\frac{2}{3}$

11. Compute 250% of 40.

    a. 1,000

    b. 100

    c. 10,000

    d. 10

12. Compute the product of $1\frac{1}{2}$ and $2\frac{1}{3}$.

    a. $\frac{6}{21}$

    b. $\frac{9}{14}$

    c. $2\frac{1}{6}$

    d. $\frac{7}{2}$

13. Compute $\frac{33}{5} \div \frac{1}{25}$.

    a. $\frac{125}{33}$

    b. $\frac{1}{165}$

    c. 165

    d. $\frac{33}{125}$

14. Compute 0.2% of 2,000.

    a. 4

    b. 400

    c. 40

    d. 40,000

For questions 15 through 24, an exact answer is not expected. Complete these problems mentally and give the best estimate. Write nothing down when solving these problems.

15. Which is the best estimate of $(5.92)^2$?

    a. 25

    b. 36

    c. 38

    d. 40

16. Determine the closest sum to $4\frac{5}{6} + 3\frac{7}{8} + 9\frac{8}{9}$.

    a. 16

    b. 17

    c. 19

    d. 21

17. Determine the closest estimate of $4(2.1 + 3.1) + 3(5.8 + 13.9)$.

    a. 80

    b. 100

    c. 60

    d. 160

18. Determine the closest estimate of $9,105 - 3,879$.

    a. 6,500

    b. 7,000

    c. 6,000

    d. 5,000

19. Determine the closest estimate of $459 \div 9$.

    a. 70

    b. 60

    c. 50

    d. 40

20. Determine the closest estimate of 4.8% of 402.

    a. 4

    b. 40

    c. 16

    d. 20

21. Your friend can mow 110 square feet of lawn per minute. Which is the best approximation of how long it would take him to mow 5,000 square feet of lawn?

  a. $\frac{3}{4}$ hour
  b. 30 minutes
  c. 1.34 hours
  d. 34% of an hour

22. You earn $160 per month babysitting and invest the first month's earnings in a savings account that earns 4% annually. What is the amount in the account after 1 year?

  a. $166.40
  b. $224
  c. $64
  d. $6.40

23. A recent study of baseball cards revealed that about 0.5% of all baseball cards manufactured have some type of misprint. If a shipment includes 20,000 baseball cards, how many would you expect to have an error?

  a. 10,000
  b. 1,000
  c. 100
  d. 10

24. You have a 5-pound bag of sugar for use in holiday baking. One-fourth of it is needed for candy, one-third is needed for cookies, and another three-eighths is needed for fruitcake. What fraction of the bag remains after all the baking is done?

  a. $\frac{2}{3}$
  b. $\frac{1}{24}$
  c. $\frac{5}{12}$
  d. $\frac{3}{8}$

Use the following bar graph for questions 25 and 26, which depicts the number of basketball foul shots that Bob, Cara, and Geoff made in a foul-shot square-off each week during the month of February.

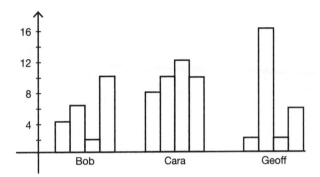

25. How many foul shots did Cara make during the four different square-offs in February?

  a. 22
  b. 32
  c. 12
  d. 40

26. How many more baskets did Geoff make in week 4 than Bob made in week 3?

  a. 14
  b. 8
  c. 4
  d. 6

27. Which of the following numbers is NOT prime?

  a. 83
  b. 71
  c. 259
  d. 1,005

28. Simplify the following expression: $-(8-3)^2 - 5 \times 5$.

  a. −75
  b. −150
  c. −10
  d. −50

29. Which of the following is a factor of 518?
  a. 4
  b. 74
  c. 16
  d. 209

30. You need to put up 410 advertisements as evenly as possible along 11 different hallways of your school. What is the least number of advertisements each hallway should get?
  a. 12
  b. 10
  c. 37
  d. 11

31. Determine the value of x such that $348 \div x = 6$.
  a. $\frac{1}{56}$
  b. 2,088
  c. 342
  d. 58

32. Which of the following is a multiple of 13?
  a. 260
  b. 141
  c. 246
  d. 415

33. Convert $\frac{3}{14}$ to a decimal and round to the nearest thousandth.
  a. 0.214
  b. 0.200
  c. 0.210
  d. 4.667

34. Compute 2^6.
  a. 36
  b. 64
  c. 12
  d. 32

35. You earn a weekly stipend (for 30 hours) during your summer job of $335, before taxes, plus $8 per hour for every hour that you work beyond 30. If you work 42 hours in one week, what would you earn before taxes?
  a. $671
  b. $351
  c. $347
  d. $431

36. Katie is able to pitch a tent in $\frac{4}{5}$ the time it takes Mandy to do so, and it takes Nina $1\frac{2}{5}$ the time it takes Katie to do so. If the sum of the times it takes the three of them to pitch their tents is 73 minutes, how long does it take Nina to pitch her tent?
  a. 25 minutes
  b. 28 minutes
  c. 20 minutes
  d. 53 minutes

37. The value of a collectible, sealed, extremely rare Atari 2600 video game was listed on eBay at $210 at the beginning of an auction. By the end, the price had increased by 350%, at which point it sold. What was the selling price?
  a. $945
  b. $735
  c. $560
  d. $350

38. As part of a dance marathon, Jane and her partner Ken started dancing at 5:30 P.M. Tuesday evening, and stopped the next morning at 3:45 A.M. If an average song is 4 minutes long, for how many full songs did they dance?
  a. 97
  b. 169
  c. 168
  d. 675

39. Walter spent $550 on food during his vacation. His friend, Valerie, spent 22% less. What is the difference in the amount that they spent on food?

a. $12.10
b. $537.90
c. $121
d. $429

40. The blueprint of a new building lists the dimensions of a window as 1 inch by 2 inches. In reality, the window's dimensions are 2 feet by 4 feet. What is the ratio of the area of the blueprint representation of the window to the area of the actual window?

a. 1:576
b. 8:2
c. 1:4
d. 3:2

41. Ralph would like to purchase the collector's edition of the game *Alien Showdown*. It costs $149, and he currently has $40 saved. He earns $20 per week delivering newspapers and is always paid at the end of the week. How many weeks must he work in order to save enough money to buy the game, assuming that sales tax is already included in the price?

a. 6 weeks
b. 5 weeks
c. 8 weeks
d. 7 weeks

42. Sam varies his workout schedule throughout the week. On Monday, he lifts weights for $1\frac{1}{2}$ hours; on Tuesday, he jogs for 2 hours; on Wednesday, he plays racquetball for $1\frac{1}{4}$ hours; and on Thursday, he swims for 45 minutes. What is the average amount of time he spends exercising on these four days?

a. $5\frac{1}{4}$ hours
b. $1\frac{5}{6}$ hours
c. $1\frac{1}{10}$ hours
d. $1\frac{3}{8}$ hours

Use the following chart to answer questions 43 and 44.

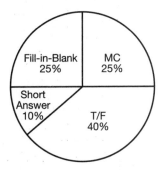

43. The circle graph shows the composition of questions for the history final exam. If the final exam is comprised of 80 questions, how many of them are true/false?

a. 40
b. 8
c. 32
d. 20

44. What is the ratio of the number of true/false questions to the number of short answer questions?

a. 4:1
b. 1:1
c. 8:5
d. 1:4

Use the following bar chart to answer questions 45 and 46. The following shows the amount of time an average hiker can expect to take to complete various trails in a state park.

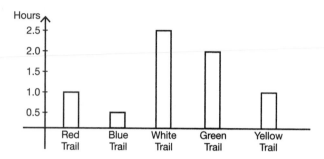

45. What is the average amount of time needed to complete these trails?
   a. 1 hour
   b. 2.5 hours
   c. 1.4 hours
   d. 1.75 hours

46. What is the percentage increase in the time required to complete the white trail as compared to the blue trail?
   a. 200%
   b. 400%
   c. 4%
   d. 2%

Use the following chart to answer questions 47 and 48.

NUMBER OF STUDENTS RECEIVING PERFECT ATTENDANCE AWARDS				
	2009	2010	2011	2012
Freshmen	2	5	6	2
Sophomores	5	1	5	4
Juniors	2	2	0	4
Seniors	0	0	2	0

47. Approximately what percentage of all students receiving this award in the years 2009 through 2012 were seniors?
   a. 95%
   b. 15%
   c. 5%
   d. 2%

48. How many fewer awards were given to juniors than to freshmen?
   a. 13
   b. 0
   c. 6
   d. 7

Use the following chart to answer questions 49 and 50.

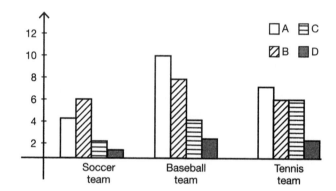

49. What is the average number of gallons of type A drink used by these three teams?
   a. 7
   b. 4
   c. 10
   d. 12

50. Which sports drink was used most heavily across all teams?
   a. A
   b. B
   c. C
   d. D

Ability

1. Find the next term: $2\frac{1}{3}, 1\frac{2}{3}, 1,$ _____
   a. $\frac{1}{3}$
   b. $\frac{2}{3}$
   c. 0
   d. $1\frac{2}{3}$

2. Find the next term: $4\frac{3}{4}, 3\frac{3}{4}, 3\frac{1}{4}, 3,$ _____
   a. $2\frac{1}{2}$
   b. $2\frac{3}{4}$
   c. $2\frac{15}{16}$
   d. $2\frac{7}{8}$

3. Find the next two terms: 0.002, 0.5, 0.02, 1.0, 0.2, 1.5, _____, _____
   a. 2, 2.5
   b. 2, 2.0
   c. 0.2, 2.0
   d. 20, 2

4. Find the next two terms: $10\frac{3}{8}, 3\frac{1}{4}, 8\frac{3}{4}, 2\frac{1}{2},$ $7\frac{1}{8}, 1,$ _____, _____
   a. $5\frac{1}{4}, \frac{3}{4}$
   b. $5\frac{3}{4}, 1\frac{1}{4}$
   c. $6\frac{1}{2}, 1$
   d. $5\frac{1}{2}, 1$

5. Find the missing term: 6.2, 7.5, 8.8, _____, 11.4, 12.7
   a. 10
   b. 10.5
   c. 10.1
   d. 9.3

6. Find the missing term: 1.3, 1.2, 1.0, _____, 0.4
   a. 0.7
   b. 0.8
   c. 0.9
   d. 0.6

7. Find the next term: 2.1, 0.7, 2.2, 0.65, 2.3, 0.6, _____
   a. 0.55
   b. 2.4
   c. 2.35
   d. 2.5

8. Find the next term: LXX, LVIII, XLVI, _____
   a. XXXIV
   b. XXXIII
   c. XXLVI
   d. XXIV

9. Find the missing term: XXIV, XXXII, XL, _____, LVI
   a. LXIIIV
   b. XLIV
   c. XLVIII
   d. LXXVIII

10. Find the next two terms: XC, $2\frac{1}{3}$, LXXXVIII, $2\frac{7}{12}$, LXXXVI, $2\frac{5}{6}$, _____, _____
   a. LXXIV, $2\frac{11}{12}$
   b. LXXXIV, $2\frac{3}{5}$
   c. LXXXIV, $3\frac{1}{12}$
   d. LXXXVI, $3\frac{1}{6}$

11. Find the missing terms: XXVI, 3, XXXVI, 6, XLVI, 12, _____, _____, LXVI, 48
   a. LVI, 24
   b. LVI, 36
   c. LXVI, 24
   d. LI, 30

12. Find the missing term: 24, 18, 21, 22, 18, 26, _____

    a. 15
    b. 30
    c. 18
    d. 29

13. Find the next term: 31, 29, 37, 27, 46, 25, 58, _____

    a. 73
    b. 21
    c. 23
    d. 70

14. Find the missing term: 101, 112, 123, _____, 145

    a. 132
    b. 134
    c. 136
    d. 138

Patterns

In questions 15 through 25, the first three figures are alike in some way. Select the choice that goes with these three figures.

15.

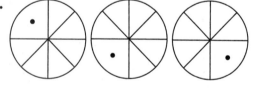

    a.   **b.**   **c.**   **d.**   **e.**

16.

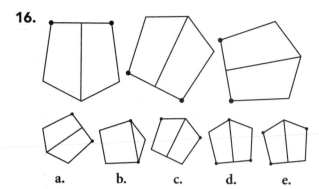

    a.   **b.**   **c.**   **d.**   **e.**

17.

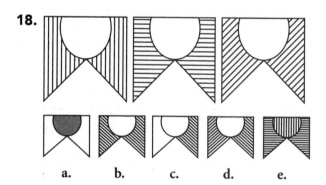

    a.   **b.**   **c.**   **d.**   **e.**

18.

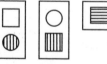

    a.   **b.**   **c.**   **d.**   **e.**

19.

    a.   **b.**   **c.**   **d.**   **e.**

20.

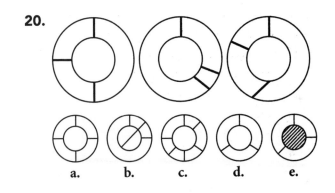

21.

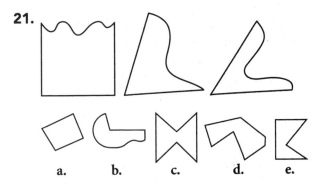

22.

23.

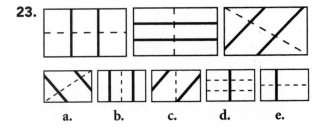

24.

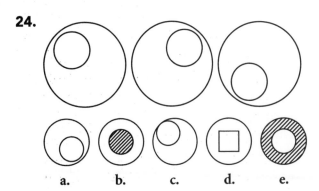

25.

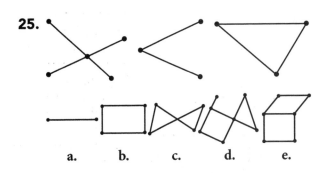

Analogy

For questions 26 through 37, the first figure is changed into the second figure. The third figure is changed in the same way to make one of the answer choices. Choose the answer that goes with the third figure.

26.

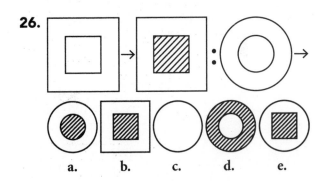

27.

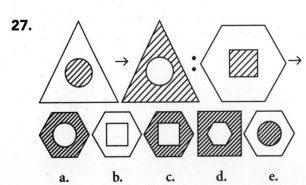

28.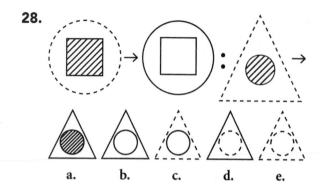

29.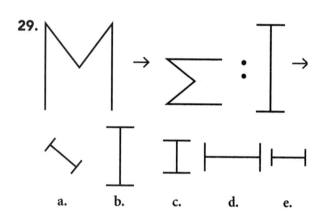

30.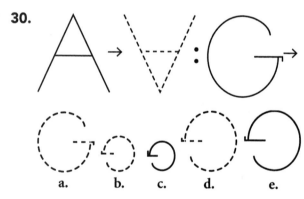

31.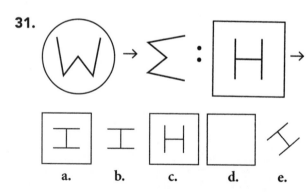

32.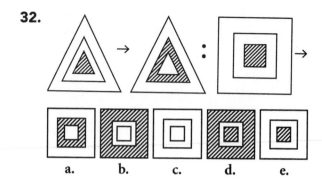

33.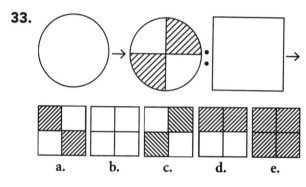

34.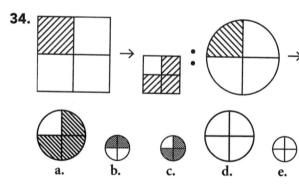

35.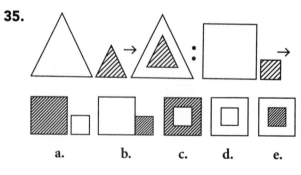

36.

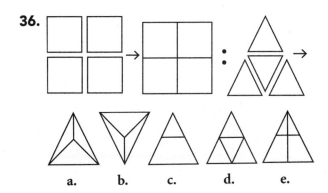

    a.   b.   c.   d.   e.

37.

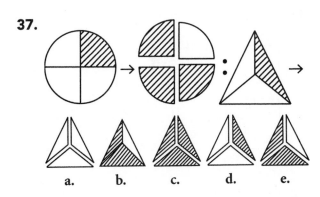

    a.   b.   c.   d.   e.

For questions 38 through 50, a piece of paper is folded (as shown in the first diagram) and then holes are punched (as shown in the second diagram). If the paper is then unfolded, choose the answer choice that shows exactly what holes would appear on the entire piece of paper.

38.

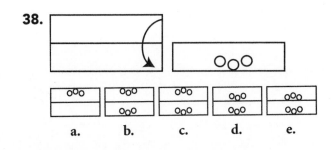

    a.   b.   c.   d.   e.

39.

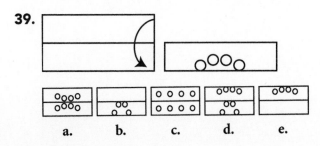

    a.   b.   c.   d.   e.

40.

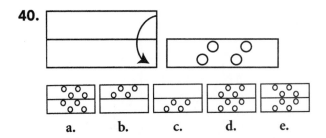

    a.   b.   c.   d.   e.

41.

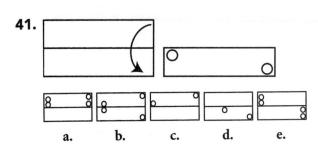

    a.   b.   c.   d.   e.

42.

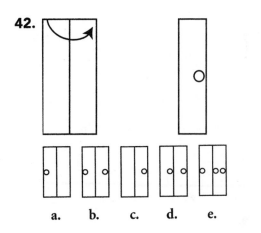

    a.   b.   c.   d.   e.

43.

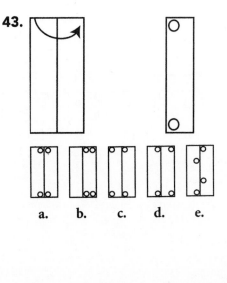

    a.   b.   c.   d.   e.

44.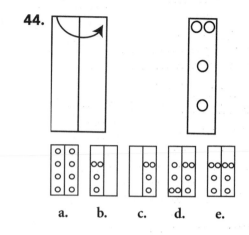

    a.   b.   c.   d.   e.

48.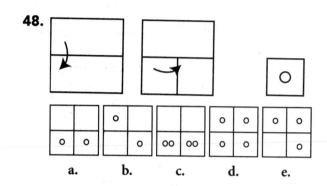

    a.   b.   c.   d.   e.

45.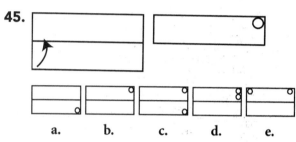

    a.   b.   c.   d.   e.

49.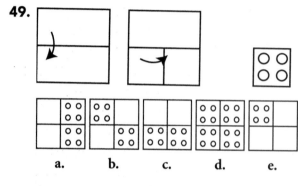

    a.   b.   c.   d.   e.

46.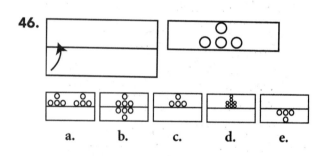

    a.   b.   c.   d.   e.

50.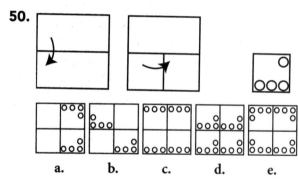

    a.   b.   c.   d.   e.

47.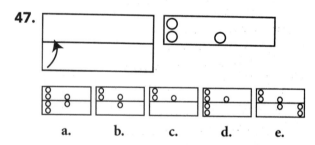

    a.   b.   c.   d.   e.

Answers

Reading: Part 1

1. c. *Function* means a use or *purpose.*

2. b. *Uproar* means noisy *chaos.* The root word "roar" is a clue to this definition.

3. b. *Subordinate* means *lesser.* The prefix "sub," meaning "under," is a clue to this definition.

4. c. *Distasteful* means *unpleasant.* The prefix "dis," meaning "not," is a clue to this definition.

5. d. *Wily* means crafty, sly, or *cunning.*

6. a. *Neglectful* means the opposite of *attentive.* Careful has the same meaning as attentive, not the opposite meaning, which is why choice **c** is incorrect.

7. b. *Add* means the opposite of *eliminate.* Remove has the same meaning as eliminate, not the opposite meaning, which is why choice **d** is incorrect.

8. d. *Current* means the opposite of *obsolete.* Extinct has the same meaning as obsolete, not the opposite meaning, which is why choice **a** is incorrect.

9. a. *Stupid* means the opposite of *ingenious.*

10. c. *Rude* means the opposite of *genial.* Friendly has the same meaning as genial, not the opposite meaning, which is why choice **b** is incorrect.

11. a. *Play* has the most similar meaning to *frolic.* Work means the opposite of frolic, so choice **b** is incorrect. Squirrels cannot actually dance, so choice **d** is not the best answer.

12. d. *Immerse* means *plunge* or dunk. Hover has the opposite meaning, so choice **a** is incorrect. One immerses oneself while swimming, but swim and immerse are not synonyms, which is why choice **c** is incorrect.

13. b. *Shrink* has the same meaning as *diminish.* Fall suggests a lessening in height, not in size, so choice **d** is not the best one. *Expand* has the opposite meaning of diminish, so choice **a** is incorrect.

14. a. In this sentence, *sanctuary* means a *safe place.* Although sanctuary can mean a holy building, this is not how it is used in the sentence, so choice **c** is incorrect. A dangerous room is the opposite of a sanctuary, so choice **b** is incorrect.

15. d. *Terminate* means *end.* Extend means the opposite of terminate, so choice **a** can be eliminated.

16. c. The use of the word *antique* implies that the car's problem is its age. Since *contemporary* means new, choice **c** is the best answer. Ancient means old, so choice **a** does not make much sense. Luxurious and expensive are not opposites of antique, so choices **b** and **d** do not make the most sense in context.

17. a. A storm would interrupt a picnic, and *disrupt* means *interrupt.* The other answer choices do not make much sense in this sentence.

18. b. Something might fall apart if it is not put together carefully or thoroughly, and *haphazard* means the opposite of careful and thorough. This is why choices **a** and **d** are incorrect. Although putting together something in a speedy way may mean it hasn't been put together carefully, this is not always the case, so choice **c** is not the very best answer.

19. d. Neighbors are most likely to complain when music is turned to its highest volume, and *maximum* means the highest. Lowest is the opposite of maximum, so choice **a** is incorrect.

20. c. Babies can often speak, but they cannot make sense. *Nonsense* is the opposite of sense. Since a baby cannot speak distinctly or intelligently, choices **a** and **b** can be eliminated. Choice **d**, pleasantly, does not make as much sense in the context of this sentence as choice **c**.

Reading: Part 2

1. a. The passage both makes a case for the importance of tracing genealogy and explains how to go about it. Although such a project may involve visiting a cemetery, this is not the main point of the passage, so choice **b** is not the best answer. The first paragraph refers to booting up a computer, but the main idea of the passage is not that people would rather use computers than trace genealogy, so choice **c** is not the best answer. Although the passage gives several reasons why you might want to trace your genealogy, fun is not one of them, so choice **d** is incorrect.

2. b. *Honor* makes the most sense in the context of the third sentence. Dismiss is the opposite of *honor*, so choice **a** is incorrect. Prove and describe do not make much sense in place of commemorate, so choices **c** and **d** can be eliminated.

3. d. The passage does not make a judgment about the best source for genealogy information, so choice **d** is not necessarily true, and therefore, the best answer. Choice **a** is stated in the second paragraph directly. Choice **b** is stated in the third paragraph. Choice **c** is stated in the first paragraph.

4. d. A process that involves research, field trips, and interviews can be time-consuming, and not necessarily easy, which is why choice **c** is incorrect. The passage does not suggest it is best to be a certain age to trace genealogy, so choice **a** is incorrect. Newspapers are never mentioned in the passage, so choice **b** is incorrect.

5. a. *Multilayered*, meaning "involving several steps," is used to describe the task of tracing genealogy in the first sentence of paragraph 2. The passage describes storytelling as a lost art, not tracing genealogy, so choice **b** is incorrect. *Great* is used to describe the idea of tracing genealogy, not the process itself, so you can eliminate choice **c**. Although the passage describes relatives as wonderful resources for information, it does not state that tracing genealogy is wonderful, so choice **d** is not the best answer.

6. c. In the context of this sentence, *benefit* means *advantage*. The other choices do not make sense in the context of the sentence, nor do they have the same meaning as benefit.

7. b. The author describes the Chunnel as a success and a remarkable feat of architecture, so she or he clearly thinks that it was good that France and England did not give up on the idea. This also means that choice **a** is not a good answer. While the Chunnel could have been dangerous had it not been well made, the author never suggests that the completed structure is dangerous, so choice **c** is not the best answer. The author points out the inconveniences of using ferries and airplanes, so choice **d** is incorrect.

8. a. The author says the Chunnel provides an alternative to the high transportation fees involved in air travel. People can travel from England to France on airplanes or boats, so choice **b** is incorrect. The author does not suggest that air travel is less safe than traveling through the Chunnel, so choice **c** is incorrect. Seasickness is an inconvenience of traveling by boat, not traveling by airplane, so choice **d** can be eliminated.

9. c. This information is in the second paragraph. 1988 is when construction began and 1994 is when the Chunnel opened, so choices **b** and **d** are incorrect.

10. d. This is stated in the final paragraph. The other answer choices are not supported by any information in the passage.

11. b. Since trade was one of the main reasons for building the Chunnel, you can conclude that it is an important trade route now that it has been constructed. The paragraph states that people debated about the construction for decades, so choice **a** is incorrect. The Chunnel was ultimately built, so choice **c** does not make much sense. There is no evidence in the passage to support choice **d**.

12. c. The purpose of the Chunnel is to link England and France, so choice **c** is a good alternate title. Before the Chunnel was built, people had already been traveling by sea on boats, so choice **a** does not do a good enough job of describing why the Chunnel was unique. Although the author does mention the dangers of storms at sea, this is not the most important idea in the passage, so choice **b** is a poor answer. The same thing is true of choice **d**.

13. d. This passage is about a valuable right—the right to vote—and how many Americans waste that right by not voting. While this passage is about voting, and voting is an American institution, its main focus is how many Americans do not take advantage of their right to vote, so choice **a** is not the best answer. Although the battle cry "No taxation without representation" is mentioned in the passage, this is just a detail and not the most important idea, so it would not make a good title and choice **b** can be eliminated. The 2012 election is never mentioned in the passage, so choice **c** is incorrect.

14. a. *Right* is the choice closest in meaning to *privilege*.

15. c. By voting, we help elect the leaders who make policies. Those who fail to vote fail to get involved in making policies. Some people who do not vote believe that voting does not matter, but failing to vote does not *prove* that opinion, so choice **a** is incorrect. Choice **b** is wrong because voting is a clearer way to express one's opinion than not voting. Not voting does not necessarily mean that war will be more likely in the future, so choice **d** is wrong.

16. c. Although some people do not believe that individual votes matter, this is an opinion, not a fact. The other choices all describe facts, not opinions.

17. a. The passage states, "Eighteen-year-olds clamored for the right to vote, saying that if they were old enough to go to war, they should be allowed to vote." Driver's licenses are never mentioned in the passage, so there is no evidence to support choice **b**. Although wars were fought to win the privilege of voting, the passage gives another reason for why eighteen-year-olds believed they deserved that privilege, so choice **c** is not the best answer. Eighteen-year-olds do have the right to express their opinions, but this is not the reason why they said they should have the right to vote that the passage gives, so choice **d** is incorrect.

18. b. The passage states, "Interviewing people about their voting habits is revealing."

19. d. The author begins the passage by stating that "Cuttlefish are intriguing little animals" before describing all the qualities that make them interesting or unique. That cuttlefish can change their skin color is just one interesting fact about them and not the main idea of the entire passage, so choice **a** is incorrect. Choice **b** only describes the main idea of the second paragraph, not the entire passage. Choice **c** is not mentioned in the passage at all.

20. b. The passage uses the word *jet* to describe a spout on the cuttlefish that helps it move. Although the other choices are all synonyms of jet, none indicate how the word is used in this particular passage.

21. d. Choice **d** is not a fact, it is an opinion because someone might think another characteristic is more intriguing. The other choices are all facts, not opinions.

22. a. The passage states that cuttlefish, "like the octopus," is "a member of the order of cephalopods." Choices **b** and **c** only describe the cuttlefish, not the octopus. Choice **d** is simply wrong; the cuttlefish and the octopus both live in water.

23. c. The author writes of cuttlefish, "it is hard not to believe they paint themselves so beautifully just for the sheer joy of it." Scientists believe cuttlefish change their appearance as a way to communicate, so choice **a** is incorrect. The author says that cuttlefish are intriguing animals that must have the most "sparkling" conversation in the sea, which implies that their lives are anything but dull, so choice **b** is incorrect. Choice **d** is wrong because the passage states, "The cuttlefish resembles a rather large squid."

24. b. The passage is full of facts about the cuttlefish, which is a kind of cephalopod. Choices **a** and **c** describe single characteristics of the cuttlefish and fail to sum up the main idea of the passage. Although the author writes that the cuttlefish's eye is similar to that of a human, the passage is not about the human eye, so choice **d** is wrong.

25. a. As it is used in the first paragraph, *trend* means *development*.

26. c. The passage states that the school provides students with their own laptops to help them "stay on top of the latest computer technology." A laptop is probably more expensive than a textbook, so choice **a** does not make sense. Although students are allowed to store music on their laptops, this is not the main reason the school issued laptops, so choice **b** is not the best answer. Choice **d** is not mentioned in the passage.

27. d. As it is used in this passage, *materials* means *notes*. Although the other choices are all synonyms of *materials*, none indicate how the word is used in this particular passage.

28. c. An innovation is something new, and since Empire High School has figured out a new way to educate, choice **c** is a good title. Although laptops make it more difficult to cheat, this is not the most important idea in the passage, and therefore, choice **a** is a poor title. This passage does not instruct you how to buy your own laptop, so choice **b** does not make sense. The passage only discusses one detail about Empire High School, not the school's entire history, so choice **d** is not the best answer.

29. b. The passage never suggests that students use their laptop computers to chat with friends. The other answer choices are all discussed in the passage.

30. b. The passage states, "Instead of handing in reports and homework on paper, these Arizona students just e-mail it to their individual teachers."

Language

1. a. *Whose* is a possessive form of *who*; this sentence requires the contraction of *who is*, which is *who's*.

2. b. When used in the possessive form, *its* is the correct spelling; *it's* is a contraction of *it is*.

3. c. When used as a title, *uncle* should be capitalized.

4. a. This is a run-on sentence that should have a semicolon between *shoes* and *I*.

5. d. All the answer choices are correct.

6. d. All the answer choices are correct.

7. b. This is a question that should end with a question mark.

8. c. The word *woman* is singular; it should be *women*.

9. a. *Paddington Theater* is the proper name of an establishment, so it should be capitalized.

10. b. Remove *Ingrid* from the sentence and you will see that *Me went to the beach* is incorrect. The sentence should read *Ingrid and I went to the beach*.

11. d. All the answer choices are correct.

12. c. There is no subject-verb agreement; the subject, *sun*, is singular so it requires the singular verb *is*.

13. b. There should be a comma before the quotation.

14. a. *Bodega Bay* is a proper noun, so *bay* should be capitalized.

15. d. All the answer choices are correct.

16. d. All the answer choices are correct.

17. a. The comma is unnecessary and should be deleted.

18. a. *Earthquake* is a compound word, so there should not be a space between *earth* and *quake*.

19. c. *Slide* is an irregular verb and should be written *slid* in the past tense.

20. b. The commas are missing from this series of adjectives.

21. c. There should be an apostrophe in the word *boy's* because it is the possessive form.

22. d. All the answer choices are correct.

23. a. This is a fragment.

24. b. This sentence makes an illogical shift from the present tense to the past tense.

25. c. *High school* should be capitalized when it is part of a proper name, such as *Monterey High School*.

26. d. All the answer choices are correct.

27. a. A colon, not a comma, precedes a list.

28. c. The word *the* should not be capitalized in a title unless it is the first word.

29. d. All the answer choices are correct.

30. b. This is not a question, so it should not end with a question mark.

31. c. amendment

32. a. finally

33. a. questionnaire

34. b. suitable

35. c. productivity

36. d. All the words are spelled correctly.

37. c. crystal

38. a. supervise

39. b. portfolio

40. c. suede

41. d. *However* is the only logical choice. It shows that there has been a change between the first sentence and the second one. The other choices do not show this relationship.

42. b. The second part of this thought is consistent with the first thought. *And* is the conjunction that indicates this relationship. Choices **a** and **c** indicate a change between the two thoughts. Choice **d** indicates a causal relationship that does not exist between the two thoughts.

43. a. Choice **a** is the only clear and correct sentence. Choice **b** is missing its subject. The syntax of choice **c** is confusing. Choice **d** is a run-on sentence.

44. c. Choice **c** is the only one that is clear and correct. Choices **a** and **d** have confusing syntax. The sentence is not a question, so it should not end with a question mark as choice **b** does.

45. b. Choice **b** is the only one that is clear and correct. Choice **a** is missing a crucial comma. Choice **c** does not have clear syntax. Choice **d** mistakenly uses the singular form of *book* when the plural, *books*, is required.

46. d. Choice **d** is the only one that is clear and correct. The other choices are awkward and difficult to read.

47. a. The other answer choices are much too broad to adequately discuss in a short essay.

48. b. Only choice **b** is relevant to the topic of "why recycling is important." Choice **a** refers to what should be recycled, Choice **c** merely lists some items that can be recycled. Choice **d** refers to pickup schedules.

49. d. Every sentence is about red foxes as an invasive species except for sentence 4, which is about their hearing.

50. c. The sentence develops the idea of learning to play notes. So it best follows sentence 2, which introduces the idea of notes. You cannot play notes until you know where they are, so it should also be placed before sentence 3, which introduces the idea of playing notes.

Math

1. c. Choice **a** is incorrect because you mistakenly borrowed from the hundreds place. Choice **b** is incorrect because you mistakenly borrowed from the hundreds place and did not borrow correctly from the tens place. Choice **d** is incorrect because you did not borrow correctly from the tens place.

2. a. Choice **b** is incorrect because you did not insert a zero place holder in the tens place after the initial division of 9 into 63. Choice **c** is incorrect because you transposed the last two digits of the quotient. Choice **d** is incorrect because the initial division of 9 into 63 is wrong; it goes in 7 times evenly, not 6.

3. d. Choice **a** is incorrect because you did not carry properly to the tens or the hundreds places. Choice **b** is incorrect because you did not carry properly to the hundreds place. Choice **c** is incorrect because you did not carry properly to the tens place.

4. b. Choice **b** is correct because $55 + 85 + 300 = (55 + 85) + 300 = 140 + 300 = 440$. Choice **a** is incorrect because you did not carry properly to the hundreds place. Choice **c** is incorrect because you did not carry properly to the tens place. Choice **d** is incorrect because you did not carry properly to the hundreds place.

5. c. Choice **c** is correct because $(1.1)2 = (1.1)(1.1) = 1.21$. Choice **a** is incorrect because the decimal place is in the wrong location; it should be one more place to the left. Choice **b** is incorrect because you multiplied base times exponent. Choice **d** is incorrect because this is $(1.2)^2$, not $(1.1)^2$.

6. b. Choice **b** is correct because $3 \div 0.15 = 300 \div 15 = 20$. Choice **a** is incorrect because you did not properly move the decimal point. Choice **c** is incorrect because you multiplied instead of dividing. Choice **d** is incorrect because you divided the numbers in the wrong order.

7. b. Choice **b** is correct because $2(5.3 - 2.2) + 4(1.9 - 1.7) = 2(3.1) + 4(0.2) = 6.2 + 0.8 = 7.0$. Choice **a** is incorrect because you subtracted the second main expression from the first one instead of adding them together. Choice **c** is incorrect because you did not simplify the second main expression correctly; it should be 0.8 instead of 0.08. Choice **d** is incorrect because you did not account for the second term in the sum.

8. c. Choice **c** is correct because $2\frac{1}{3} + 4\frac{7}{9} = 2\frac{3}{9} + 4\frac{7}{9} = (2 + 4) + (\frac{3}{9} + \frac{7}{9}) = 6\frac{10}{9} = 7\frac{1}{9}$. Choice **a** is incorrect because you computed this sum by adding the numerators and denominators straight across; you must first get a least common denominator. Choice **b** is incorrect because you added the fractional parts incorrectly. Choice **d** is incorrect because you did not interpret the mixed numbers correctly.

9. d. Choice **d** is correct because you multiplied 6 times 9, and moved the decimal point five units to the left. Choice **a** is incorrect because you completely ignored the decimal point. Choice **b** is incorrect because the decimal point is in the wrong location. Choice **c** is incorrect because there is one too few zeros after the decimal point.

10. b. Choice **b** is correct because $15 - \frac{11}{6} = \frac{90}{6} - \frac{11}{6} = \frac{79}{6} = 13\frac{1}{6}$. Choice **a** is incorrect because when you converted 15 to an improper fraction with denominator 6, you wrote $\frac{80}{6}$ instead of $\frac{90}{6}$. Choice **c** is incorrect because you did not convert the improper fraction obtained upon subtracting to a mixed number correctly. Choice **d** is incorrect because you did not first get a least common denominator before subtracting.

11. b. Choice **b** is correct because $2.5(40) = 100$. Choice **a** is incorrect because $250\% = 2.5$, not 25. Choice **c** is incorrect because you multiplied 250 times 40, instead of 2.5 times 40. Choice **d** is incorrect because $250\% = 2.5$, not 0.25.

12. d. Choice **d** is correct because $1\frac{1}{2} \times 2\frac{1}{3} = \frac{3}{2} \times \frac{7}{3} = \frac{21}{6} = \frac{7}{2}$. Choice **a** is incorrect because this is the reciprocal of the correct answer. Choice **b** is incorrect because you divided instead of multiplying. Choice **c** is incorrect because you did not treat the mixed numbers correctly.

13. c. Choice **c** is correct because $\frac{33}{5} \div \frac{1}{25} = \frac{33}{5} \times 25 = 33 \times 5 = 165$. Choice **a** is incorrect because you multiplied instead of dividing, and then took the reciprocal of that result. Choice **b** is incorrect because this is the reciprocal of the correct answer. Choice **d** is incorrect because you multiplied instead of dividing.

14. a. Choice **a** is correct because $0.002(2000) = 4$. Choice **b** is incorrect because $0.2\% = 0.002$, not 0.2. Choice **c** is incorrect because $0.2\% = 0.002$, not 0.02. Choice **d** is incorrect because $0.2\% = 0.002$, not 20. You moved the decimal point the wrong way.

15. b. Choice **b** is correct because 5.92 is very close to 6, so that $(5.92)^2$ is very close to 6^2, or 36. Choice **a** is incorrect because 5.92 is much closer to 6 than to 5, so 5^2, or 25, is not the best estimate. Choice **c** is incorrect because $(5.92)^2 < 6^2 = 36$, so that 36 is a better estimate than 38. Choice **d** is incorrect because $(5.92)^2 < 6^2 = 36$, so that 36 is a better estimate than 40.

16. c. Choice **c** is correct because each of the fractional parts is close to 1, so that the sum of them is close to 3. Adding this to the sum of the three whole parts suggests 19 is a good estimate. Choice **a** is incorrect because this does not account for the fractional parts, only the whole parts of the mixed numbers. Choice **b** is incorrect because the sum of the fractional parts is close to 3, not 1. So, 19 is the better estimate. Choice **d** is incorrect because this is too large. The sum is less than 19, so that 19 is the better estimate.

17. a. Choice **a** is correct because the given sum is close to $4(5) + 3(20) = 20 + 60 = 80$. Choice **b** is incorrect because you rounded (2.1 + 3.1) to the nearest 10, not nearest ones place. This results in a much larger estimate. Choice **c** is incorrect because this estimate is too small; this would be a good estimate only for the second main expression in the given sum, but not the entire sum. Choice **d** is incorrect because this is a good estimate for double the sum.

18. d. Choice **d** is correct because $9,000 - 4,000 = 5,000$. Choice **a** is incorrect because choice **d** is a better estimate. Choice **b** is incorrect because 9,105 is close to 9,000 and 3,879 is close to 4,000; so, choice **d** is better. Choice **c** is incorrect because 3,879 is closer to 4,000 than it is to 3,000. So, 5,000 is a better estimate of this difference.

19. c. Choice **c** is correct because the actual quotient is 51, and note that $50(9) = 450$. Choice **a** is incorrect because this estimate is way too large; note that $70(9) = 630$, which is not close to 459. Choice **b** is incorrect because this estimate is too large; note that $60(9) = 540$, which is not close to 459. Choice **d** is incorrect because the actual quotient is 51, so that choice **c** is better. Note also that $40(9) = 360$, which is not as close as $50(9) = 450$ is to 459.

20. d. Choice **d** is correct because we estimate the given quantity by 5% of 400, which is 20. Choice **a** is incorrect because this is close to 1% of 400, so that choice **d** is better. Choice **b** is incorrect because this is close to 10% of 400, so that choice **d** is better. Choice **c** is incorrect because this is closer to 4% of 400, so that choice **d** is better.

21. a. Choice **a** is correct because $\frac{5,000}{110} = 45.45$ minutes, and converting this to hours yields $\frac{45.45}{60}$ hours, which is approximately $\frac{3}{4}$ hour. Choice **b** is incorrect because this accounts for mowing only 3,300 square feet of lawn. Choice **c** is incorrect because this is approximately $60 + 18 = 78$ minutes of mowing, which would yield 8,580 square feet. Choice **d** is incorrect because this would correspond to $0.34(60) = 20$ minutes, which only would yield 2,200 square feet of mowing.

22. a. Choice **a** is correct because the amount of interest is $160(0.04) = \$6.4$. This, added to the original amount of $160, is $166.40. Choice **b** is incorrect because this would be the amount had the interest rate been 40%, not 4%. Choice **c** is incorrect because this is 40% of the original amount, not the original amount plus 4%. Choice **d** is incorrect because this is the amount of interest earned.

23. c. Choice **c** is correct because $0.005(20,000) = 100$. Choice **a** is incorrect because $5\% = 0.005$, not 0.5. Choice **b** is incorrect because $5\% = 0.005$, not 0.05. Choice **d** is incorrect because $5\% = 0.005$, not 0.0005.

24. b. Choice **b** is correct because $\frac{1}{4} + \frac{1}{3} + \frac{3}{8} = \frac{6+8+9}{24} = \frac{23}{24}$ of the bag is used for the baking, so that $1 - \frac{23}{24} = \frac{1}{24}$ of the bag remains. Choice **a** is incorrect because you added the fractions incorrectly by simply adding the numerators and the denominators; you must first get a least common denominator. Choice **c** is incorrect because you did not account for the portion of the bag used for baking fruitcake. Choice **d** is incorrect because you did not account for the portion of the bag used to make candy.

25. d. Choice **d** is correct because summing the heights of the bars yields $8 + 10 + 12 + 10 = 40$. Choice **a** is incorrect because this is the number that Bob made, not Cara. Choice **b** is incorrect because this is not the sum of the four heights of the bar graphs for Cara's foul shots for these four weeks. Choice **c** is incorrect because this is the maximum number she made for a given square-off during the four weeks, not the total number of foul shots that she made.

26. c. Choice **c** is correct because subtracting the heights of the corresponding bars yields $6 - 2 = 4$. Choice **a** is incorrect because this is the maximum number of foul shots that Geoff made minus the minimum number that Bob made. Choice **b** is incorrect because you did not subtract the number of foul shots Bob made from the number that Geoff made. Choice **d** is incorrect because you are not using the correct bars in the bar graph.

27. d. Choice **d** is correct because 1,005 is divisible by 5. Choice **a** is incorrect because this number is prime. Choice **b** is incorrect because this number is prime. Choice **c** is incorrect because this number is prime.

28. d. Choice **d** is correct because $-(8 - 3)^2 - 5 \times 5 = -5^2 - 5 \times 5 = -25 - 25 = -50$. Choice **a** is incorrect because you incorrectly simplified $(8 - 3)^2$ as 5 times 2 instead of 5^2. Then, you subtracted 5 immediately rather than first computing 5×5. Choice **b** is incorrect because after you correctly simplified $-(8 - 3)^2$ as -25, you immediately subtracted 5 from it rather than first computing 5×5. Remember to follow the order of operations. Choice **c** is incorrect because you incorrectly simplified $(8 - 3)^2$ as 5 times 2 instead of 5^2.

29. b. Choice **b** is correct because $518 = 2(7)(37) = 7(74)$, so 74 divides 518 evenly. Choice **a** is incorrect because 4 does not divide 518 evenly. Choice **c** is incorrect because 16 does not divide 518 evenly. Choice **d** is incorrect because 209 does not divide 518 evenly.

30. c. Choice **c** is correct because $\frac{410}{11} = 37.27$. So each hallway must get 37 to make certain the distribution is as even as possible; some hallways will get one extra because of the remainder. Choice **a** is incorrect because this is one too many. Choice **b** is incorrect because this is one too few. Choice **d** is incorrect because this is the number of hallways—you need to divide 410 by 11.

31. d. Choice **d** is correct because $\frac{348}{58} = 6$. Choice **a** is incorrect because you divided in the wrong order. Choice **b** is incorrect because you multiplied both sides by 348 instead of dividing by x. Choice **c** is incorrect because you subtracted 6 from both sides.

32. a. Choice **a** is correct because $\frac{260}{13} = 20$. Choice **b** is incorrect because 13 does not divide 141 evenly. Choice **c** is incorrect because 13 does not divide 246 evenly. Choice **d** is incorrect because 13 does not divide 415 evenly.

33. a. Choice **a** is correct because $\frac{3}{14}$ is approximately 0.2142, so the correct estimate is 0.214. Choice **b** is incorrect because you rounded to the nearest tenth. Choice **c** is incorrect because you rounded to the nearest hundredth. Choice **d** is incorrect because you divided 14 by 3, not the other way.

34. b. Choice **b** is correct because $2^6 = 2(2)(2)(2)(2)(2) = 64$. Choice **a** is incorrect because this is 6^2, not 2^6. Choice **c** is incorrect because you multiplied 2 times 6, but this is not how you compute a power. Choice **d** is incorrect because this is 2^5, not 2^6.

35. d. Choice **d** is correct because $335 + (42 - 30)(\$8) = \$431$. Choice **a** is incorrect because you treated all 42 hours as though they were overtime. Choice **b** is incorrect because you only accounted for 2 hours overtime beyond 30, not 12. Choice **c** is incorrect because you forgot to multiply 12 hours times $8.

36. b. Let x be the time it takes Mandy to pitch the tent. Then,
$$\frac{4}{5}x + x + \frac{7}{5}\left(\frac{4}{5}x\right) = 73$$
$$20x + 25x + 28x = 73(25)$$
$$73x = 73(25)$$
$$x = 25$$
Thus, Nina's time is $\frac{7}{5}\left(\frac{4}{5} \times 25 \text{ minutes}\right) =$ 28 minutes. Choice **a** is incorrect because this is Mandy's time. Choice **c** is incorrect because this is Katie's time. Choice **d** is incorrect because this is the sum of Mandy's and Nina's times.

37. a. Choice **a** is correct because $\$210 + \$210(3.5) = \$945$. Choice **b** is incorrect because this is the amount the price increased beyond the listed price; you should have added the original listed price to this amount. Choice **c** is incorrect because you added the original listed price to the percentage rather than to the percentage applied to the listed price. Choice **d** is incorrect because this is just the percentage amount given in dollars.

38. c. Choice **c** is correct because there are 6.5 hours from 5:30 P.M. to midnight, and 3.75 hours from midnight to 3:45 A.M. So, they dance for 11.25 hours, which is equivalent to $11.25(60) = 675$ minutes. Since each song lasts about 4 minutes, the number of full songs during which they dance is the whole part of the quotient $\frac{675}{4}$, which is 168. Choice **a** is incorrect because this only accounts for the time period from 5:30 P.M. to midnight. Choice **b** is incorrect because they wouldn't get all the way through the 169th song. Choice **d** is incorrect because this is the number of minutes that they are dancing.

39. c. Choice **c** is correct because $\$550(0.22) = \$121$. Choice **a** is incorrect because 22% = 0.22, not 0.022. Choice **b** is incorrect because 22% = 0.22, not 0.022, and this would have represented the amount Valerie spent on food in such case. Choice **d** is incorrect because this is the amount Valerie spent on food, not the difference in the amounts they both spent.

40. a. Choice **a** is correct because the area of the blueprint representation of the window is 2 square inches and the area of the actual window is 24 inches × 48 inches = 1,152 square inches. So, the ratio of these areas is 2:1,152, or 1:576. Choice **b** is incorrect because this is written backward (since the smaller area is to come first from the statement of the problem), and you didn't convert feet to inches when forming the ratio. Choice **c** is incorrect because you did not convert feet to inches. Choice **d** is incorrect because the number that comes first in this ratio must be no larger than the second one (based on the ratio for which the problem asks).

41. a. Because $149 – $40 = $119 is the amount he must yet earn. Since he earns $20 per week, dividing this by $20 yields the number of weeks he must work in order to earn this much more money. This division results in 5 R9. So, he must work 6 weeks. Choice **b** is incorrect because you forgot to account for the remainder. He would only have earned $100 by the end of 5 weeks. Choice **c** is incorrect because you did not account for the $40 he already saved. Choice **d** is incorrect because you did not account for the $40 he already saved, and you did not account for the remainder.

42. d. Note that 45 minutes = $\frac{3}{4}$ hour. As such, we add the four times and divide the sum by 4 to get the average, as follows:

$$\frac{1\frac{1}{2} + 2 + 1\frac{3}{4} + \frac{3}{4}}{4} = \frac{\frac{3}{2} + 2 + \frac{5}{4} + \frac{3}{4}}{4}$$

$$= \frac{6 + 8 + 5 + 3}{16}$$

$$= \frac{22}{16} = 1\frac{6}{16} = 1\frac{3}{8} \text{ hours.}$$

Choice **a** is incorrect because this is the total time he spent exercising during the week, not the average amount of time on each of the four days. Choice **b** is incorrect because you divided by 3, not 4. Choice **c** is incorrect because you divided by 5, not 4.

43. c. Choice **c** is correct because 40% of 80 = 80(0.40) = 32. Choice **a** is incorrect because 40% is not equal to 40. You need to take 40% of 80. Choice **b** is incorrect because this is 10% of 80 and equals the number of short answer questions. Choice **d** is incorrect because this is 25% of 80, and could be either the number of fill-in-the-blank questions or the number of multiple-choice questions.

44. a. Choice **a** is correct because there are 0.40(80) = 32 true/false questions and 0.10(80) = 8 short answer questions, which gives the ratio as 32:8 or 4:1. Choice **b** is incorrect because this would mean there was the same number of true/false questions as there were short answer questions. Choice **c** is incorrect because you used the wrong type of questions when forming the ratio. Choice **d** is incorrect because you wrote the ratio backward.

45. c. Choice **c** is correct because summing the five times and dividing by 5 yields $\frac{1 + 0.5 + 2.5 + 2 + 1}{5} = \frac{7}{5} = 1.4$ hours. Choice **a** is incorrect because this is the median time, not the average. Choice **b** is incorrect because this is the maximum time, not the average. Choice **d** is incorrect because you divided the sum of the five times by 4, not 5.

46. b. Choice **b** is correct because $\frac{2.5 - 0.5}{0.5} \times 100\%$ = 400%. Choice **a** is incorrect because you did not divide the difference in time by 0.5. Choice **c** is incorrect because you did not multiply by 100%. Choice **d** is incorrect because you did not multiply by 100%, and you divided by 0.5.

47. c. Choice **c** is correct because $\frac{2}{40}$. Choice **a** is incorrect because this is the percentage of all students who received such awards who were NOT seniors. Choice **b** is incorrect because you divided 2 by 13; this is how to determine the percentage of all students in 2011 receiving these awards who were seniors, not in all four years. Choice **d** is incorrect because 2 is the number of seniors, but you need to divide by the number receiving the award (namely 40).

48. d. Choice **d** is correct because 15 freshmen received awards and 8 juniors received awards; so the difference is $15 - 8 = 7$. Choice **a** is incorrect because this corresponds to either freshmen minus seniors, or sophomores minus seniors. Choice **b** is incorrect because this would suggest that the same number of awards were given to freshmen and juniors. Choice **c** is incorrect because this represents juniors minus seniors.

49. a. Choice **a** is correct because $\frac{4 + 10 + 7}{3} = \frac{21}{3} = 7$. Choice **b** is incorrect because this is the minimum number across all teams, not the average. Choice **c** is incorrect because this is the maximum number across all teams, not the average. Choice **d** is incorrect because this exceeds even the maximum number across all teams and so, cannot possibly be the average.

50. a. Choice **a** is correct because 21 gallons of this drink were used, which exceeds all of the others. Choice **b** is incorrect because 20 gallons of this drink were used, and drink A was used slightly more. Choice **c** is incorrect because 12 gallons of this drink were used, and drinks A and B were both used more. Choice **d** is incorrect because only 5 gallons of this drink were used, which is the least used drink of the four.

Ability

1. a. Choice **a** is correct because you obtain the next term by subtracting $\frac{2}{3}$ from the previous term. Choice **b** is incorrect because you subtracted $\frac{1}{3}$, not $\frac{2}{3}$, from the previous term. Choice **c** is incorrect because you subtracted 1, not $\frac{2}{3}$, from the previous term. Choice **d** is incorrect because you added $\frac{2}{3}$ to the previous term instead of subtracting it.

2. d. Choice **d** is correct because the pattern is to subtract 1, then $\frac{1}{2}$, then $\frac{1}{4}$, and then $\frac{1}{8}$, always from the previous term. Choice **a** is incorrect because you subtracted $\frac{1}{2}$, not $\frac{1}{8}$, from the previous term. Choice **b** is incorrect because you subtracted $\frac{1}{4}$, not $\frac{1}{8}$, from the previous term. Choice **c** is incorrect because you subtracted $\frac{1}{16}$, not $\frac{1}{8}$, from the previous term.

3. b. Choice **b** is correct because the sequences are interlaced. For the 1st, 3rd, 5th, and 7th terms, you multiply the previous term by 10 to get the next one; for the 2nd, 4th, 6th, and 8th terms, you add 0.5 to the previous term to get the next one. So, to get the first missing term, multiply 0.2 times 10 to get 2; to get the second missing term, add 0.5 to 1.5 to get 2.0. Choice **a** is incorrect because the second term is wrong; you should have added 0.5 to 1.5. Choice **c** is incorrect because the first term is wrong; you should have multiplied it by 10. Choice **d** is incorrect because the first term is wrong; you should have multiplied it by 10, not 100.

4. d. Choice **d** is correct because the sequences are interlaced. For the 1st, 3rd, 5th, and 7th terms, you subtract $1\frac{5}{8}$ from the previous term to get the next one; for the 2nd, 4th, 6th, and 8th terms, you subtract $\frac{3}{4}$ from the previous term to get the next one. This yields the two terms listed in this choice. Choice **a** is incorrect because you subtracted too much from both terms. Choice **b** is incorrect because you did not follow the pattern. For the 1st, 3rd, 5th, and 7th terms, you subtract $1\frac{5}{8}$ from the previous term to get the next one; for the 2nd, 4th, 6th, and 8th terms, you subtract $\frac{3}{4}$ from the previous term to get the next one. Choice **c** is incorrect because while you followed the correct pattern, you subtracted $1\frac{5}{8}$ incorrectly from $7\frac{1}{8}$.

5. c. Choice **c** is correct because the pattern is to add 1.3 to the previous term to get the next one. Choice **a** is incorrect because you added 1.2 to 8.8 instead of 1.3. Choice **b** is incorrect because you added 1.7 to 8.8 instead of 1.3. Choice **d** is incorrect because you did not assess the pattern correctly.

6. a. Choice **a** is correct because the pattern is to subtract 0.1 from the first to second term, second 0.2 from the second to third term, subtract 0.3 from the third to fourth term, and so on. Choice **b** is incorrect because you subtracted 0.2 from the previous term when you should have subtracted 0.3. Choice **c** is incorrect because you subtracted 0.1 from the previous term when you should have subtracted 0.3. Choice **d** is incorrect because you subtracted 0.4 from the previous term when you should have subtracted 0.3.

7. b. Choice **b** is correct because the sequence is interlaced. For the 1st, 3rd, 5th, and 7th terms, you add 0.1 to the previous term to get the next one; for the 2nd, 4th, 6th, and 8th terms, you subtract 0.5 from the previous term to get the next one. This yields the two terms listed in this choice. Choice **a** is incorrect because this would be the term after the one being asked for. Choice **c** is incorrect because you added 0.05 to 2.3 when you should have added 0.1. Choice **d** is incorrect because you added 0.2 to 2.3 when you should have added 0.1.

8. a. Choice **a** is correct because converting these to whole numbers gives the equivalent sequence 70, 58, 46, from which it is clear that we subtract 12 from the previous term to get the next one. So, the next term is 34, which is XXXIV in Roman numerals. Choice **b** is incorrect because this corresponds to the whole number 33, which is one off from the actual next term in the sequence. Choice **c** is incorrect because this is not a properly formed Roman numeral. Choice **d** is incorrect because this corresponds to the whole number 24, not 34.

9. c. Choice **c** is correct because converting these to whole numbers gives the equivalent sequence 24, 32, 40, ____, 56. From this, it is clear that we add 8 to the previous term to get the next one. Choice **a** is incorrect because you transposed the Roman numerals for 50 and 8. Choice **b** is incorrect because this corresponds to the whole number 44, not 48. Choice **d** is incorrect because this corresponds to the whole number 78, not 48.

10. c. Choice **c** is correct because you subtract II from the previous Roman numeral to get to the next one; and you add $\frac{1}{4}$ to the previous fraction to get to the next one. Choice **a** is incorrect because both terms are wrong. Choice **b** is incorrect because the second term is wrong—you added $\frac{5}{6}$ and $\frac{1}{4}$ incorrectly. Choice **d** is incorrect because both terms are wrong.

11. a. Choice **a** is correct because you add X to the previous Roman numeral to get to the next one; and you multiply the previous whole number by 2 to get the next one. Choice **b** is incorrect because the second term is wrong. You should have multiplied 12 times 2, not 3. Choice **c** is incorrect because the first term is wrong; you added XX rather than X. Choice **d** is incorrect because both terms are wrong.

12. a. Choice **a** is correct because the sequence is interlaced. For the 1st, 3rd, 5th, and 7th terms, you subtract 3 from the previous term to get the next one; for the 2nd, 4th, 6th, and 8th terms, you add 4 to the previous term to get the next one. Choice **b** is incorrect because you added 4, but should have subtracted 3. Choice **c** is incorrect because you didn't follow the pattern. Choice **d** is incorrect because you added 3 instead of subtracting it.

13. c. Choice **c** is correct because the sequence is interlaced. For the 2nd, 4th, and 6th terms, you subtract 2 from the previous term. Choice **a** is incorrect because this is the next term beyond what was asked for. Choice **b** is incorrect because you subtracted 4 instead of 2. Choice **d** is incorrect because this is two terms beyond what has been asked for.

14. b. Choice **b** is correct because the pattern is to add 11 to the previous term. Choice **a** is incorrect because you should have added 11 to 123. Choice **c** is incorrect because you should have added 11 to 123. Choice **d** is incorrect because you should have added 11 to 123.

15. a. Choice **a** is correct because all the figures are rotations of each other. Choice **b** is incorrect because a diagonal line is missing from the figure. Choice **c** is incorrect because there are too many dots. Choice **d** is incorrect because the figure is missing a diameter. Choice **e** is incorrect because the figure is missing a dot.

16. a. Choice **a** is correct because all the figures are rotations of each other. Choice **b** is incorrect because this figure does not have two consecutive vertices being highlighted like the others. Choice **c** is incorrect because this figure does not have two consecutive vertices being highlighted, and the dividing line is incorrectly placed. Choice **d** is incorrect because the vertex at one endpoint of the line segment should not be highlighted. Choice **e** is incorrect because there are too many vertices highlighted, and the dividing line is incorrectly placed.

17. b. Choice **b** is correct because like the others, there is an odd number of parts shaded. Choice **a** is incorrect because there is an even number of parts shaded. Choice **c** is incorrect because there is an even number of parts shaded. Choice **d** is incorrect because there is an even number of parts shaded. Choice **e** is incorrect because none of the parts is shaded.

18. b. Choice **b** is correct because the correct part is shaded and both disjoint pieces are shaded in the same direction. Choice **a** is incorrect because the wrong part is shaded. Choice **c** is incorrect because not enough of the figure is shaded. Choice **d** is incorrect because while the correct portion of the figure is shaded, the shading is done in different directions (unlike in choice **b**). Choice **e** is incorrect because too much of the figure is shaded.

19. a. Choice **a** is correct because all of the figures are rotations of each other, as is this one. Choice **b** is incorrect because the wrong figure is shaded. Choice **c** is incorrect because the square should not be shaded. Choice **d** is incorrect because neither shape is shaded. Choice **e** is incorrect because the circle is shaded, but in the wrong direction, so this is not a proper rotation of the figures in the grouping.

20. d. Choice **d** is correct because this figure contains three segments in the outer ring, just like the others in the grouping. Choice **a** is incorrect because this figure contains 4 segments rather than 3. Choice **b** is incorrect because one of the segments intersects the inner circle, unlike those in the grouping. Choice **c** is incorrect because this figure contains 6 segments rather than 3. Choice **e** is incorrect because the inner circle is shaded.

21. b. Choice **b** is correct because this figure contains a curved portion like the others, and no other choice does. Choice **a** is incorrect because this figure does not contain a curved portion. Choice **c** is incorrect because this figure does not contain a curved portion. Choice **d** is incorrect because this figure does not contain a curved portion. Choice **e** is incorrect because this figure does not contain a curved portion.

22. d. Choice **d** is correct because the shapes are the same and the correct region is shaded. Choice **a** is incorrect because the inside shape would need to be a circle in order for this to match the pattern. Choice **b** is incorrect because the shapes need to be the same, and the region between the shapes would need to be shaded. Choice **c** is incorrect because the wrong portion is shaded. Choice **e** is incorrect because there is no shading.

23. a. Choice **a** is correct because the figure contains two parallel bold lines and one dotted line that intersects both of them. Choice **b** is incorrect because the dotted line does not intersect either of the bold lines. Choice **c** is incorrect because the dotted line does not intersect both of the bold lines, as it does in all the given figures. Choice **d** is incorrect because the figure has the wrong number of dotted and bold lines. Choice **e** is incorrect because there needs to be one more bold line parallel to the one already present.

24. **a.** Choice **a** is correct because the two shapes are the same, and the one inside does not intersect the larger one encompassing it. Choice **b** is incorrect because there should be no part of the figure shaded. Choice **c** is incorrect because the inside smaller circle touches the one encompassing it, unlike those given. Choice **d** is incorrect because the shapes are not the same. Choice **e** is incorrect because the shapes are not the same, and no part of the region should be shaded.

25. **d.** Choice **d** is correct because there is an odd number of vertices. Choice **a** is incorrect because there is an even number of vertices, but all the given figures have an odd number. Choice **b** is incorrect because there is an even number of vertices, but all the given figures have an odd number. Choice **c** is incorrect because there is an even number of vertices, but all the given figures have an odd number. Choice **e** is incorrect because there is an even number of vertices, but all the given figures have an odd number.

26. **a.** Choice **a** is correct because the only change is that the region bounded by the inner shape be shaded, which occurs with the figure in this choice. Choice **b** is incorrect because the wrong shape is being used; it should have been a circle. Choice **c** is incorrect because no inner shape is shaded. Choice **d** is incorrect because the wrong portion is shaded. Choice **e** is incorrect because the inner shape is wrong; it should be a circle.

27. **c.** Choice **c** is correct because the shapes are correct and the shading follows the pattern provided. Choice **a** is incorrect because the inner shape is wrong. Choice **b** is incorrect because there is no shading between the inner and outer shapes. Choice **d** is incorrect because the shapes are swapped; the inner one should be a square and the outer a hexagon, not the other way around. Choice **e** is incorrect because this figure contains the wrong inner shape and shading.

28. **b.** Choice **b** is correct because the shapes are correct, the boundary is in bold (not dotted), and the lack of shading is correct. Choice **a** is incorrect because the inside of the circle should not be shaded. Choice **c** is incorrect because the outer triangle should be solid, not dotted. Choice **d** is incorrect because the inner circle should not be dotted. Choice **e** is incorrect because neither shape should be dotted.

29. **e.** Choice **e** is correct because the figure has been shrunk and rotated by the correct amount. Choice **a** is incorrect because the figure has been rotated by an incorrect amount. Choice **b** is incorrect because the figure has been neither rotated nor shrunk. Choice **c** is incorrect because the figure has not been rotated. Choice **d** is incorrect because the figure has not been shrunk.

30. **d.** Choice **d** is correct because the figure is dotted and has been rotated. Choice **a** is incorrect because the figure has not been rotated. Choice **b** is incorrect because the figure should not have been shrunk. Choice **c** is incorrect because the figure should not have been shrunk, and it should be dotted. Choice **e** is incorrect because the figure should be dotted.

31. b. Choice **b** is correct because the letter has been rotated by the proper amount and the outer shape has been removed. Choice **a** is incorrect because the outer shape should have been removed. Choice **c** is incorrect because the letter has not been rotated and the outer shape has not been removed. Choice **d** is incorrect because the letter was removed rather than the shape. Choice **e** is incorrect because the letter was rotated by an improper amount.

32. a. Choice **a** is correct because the shapes are all correct and the correct region has been shaded. Choice **b** is incorrect because the wrong portion has been shaded. Choice **c** is incorrect because there is no shading. Choice **d** is incorrect because the wrong portion has been shaded. Choice **e** is incorrect because the wrong portion has been shaded.

33. c. Choice **c** is correct because the correct parts are shaded. Choice **a** is incorrect because the wrong parts of the figure are shaded. Choice **b** is incorrect because there is no shading. Choice **d** is incorrect because the wrong parts of the figure are shaded. Choice **e** is incorrect because too much of the figure is shaded.

34. c. Choice **c** is correct because the shape has been shrunk and the correct parts are shaded. Choice **a** is incorrect because you did not shrink the shape. Choice **b** is incorrect because the shading is wrong. Choice **d** is incorrect because there is no shading and the shape has not been shrunk. Choice **e** is incorrect because there is no shading.

35. e. Choice **e** is correct because the smaller square has been shaded and it is inside the larger one. Choice **a** is incorrect because the smaller square should be inside the larger one, and the shading reversed. Choice **b** is incorrect because the small shaded square should be inside the larger square. Choice **c** is incorrect because the shading is wrong. Choice **d** is incorrect because the smaller square should be shaded.

36. d. Choice **d** is correct because the figure is partitioned into the correct number of pieces and the shapes of these pieces are all correct. Choice **a** is incorrect because the figure has been partitioned incorrectly. Choice **b** is incorrect because the figure is upside down and partitioned incorrectly. Choice **c** is incorrect because the figure has been partitioned incorrectly—there need to be four distinct pieces, not just 2, and they all need to be triangles. Choice **e** is incorrect because the shapes into which the figure is partitioned are not correct.

37. e. Choice **e** is correct because the figure has been pulled apart correctly and the correct pieces shaded. Choice **a** is incorrect because there is no shading. Choice **b** is incorrect because the smaller pieces have not been pulled apart as in the given pattern. Choice **c** is incorrect because too many of the pieces have been shaded. Choice **d** is incorrect because the wrong piece has been shaded.

38. c. Choice **c** is correct because there should be six distinct holes, and those below the fold have been correctly reflected across the fold to get those above it. Choice **a** is incorrect because the holes below the fold do not appear. Choice **b** is incorrect because the holes do not reflect across the fold correctly. Choice **d** is incorrect because the holes above the fold are too close to the fold, and their alignment should be a reflection of what is shown. Choice **e** is incorrect because the holes above the fold are too close to the fold.

39. a. Choice **a** is correct because the number of holes and alignment of them across the fold is correct. Choice **b** is incorrect because the holes above the fold are missing. Choice **c** is incorrect because the spacing of both sets of holes on either side of the fold is incorrect. Choice **d** is incorrect because the holes above the fold have not been reflected correctly. Choice **e** is incorrect because the holes below the fold are missing.

40. e. Choice **e** is correct because the number of holes is correct, and the reflection of the holes below the fold to those above it is correct. Choice **a** is incorrect because the holes below the fold are not aligned correctly. Choice **b** is incorrect because the holes below the fold are missing, and those above it are not aligned correctly. Choice **c** is incorrect because the holes above the fold are missing. Choice **d** is incorrect because the holes below the fold have not been reflected across the fold correctly.

41. b. Choice **b** is correct because the number of holes and their placement on both sides of the fold is correct. Choice **a** is incorrect because the holes should not all occur on the same side of the fold. Choice **c** is incorrect because the holes below the fold are missing. Choice **d** is incorrect because the holes above the fold are missing. Choice **e** is incorrect because the holes are not properly aligned on either side of the fold.

42. b. Choice **b** is correct because the number and placement of the holes on both sides of the fold are correct. Choice **a** is incorrect because the hole on the right side of the fold is missing. Choice **c** is incorrect because the hole on the left side of the fold is incorrect. Choice **d** is incorrect because the hole on the left side of the fold is too close to the fold. Choice **e** is incorrect because there is one hole too many.

43. a. Choice **a** is correct because the number and placement of the holes on both sides of the fold is correct. Choice **b** is incorrect because all four holes should not be on the same side of the fold. Choice **c** is incorrect because the holes on the left side of the fold should be closer to the fold. Choice **d** is incorrect because the holes on the right side of the fold should be closer to the fold. Choice **e** is incorrect because the holes on the left side of the fold should be directly across from those on the right side of the fold.

44. e. Choice **e** is correct because the number and placement of holes on both sides of the fold are correct. Choice **a** is incorrect because the original alignment of the holes was not preserved. Choice **b** is incorrect because the holes on the right side of the fold are missing. Choice **c** is incorrect because the holes on the left side of the fold are missing. Choice **d** is incorrect because the holes on the left side are flipped upside down from what they ought to be.

45. c. Choice **c** is correct because the number and placement of holes on both sides of the fold are correct. Choice **a** is incorrect because the hole above the fold is missing. Choice **b** is incorrect because the hole below the fold is missing. Choice **d** is incorrect because both holes should not occur on the same side of the fold. Choice **e** is incorrect because the leftmost hole is misplaced.

46. b. Choice **b** is correct because the number and placement of the holes on both sides of the fold is correct. Choice **a** is incorrect because the holes were not reflected over the indicated fold. Choice **c** is incorrect because the holes below the fold are missing. Choice **d** is incorrect because all the holes should not be above the fold. Choice **e** is incorrect because the holes above the fold are missing.

47. a. Choice **a** is correct because the number and placement of the holes on both sides of the fold is correct. Choice **b** is incorrect because the leftmost holes above the fold have not been reflected over the fold. Choice **c** is incorrect because the holes below the fold are missing. Choice **d** is incorrect because the middle hole closest to the fold was not reflected across the fold. Choice **e** is incorrect because the holes were reflected over the wrong line.

48. d. Choice **d** is correct because number and placement of the holes on all sides of the folds is correct. Choice **a** is incorrect because the holes arising from the horizontal fold are missing. Choice **b** is incorrect because the holes along the other diagonal through the center are missing. Choice **c** is incorrect because two of the four holes should be on the opposite side of the horizontal fold. Choice **e** is incorrect because one hole in the lower left corner is missing.

49. d. Choice **d** is correct because the number and placement of the holes on all sides of the folds is correct. Choice **a** is incorrect because the holes to the left of the vertical fold are missing. Choice **b** is incorrect because the holes in the other two squares are missing. Choice **c** is incorrect because the holes above the horizontal fold are missing. Choice **e** is incorrect because all four squares should have holes with the same placement as in the upper left square.

50. e. Choice **d** is correct because the number and placement of holes on all sides of the folds is correct. Choice **a** is incorrect because the holes to the left of the vertical fold are missing. Choice **b** is incorrect because the two empty squares should also have holes punched out. Choice **c** is incorrect because the single hole closest to the fold is missing in all places. Choice **d** is incorrect because the original set of holes is not reflected across the folds correctly.

Scoring

Your raw score on the TACHS will be converted into a standard score used by schools to compare you with other test takers, but for the purpose of seeing how you did on this practice test, just consider simple percentages.

First, find the number of questions you got right in each section. Questions you skipped or answered incorrectly don't count; just add up how many questions you got right in each section. Then, divide the number of questions you got right by the number of questions in each section:

Reading: Part 1
_____ correct divided by 20 = _____%

Reading: Part 2
_____ correct divided by 30 = _____%

Language
_____ correct divided by 50 = _____%

Math
_____ correct divided by 50 = _____%

Ability
_____ correct divided by 50 = _____%

It is up to the individual high schools to decide what is an acceptable score for admission as a high school freshman. You want to try for the best possible score you can reach to ensure you get into the school you choose. You can use the percentage scores to show you your strong and weak areas. You should study all the lessons of this book that relate to the TACHS exam, but spend more time on the lessons that relate to the parts of the exam that troubled you most.

Later, when you take the second TACHS exam in this book, you can compare your percentages on that exam with this first exam to see how much you've improved.

7 ▶ READING COMPREHENSION

LESSON SUMMARY
Reading is a vital skill, and the HSPT, COOP, and TACHS include reading comprehension sections that test your ability to understand what you read. The tips and exercises in this lesson will help you improve your comprehension of written passages so you can increase your score in this area.

ew, more advanced textbooks; complicated directions for tests and papers; novels, stories, and essays—these are all things you'll be reading when you go to high school. Being able to understand written materials is vital to academic success. That's why the exams attempt to measure how well students understand what they read.

Reading comprehension tests are usually in a multiple-choice format and ask questions based on brief passages. For that matter, almost all standardized test questions test your reading skill. After all, you can't answer the question if you can't read it! Similarly, you can't study your textbooks or learn the subjects you'll encounter in high school if you can't read well. So reading comprehension is vital not only on the test, but also for the rest of your school career and beyond.

Types of Reading Comprehension Questions

You have probably encountered reading comprehension questions before, where you are given a passage to read and then have to answer multiple-choice questions about it. This kind of question has a big advantage for you as a test taker:

> You don't have to know anything about the topic of the passage because *you're being tested only on the information the passage provides.*

But the disadvantage is that you have to know where and how to find that information quickly in an unfamiliar text. This makes it easy to fall for one of the wrong answer choices, especially because they're designed to mislead you.

The best way to do well on this passage/question format is to be very familiar with the kinds of questions that are typically asked on the test. Questions most frequently ask you to:

- identify a specific **fact or detail** in the passage
- note the **main idea** of the passage
- make an **inference** based on the passage
- define a **vocabulary** word from the passage

For you to do well on a reading comprehension test, you need to know exactly what each question is asking. **Facts and details** are the specific pieces of information that support the passage's **main idea**. The main idea is the thought, opinion, or attitude that governs the whole passage. Generally, facts and details are indisputable—things that don't need to be proven, like statistics (18 million people) or descriptions (a green overcoat). Let's say, for example, you read a sentence in a magazine that says, "After Coach Susan Richmond signed on, the team's batting average improved by 50%." This sentence gives you the fact that the team's average improved by 50%. It

might support a main idea, such as "Coach Susan Richmond is an excellent coach." Notice, though, that this main idea is something that could be disputed; it is an opinion. The writer believes that Coach Richmond is wonderful, and because this is the writer's *opinion* (and maybe not everyone shares it), he or she needs to *back it up* with facts and details. For example, the writer might point to previous teams handled by Coach Richmond, which had superb batting averages, or the writer might gather testimonials from members of the current team.

An **inference**, on the other hand, is a *conclusion that can be drawn based on fact or evidence.* For example, you can infer that the previous coach was not nearly as good based on the fact that the team's batting average improved by 50% after Coach Richmond took over. There may, of course, have been other reasons, but we can infer only one from this sentence.

As you might expect, **vocabulary** questions ask you to determine the meaning of particular words. Often, if you've read carefully, you can determine the meaning of such words from their context—that is, how the word is used in the sentence or paragraph.

Practice Passage 1: Using the Four Question Types

The following is a sample test passage, followed by four questions. Read the passage carefully, and then answer the questions, based on your reading of the text, by circling your choice. Then refer to the previous list and note under your answer which type of question has been asked. Correct answers appear immediately after the questions.

Bicycles

Today, bicycles are elegantly simple machines that are common around the world. Many people ride bicycles for fun, and many others use them as a means of transportation. But two hundred years ago, bicycles didn't even exist. The first bicycle, called a *draisienne*, was invented in Germany in 1818 by Baron Karl de Drais de Sauerbrun. It was made of wood and wasn't very durable, and it didn't even have pedals. Riders moved it by pushing their feet against the ground.

In 1839, Kirkpatrick Macmillan, a Scottish blacksmith, invented a much better bicycle. Macmillan's machine had tires with iron rims to keep them from getting worn down. He also used foot-operated cranks similar to pedals so his bicycle could be ridden at a quick pace. It didn't look much like a modern bicycle, though, because its back wheel was substantially larger than its front wheel. Macmillan's bicycles could be ridden easily, but they were never produced in large numbers.

In 1861, Frenchman Pierre Michaux and his brother Ernest invented a bicycle with an improved crank mechanism. They called their bicycle a *vélocipède*, but most people called it a "bone shaker" because of the jarring effect of the wood and iron frame. Despite the unflattering nickname, the *vélocipède* was a hit. After a few years, the Michaux family was making hundreds of the machines annually, mostly for fun-seeking young people.

Ten years later, James Starley, an English inventor, made several innovations that revolutionized bicycle design. He made the front wheel many times larger than the back wheel, put a gear on the pedals to make the bicycle more efficient, and lightened the wheels by using wire spokes. This bicycle was much lighter and less tiring to ride, yet it was still clumsy, extremely top-heavy, and ridden mostly for entertainment.

It wasn't until 1874 that the first truly modern bicycle appeared on the scene, invented by another Englishman, H.J. Lawson. The *safety bicycle* would look familiar to today's cyclists—it had equal-sized wheels, which made it much less prone to toppling over. Lawson also

attached a chain to the pedals to drive the rear wheel. By 1893, the safety bicycle had been further improved with air-filled rubber tires, a diamond-shaped frame, and easy braking. With the improvements provided by Lawson, bicycles became extremely popular and useful for transportation. Today, they are built, used, and enjoyed all over the world.

1. The first person to use a gear system on bicycles was
   a. H.J. Lawson.
   b. Kirkpatrick Macmillan.
   c. Pierre Michaux.
   d. James Starley.

2. The safety bicycle was less hazardous than Starley's bicycle because it
   a. had pedals.
   b. had an iron frame.
   c. was much more stable.
   d. had wire-spoked wheels.

3. This passage was most likely written in order to
   a. persuade readers to use bicycles for transportation.
   b. describe the problems that bicycle manufacturers encounter.
   c. compare bicycles used for fun with bicycles used for transportation.
   d. tell readers a little about the history of the bicycle.

4. Today, bicycles are <u>elegantly</u> simple machines that are common around the world.
   As it is used in the sentence, the word *elegantly* most nearly means
   a. nicely painted.
   b. well-designed.
   c. long and thin.
   d. oversized and clumsy.

Answers and Explanations for Practice Passage 1

Don't just look at the right answers and move on. The explanations are the most important part, so read them carefully. Use these explanations to help you understand how to tackle each kind of question the next time you come across it.

1. **d.** Question type: **fact or detail**. The fourth paragraph states that James Starley added a gear to the bicycles. Don't be misled by the names of the other inventors, because this may lead you to choose the wrong answer.

2. **c.** Question type: **inference**. According to the fourth and fifth paragraphs, Starley's bicycle was "top-heavy," but the safety bicycle was "less prone to toppling over." Choice **a** is incorrect because Starley's bicycle had pedals. Choice **d** is incorrect because both bicycles had wire-spoked wheels. There is no support for choice **b**.

3. **d.** Question type: **main idea**. The passage gives the history of the bicycle. Choice **a** is incorrect because few opinions are included in the passage. There is no support for choices **b** and **c**.

4. **b.** Question type: **vocabulary**. The paragraph does not address the appearance of modern bicycles—either in color (choice **a**) or shape (choices **c** and **d**). Choice **b** is the only possible choice, based on context.

Detail and Main Idea Questions

Main idea questions and **fact or detail** questions are both asking you for information that's right there in the passage. All you have to do is find it.

Detail or Fact Questions

In **detail or fact** questions, you have to identify a specific item of information from the test. This is usually the simplest kind of question. You just have to be able to separate important information from less important information. However, the choices may often be very similar, so you must be careful not to get confused.

Be sure to read the passage and questions carefully. Here's a tip: By reading the questions first, you'll know what details to look out for, and you'll be able to answer the questions more accurately.

Main Idea Questions

The **main idea** of a passage, like that of a paragraph or a book, is what it is *mostly* about. The main idea is like an umbrella that covers all the ideas and details in the passage, so it is usually something general, not specific. For example, in Practice Passage 1, question 3 asked you why the passage was written, and the correct answer was to tell readers a little about the history of the bicycle. This is the best answer because it's the only one that does not try to persuade, describe, or compare. It is the only one that explains.

Sometimes, the main idea is stated clearly, often in the first or last sentence of the passage. The sentence that expresses the main idea is often referred to as the *topic sentence.*

At other times, the main idea is not stated in a topic sentence but is *implied* in the overall passage, and you'll need to determine the main idea by inference. There may be much information in the passage, so the trick is to understand what all that information adds up to—the gist of what the author wants you to know. Often, some of the wrong answers on main idea questions are specific facts or details from the passage. A good way to test yourself is to ask, "Can this answer serve as a *net* to hold the whole passage together?" If not, chances are you've chosen a fact or detail, not a main idea.

Practice Passage 2: Detail and Main Idea Questions

Practice answering **main idea** and **detail** questions by working on the questions that follow this passage.

Circle the answers to the questions, and then check your answers against the key that appears immediately after the questions.

First Aid

There are three different kinds of burns: first degree, second degree, and third degree. It is important for healthcare workers to be able to recognize each of these types of burns so that they can be sure burn victims are given proper medical treatment. The least serious burn is the first-degree burn, which causes the skin to turn red but does not cause blistering. A mild sunburn is a good example of a first-degree burn, and like a mild sunburn, first-degree burns generally do not require medical treatment other than a gentle cooling of the burned skin with ice or cold tap water. Second-degree burns, on the other hand, do cause blistering of the skin and should be treated immediately. These burns should be immersed in warm water and then wrapped in a sterile dressing or bandage. (Do not apply butter or grease to these burns; despite the old wives' tale, butter does *not* help burns heal and actually increases chances of infection.) If second-degree burns cover a large part of the body, then the victim should be taken to the hospital immediately for medical care. Third-degree burns are those that char the skin and turn it black, or burn so deeply that the skin shows white. These burns usually result from direct contact with flames and have a great chance of becoming infected. All third-degree burns should receive immediate hospital care. They should not be immersed in water, and charred clothing should not be removed from the victim. If possible, a sterile dressing or bandage should be applied to burns before the victim is transported to the hospital.

1. Which of the following would be the best title for this passage?
   a. Dealing with Third-Degree Burns
   b. How to Recognize and Treat Different Burns
   c. Burn Categories
   d. Preventing Infection in Burns

2. Second-degree burns should be treated with
   a. butter.
   b. nothing.
   c. cold water.
   d. warm water.

3. First-degree burns turn the skin
   a. red.
   b. blue.
   c. black.
   d. white.

4. Which of the following best expresses the main idea of the passage?
   a. There are three different types of burns.
   b. Healthcare workers should always have cold compresses on hand.
   c. Different burns require different types of treatment.
   d. Butter is not good for healing burns.

Answers and Explanations for Practice Passage 2

1. b. A question that asks you to choose a title for a passage is a **main idea** question. This main idea is expressed in the second sentence, the topic sentence: "It is important for healthcare workers to be able to recognize each of these types of burns so that they can be sure burn victims are given proper medical treatment." Choice **b** expresses this idea and is the only title that sums up all the ideas expressed in the passage. Choice **a** is too limited; it deals only with one of the kinds of burns discussed in the passage. Likewise, choices **c** and **d** are too limited. Choice **c** covers types of burns but not their treatment, and choice **d** deals only with preventing infection, which is a secondary part of the discussion of treatment.

2. d. The answer to this **fact** question is clearly expressed in the sentence, "These burns should be immersed in warm water and then wrapped in a sterile dressing or bandage." The hard part is keeping track of whether "These burns" refers to the kind of burns in the question, which is second-degree burns. It's easy to choose a wrong answer here because all the answer choices are mentioned in the passage. You need to read carefully to be sure you match the right burn to the right treatment.

3. a. This is another **fact or detail** question. The passage says that a first-degree burn "causes the skin to turn red." Again, it's important to read carefully because all the answer choices are listed elsewhere in the passage (except choice **b**, which can be eliminated immediately).

4. c. Clearly, this is a **main idea** question, and choice **c** is the only answer that encompasses the whole passage. Choices **b** and **d** are limited to particular burns or treatments, and choice **a** discusses only burns and not their treatment. In addition, the second sentence tells us, "It is important for healthcare workers to be able to *recognize each of these types of burns so that they can be sure burn victims are given proper medical treatment.*"

Inference and Vocabulary Questions

Questions that ask you about the meaning of vocabulary words in the passage and those that ask what the passage *suggests* or *implies* (inference questions) are different from detail or main idea questions. In **vocabulary** and **inference** questions, you usually have to pull ideas from the passage, sometimes from more than one place in the passage.

Inference Questions

Inference questions can be the most difficult to answer because they require you to draw meaning from the text when that meaning is implied rather than directly stated. Inferences are conclusions that we draw based on the clues the writer has given us. When you draw inferences, you have to be something of a detective, looking for such clues as *word choice, tone,* and *specific details* that suggest a certain *conclusion, attitude,* or *point of view.* You have to read between the lines in order to make a judgment about what an author is implying in the passage.

A good way to test whether you've drawn a good inference is to ask, "What evidence do I have for this inference?" If you can't find any, you probably have the wrong answer. You need to be sure that your inference is logical and based on something that is suggested or implied in the passage itself—not on what you or others might think. Like a good detective, you need to base your conclusions on evidence—facts, details, and other information—not on random hunches or guesses.

Vocabulary Questions

Questions designed to test vocabulary are really trying to measure how well you can figure out the meaning of an unfamiliar word from its context. *Context* refers to the words and ideas surrounding a vocabulary word. If the context is clear enough, you should be able to substitute a nonsense word for the one being sought and still make the right choice because you could determine meaning strictly from the sense of the sentence. For example, you should be able to determine the meaning of the italicized nonsense word in the following sentence based on its context:

> The principal noted that it gave her great *terivinix* to announce that Kevin was the winner of the nationwide spelling bee.

> In this sentence, *terivinix* most likely means

> **a.** pain.
> **b.** sympathy.
> **c.** pleasure.
> **d.** anxiety.

Clearly, the context of winning a nationwide contest makes choice **c**, *pleasure*, the best choice. Winning contests doesn't usually bring pain, sympathy, or anxiety.

When confronted with an unfamiliar word, try substituting a nonsense word and see whether the context gives you the clue. If you're familiar with prefixes, suffixes, and word roots, you can also use this knowledge to help you figure out the meaning of an unfamiliar word.

You should be careful not to guess at the answer to vocabulary questions based on how you may have seen the word used before or what you *think* it means. Many words have more than one possible meaning,

depending on the context in which they're used, and a word you've seen used one way may mean something else in a test passage. Also, if you don't look at the context carefully, you may make the mistake of confusing the vocabulary word with a similar word. For example, the vocabulary word may be *taut* (meaning *tight*), but if you read too quickly or don't check the context, you might think the word is *taunt* (meaning *tease*). Always make sure that you read carefully and that what you think the word means fits into the context of the passage on which you're being tested.

Practice Passage 3: Inference and Vocabulary Questions

The questions that follow this passage are strictly **vocabulary** and **inference** questions. Circle the answers to the questions, and then check your answers against the key that appears immediately after the questions.

> The ocean's tides are caused in part by the magnetic pull of the moon, and the tides themselves follow a pattern of waxing and waning that is similar to the cycles of the moon. The moon is said to be waxing as it becomes more visible each night, and we see less and less of it each night when it is waning. The tides follow a similar pattern of rise and fall, ebb and flow.

1. According to the passage, magnetic forces from the moon
   a. cause it to wax and wane.
   b. affect the earth's rotation.
   c. never change.
   d. pull and push the ocean's waters.

2. It can be inferred from the passage that the ocean's tides are
   a. always the same.
   b. affected by the moon's cycles.
   c. often unpredictable.
   d. unaffected by external influences.

3. The word *ebb*, as it is used in this passage, means
   a. outgoing tide.
   b. dark color.
   c. egg shaped.
   d. deep water.

Answers and Explanations for Practice Passage 3

1. **d.** This is an **inference** question. According to the passage, the moon's magnetism influences the tides, which is addressed only in choice **d.**

2. **b.** The passage implies that there is a connection between the cycles of the moon and the ocean's tides, so we can infer that the moon's cycles affect the tides.

3. **a.** The passage makes a connection between the words *waning, fall,* and *ebb,* so the context suggests that it refers to the outgoing tide.

Review: Putting It All Together

A good way to solidify what you've learned about reading comprehension questions is for *you* to write the questions. Here's a passage, followed by space for you to write your own questions. Write one question of each of the four types: fact or detail, main idea, inference, and vocabulary.

(The following passage is an advertisement for Mercury Shoes.)

Help your feet take flight! Mercury Shoes promises you high quality and can save you from the aches and pains that runners often suffer.

Running magazine has awarded Mercury Shoes its "High Quality" rating for our breakthrough in shoe technology! By studying the feet of track-and-field champions and ultra-marathoners, we have developed a revolutionary sole construction that offers complete support for dedicated runners. Our <u>unique</u> construction of gel and air cushioning provides greater stability and incredible comfort.

All Mercury Shoes feature our greatly improved Lacing System, which individually molds each shoe, holding the foot firmly in place. Used properly, the Lacing System can dramatically decrease the occurrence and severity of blisters.

Three types of Mercury Shoes are now available:

Cheetahs
- This racing shoe combines light weight with real support.
- Shave minutes off your best time and prevent aching feet.

Mountain Goats
- This superior trail-running shoe has great traction and stability, even on muddy or slick trails.
- Say good-bye to turned ankles and enjoy the scenery when you're wearing Mountain Goats.

Gray Wolves
- This shoe gives maximum support in order to minimize common injuries caused by mile after mile of training runs on hard pavement.
- Feel the comfort and cushioning as you run in Gray Wolves.

1. Detail question: _____
_____

    a.

    b.

    c.

    d.

2. Main idea question: _____
_____

    a.

    b.

    c.

    d.

3. Inference question: _____
_____

    a.

    b.

    c.

    d.

4. Vocabulary question: _____
_____

    a.

    b.

    c.

    d.

IF ENGLISH ISN'T YOUR FIRST LANGUAGE

If you grew up speaking a language other than English, you may be at a disadvantage when taking a standardized test in English. You have not had certain culture-based experiences that your fellow students may have had. You may not know slang words or idioms that mean something other than they say—phrases like "That blows me away," for instance. Here are tips that can help:

- Read as much as possible. Magazines, newspapers, comic books, and the directions on appliances or packages of frozen foods will help you increase your vocabulary.
- When you read, watch TV, or go to the movies, be alert for new words that creep into the language from the popular media, or words that have changed meaning. *Awesome*, for example, used to refer only to something grand, such as a wonderful sunset or a cathedral—now the word can be used to describe running shoes.
- If you have access to a computer, take advantage of the Internet, which is full of interesting and even humorous reading material.
- Look up new words in a standard dictionary, or try browsing through a slang dictionary. The latter will help you increase your vocabulary and is actually fun.
- Hold as many conversations as you can with native English speakers, and don't be afraid to ask the meaning of a word you don't understand. This can be hard, but it really is one of the best ways to learn, and there is no shame in not understanding every word. Remember that most English-speaking people would be just as lost if they suddenly had to speak or understand your native language.

Possible Questions

Here is one question of each type based on the Mercury Shoes advertisement. Your questions may be very different, but these will give you an idea of the kinds of questions that could be asked.

Answers
1. b.
2. b.
3. a.
4. d.

1. **Detail question:** There is enough information in the ad to show that
   a. Mercury Shoes makes many different products.
   b. no other shoes are good for your feet.
   c. Mercury Shoes work best on hard surfaces.
   d. all running shoes should have gel cushioning.

2. **Main idea question:** Which of the following best expresses the main idea of the passage?
   a. Even minor heel blisters will appear.
   b. Mercury Shoes are the best running shoes.
   c. People should comparison shop for running shoes.
   d. Mercury Shoes are available in limited stores.

3. **Inference question:** The passage suggests that wearing Cheetahs allows the runner to
   a. run a faster race.
   b. avoid running injuries.
   c. eliminate heel blisters
   d. run safely when it rains.

4. **Vocabulary question:** In this passage, *unique* most nearly means
   a. always the same.
   b. joining together.
   c. having two sides.
   d. the only one of its kind.

8 ▶ VOCABULARY

LESSON SUMMARY

Vocabulary is tested on the HSPT in the form of synonyms and antonyms (in the Verbal Skills section) and context questions (in the Reading section). The TACHS tests it in synonyms and antonyms, context questions, and sentence completion questions. This lesson provides tips and exercises to help you improve your score in both areas.

A good vocabulary will strengthen your ability to express ideas clearly and precisely. For almost any high school course, you must have a good vocabulary to understand assignments and subject matter. That's why the HSPT includes vocabulary questions.

Kinds of Vocabulary Questions

- **Synonyms and antonyms:** Identify words that mean the *same* or the *opposite* of given words.
- **Context:** Determine the meaning of a word or phrase by noting how it is *used* in a sentence or paragraph.
- **Sentence completion:** Choose the best word to complete a given sentence.

Synonym and Antonym Questions

A word is a *synonym* of another word if it has the *same* or *nearly the same* meaning as the other word. *Antonyms* are words with *opposite* meanings. Test questions often ask you to find the synonym or antonym of a word. If you're lucky, the word will be given in a sentence that helps you guess what the word means. If you're less lucky, you'll just get the word, and then you'll have to figure out what the word means without any help.

Questions that ask for synonyms and antonyms can be tricky because they require you to recognize words that may be unfamiliar—words not only in the questions, but also the answer choices. Usually, the best strategy is to *look* at the structure of the word and to *listen* for its sound. See whether a part of a word looks familiar. Think of other words that have similar key elements. How could those words be related?

Synonym Practice

Try your hand at identifying the word parts and related words in these sample synonym questions. Circle the word that means the *same* or *about the same* as the underlined word. Answers and explanations appear right after the questions.

1. a <u>partial</u> answer
   a. identifiable
   b. incomplete
   c. visible
   d. enhanced

2. <u>substantial</u> advice
   a. inconclusive
   b. weighty
   c. proven
   d. alleged

3. <u>corroborated</u> the statement
   a. confirmed
   b. negated
   c. denied
   d. challenged

4. <u>ambiguous</u> questions
   a. meaningless
   b. difficult
   c. simple
   d. vague

Answers to Synonym Questions

The explanations are just as important as the answers, because they show you how to go about choosing a synonym if you don't know the word.

1. **b.** *Partial* means incomplete. The key part of the word here is *part*. A partial answer is only *part* of the whole.
2. **b.** *Substantial* advice is weighty. The key part of the word here is *substance*. Substance has weight.
3. **a.** *Corroboration* is confirmation. The key part of the word here is the prefix *co-*, which means with or together. Corroboration means that one statement fits *with* another.
4. **d.** *Ambiguous* questions are *vague* or uncertain. The key part of this word is *ambi-*, which means two or both. An ambiguous question can be taken *two* ways.

Antonym Practice

The main danger in answering questions with antonyms is forgetting that you are looking for *opposites* rather than synonyms. Most questions will include one or more synonyms as answer choices. The trick is to keep your mind on the fact that you are looking for the opposite of the word. If you're allowed to mark in the books or on the test papers, circle the word *antonym* or *opposite* in the directions to help you remember.

Otherwise, the same tactics that work for synonym questions work for antonyms: Try to determine the meaning of part of the word or to remember a context where you've seen the word before.

Circle the word that means the *opposite* of the underlined word in the following sentences. Answers are immediately after the questions.

5. <u>zealous</u> pursuit
  a. envious
  b. eager
  c. idle
  d. comical

6. <u>inadvertently</u> left
  a. mistakenly
  b. purposely
  c. cautiously
  d. carefully

7. <u>exorbitant</u> prices
  a. expensive
  b. unexpected
  c. reasonable
  d. outrageous

8. <u>combative</u> workers
  a. angry
  b. cooperative
  c. opposed
  d. comprehensive

9. <u>belligerent</u> attitude
  a. hostile
  b. reasonable
  c. instinctive
  d. ungracious

Answers to Antonym Questions

Be sure to read the explanations as well as the right answers.

5. c. *Zealous* means eager, so *idle* is most nearly opposite. Maybe you've heard the word *zeal* before. One trick in this question is not to be misled by the similar sounds of *zealous* and *jealous*. The other is not to choose the synonym, *eager*.

6. b. *Inadvertently* means by mistake, so *purposely* is the antonym. The key element in this word is the prefix *in-*, which usually means *not, the opposite of*. As usual, one of the answers (choice **a**) is a synonym.

7. c. The key element here is *ex-*, which means out of or away from. *Exorbitant* literally means "out of orbit." The opposite of an *exorbitant* or outrageous price would be a *reasonable* one.

8. b. The opposite of *combative* is *cooperative*. Here, you encounter three words with the same suffix, *-ive*, but they do not all mean the same thing. The root of *combative* is *combat*, so choices **a** and **c** are synonyms.

9. b. The key element in this word is the root *belli-*, which means warlike. The synonym choices, then, are hostile and ungracious; the antonym is *reasonable*.

Context Questions

Context is the surrounding text in which a word is used. Most people use context to help them determine the meaning of an unknown word. A vocabulary question that gives you a sentence around the vocabulary word is usually easier to answer than one with little or no context. The surrounding text can help you as you look for synonyms for the specified words in the sentences.

The best way to take meaning from context is to look for key words in sentences or paragraphs that convey the meaning of the text. If nothing else, the context will give you a means to eliminate wrong answer choices that clearly don't fit. The process of elimination will often leave you with the correct answer.

Context Practice

Try these sample questions. Circle the word that best describes the *meaning* of the underlined word in the sentence. Answers are immediately after the questions.

10. The clerks in the store were <u>appalled</u> by the angry customer's wild and uncontrolled behavior.
  a. horrified
  b. amused
  c. surprised
  d. dismayed

11. Despite the fact that he appeared to have financial resources, the client claimed to be <u>destitute</u>.
  a. wealthy
  b. ambitious
  c. solvent
  d. impoverished

12. Although she was <u>distraught</u> over the disappearance of her child, the woman was calm enough to give the officer her description.
  a. punished
  b. distracted
  c. composed
  d. anguished

13. He had a sense of <u>foreboding</u> as he entered the dark alley.
  a. prohibition
  b. warning
  c. humor
  d. formality

Some tests may ask you to fill in the blank by choosing a word that fits the context. In the following questions, circle the word that best completes the sentence.

14. Professor Washington was a very _____ man known for his reputation as a scholar.
  a. stubborn
  b. erudite
  c. illiterate
  d. disciplined

15. His _____ was demonstrated by his willingness to donate large amounts of money to worthy causes.
  a. honesty
  b. loyalty
  c. selfishness
  d. altruism

Answers to Context Questions

Check to see whether you were able to pick out the key words that help you define the target word, as well as whether you got the right answer.

10. a. The key words *wild* and *uncontrolled* signify *horror* rather than the milder emotions described by the other choices.
11. d. The key words here are *financial resources*, but this is a clue by *contrast*. The phrase *Despite the fact* signals that you should look for the opposite of having financial resources.
12. d. The key words here are *Although* and *disappearance of her child*, signaling that you are looking for an opposite of calm in describing how the mother spoke to the officer. The only word strong enough to match the situation is *anguish*.

13. b. *Foreboding* means a sense of *warning* or anticipation of coming events. The word looks similar to forbidding, and the two are often confused. The prefix *fore-* means *in advance*, but don't be misled by formal, the root word of choice **d.**

14. b. The key words here are *professor* and *scholarly*. Even if you don't know the word *erudite*, the other choices don't fit the description of the professor.

15. d. The key words here are *large amounts of money to worthy causes*. They give you a definition of the word you're looking for. Again, even if you don't know the word *altruism*, the other choices seem inappropriate to describe someone so generous.

Some Tips about Word Parts

Some tests may ask you to find the meaning of a part of a word: *roots,* which are the main part of the word; *prefixes,* which go before the root word; or *suffixes,* which go after. Any of these elements can carry meaning or change the use of a word in a sentence. For instance, the suffix *-s* or *-es* can change the meaning of a noun from singular to plural: *boy, boys.* The prefix *un-* can change the meaning of a root word to its opposite: *necessary, unnecessary.* Even if your test doesn't include word parts—and the HSPT does not—knowing about them will help you answer other kinds of vocabulary questions.

To identify most parts of words, the best strategy is to think of words that carry the same root, suffix, or prefix. Let what you know about those words help you to see the meaning in words that are less familiar.

Word Part Practice

Circle the word or phrase that best describes the meaning of the underlined portion of the word. Answers appear after the questions.

16. <u>pro</u>active
 a. after
 b. forward
 c. toward
 d. behind

17. <u>re</u>cession
 a. against
 b. see
 c. under
 d. back

18. <u>con</u>temporary
 a. with
 b. over
 c. apart
 d. time

FOR NON-NATIVE SPEAKERS OF ENGLISH

Be very careful not to be confused by the sound of words that may mislead you. Be sure to look at the word carefully, and pay attention to the structure and appearance of the word as well as its sound. You may be used to hearing English words spoken with an accent. The sounds of those words may be misleading in choosing a correct answer.

19. etym*ology*
    a. state of
    b. prior to
    c. study of
    d. quality of

20. vandal*ize*
    a. to make happen
    b. to stop
    c. to fill
    d. to continue

Answers to Word Part Questions

Even if the word in the question was unfamiliar, you might have been able to guess the meaning of the prefix or suffix by thinking of some other word that has the same prefix or suffix.

16. b. Think of *propeller:* A propeller sends an airplane *forward.*

17. d. Think of *recall:* Manufacturers *recall* or *bring back* cars that are defective; people *recall* or *bring back* past events in memory.

18. a. Think of *congregation:* A group of people gather *with* one another in a house of worship.

19. c. Think of *biology:* the *study of* life.

20. a. Think of *scandalize:* to *make* something shocking *happen.*

Words That Are Easily Confused

Vocabulary tests of any kind often contain words that are easily confused with each other. A smart test taker will be aware of these easily mixed up words or phrases:

accept: to receive willingly	**except:** exclude or leave out
allusion: an indirect reference	**illusion:** a misconception
alternately: in turn; one after the other	**alternatively:** one or the other
beside: next to	**besides:** also
capital: the city or town that is the seat of government, or an accumulation of wealth	**capitol:** the building in which the legislative assembly meets
cite: to quote as an authority or example, or to recognize formally	**site:** location
complement: to complete	**compliment:** to say something flattering
concurrent: simultaneous or happening at the same time as something else	**consecutive:** successive or following one after the other
connote: to imply or suggest	**denote:** to indicate or refer to specifically
contemptuous: having an attitude of contempt	**contemptible:** worthy of contempt
continuous: without interruption	**continual:** from time to time
council: a group that makes decisions	**counsel:** to give advice
discreet: prudent, circumspect, or modest	**discrete:** separate or individually distinct

disinterested: unbiased or impartial

uninterested: not interested or indifferent

effect: a result

affect: to have an influence on

elicit: to draw out

illicit: unlawful

emigrate: to move from

immigrate: to move to

farther: to or at a more distant point

further: to or at a greater extent or degree, or in addition

few: small in number; used with countable objects

less: small in amount or degree; used with objects of indivisible mass

figuratively: metaphorically or symbolically

literally: actually or according to the exact meaning of the words

flaunt: to show off shamelessly

flout: to show scorn or contempt

foreword: an introductory note or preface

forward: toward the front or to send on

historic: what is important in history

historical: whatever existed in the past, whether it was important or not

ingenious: something clever

ingenuous: guileless or naive

lightening: illuminating, or decreasing in weight

lightning: electrical charges that cause flashes of light during storms

oral: pertaining to the mouth

verbal: pertaining to language

passed: the past tense and past participle of pass

past: time gone by

persecute: to oppress someone

prosecute: to bring a legal action against someone

principal: a person who holds a high position

principle: a rule or standard

stationary: fixed or unmoving

stationery: writing materials

HOW TO ANSWER VOCABULARY QUESTIONS

- **Notice and connect** what you do know to what you may not recognize.
- **Know your word parts.** You can recognize or make a good guess at the meanings of words when you see some suggested meaning in a root word, prefix, or suffix.
- **Note directions very carefully.** Remember when you are looking for opposites rather than synonyms.
- **Use a process of elimination.** Think of how the word makes sense in the sentence.
- **Don't be confused by words that sound like other words,** but may have no relation to the word you need.

A List of Word Parts

Following are some of the word elements seen most often in vocabulary tests. Simply reading them and their examples five to ten minutes a day will give you the quick recognition you need to make a good association with the meaning of an unfamiliar word.

WORD ELEMENT	MEANING	EXAMPLE
ama	love	amateur
ambi	both	ambivalent, ambidextrous
aud	hear	audition
belli	war	belligerent, bellicose
bene	good	benefactor
cid/cis	cut	homicide, scissors
cogn	know	recognize
curr	run	current
flu/flux	flow	fluid, fluctuate
gress	to go	congress, progress
in	not, in	ingenious
ject	throw	inject, reject
luc/lux	light	lucid, translucent
neo	new	neophyte
omni	all	omnivorous, omniscient
pel/puls	push	impulse, propeller
pro	forward	project
pseudo	false	pseudonym
rog	ask	interrogate
spec/spic	look, see	spectator
sub	under	subjugate
super	over	superfluous
temp	time	contemporary, temporal
un	not, opposite	uncoordinated
viv	live	vivid

More Practice in Vocabulary

Here is a second set of practice exercises with samples of vocabulary questions covered in this lesson. Answers to all questions are at the end of the lesson.

Circle the word that means the *same* or *nearly the same* as the underlined word.

21. convivial company
    a. lively
    b. dull
    c. tiresome
    d. dreary

22. divisive behavior
    a. friendly
    b. unpredictable
    c. contradictory
    d. outrageous

23. meticulous record keeping
    a. dishonest
    b. casual
    c. painstaking
    d. careless

24. superficial wounds
    a. life-threatening
    b. bloody
    c. severe
    d. shallow

25. capricious actions
    a. dancing
    b. unpredictable
    c. formal
    d. cowardly

Circle the word that is most nearly opposite in meaning to the underlined word.

26. superseded information
    a. up-to-date
    b. inferior
    c. slow
    d. large

27. lucid opinions
    a. clear
    b. strong
    c. hazy
    d. heartfelt

28. traveling incognito
    a. unrecognized
    b. alone
    c. by night
    d. publicly

29. incisive reporting
    a. mild
    b. sharp
    c. dangerous
    d. insightful

30. reticent response
    a. talkative
    b. angry
    c. unthinking
    d. belligerent

Using the context, choose the word that means the *same* or *nearly the same* as the underlined word.

31. Although he had little time, the student took <u>copious</u> notes in preparation for the test.
  a. limited
  b. plentiful
  c. illegible
  d. careless

32. Although flexible about homework, the teacher was <u>adamant</u> that papers be in on time.
  a. liberal
  b. casual
  c. strict
  d. pliable

33. The <u>intrepid</u> soldier went into battle, even though he was wounded.
  a. brave
  b. injured
  c. lazy
  d. clumsy

Choose the word that best completes the following sentences.

34. Her position as a(n) _____ teacher took her all over the city.
  a. primary
  b. secondary
  c. itinerant
  d. permanent

35. Jane was _____ about which dress to wear, since both looked old-fashioned.
  a. ambivalent
  b. opinionated
  c. tasteful
  d. neutral

Choose the word or phrase closest in meaning to the underlined part of the word.

36. <u>uni</u>verse
  a. one
  b. three
  c. under
  d. opposite

37. incongru<u>ous</u>
  a. condition of being
  b. outdated
  c. direction
  d. set in motion

38. <u>bene</u>fit
  a. bad
  b. suitable
  c. beauty
  d. good

39. educat<u>ion</u>
  a. something like
  b. state of
  c. to increase
  d. unlike

40. urban<u>ite</u>
  a. resident of
  b. relating to
  c. that which is
  d. possessing

Answers to Practice Questions

21. a.
22. c.
23. c.
24. d.
25. b.
26. a.
27. c.
28. d.
29. a.
30. a.
31. b.
32. c.
33. a.
34. c.
35. a.
36. a.
37. a.
38. d.
39. b.
40. a.

LANGUAGE SKILLS

LESSON SUMMARY

This lesson reviews skills that are tested on the exams, including capitalization and punctuation, subject–verb agreement, and verb tenses. It also offers suggestions on choosing the sentence that is most clearly written, identifying topic sentences, and recognizing effective paragraph development.

K nowing how to use written language is vital. It helps you do well on exams and helps you achieve success during your whole high school career. Almost every high school class involves some writing; therefore, all the exams include questions that test your grammar and your ability to tell a well-written sentence or paragraph from a poorly written one.

In this lesson, you'll see examples of the kinds of language questions you'll see on the exams. After that is a review of the language skills you'll need to succeed. Later, this lesson also covers HSPT and TACHS questions that deal with punctuation and capitalization, spelling, and composition.

What COOP Language Arts Questions Are Like

The Language Arts portion of the COOP measures your knowledge of English usage and grammar. There are six different question types. An example of each type follows. The answers follow the questions.

Sample Questions

Choose the word that best completes the sentence.

1. I ate two bowls of chili for lunch _____ I had skipped breakfast.
   a. therefore
   b. because
   c. instead
   d. until

Choose the sentence that is complete and correctly written.

2. a. The computer technician repaired Winona's computer and it worked like brand-new which she told everyone.
   b. After the computer technician repaired it, Winona telling everyone that her computer worked like brand-new.
   c. Her computer worked like brand-new, Winona told everyone. After the computer technician repaired it.
   d. After the computer technician repaired Winona's computer, she told everyone that it worked like brand-new.

Choose the sentence that uses verbs correctly.

3. a. The sun was shining and there isn't a cloud in the sky.
   b. I drink too many grape sodas and felt sick.
   c. The man in front of me was wearing a hat, so I couldn't enjoy the movie.
   d. By the time we got to the state fair, all the blue ribbons have been awarded.

Choose the sentence that best combines the two underlined sentences into one.

4. I was angry about the new rules at the park. I wrote a letter to the mayor.
   a. I wrote a letter, angry about the new rules at the park, to the mayor.
   b. I wrote a letter to the mayor because I was angry about the new rules at the park.
   c. Angered, my letter to the mayor was about the new rules at the park.
   d. Writing a letter to the mayor, the new rules at the park made me angry.

Choose the topic sentence that best fits the paragraph.

5. _____. They may not be comfortable, but comfort is not as important as safety. Seat belts are an important feature in every car.
   a. Wearing seat belts can save your life.
   b. Seat belts and comfort don't mix.
   c. Seat belts were invented in 1952.
   d. Cars with airbags don't need seat belts.

Choose the pair of sentences that best develops the topic sentence.

6. Japanese green tea is considered a gourmet treat by many tea drinkers, but it is much more than that.

  a. Tea lovers think green tea is smooth-tasting. They also find it to be more palatable than other teas.

  b. But green tea is not often a first choice at tea- and coffeehouses. A taste for green tea must be acquired.

  c. Studies show that this relaxing drink may have disease-fighting properties. Green tea inhibits some viruses and may protect people from heart disease.

  d. The Japanese have been consuming this drink for centuries. For those who do not like the taste, green tea can now be purchased in capsule form.

Answers

1. b. The word *because* is the only choice that logically connects the two clauses.

2. d. This is the only choice that is complete and correctly written. Choice **a** has a misplaced modifier. Choices **b** and **c** contain sentence fragments.

3. c. This is the only choice that uses proper parallelism. In other words, the verbs in both clauses are in the same tense—in this case, past tense. Each of the other choices contains an illogical shift in tense. The shift in choice **a** is from past tense to present tense. In choice **b**, it is from present to past. In choice **d**, it is from past to present perfect.

4. b. This answer best establishes the causal relationship between the two sentences. Choices **a** and **c** really say that it was the letter that was angry. Although we know better, the construction is awkward and ungrammatical. Choice **d** really means that the new rules at the park wrote the letter, which makes no sense.

5. a. This paragraph develops the idea that seat belts increase safety. Choice **a** is the only sentence that addresses this idea.

6. c. This is the only choice that follows up on the idea that green tea is *much more than* a gourmet drink—green tea actually fights disease.

What HSPT and TACHS Usage Questions Are Like

HSPT and TACHS usage questions ask you to do the following:

Find the sentence (or the sentence within a paragraph) that has an error in usage. If you find no mistake, mark choice **d** as your answer.

Sample Question

7. a. Will you join me for dinner?
  b. Molly had chose not to attend.
  c. I am wearing my sister's coat.
  d. No mistakes.

Answer

7. b. The correct verb form is *had chosen*.

As you can see, the Language Arts section of the COOP and the Usage section of the HSPT and TACHS present similar challenges. We begin by talking about the similarities. For both kinds of questions, you need to know how to make complete sentences, use verbs correctly, avoid problems with pronouns, and use a lot of basic grammatical skills that you can review in the following sections.

A little later in this lesson, we tackle the additional tasks that you'll face when you come to the punctuation and capitalization, spelling, and composition sections of the HSPT and TACHS.

Complete Sentences

The sentence is the basic unit of written language. Most writing is done using complete sentences, so it's important to distinguish them from fragments. You also need to learn to avoid writing two sentences as if they were one, which is called a *run-on sentence.*

Sentence Fragments

A complete sentence expresses a complete thought, while a fragment needs something more to express a complete thought.

MAKING COMPLETE SENTENCES	
FRAGMENT	COMPLETE SENTENCE
The dog walking down the street.	The dog was walking down the street.
Exploding from the bat for a home run.	The ball exploded from the bat for a home run.

These examples show that a sentence must have a subject and a verb to complete its meaning. The first fragment has a subject, but not a verb. *Walking* looks like a verb, and in some sentences **is** a verb, but as used here, it is actually an adjective describing *dog* (or more specifically, what the dog is doing). The second fragment has neither a subject nor a verb. *Exploding* looks like a verb; however, it is also an adjective describing something not identified in the word group. In English, these are called *progressive forms* of verbs. You need not memorize the term, but when you see a word ending in *-ing,* look to see whether a "helping" verb is with it. *The dog walking* is not a sentence, because there is no helping verb. *The dog is walking* is a sentence, because of the helping verb *is.*

Now look at the following sets of word groups. Can you identify the complete sentences?

8. a. We saw the tornado approaching.
   b. When we saw the tornado approaching.

9. a. Before the house was built in 1972.
   b. The house was built in 1972.

10. a. The mouse stealing the potato chips.
   b. The mouse had been stealing the potato chips.

11. a. We are leaving in the morning.
   b. Because we are leaving in the morning.

If you chose **8. a**, **9. b**, **10. b**, and **11. a**, you were right. Notice that in **8**, **9**, and **11**, the groups of words are the same in choices **a** and **b** in all three examples, but in **10. a**, there is no helping verb. In **8**, **9**, and **11**, the fragments have an extra word at the beginning, a subordinating conjunction.

Let's take another example: If your friend said, "I opened the box," you'd know exactly what she meant. However, if she said, "When I opened the box . . . ," you'd wait for her to complete the sentence. If she didn't, you might become impatient and demand, "When you opened the box, *WHAT?*" Similarly, if she said, "I opened the box after," you'd want to know "*AFTER WHAT?*"

So as you can see, the sentence "I opened the box" is no longer a sentence when *before, after, when,* or *where* is tacked onto the front or at the end of it. Such words are called *subordinating conjunctions.*

Run-On Sentences

If you can tell when a group of words isn't a sentence, then you can tell when one or more sentences have been run together, sometimes with a comma in between. Some tests will ask you to find *run-on sentences*. Each of the following sentences is a run-on sentence. Can you find where to put a period and begin a new sentence?

12. We went to the beach, we had a good time.

13. Melvin obeyed his stepmom's rule he kept his room clean.

14. Emily wanted to stay home with her new hamster, her mom said she had to go to school.

A new sentence begins after *beach* in the first sentence, after *rule* in the second, and after *hamster* in the third.

Certain questions on the COOP and HSPT will test your ability to distinguish a sentence from a fragment or a run-on. Approach these questions by taking the following steps:

- Check to see that the group of words has both a subject and a verb.
- Make sure that what looks like a verb isn't actually an adjective (or adjectival phrase) describing the noun that precedes it.
- Check to see whether a subordinating conjunction precedes the group of words.

Now let's look more closely at the individual parts of a sentence. Knowing as much as you can about the separate parts can make your identification of the whole much easier.

Verbs

Subject–Verb Agreement

In written language, a subject must agree with its verb *in number*. In other words, if a subject is singular, the verb must be singular. If the subject is plural, the verb must be plural. If you are unsure whether a verb is singular or plural, you can test it in a very simple way. Fill in the blanks in the following two sentences with the correct form of a verb—any verb. The verb form that best completes the first sentence is singular. The verb form that best completes the second sentence is plural.

One person _____. [singular]
Two people _____. [plural]

Now fill in the blanks, using the verbs *speak* and *do*.

One person *speaks*. One person *does*.
Two people *speak*. Two people *do*.

Verb Tense

The tense of a verb tells a reader when the action occurs. Present tense verbs tell the reader to imagine that action is happening as it is being read, while past tense verbs tell the reader the action has already happened. Read the following two paragraphs. The first one is written in the present tense, the second in the past tense. Notice the difference in the verbs. They are boldface to make them easier to locate.

As Horace **opens** the door, he **glances** around cautiously. He **sees** signs of danger everywhere. The centerpiece and placemats from the dining room table **are scattered** on the floor next to the table. An end table in the living room **is lying** on its side. He **sees** the curtains flapping and **notices** glass on the carpet in front of the window.

As Horace **opened** the door, he **glanced** around cautiously. He **saw** signs of danger everywhere. The centerpiece and placemats from the dining room table **were scattered** on the floor next to the table. An end table in the living room **was lying** on its side. He **saw** the curtains flapping and **noticed** glass on the carpet in front of the window.

It's easy to distinguish present tense from past tense by simply fitting the verb into a sentence. The important thing to remember about verb tense is to keep it consistent. If a passage begins in the present tense, keep it in the present tense unless there is a specific reason to change—to indicate that some action occurred in the past, for instance. If a passage begins in the past tense, it should remain in the past tense. Verb tense should never be mixed as it is in the following sentence.

Wrong: Terry **opens** the door and **saw** the crowd.
Correct: Terry **opens** the door and **sees** the crowd. Terry **opened** the door and **saw** the crowd.

However, sometimes it is necessary to use a different verb tense in order to clarify when an action occurred. Read the following sentence and the explanation following it.

The game warden **sees** the fish that you **caught**. [The verb **sees** is in the present tense, indicating that the action is occurring in the present. However, the verb **caught** is in the past tense, indicating that the fish was caught earlier.]

Clear Sentences

On your exam, you may be asked to read two or more written versions of the same information and to choose the one that most clearly presents accurate information. It may be that all the choices are more or less grammatically correct, but some of them are so poorly written that they're hard to understand. You want the best option, the one that's clearest and most accurate. Check for accuracy first. If the facts are wrong, the answer is wrong, no matter how well written the answer choice is. If the facts are accurately represented in several of the answer choices, then you must evaluate the writing itself. Here are three tips for choosing the best answer.

1. The **best** answer will be written in plain English in such a way that most readers can understand it the first time through. If you read through an answer choice and need to reread it to understand what it says, look for a better option.
2. The **best** option will present the information in logical order, usually chronological order. If the order seems questionable or is hard to follow, look for a better option.
3. The **best** option will be written with active voice rather than passive voice. Answer choices written with passive voice sound formal and stuffy. Look for an option that sounds like normal conversation. Here's an example.

Passive Voice
At 8:25 P.M., Robert was walking down Main Street where a movie was being filmed. MGM was the producer.

Active Voice
At 8:25 P.M., Robert turned the corner on Main Street and found MGM filming a movie.

The first version uses the passive phrases "was walking" and "was being filmed" rather than active verbs. The second version uses the active verbs "turned" and "found."

As you take the portion of the test that assesses your writing skills, apply what you know about the rules of grammar:

- Look for complete sentences.
- Check for endmarks, commas, and apostrophes.
- Look for subject-verb agreement and consistency in verb tense.

HSPT and TACHS Punctuation and Capitalization

All the HSPT and TACHS punctuation and capitalization questions ask you to do the same thing—to recognize when there are punctuation and capitalization mistakes in a sentence and (just as important) to recognize when there are no errors. Read the following question for an example:

Sample Question

For question 15, find the sentence that has a mistake in capitalization, punctuation, or usage. If you find no mistakes, mark choice **d**.

15. **a.** Doug's least favorite subject is gym.
    b. In april, I had a bike accident.
    c. We told Alice to go home and wash her face.
    d. No mistakes.

Answer

15. **b.** Choice **b** contains a capitalization error. The word *April* should be capitalized.

Let's look more closely at English capitalization and punctuation.

Capitalization

You may encounter questions that test your ability to capitalize correctly. Here is a quick review of the most common capitalization rules. (See also the following table.)

- Capitalize the first word of a sentence. If the first word is a number, write it as a word.
- Capitalize the pronoun *I*.
- Capitalize the first word of a quotation: I said, "What's the name of your dog?" Do not capitalize the first word of a partial quotation: He called me "the best friend" he ever had.
- Capitalize proper nouns and proper adjectives.

Punctuation
Periods

Here is a quick review of the rules regarding the use of a period.

- Use a period at the end of a sentence that is not a question or an exclamation.
- Use a period after an initial in a name: Millard K. Furham.
- Use a period after an abbreviation, unless the abbreviation is an acronym.
  - Abbreviations: Mr., Ms., Dr., A.M., General Motors Corp., Allied Inc.
  - Acronyms: NASA, AIDS
- If a sentence ends with an abbreviation, use only one period: *We brought food, tents, sleeping bags, etc.*

CAPITALIZATION	
CATEGORY	EXAMPLE (PROPER NOUNS)
days of the week, months of the year	Friday, Saturday; January, February
holidays, special events	Christmas, Halloween; Two Rivers Festival, Dilly Days
names of individuals	John Henry, George Billeck
names of structures, buildings	Lincoln Memorial, Principal Building
names of trains, ships, aircraft	Queen Elizabeth, Chicago El
product names	Corn King hams, Dodge Intrepid
cities and states	Des Moines, Iowa; Juneau, Alaska
streets, highways, roads	Grand Avenue, Interstate 29, Deadwood Road
landmarks, public areas	Continental Divide, Grand Canyon, Glacier National Park
bodies of water	Atlantic Ocean, Mississippi River
ethnic groups, languages, nationalities	Asian American, English, Arab
official titles	Mayor Daley, President Johnson
institutions, organizations, businesses	Dartmouth College, Lions Club, Chrysler Corporation
proper adjectives	English muffin, Polish sausage

Commas

Using commas correctly can make the difference between presenting information clearly and distorting the facts. The following chart demonstrates the necessity of commas in written language. See how commas make a difference in the following sentences.

Here is a quick review of the most basic rules regarding the use of commas.

- Use a comma before *and, but, or, for, nor,* and *yet* when they separate two groups of words that could be complete sentences.
  Example: The coaches laid out the game plan, and the team executed it to perfection.
- Use a comma to separate items in a series.
  Example: The student driver stopped, looked, and listened when she got to the railroad tracks.
- Use a comma to separate two or more adjectives modifying the same noun.
  Example: The hot, black, rich coffee tasted great after an hour in below-zero weather. [Notice that there is no comma between *rich* (an adjective) and *coffee* (the noun *rich* describes).]
- Use a comma after introductory words, phrases, or clauses in a sentence.
  Examples: Usually, the class begins with a short writing assignment. [Word]
  Racing down the street, the yellow car ran a stoplight. [Phrase]
  After we found the source of the noise, we relaxed and enjoyed the rest of the evening. [Clause]
- Use a comma after a name followed by Jr., Sr., or some other abbreviation.
  Example: The class was inspired by the speeches of Martin Luther King, Jr.

- Use a comma to separate items in an address.
  Example: The car stopped at 1433 West G Avenue, Orlando, Florida 36890.
- Use a comma to separate a day and a year, as well as after the year.
  Example: I was born on July 21, 1954, during a thunderstorm.
- Use a comma after the greeting of a friendly letter and after the closing of any letter.
  Examples: Dear Uncle Jon, Sincerely yours,
- Use a comma to separate contrasting elements in a sentence.
  Example: Your essay needs strong arguments, not strong opinions, to convince me.
- Use commas to set off appositives (words or phrases that explain or identify a noun).
  Example: My cat, a Siamese, is named Ron.

COMMAS AND MEANING	
Number undetermined	My sister Diane John Carey Melissa and I went to the fair.
Four people	My sister Diane, John Carey, Melissa, and I went to the fair.
Five people	My sister, Diane, John Carey, Melissa, and I went to the fair.
Six people	My sister, Diane, John, Carey, Melissa, and I went to the fair.

Apostrophes

Apostrophes communicate important information in written language. Here is a quick review of the two most important rules regarding the use of apostrophes.

- Use an apostrophe to show that letters have been omitted from a word to form a contraction.
- Use an apostrophe to show possession.

APOSTROPHES TO SHOW POSSESSION		
SINGULAR NOUNS (ADD 'S)	PLURAL NOUNS ENDING IN S (ADD ')	PLURAL NOUNS NOT ENDING IN S (ADD 'S)
boy's	boys'	men's
child's	kids'	children's
lady's	ladies'	women's

HSPT Spelling

The HSPT spelling section is in a multiple-choice format. You will be given three sentences labeled **a**, **b**, and **c**. One (and only one) of these sentences *may* contain a misspelled word. A fourth choice, **d**, reads, "No mistakes." For this part of the test, you must be able to see very fine differences between word spellings. The best way to prepare for a spelling test is to have a good grasp of the fundamental spelling rules—and to be able to recognize when those rules don't apply.

The HSPT test is mainly looking to ensure three things:

1. that you know and can apply the basic rules of spelling
2. that you remember that English spelling is full of exceptions to the rules
3. that you have developed a good eye for spotting spelling errors

Here are some of the basic rules to review:

- *i* before *e*, except after *c* or when *ei* sounds like *a*
  Examples: piece, receive, neighbor
- *gh* can replace *f* or be silent.
  Examples: *enough, night*
- Double the consonant when you add an ending.
  Examples: forget/forgettable, shop/shopping
- Drop the *e* when you add *-ing*.
  Example: hope/hoping
- The spelling of prefixes and suffixes generally doesn't change.
  Examples: project, propel, proactive

Sample Question

Here is an example of how spelling questions will appear on the HSPT, in Part 5, Language Skills.

For question 16, look for mistakes in spelling only.

16. **a.** Most animals wear fur coats.
  b. The radiator is very hot.
  c. My nieghbor bought a new car.
  d. No mistakes.

Answer

16. **c.** The word *nieghbor* is misspelled.

How to Answer Spelling Questions

Keep in mind the basics that you probably learned a long time ago—that is, the English alphabet is made up of:

Vowels: *a, e, i, o, u,* and sometimes *y*
Consonants: all the other letters

Now here are some tips on how to approach the spelling questions on the HSPT.

Sound Out the Word in Your Mind

Remember that long vowels inside words usually are followed by single consonants; for example:

- *sofa* (*o* followed by a single *f*)
- *total* (*o* followed by a single *t*)

Short vowels inside words usually are followed by double consonants; for example:

- *dribble* (*i* followed by *bb*)
- *scissors* (*i* followed by *ss*)

Sounding out the words will help you "hear" whether you're dealing with a long or short vowel.

Give Yourself Auditory (Listening) Clues

As you're learning how to spell words, repeat the word in your mind, but say it the way it's spelled. For example, say *Wed-nes-day* instead of *Wensdy* or *lis-ten* instead of *lissen* or *bus-i-ness* instead of *biznus*. That way, you'll remember to add letters you do not hear in ordinary conversation.

Look at Each Part of a Word

See if there is a root, prefix, or suffix that will always be spelled the same way. For example, in *uninhabitable*, there is the prefix *un-*, the prefix *in-*, and the suffix *-able*, leaving the root word *habit*, which is easy to spell. Examples of words that are changed in meaning by the addition of prefixes and suffixes are shown in the following tables.

PREFIX	ROOT	WORD
dis	agree	disagree
un	usual	unusual
mis	used	misused
re	emphasize	reemphasize

ROOT	SUFFIX	WORD
mark	er	marker
start	ing	starting
play	ful	playful
agree	able	agreeable

Use a Spelling List

Ask a parent or teacher for a spelling list, or make up one of your own, then do the following:

- **Cross out** or discard any words you already know for certain.
- **Divide** the remaining list into groups of three to five words, and **concentrate** on those until you know them, then move on. Another good approach is to **make flash cards** of words you don't know.
- **Highlight** or circle the tricky elements in each word. For example, if you are learning to spell the word *psychology*, circle the *p*, because the word is pronounced *sychology* even though it is spelled *psychology*.
- **Say** the words aloud as you read them. Remember to pronounce them as they're spelled, not as they're spoken in everyday language: *deb-t*, rather than *det*, *p-sychology* rather than *sycology*, and so on. (Of course, you will not want to forget how the words are really pronounced, once you learn how to spell them!)
- **Spell** each word out in your mind so you can "hear" the spelling.

HSPT Composition

Besides asking you to recognize errors in punctuation, capitalization, usage, and spelling, the Language Skills section of the HSPT will ask you to recognize effective composition of sentences and paragraphs, and to spot poor composition.

Paragraph Development

Here is a well-developed, logical, coherent paragraph:

(1) Many myths about bats need to be dispelled if we are to come to appreciate these fascinating creatures. For example, bats are not "flying mice," as they have sometimes been described. In fact, they are not rodents at all. It is true that they look a little like winged mice, but this is only surface appearance. Actually, according to biologists, bats are more closely related to primates (meaning humans like you and me) than they are to the rodents. The anatomy of their arms and hand bones is very like our own, and they have canine teeth instead of the huge incisors of rodents. Another myth sometimes repeated by people who do not understand bats is that, because they are blind, they are apt to run into people and become entangled in their hair. Actually, bats are NOT blind, and they have a highly developed radar system that enables them to detect, with precision, objects of interest to them—such as a small insect they might have for dinner or a large obstacle they very much want to avoid, such as a tree, a telephone pole, or a person.

Now suppose the paragraph were written like this:

(2) In fact, they are not rodents at all. The anatomy of their arms and hand bones is very like our own, and they have canine teeth instead of the huge incisors of rodents. It is true that they look a little like winged mice, but this

is all surface appearance. You can learn many interesting facts from an encyclopedia. Another myth repeated by people who do not understand bats is that, because they are blind, they are apt to run into people and become entangled in their hair. Actually, according to biologists, bats are more closely related to primates (that includes humans, you and me) than they are to the rodents. Many myths about bats should be dispelled. For example, bats are not "flying mice," as they have sometimes been described. Actually, bats are NOT blind, and they have a highly developed radar system that enables them to detect, with precision, objects of interest to them—such as a small insect they might like to have for dinner or a large obstacle they very much want to avoid, such as a tree, a telephone pole, or a person.

With the exception of the inclusion of one irrelevant sentence (*You can learn many interesting facts from an encyclopedia*), the second paragraph is exactly like the first—except that its sentences have been scrambled, so that it is now annoyingly difficult to read.

Suppose, besides being incoherent, the paragraph were made up of individual sentences that were mangled. Take a look at this:

(3) The anatomy is similar to ours, with arms and hand bones and, unlike rodents that have huge incisors, canine teeth. In surface appearance, you could say they are like winged mice and that is true. Many interesting facts can be learned from an encyclopedia. Not rodents at all, biologists say bats closely relate to humans, as primates, than they relate to rodents. Bats as "flying mice" is one of the myths about bats that should be dispelled, as they are sometimes described . . .

We'll stop there. It's doubtful you'd ever find such a paragraph in a book on bats or on anything else, but if you did, you'd probably put the book back on the shelf without finishing even one paragraph.

Characteristics of Good Paragraphs

An effective paragraph has the following characteristics:

- A clear, controlling idea—usually expressed in the topic sentence. In the first paragraph on page 187, the topic sentence is easy to spot: *Many myths about bats need to be dispelled if we are to come to appreciate these fascinating creatures.* This sentence controls the paragraph.
- A pattern of organization that clearly relates to (and usually supports) that idea. The paragraph about bats is organized with a topic sentence first, dealing with myths about bats, followed by examples of mistaken myths that tend to "prove" the main idea. There are other types of paragraph organization—the main thing to look for in all is clarity.
- Sentences that are correctly written and coherent. To see the difference between clearly written and poorly constructed sentences, compare the preceding first and third paragraphs.

What the HSPT Composition Questions Look Like

Here are the directions for the questions we've been discussing. (For examples of the questions themselves, see Lessons 4 and 13, HSPT Practice Tests 1 and 2, Part 5 of each.)

For questions 1 through 7, follow the directions.

These directions will be followed by seven basic question types. Here are some examples:

1. Choose the word that best joins the thoughts together.
2. Which of these expresses the idea most clearly?
3. Choose the group of words that best completes this sentence.

4. Which of these best fits under the topic, "The Insect Is Our Friend?"

5. Which sentence does NOT belong in the paragraph?

6. Where should the sentence, *Why is it that we think ladybugs are cute, whereas we detest cockroaches?* be placed in the following paragraph?

7. Which of the following topics would be best for a one-page essay?

Summary

In order to have success on the Language portion of these exams, you will need the skill to recognize:

- what makes an effective, coherent, and mechanically correct sentence
- what makes a logically developed paragraph

As you probably already know, the best way to acquire skill—whether in English or in basketball—is not just to read about it, but to **practice**. So be sure to do all the practice exams in this book. You'll be amazed at how rapidly your skills—and your self-confidence—will grow!

10 ▶ VERBAL REASONING

LESSON SUMMARY

This lesson gives hints on how to deal with questions you will encounter on the Verbal Reasoning section of the COOP and on the Verbal Analogies, Logic, and Verbal Classification sections of the HSPT. These parts of the two exams test your general ability to reason about the relationships between words. These skills will also help you on the Reading and Language sections of the TACHS.

Besides having a good vocabulary, you will need the ability to see relationships between words and between ideas to achieve success in high school. This is the ability that is tested on the Verbal Reasoning section of the COOP and on the Verbal Skills portion of the HSPT. There is some overlap between these sections of the two tests; however, for simplicity, we'll discuss them separately here.

COOP: Verbal Reasoning—Words and Context

The COOP contains several question types that test your ability to reason with words. Following are the directions for each kind of question, accompanied by examples and tips on how to approach the questions.

Necessary Part Questions

Directions for the first type of question on the Verbal Reasoning—Words portion of the COOP will read as follows:

Find the word that names a necessary part of the underlined word.

A good way to approach this kind of question is by saying the following sentence to yourself: "A _____ could not exist without _____." Take a look at this example.

1. <u>tree</u>
   a. fruit
   b. forest
   c. roots
   d. shade

Now look at what happens when you put each of the answer choices into a sentence:

   a. *A tree could not exist without fruit.* As you know, many trees do not have fruit hanging from them, so you can move on to the next answer choice.
   b. *A tree could not exist without a forest.* This is wrong, too, of course. What about that lone elm in your best friend's backyard?
   c. *A tree could not exist without roots.* True, right? All trees are nourished through their roots. Without roots, they would die.
   d. *A tree could not exist without shade.* Another wrong choice, because at night, there's no shade, but the tree's still there.

So, the answer is choice **c**.

1. c. The essential part of a tree is its roots. Choices **a** and **d** are incorrect because they are by-products of trees. Choice **b** is wrong because being in a forest is not essential to the growth of a tree.

The Underlined Words

Directions for the second type of question on the Verbal Reasoning—Words portion of the COOP will read as follows:

Find the word that is most like the underlined word.

2. <u>clean</u>　　　<u>spotless</u>　　　<u>neat</u>
   a. efficient
   b. careful
   c. tidy
   d. hazardous

First, you need to think about what the three words have in common. In the previous example, all three are adjectives with the same meaning—<u>clean</u>. Now, consider the choices. Is *efficient* clean? No, it is not (*efficient* means competent). Does *careful* mean clean? No (*careful* means alert, cautious). Is *tidy* clean? Yes, it is. But always be sure to check all the other choices to make sure you picked the best one. Does *hazardous* mean clean? No, it does not. (*Hazardous* means dangerous.)

The Word That Does Not Belong

Directions for this third type of question on the Verbal Reasoning—Words portion of the COOP will read as follows:

3. Which word does NOT belong with the others?
   a. flute
   b. violin
   c. saxophone
   d. trumpet

The only way to approach this type of question is by trying to figure out what all the words have in common and choosing the one that does not belong in that category. In this particular instance, a flute, a saxophone, and a trumpet all happen to be wind instruments, while a violin is a stringed instrument.

Let's look at another example:

4. Which word does NOT belong with the others?
   a. noun
   b. preposition
   c. punctuation
   d. adverb

Again, let's figure out what all the words have in common. A noun, a preposition, and an adverb are all classes of words that make up a sentence. Punctuation belongs in a sentence, but punctuation is not a class of a word.

Word Relationship Questions

Now let's look at the fourth type of question on the Verbal Reasoning—Words portion of the COOP. The directions for this type will read:

In question 5, the words in the top row are related in some way. The words in the bottom row are related in the same way. Find the word that completes the bottom row of words.

5. shirt   coat   clothing
   _____
   ring   bracelet   _____
   a. necklace
   b. jewelry
   c. earring
   d. silver

The next step is a bit more complicated. Your approach will depend on what the first three words are; however, for all questions of this type, there are three main steps to take. For example:

1. Form mental pictures based on the first three words (shirt, coat, clothing).
2. Make up a sentence using the first three words.
3. Insert the second two words (ring, bracelet) and each of the answer choices (a, b, c, d) into that sentence.

It's easy to picture a particular *shirt* and a particular *coat*, but to picture *clothing* is harder, because the word is less specific; it's not an object but a category that can include a shirt, or a coat, or shoes, or trousers, and so on. By now, you have noticed that a *shirt* and a *coat* both belong to the category *clothing*.

Now you're ready to form sentences, beginning with the first three words: *A shirt and a coat are both clothing.* Now look at the second line and the answer choices and make up a similar sentence:

a. *A ring and a bracelet are both necklaces.* "No," you'll say to yourself. "That's silly." And you'll move on.
b. *A ring and a bracelet are both jewelry.* Aha! This seems right. But check the other choices just to make sure there isn't something better.
c. *A ring and a bracelet are both earrings.* Nope. Silly again.
d. *A ring and a bracelet are both silver.* Well, they might be, but not necessarily. Choice **b** is still the best answer.

Since there are several possible variations on this type of question, let's try another example.

6. honeybee   angel   bat
   _____
   kangaroo   rabbit   _____
   a. mermaid
   b. possum
   c. grasshopper
   d. sprinter

First, form your mental picture. The one that springs immediately to mind might be of a *honeybee* sitting on a flower and an *angel* sitting on a cloud. But when you come to picturing a *bat*, you're stopped in your tracks and have to go back. Now you see a honeybee buzzing around a flower, an angel flying through clouds. Aha! That's it. In your mind's eye, a bat comes swooping out of a cave.

They all can fly. So your sentence will be: *A honey-bee, an angel, and a bat can all fly.*

Now move on to *kangaroo* and *rabbit*. Chances are you'll immediately see the rabbit and the kangaroo hopping. Examine the answer choices now. When you picture a *mermaid*, a *possum*, or a *sprinter*, you'll probably see no similarity; however, a *grasshopper* (choice **c**) definitely hops. A *honeybee*, an *angel*, and a *bat* are all capable of flight. A *kangaroo*, a *rabbit*, and a *grasshopper* are all capable of hopping.

Must-Be-True Questions

Now we'll look at the fifth type of question you'll find on the Verbal Reasoning—Context portion of the COOP. Here are the directions and a sample question:

Find the statement that must be true according to the given information.

7. Jenna lives in a large city on the East Coast. Her younger cousin Marlee lives in the Midwest, in a small town with fewer than 1,000 residents. Marlee has visited Jenna several times during the past five years. In the same period of time, Jenna has visited Marlee only once.
    a. Marlee likes Jenna better than Jenna likes Marlee.
    b. Jenna thinks small towns are boring.
    c. Jenna is older than Marlee.
    d. Marlee wants to move to the East Coast.

In approaching this type of question, the important thing is to avoid any answer choice that is not written *explicitly* (that is, plainly) in the short informational passage. These questions do not test your ability to make inferences or draw conclusions, *only* to look at what is on the page. You have to find the statement that **must be true**. The best way to approach this problem is to read the answer choices in turn, going back each time to look for that exact information in the short passage. For example:

a. *Marlee likes Jenna better than Jenna likes Marlee.* Now look at the informational passage. There is nothing in it about who likes whom. So move on.
b. *Jenna thinks small towns are boring.* Look again at the passage. There is nothing in it about how either girl feels about small towns.
c. *Jenna is older than Marlee.* Aha! Reading carefully, you'll see that Marlee is Jenna's *younger* cousin.
d. *Marlee wants to move to the East Coast.* According to the passage, Marlee was *visiting*, and there was never a statement about her wanting to move.

Since there is only one right answer, you can stop right here. The answer is choice **c**.

HSPT and TACHS: Verbal Skills

There are five types of questions on the verbal skills portions of the HSPT and TACHS exams:

1. verbal analogies
2. synonyms
3. logic
4. verbal classification
5. antonyms

Synonyms and antonyms are covered in Lesson 8 of this book. In this lesson, we will look at the rest of the list: verbal analogies, logic, and verbal classification.

Verbal Analogies

In an *analogy,* two sets of words are related to each other in a specific similar way. The verbal analogy portion of the HSPT tests your ability to see these word relationships. You will be given a set of two words that are related, followed by a third word and four answer choices. Of the four choices, you must identify the one that would best complete the second set so that it expresses the same relationship as in the first set. Each question is constructed the same way.

8. Aspirin is to headache as bandage is to
   a. injection.
   b. sprain.
   c. wound.
   d. welt.

The correct answer is choice **c**, *wound*. This is a "use or function" analogy: In both sets of words—aspirin and headache, bandage and wound—something is **used for** something else. *Aspirin* is used to treat a *headache*; a *bandage* is used to treat a *wound*. All the other choices in this question are loosely associated with injury or illness, but the *best* answer is choice **c**.

Analogies can be difficult, but you can conquer them with the following steps.

Look at the Literal Meaning of the Words

The first challenge is to know what all the words mean in the analogy question. For this, there is no substitute for *reading*. Between now and the time of the actual test, you should read everything you can get your hands on, from textbooks to comic books, from directions on products you find around the house to newspapers and magazines. If you come upon a word you don't know, look it up. In addition, use the skills you acquired in Lesson 8, in the part called "How to Prepare for Synonym and Antonym Questions." Pay particular attention to word parts when you encounter an unfamiliar word.

Look at the Exact Relationship between the Words

After figuring out the meaning of each word in the analogy, you must master the art of seeing the relationship between the words. In the practice section that follows, each answer explanation tells what type of analogy is involved—that is, what kind of relationship the question represents. Be sure to read these answer explanations so you will be familiar with the various types of relationships that are possible.

Make Up a Sentence

A good way to figure out the relationship in a given question is to make up a sentence. You must first read each question carefully, as it is easy to mistake one kind of analogy for another and make the wrong answer choice. Formulating a sentence that expresses the relationship is the best way to avoid this mistake. Take question 8 as an example. The following are sentences you might make up when approaching the analogy.

- *Aspirin* is used to treat a *headache*. A *bandage* is used to treat an *injection*? Nope. As soon as you say the sentence, you know that choice **a** is wrong. So you must try again.
- . . . A *bandage* is used to treat a *sprain*. Again, no. You might use one of those wrap bandages, but not a regular bandage.
- . . . A *bandage* is used to treat a *wound*. Yes, of course. Your sentence tells you this is the right choice. But wait! Take the time to look at the last choice, just to make sure it's not better.
- . . . A *bandage* is used to treat a *welt*. If you're not sure exactly what a *welt* is, you're out of luck. But if you know, from your wide reading, that a welt is a bump such as a bee sting might leave, then you'll know that the word *wound* is better—an injury in which the skin is torn or broken.

Remember That a Word May Have Several Meanings

Words often have more than one meaning or varying shades of meaning. For example, you might encounter an analogy that includes the word *shoulder,* which can be a part of the body or the side of a road. Making up a sentence will help you avoid confusion.

Watch Your Time

The analogy questions in the Verbal Skills section of the HSPT are generally considered the hardest (with logic questions a close second), so don't dawdle on simple synonym and antonym questions. In fact, when you're doing the practice tests in this book, try skimming through and doing the analogy questions first. See whether that approach works for you, and if it does, use it when you take the actual test.

Practice, Practice, Practice

The very best way to hone your skills for the verbal analogy portion of the HSPT is to practice. Some sample analogy questions follow, and after the questions are a set of answers, each including a short explanation of the answer and the type of analogy involved. There are many types of analogies, and they're not all included here, but the mention of some of the various categories should help. The practice you do on the sample tests in this book will also sharpen your skills.

Practice Analogy Questions

9. Groom is to wedding as lawyer is to
   a. crime.
   b. accident.
   c. trial.
   d. client.

10. Hat is to clothing as apple is to
    a. pie.
    b. pear.
    c. fruit.
    d. core.

11. Hurricane is to thunderstorm as rage is to
    a. anger.
    b. murder.
    c. calmness.
    d. madness.

12. Weeping is to grief as tantrum is to
    a. fit.
    b. kicking.
    c. loudness.
    d. rage.

13. Love is to hate as optimism is to
    a. depression.
    b. meanness.
    c. pessimism.
    d. realism.

14. Teeth are to mouth as brick is to
    a. kiln.
    b. wall.
    c. clay.
    d. masonry.

15. Christmas is to gifts as beach is to
    a. swimming.
    b. ocean.
    c. summer.
    d. sandbox.

16. Lukewarm is to hot as big is to
    a. small.
    b. delicate.
    c. immense.
    d. size.

17. Fire is to burn as medicine is to
    a. pill.
    b. disease.
    c. taste.
    d. recovery.

18. Organ is to heart as dog is to
    a. canine.
    b. poodle.
    c. breed.
    d. mammal.

Answers to Practice Questions

9. c. You can think of this as a "part-to-whole" analogy. A sentence describing the nature of the analogy might go like this: A *groom* is a member of (or a part of) a *wedding*; a *lawyer* is a part of a _____. The correct answer is *trial* (choice **c**), as this is the only word that would logically complete the sentence.

10. c. This is a "classification" analogy, where one word is a general classification—such as *clothing*—and the other word is an example of that classification. A *hat* is a type of *clothing*, and an *apple* is a type of *fruit*.

11. a. This is a "proportion or degree" analogy, in which one word may represent an increase or decrease of the other; or there may be a difference in degree between the two words in the set. The same difference will then exist between the two words in the other set, although there may be no other relationship between the two sets of words. A *hurricane* is more powerful and destructive than a *thunderstorm*, just as *rage* is more extreme than *anger*.

12. d. This analogy is based on "cause and effect." *Weeping* is caused by *grief*; a *tantrum* is caused by *rage*, so choice **d** is correct. Always look for the relationship between the words. A *tantrum* is a kind of *fit*, but it is not caused by a fit, and so the two words *tantrum* and *fit* are not related in the same way as the words *weeping* and *grief*.

13. c. Analogies may express a "similarity or difference." In this type, the second word will be a synonym or antonym of the first word, and so you will have to look for an answer choice that is also a synonym or antonym. *Love* and *hate* are opposite emotions; *optimism* and *pessimism* are opposite temperaments. Thus, the correct answer is choice **c**. This kind of question will test your vocabulary as well as your ability to reason about the relationships of words. If you didn't know what *optimism* was, you might have a tough time choosing the correct answer.

14. b. This analogy relies on a "part-to-whole" or "whole-to-part" relationship. That is, the second word may be a part of the thing expressed in the first word, or vice versa. Choice **b** is correct. The *teeth* are a part of the *mouth*; a *brick* may be part of a *wall*.

15. a. The relationship in an analogy may express "a strong association or a connection" between the meanings of the two words. There is a strong association between *Christmas* and *gifts* and between *beach* and *swimming*, so the correct answer is choice **a**.

16. c. This analogy concerns "proportion or degree." *Hot* is warmer than *lukewarm*, just as an *immense* object is larger than a *big* object.

17. d. This is a "cause and effect" analogy. *Fire* can cause a *burn*, and *medicine* can cause *recovery* from illness.

18. b. This is a "classification" analogy. A *heart* is a type of *organ*. A *poodle* is a type of *dog*. Note that the order of the words in the analogy is important. In this case, the word *organ* comes first, then the subtype *heart*; similarly, the word *dog* comes first, so you want a subtype. Thus, choice **d** is wrong; although a dog is a type of mammal, a mammal is not a type of dog.

Logic Questions

The logic portion of the HSPT may appear daunting at first. However, solving the logic problems can really be done in the most straightforward way. Simply "translate" the abstract relationships in the question into real-world relationships, so you can see the facts more clearly. Here is an example.

19. Corn flakes cost less than wheat flakes. Oat flakes cost more than wheat flakes. Oat flakes cost less than corn flakes. If the first two statements are true, the third statement is
  a. true.
  b. false.
  c. uncertain.
  d. repetitive.

Approach this problem by making a little grid with all the information on it, translated into simple "real-world" terms:

Wheat flakes	$2.50
Corn flakes (less than wheat)	$2.00
Oat flakes (more than wheat)	$2.75

The statement that "oat flakes (at $2.75) cost less than corn flakes (at $2.00)" is clearly false, and the answer is choice **b.**

Now look at a second example:

20. Gloria is younger than Francesca. Yvonne is older than Gloria. Yvonne is older than Francesca. If the first two statements are true, the third statement is
  a. true.
  b. false.
  c. uncertain.
  d. repetitive.

Write down the information you know and try to fill in what you don't. You'll get something like this:

Gloria	12 years old
Francesca	14 years old (older than Gloria)
Yvonne	13 (older than Gloria, but younger than Francesca)

OR

Yvonne	19 (older than Gloria and older than Francesca)

So the statement "Yvonne is older than Francesca" is uncertain. The correct answer is choice **c.**

Practice Logic Questions

Now try a couple more of these logic questions:

21. Marshalltown is east of Susanville. Halsted is north of Marshalltown. Susanville is southeast of Halsted. If the first two statements are true, the third statement is
  a. true.
  b. false.
  c. uncertain.
  d. repetitive.

22. The blue box is smaller than the red box, but larger than the green one. The yellow box is the largest of all. The red box is larger than the green box. If the first two statements are true, the third statement is
  a. true.
  b. false.
  c. uncertain.
  d. repetitive.

Answers to Practice Questions

21. b. Drawing a very simple map will help with this one. It will show Susanville is actually south*west* of Halsted.

22. a. Another real-world example will help:

blue   10 inches
red   12 inches
green   8 inches
yellow   15 inches

Quickly reorder this list by size:

yellow
red
blue
green

It instantly becomes apparent that the red box is larger than the green one, making the third statement true.

Verbal Classification

The final type of verbal reasoning question on the tests is the verbal classification question. Here is an example:

23. Which word does NOT belong with the others?
   a. jury
   b. judge
   c. courtroom
   d. bailiff

The important thing (as the name "verbal classification" indicates) is to *classify* the words in the four answer choices. Three of the words will be in the same classification; the remaining one will not be.

In this question, all four choices have to do with legal proceedings, so the classification "legal" is no help. You must look more closely. Note that three of the choices are people: a jury, a judge, and a bailiff. A courtroom, choice **c**, is a place. This is the one that doesn't fit.

Practice Logic Questions

Now try these practice questions.

24. Which word does NOT belong with the others?
   a. butter
   b. cream
   c. cheese
   d. margarine

25. Which word does NOT belong with the others?
   a. vanish
   b. evade
   c. dodge
   d. avoid

26. Which word does NOT belong with the others?
   a. book
   b. tome
   c. volume
   d. library

Answers to Practice Questions

24. d. *Butter, cream,* and *cheese* all belong to the classification "products made from milk." Margarine is not made from milk, but from vegetable oils.

25. a. *Evade, dodge,* and *avoid* are all synonyms that mean "staying out of the way." Vanish means to disappear.

26. d. *Book, tome,* and *volume* are all individual books, while a library holds many books.

11 ▶ NONVERBAL REASONING

LESSON SUMMARY

This lesson will introduce you to the Nonverbal Reasoning section of the COOP, Quantitative Skills portion of the HSPT (except for the Number Manipulation questions, which are really algebra problems covered in Lesson 12), and the Ability section of the TACHS.

As you will see in the following, there is a great deal of similarity between the Nonverbal Reasoning section of the COOP, the Quantitative Skills section of the HSPT and the Ability section of the TACHS. No matter which test you will be taking, you should read this whole lesson and do all the practice questions at the end. The main thing to do is to treat the questions as puzzles, and relax and have fun solving them!

COOP and TACHS Analogies

In the Analogy questions on the COOP and TACHS, you will be presented with a set of two pictures that are related to each other in some way. Along with this set, you'll be given a third picture and four answer choices, which are also pictures. Of the four choices, you must identify the one that would best complete the second set of pictures so that it expresses the same relationship as in the first set. Each question looks the same. An example is shown on the next page.

Sample COOP Question

1.

a.   b.   c.   d.

Answer

1. b. The answer is a *soup bowl*. Milk is served in a drinking glass. Soup is served in a soup bowl.

Preparing for COOP Analogy Questions

There are three steps that will make you successful in answering COOP analogy questions.

Translate the Pictures into Words

There is essentially no difference between verbal and picture analogies, except that you have to take this extra first step of naming each picture. If you deal better with pictures than with words, you can skip this step, but make sure you understand the relationship between the first set of pictures.

Look for the Relationship

Analogy questions are meant to measure your ability to see relationships between concepts. The relation-

ship between the first set of words will guide you to the relationship in the second set, so figuring out the first relationship is the most important part.

Make up a sentence that describes the relationship between the first two sets of words. In our previous example, your sentence would be: *Milk is served in (or drunk from) a drinking glass.* Now use the same sentence to describe the possible relationships between the third picture and each of the answer choices.

- *Soup is served in (or eaten from) a box of cereal.* Nope. There is no relationship between soup and cereal, so move on to the next choice.
- *Soup is served in (or eaten from) a soup bowl.* This is almost certainly it! But just to make sure, continue on. You may find a closer relationship.
- *Soup is served in (or eaten from) a cooking pan.* There is a relationship here, but it is not, after all, exactly the same kind. *Soup bowl* is still a better choice.
- Finally, *soup is served in (or eaten from) a cooking stove.* This does not make sense at all. So you can settle on *soup bowl* as the correct answer.

There are many different types of analogy relationships. Following are just some of the possibilities:

- use or function
- part-to-whole
- classification
- proportion or degree
- cause and effect
- similarity or difference
- strong association or connection

For examples of each of these different types of analogies, be sure to turn to Lesson 10 of this book (which deals with word analogies) and read the section called "How to Prepare for Analogy Questions."

Practice!

The very best way to learn how to approach analogies—whether presented as pictures or as words—is to practice. So be sure to work through all the analogy questions in Lessons 5, 6, 14, and 15.

Sequences

The sequences questions on the COOP and TACHS and the number series portion of the HSPT and TACHS presents test takers with nearly identical challenges.

The directions for the sequences questions will read something like:

For questions 2 through 4, choose the part that would continue the pattern or sequence.

Three question types are used to measure your ability to reason with number, letter, and symbol sequences.

Number Sequences

One type of Sequences question involves a series of **numbers**, which may entail addition, subtraction, multiplication, division, and/or identification of a random number inserted in the sequence; for example: 12 24 48 9 3 6 12 9 . . . Here, the first numbers are multiplied by 2, then the random number 9 is inserted, then you multiply by 2 again, and then 9 is inserted. Every fourth number is 9. Here is an example of a typical number sequence question.

Sample Question

2. 3 9 6 | 7 21 18 | 10 30 ___
   a. 5
   b. 20
   c. 23
   d. 27

Answer

2. d. This is an alternating sequence, requiring multiplication and subtraction. In each set, the second number is three times the first number. The third number is three less than the second number.

Letter Sequences

Another kind of Sequences question uses a series of **letters** in a pattern. Usually, these questions use the letters' alphabetical order as a base. To make matters more complicated, sometimes a number will be thrown into the letter sequences—for example: rather than A B F, there might be $A_3B_2F_4$. Here is an example of a typical letter sequence question.

Sample Question

3. FHJ JLN NPR ___ VXZ
   a. RSU
   b. SUW
   c. RTV
   d. TUV

Answer

3. c. The letters in each set of three are in alphabetical order, but one letter is skipped. For example, the first set is F (skip G), H (skip I), J. The second set begins with J, which is the last letter of the previous set. This pattern repeats. Note that this item asks you to fill in the blank and not to add to the end of the sequence. The last letter repeats, so the set that is missing must begin with an "R." Immediately, this rules out choices **b** and **d**.

Symbol Sequences

Finally, a COOP sequences question may use a series of nonverbal, non-number **symbols** in a pattern; for example: ∞ ♣ ∩. Here is an example of a typical symbol sequence question on the COOP.

Sample Question

4. + x + | x + x | + x + | _____
   a. x + x
   b. + x +
   c. + x
   d. x +

Answer

4. **a.** This is a simple alternating sequence. In the first set, the **x** is in the middle; in the second set, the **+** is in the middle; and then the pattern repeats.

HSPT and TACHS Number Series

Only one question type is used to measure your ability to reason with sequences on the HSPT and TACHS—that is, the number series question type. It is quite similar to the COOP sequences, although the way it is presented will look different. There are no overall directions for the HSPT and TACHS number series questions; each question has its own directions. The following are typical examples.

Sample Questions

5. Look at this series: 37 35 33 31 29 27 25...
   What two numbers should come next?
   a. 24 23
   b. 24 22
   c. 23 21
   d. 22 20

Here's a more complex item of this type.

6. Look at this series: 10 12 50 15 17 50 20...
   What two numbers should come next?
   a. 50 21
   b. 21 50
   c. 50 22
   d. 22 50

Answers

5. **c.** Say the numbers silently in your head, and you may begin to "hear" a rhythm that supplies the missing numbers in the sequence: "37 (36) 35 (34) 33 (32) 31 (30) 29 (28) 27 (26) 25 (24) 23 (22) 21" and so forth.

6. **d.** Chances are, this series is too complex to be solved simply by reading the string of numbers. So you will want to begin by looking for *repetition*. By doing this, you'll see that the *random number* 50 has been introduced (10 12 **50** 15 17 **50** 20). To figure out the rest of the series, simply read the numbers "aloud," for the time being, leaving the random number out. Doing so will show you that the series otherwise increases first by 2 (10 + **2** = 12), then by 3 (12 + **3** = 15), then by 2 (15 + **2** = 17), then by 3 again (17 + **3** = 20). Continuing the pattern would lead you to: 20 + 2 = 22; now reinsert the random number 50, which will bring you to: 20 (+2) **22** (R) **50**. The correct answer in this case is therefore choice **d**.

TIPS FOR ANSWERING SEQUENCES AND SERIES QUESTIONS

- Look carefully at the sequence—you may be lucky and spot the pattern immediately.
- If you're dealing with numbers or letters, and you don't immediately see a pattern, read the series "aloud" (that is, actually *pronounce* the numbers silently inside your head).
- If you still do not see a pattern, look at every second number, then at every third number, and see if a pattern emerges from these. Look for repeated numbers, letters, or symbols—remember, these repeated numbers may be *random numbers* that have no relationship to any of the other numbers in the series.

Geometric and Non-Geometric Comparison (HSPT and TACHS)

The geometric comparison questions and non-geometric comparison questions on the HSPT and TACHS are very similar, and the approaches that you take to them will be similar. Here is an example of each:

Sample Geometric Comparison Question

7. Examine (A), (B), and (C) and find the best answer.

   (A)   (B)   (C)

a. (A) is more shaded than (B).
b. (B) is more shaded than (C).
c. (C) is more shaded than (A).
d. (A) and (C) are equally shaded.

Answer

7. c. First, look at each figure and count the number of blocks that are shaded. In (A), four blocks are shaded; in (B), four blocks are shaded; and in (C), five blocks are shaded. Then test each answer choice to determine which one is true. Choice **c** is the only true statement.

Sample Non-Geometric Comparison Question

8. Examine (A), (B), and (C) and find the best answer.

(A) 2(2 + 2)
(B) 14 ÷ 2
(C) 3(1 + 2)

a. (B) is greater than (A).
b. (C) is less than (A).
c. (B) is less than (A) but greater than (C).
d. (C) is greater than (A) or (B).

Answer

8. d. First, determine the value of (A), (B), and (C): 2(2 + 2) is 8; 14 ÷ 2 is 7; 3(1 + 2) is 9. Then test each statement to find out which one is true.

How to Answer Comparison Questions

As you can see, the form of the geometric comparison and non-geometric comparison questions is the same. The steps to take in answering both types are also the same.

- Take these questions in *steps*, carefully, one step at a time. Otherwise, you'll get confused.
- First, work out each of the problems (A) (B) (C) separately.
- If you work each problem correctly, you can easily rule out incorrect answer choices.

Practice Questions

For practice, do this minitest. Be sure to carefully read the answer explanations that follow it. All the kinds of questions covered in this lesson are included here. You could just do the ones that appear on your test, but why not do them all? After all, the logic is the same for all these nonverbal reasoning questions.

9.

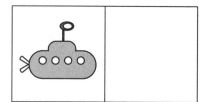

a.   b.   c.   d.

10.

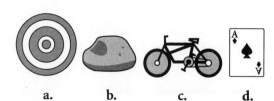

a.   b.   c.   d.

11. L_5MN OP$_4$Q R$_3$ST _____
  a. Q$_7$PR
  b. N$_3$RT
  c. UV$_2$W
  d. WV$_3$U

12. Look at this series: X, V, IV, II, XX, . . .
  What number should come next?
  a. VI
  b. IV
  c. XV
  d. X

13. Look at this series: 4, 7, 11, 18, . . .
  What number should come next?
  a. 21
  b. 23
  c. 29
  d. 44

14. Examine (A), (B), (C), and (D) and find the best answer.

(A) ————————

(B) —————————

(C) ——————————

(D) ————————

  a. (A) is longer than (D).
  b. (B) and (D) are the same length.
  c. (A) is shorter than (B) but longer than (D).
  d. (A) plus (D) is longer than (C).

15. Examine (A), (B), and (C) and find the best answer.

(A)   (B)   (C)

  a. (A) and (C) are equally shaded.

  b. (A) is more shaded than (B) but less shaded than (C).

  c. (A) is less shaded than (B) but more shaded than (C).

  d. Of the three, (A) is the least shaded.

16. Examine (A), (B), and (C) and find the best answer.

```
X X X X        X X            X X
X X X          X X X X X      X X
X X                           X X X X
X                             X       X X
  (A)            (B)            (C)
```

  a. (A) and (C) have an equal number of X's.

  b. (C) has one more X than (A) has.

  c. (A) plus (B) equals (C).

  d. (A) plus (B) minus (C) equals 5.

17. Examine (A), (B), and (C) and find the best answer.

(A) $\frac{1}{3}$ of 123

(B) $8^2 - 23$

(C) $9(9) - 40$

  a. (A), (B), and (C) are all equal.

  b. (A) plus (B) equals (C).

  c. (A) and (C) are equal, but (B) is less than both (A) or (C).

  d. (C) is one more than (A).

18. Examine (A), (B), and (C) and find the best answer.

(A)   5% of 45

(B) $\frac{1}{6}$ of 12

(C)   10% of 22

  a. (A) and (C) are equal.

  b. (A) is less than (B).

  c. (C) is less than (A).

  d. (C) is greater than (A).

Answers

  9. c. The first picture presents an airplane, a machine that flies—like the bird in the second picture. These two objects have similar abilities. The submarine in the third picture is a machine that swims underwater, and is similar only to the fish.

10. b. This picture sequence presents opposites. The match is hot, opposite of the cold ice cubes. A feather is lightweight, so the best choice is the heavy rock.

11. c. There are two sequences here. The letters are simply in alphabetical order, while the numbers are counting backward. Only choice **c** fits both the letter and number sequences.

12. d. It is a good idea to learn basic Roman numerals, since there will probably be a question or two using them on the test. This is a simple division series, but you will find it puzzling if you aren't familiar with Roman numerals. The series in Arabic numbers is: 10, 5, 4, 2, 20. The numbers are being divided by 2, so $\frac{1}{2}$ of 20 would be 10—or X in Roman numerals.

13. c. Each number in this series is added to the previous number. Thus, $7 + 4 = 11$; $11 + 7 = 18$. The next number would be $18 + 11$, which equals 29.

14. d. First, look carefully at each line. Then test each statement to determine which one is true.

15. c. First, count the shaded pieces of the pie. Then test each answer choice to find the correct one.

16. b. First, count the number of X's: (A) has 10; (B) has 7; (C) has 11. Now, test each answer choice to find out which one is true.

17. a. First, determine the value of (A), (B), and (C): $\frac{1}{3}$ of 123 is 41; $8^2 - 23$ also equals 41; $9(9) - 40$ is also 41. It is now easy to see that choice **a** is the only possible answer.

18. c. First, find values for (A), (B), and (C): 5% of 45 is 2.25; $\frac{1}{6}$ of 12 is 2; 10% of 22 is 2.2. Then test each answer choice to find out which one is true.

12 ▶ MATH SKILLS

LESSON SUMMARY

This lesson reviews the math you need to know for all the Catholic High School Entrance Exams.

f you've already taken one practice exam in this book, you probably know how much you need to improve your math skills to get a passing grade. The next step is to buckle down and start studying the math that doesn't come easy to you. That's where this lesson will help. Section by section, all the different types of math that are on the test are explained. If there are some concepts you just can't seem to understand—whether they be square roots, exponents, or fractions—you might want to do a more thorough study.

Here's what you'll find in this lesson:

Word Problems

Some of the math questions on the test are word problems. A word problem can include any kind of math, including simple arithmetic, fractions, decimals, percentages, and even algebra and geometry.

The hardest part of any word problem is translating English into math. When you read a problem, you can frequently translate it *word for word* from English statements into mathematical statements. At other times, however, a key word in the problem hints at the mathematical operation to be performed. Here are the translation rules:

EQUALS   key words: is, are, has

English	Math
Bob **is** 18 years old.	$B = 18$
There **are** seven nurses.	$N = 7$
This group **has** five families.	$F = 5$

ADDITION   key words: sum; more, greater, or older than; total; altogether

English	Math
The **sum** of two numbers is 10.	$X + Y = 10$
Karen has $5 **more than** Sam.	$K = 5 + S$
The base is 3" **greater than** the height.	$B = 3 + H$
Judi is two years **older than** Tony.	$J = 2 + T$
The **total** of three numbers is 25.	$A + B + C = 25$
How much do Joan and Tom have **altogether**?	$J + T = ?$

SUBTRACTION   key words: difference; less, fewer, or younger than; remain; left over

English	Math
The **difference** between two numbers is 17.	$X - Y = 17$
Mike has five **fewer** cats **than** twice the number Jan has.	$M = 2J - 5$
Jay is two years **younger than** Brett.	$J = B - 2$
After Carol ate three apples, how many apples **remained**?	$R = A - 3$

MULTIPLICATION   key words: of, product, times

English	Math
20% **of** the samples	$0.20 \times S$
half **of** the bacteria	$\frac{1}{2} \times B$
The **product** of two numbers is 12.	$A \times B = 12$

DIVISION   key words: per, half, divide, quotient, is divided by

English	Math
22 miles **per** gallon	$\frac{\text{miles}}{22} = \text{gallons}$
two is **divided** by five	$\frac{2}{5}$
one-**half** of eight	$\frac{8}{2}$

Solving a Word Problem Using the Translation Table

Let's try to solve the following problem using our translation rules.

Juan ate $\frac{1}{3}$ of the jelly beans. Maria then ate $\frac{3}{4}$ of the remaining jelly beans, which left 10 jelly beans. How many jelly beans were there to begin with?

a. 60

b. 80

c. 90

d. 120

e. 140

Assume Juan started with J jelly beans. Eating $\frac{1}{3}$ **of** them means eating $\frac{1}{3} \times J$ jelly beans. Maria ate a fraction of the **remaining** jelly beans, which means we must **subtract** to find out how many are left: $J - \frac{1}{3} \times J = \frac{2}{3} \times J$. Maria then ate $\frac{3}{4}$, leaving $\frac{1}{4}$ **of** the $\frac{2}{3} \times J$ jelly beans, or $\frac{1}{4} \times \frac{2}{3} \times J$ jelly beans. Multiplying out $\frac{1}{4} \times \frac{2}{3} \times J$ gives $\frac{1}{6}J$ as the number of jelly beans left. The problem states that there were **10 jelly beans left**, meaning that we set $\frac{1}{6} \times J$ **equal to** 10:

$$\frac{1}{6} \times J = 10$$

Solving this equation for J gives $J = 60$. Thus, the right answer is choice **a**.

Practice Word Problems

You will find word problems using fractions, decimals, and percentages in those sections of this lesson. For now, practice using the translation table on problems that just require you to work with basic arithmetic. Answers are at the end of the lesson.

_____ **1.** Joan went shopping with $100.00 and returned home with only $18.42. How much money did she spend?
   a. $81.58
   b. $72.68
   c. $72.58
   d. $71.68
   e. $71.58

_____ **2.** Each of five tutors at the math tutoring center works six hours per day. Each tutor can work with three students per hour. In total, how many students can be seen each day at the center?
   a. 18
   b. 30
   c. 60
   d. 75
   e. 90

_____ **3.** Rhonda drove for $4\frac{1}{2}$ hours at an average speed of 68 miles per hour. How far did she drive?
   a. 153 miles
   b. 206 miles
   c. 248 miles
   d. 306 miles
   e. 352 miles

_____ **4.** Principal Wallace is writing a budget request to upgrade his office computer. He wants to purchase $100 of additional RAM, two new software programs for $350 each, a new monitor for $249, and a new keyboard for $25. What is the total amount Principal Wallace should write on his budget request?
   a. $724
   b. $974
   c. $1,049
   d. $1,064
   e. $1,074

Number Names

There's bound to be at least one question on the math test that asks you to give numbers for words, or vice versa. This can mean easy points for you if you learn a few place names.

Numbers are made up of digits that represent different values according to their position in the number. For instance, in the number 4,312.796, the 2 is in the *ones* place and equals 2 units. The 1 is in the *tens* place and equals 1 ten (10). The 3 is in the *hundreds* place and equals 3 hundreds (300). The 4 in the *thousands* place equals 4 thousands (4,000). To the right of the decimal, the 7 is in the *tenths* place and equals seven tenths (0.7 or $\frac{7}{10}$). The 9 is in the *hundredths* place and equals 9 hundredths (0.09 or $\frac{9}{100}$). The 6 is in the *thousandths* place and equals 6 thousandths (0.006 or $\frac{6}{1000}$).

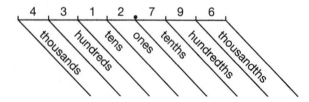

Denominator	the bottom number in a fraction. Example: 2 is the denominator in $\frac{1}{2}$.
Difference	subtract. The difference of two numbers means subtract one number from the other.
Divisible by	A number is divisible by a second number if that second number divides *evenly* into the original number. Example: 10 is divisible by 5 (10 ÷ 5 = 2, with no remainder). However, 10 is not divisible by 3. (See *multiple of*.)
Even Integer	integers that are divisible by 2, like . . . –4, –2, 0, 2, 4, . . . (See *integer*.)
Integer	numbers along the number line, like . . . –3, –2, –1, 0, 1, 2, 3, . . . Integers include the whole numbers and their opposites. (See *whole number*.)
Multiple of	A number is a multiple of a second number if that second number can be multiplied by an integer to get the original number. Example: 10 is a multiple of 5 (10 = 5 × 2); however, 10 is not a multiple of 3. (See *divisible by*.)
Negative Number	a number that is less than zero, like –1, –18.6, $-\frac{3}{4}$
Numerator	the top part of a fraction. Example: 1 is the numerator of $\frac{1}{2}$.
Odd Integer	integers that aren't divisible by 2, like . . . –5, –3, –1, 1, 3, . . .
Positive Number	a number that is greater than zero, like 2, 42, $\frac{1}{2}$, 4.63
Prime Number	integers that are divisible only by 1 and themselves, like 2, 3, 5, 7, 11, . . . All prime numbers are odd, except for 2. The number 1 is not considered prime.
Product	multiply. The product of two numbers means the numbers are multiplied together.
Quotient	the answer you get when you divide. Example: 10 divided by 5 is 2; the quotient is 2.
Real Number	all the numbers you can think of, like 17, –5, $\frac{1}{2}$, –23.6, 3.4329, 0. Real numbers include the integers, fractions, and decimals. (See *integer*.)
Remainder	the number left over after division. Example: 11 divided by 2 is 5, with a remainder of 1.
Sum	add. The sum of two numbers means the numbers are added together.
Whole Number	numbers you can count on your fingers, like 1, 2, 3, . . . All whole numbers are positive. Zero is also a whole number.

Example: Write, in numerals, *one thousand forty-nine*.

1. Notice first that there is no *hundred* included in the number name.
   Therefore, a zero will go in the hundreds place: _, 0 _ _
2. Put down a 1 in the thousands place for *one thousand*:   1,0 _ _
3. And 49 for *forty-nine*:   1,049

A question also may ask you to work the other way, from numerals to words.

Example: Write, in words, 5,678.

1. 5 is in the thousands place: *five thousand*
2. 6 is in the hundreds place: *five thousand six hundred*
3. 7 is in the tens place: *five thousand six hundred seventy*
4. And 8 is in the ones place: *five thousand six hundred seventy-eight*

Try a few problems on your own. Answers are at the end of this lesson.

5. Write, in numerals, *eight thousand seven hundred fifty-five.*

6. Write, in numerals, *two hundred one.*

7. Write, in words, 710.

8. Write, in words, 9,186.

Fraction Review

Problems involving fractions may be straightforward calculation questions, or they may be word problems. Typically, they ask you to add, subtract, multiply, divide, or compare fractions.

Working with Fractions

A fraction is a part of something.

> **Example:** Let's say that a pizza was cut into eight equal slices and you ate three slices. The fraction $\frac{3}{8}$ tells you what part of the pizza you ate. The following pizza shows this: Three of the eight pieces (the ones you ate) are shaded.

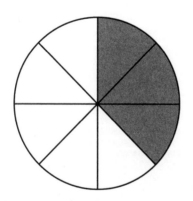

Three Kinds of Fractions

Proper fraction: The top number is *less than* the bottom number: $\frac{1}{2}$; $\frac{2}{3}$; $\frac{4}{9}$; $\frac{8}{13}$ The value of a proper fraction is less than 1.

Improper fraction: The top number is *greater than or equal to* the bottom number: $\frac{3}{2}$; $\frac{5}{3}$; $\frac{14}{9}$; $\frac{12}{12}$ The value of an improper fraction is 1 or more.

Mixed number: A fraction written *to the right of* a whole number: $3\frac{1}{2}$; $4\frac{2}{3}$; $12\frac{3}{4}$; $24\frac{3}{4}$ The value of a mixed number is more than 1: It is the sum of the whole number plus the fraction.

Changing Improper Fractions into Mixed or Whole Numbers

It's easier to add and subtract fractions that are mixed numbers rather than improper fractions. To change an improper fraction, say $\frac{13}{2}$, into a mixed number, follow these steps:

1. Divide the bottom number (2) into the top number (13) to get the whole number portion (6) of the mixed number:

$$\begin{array}{r} 6 \\ 2\overline{)13} \\ \underline{12} \\ 1 \end{array}$$

2. Write the remainder of the division (1) over the old bottom number (2): $6\frac{1}{2}$

3. Check: Change the mixed number back into an improper fraction (see the following steps).

Changing Mixed Numbers into Improper Fractions

It's easier to multiply and divide fractions when you're working with improper fractions rather than mixed numbers. To change a mixed number, say $2\frac{3}{4}$, into an improper fraction, follow these steps:

1. Multiply the whole number (2) by the bottom number (4). $\qquad 2 \times 4 = 8$
2. Add the result (8) to the top number (3). $\qquad 8 + 3 = 11$
3. Put the total (11) over the bottom number (4). $\qquad \frac{11}{4}$
4. Check: Reverse the process by changing the improper fraction into a mixed number. If you get back the number you started with, your answer is right.

Reducing Fractions

Reducing a fraction means writing it in its *lowest terms*, that is, with smaller numbers. For instance, 50¢ is $\frac{50}{100}$ of a dollar, or $\frac{1}{2}$ of a dollar. In fact, if you have 50¢ in your pocket, you say that you have *half a dollar*. Reducing a fraction does not change its value.

Follow these steps to reduce a fraction:

1. Find a whole number that divides *evenly* into both numbers that make up the fraction.
2. Divide that number into the top of the fraction, and replace the top of the fraction with the quotient (the answer you got when you divided).
3. Do the same thing to the bottom number.
4. Repeat the first three steps until you can't find a number that divides evenly into both numbers of the fraction.

For example, let's reduce $\frac{8}{24}$. We could do it in two steps: $\frac{8 \div 4}{24 \div 4} = \frac{2}{6}$; then $\frac{2 \div 2}{6 \div 2} = \frac{1}{3}$. Or we could do it in a single step: $\frac{8 \div 8}{24 \div 8} = \frac{1}{3}$.

Shortcut: When the top and bottom numbers both end in zeros, cross out the same number of zeros in both numbers to begin the reducing process. For example, $\frac{300}{4,000}$ reduces to $\frac{3}{40}$ when you cross out two zeros in both numbers.

Whenever you do arithmetic with fractions, *reduce* your answer. On a multiple-choice test, don't panic if your answer isn't listed. Try to reduce it and then compare it to the choices.

Reduce these fractions to lowest terms. Answers are at the end of the lesson.

_____ **9.** $\frac{3}{15}$

_____ **10.** $\frac{12}{36}$

_____ **11.** $\frac{6}{16}$

Raising Fractions to Higher Terms

Before you can add and subtract fractions, you have to know how to raise a fraction to higher terms. This is actually the opposite of reducing a fraction.

Follow these steps to raise $\frac{2}{3}$ to 24ths:

1. Divide the old bottom number (3) into the new one (24): $\qquad 3\overline{)24} = 8$
2. Multiply both the top and bottom number by 8: $\qquad \frac{2 \times 8}{3 \times 8} = \frac{16}{24}$
3. Check: Reduce the new fraction to see if you get back the original one: $\qquad \frac{16 \div 8}{24 \div 8} = \frac{2}{3}$

Raise these fractions to higher terms:

_____ **12.** $\frac{5}{12} = \frac{}{24}$

_____ **13.** $\frac{2}{9} = \frac{}{27}$

_____ **14.** $\frac{3}{8} = \frac{}{32}$

Adding Fractions

If the fractions have the same bottom numbers, just add the top numbers together and write the total over the bottom number.

Examples: $\frac{2}{9} + \frac{4}{9} = \frac{2+4}{9} = \frac{6}{9}$ Reduce the sum: $\frac{2}{3}$

$\frac{5}{8} + \frac{7}{8} = \frac{12}{8}$ Change the sum to a mixed number: $1\frac{4}{8}$; then reduce: $1\frac{1}{2}$

There are a few extra steps to add mixed numbers with the same bottom numbers, say $2\frac{3}{5} + 1\frac{4}{5}$:

1. Add the whole numbers: $2 + 1 = 3$

2. Add the fractions: $\frac{3}{5} + \frac{4}{5} = \frac{7}{5}$

3. Change the improper fraction into a mixed number: $\frac{7}{5} = 1\frac{2}{5}$

4. Add the results of steps 1 and 3: $1\frac{2}{5} + 3 = 4\frac{2}{5}$

Finding the Least Common Denominator

If the fractions you want to add don't have the same bottom number, you'll have to raise some or all of the fractions to higher terms so that they all have the same bottom number, called the **common denominator**. All the original bottom numbers divide evenly into the common denominator. The smallest number that they all divide evenly into is called the **least common denominator (LCD)**.

Here are a few tips for finding the LCD:

- See whether all the bottom numbers divide evenly into the biggest bottom number.
- Check out the multiplication table of the largest bottom number until you find a number that all the other bottom numbers evenly divide into.
- When all else fails, multiply all the bottom numbers together.

Example: $\frac{2}{3} + \frac{4}{5}$

1. Find the LCD. Multiply the bottom numbers: $3 \times 5 = 15$

2. Raise each fraction to 15ths: $\frac{2 \times 5}{3 \times 5} = \frac{10}{15}$
   $+\frac{4 \times 3}{5 \times 3} = \frac{12}{15}$

3. Add as usual: $\frac{22}{15}$

Try these addition problems:

_____ **15.** $\frac{3}{8} + \frac{2}{3}$

_____ **16.** $\frac{7}{8} + \frac{2}{3} + \frac{3}{4}$

_____ **17.** $4\frac{1}{3} + 2\frac{3}{4} + \frac{1}{6}$

Subtracting Fractions

If the fractions have the same bottom numbers, just subtract the top numbers and write the difference over the bottom number.

Example: $\frac{4}{9} - \frac{3}{9} = \frac{4-3}{9} = \frac{1}{9}$

If the fractions don't have the same bottom number, you'll have to raise some or all of the fractions to higher terms so that they all have the same bottom number, or LCD. If you forgot how to find the LCD, just read the section on adding fractions with different bottom numbers.

Example: $\frac{5}{6} - \frac{3}{4}$

1. Raise each fraction to 12ths because 12 is the LCD, the smallest number that 6 and 4 both divide into evenly:

$$\frac{5 \times 2}{6 \times 2} = \frac{10}{12}$$

$$-\frac{3 \times 3}{4 \times 3} = \frac{9}{12}$$

2. Subtract as usual: $\frac{1}{12}$

Subtracting mixed numbers with the same bottom number is similar to adding mixed numbers.

Example: $4\frac{3}{5} - 1\frac{2}{5}$

1. Subtract the fractions: $\frac{3}{5} - \frac{2}{5} = \frac{1}{5}$
2. Subtract the whole numbers: $4 - 1 = 3$
3. Add the results of steps 1 and 2: $\frac{1}{5} + 3 = 3\frac{1}{5}$

Sometimes, there is an extra "borrowing" step when you subtract mixed numbers with the same bottom numbers, say $7\frac{3}{5} - 2\frac{4}{5}$:

1. You can't subtract the fractions the way they are because $\frac{4}{5}$ is bigger than $\frac{3}{5}$. So you borrow 1 from the 7, making it 6, and change that 1 to $\frac{5}{5}$ because 5 is the bottom number: $7\frac{3}{5} = 6\frac{5}{5} + \frac{3}{5}$
2. Add the numbers from step 1: $6\frac{5}{5} + \frac{3}{5} = 6\frac{8}{5}$
3. Now you have a different version of the original problem: $6\frac{8}{5} - 2\frac{4}{5}$
4. Subtract the fractional parts of the two mixed numbers: $\frac{8}{5} - \frac{4}{5} = \frac{4}{5}$
5. Subtract the whole number parts of the two mixed numbers: $6 - 2 = 4$
6. Add the results of the last 2 steps together: $4 + \frac{4}{5} = 4\frac{4}{5}$

Try these subtraction problems. Answers are at the end of the lesson.

_____ **18.** $\frac{1}{4} - \frac{1}{8}$

_____ **19.** $\frac{7}{8} - \frac{1}{4} - \frac{1}{2}$

_____ **20.** $4\frac{1}{3} - 2\frac{3}{4}$

Now let's put what you've learned about adding and subtracting fractions to work in some real-life problems.

_____ **21.** Mom bought a 32-ounce box of cornflakes. Ben ate $6\frac{1}{2}$ ounces, Frieda ate $2\frac{3}{4}$ ounces, Mike ate $8\frac{1}{2}$ ounces, and Megan ate $5\frac{3}{4}$ ounces. How much cereal was left in the box?
   a. $8\frac{1}{2}$ ounces
   b. $9\frac{1}{4}$ ounces
   c. $10\frac{3}{8}$ ounces
   d. $12\frac{1}{3}$ ounces
   e. $18\frac{3}{4}$ ounces

_____ **22.** Before leaving the garage, the bus driver noted that the mileage gauge on the school bus registered $4{,}357\frac{4}{10}$ miles. When he arrived at the first stop on his route, the mileage gauge then registered $4{,}400\frac{1}{10}$ miles. How many miles did he drive from the garage to his first stop?
   a. $42\frac{3}{10}$ miles
   b. $42\frac{7}{10}$ miles
   c. $43\frac{7}{10}$ miles
   d. $47\frac{2}{10}$ miles
   e. $57\frac{3}{10}$ miles

Multiplying Fractions

Multiplying fractions is actually easier than adding them. All you do is multiply the top numbers, and then multiply the bottom numbers.

Examples:
$$\frac{2}{3} \times \frac{5}{7} = \frac{2 \times 5}{3 \times 7} = \frac{10}{21}$$
$$\frac{1}{2} \times \frac{3}{5} \times \frac{7}{4} = \frac{1 \times 3 \times 7}{2 \times 5 \times 4} = \frac{21}{40}$$

Sometimes, you can *cancel* before multiplying. Canceling is a shortcut that makes the multiplication go faster because you're multiplying with smaller numbers. It's very similar to reducing: If there is a number that divides evenly into a top number and bottom number, do that division before multiplying. If you forget to cancel, you'll still get the right answer, but you'll have to reduce it.

Example: $\frac{5}{6} \times \frac{9}{20}$

1. Cancel the 6 and the 9 by dividing 3 into both of them: $6 \div 3 = 2$ and $9 \div 3 = 3$. Cross out the 6 and the 9: $\quad \frac{5}{\cancel{6}_2} \times \frac{\cancel{9}^3}{20}$

2. Cancel the 5 and the 20 by dividing 5 into both of them: $5 \div 5 = 1$ and $20 \div 5 = 4$. Cross out the 5 and the 20: $\quad \frac{\cancel{5}^1}{\cancel{6}_2} \times \frac{\cancel{9}^3}{\cancel{20}_4}$

3. Multiply across the new top numbers and the new bottom numbers: $\quad \frac{1 \times 3}{2 \times 4} = \frac{3}{8}$

Try these multiplication problems. Answers are at the end of the lesson.

_____ **23.** $\frac{7}{8} \times \frac{3}{5}$

_____ **24.** $\frac{2}{3} \times \frac{4}{7} \times \frac{3}{5}$

_____ **25.** $\frac{3}{4} \times \frac{8}{9}$

To multiply a fraction by a whole number, first rewrite the whole number as a fraction with a bottom number of 1:

Example: $5 \times \frac{2}{3} = \frac{5}{1} \times \frac{2}{3} = \frac{10}{3}$
(Optional: Convert $\frac{10}{3}$ to a mixed number: $3\frac{1}{3}$.)

To multiply with mixed numbers, it's easier to change them to improper fractions before multiplying.

Example: $4\frac{2}{3} \times 5\frac{1}{2}$

1. Convert $4\frac{2}{3}$ to an improper fraction: $\quad 4\frac{2}{3} = \frac{4 \times 3 + 2}{3} = \frac{14}{3}$

2. Convert $5\frac{1}{2}$ to an improper fraction: $\quad 5\frac{1}{2} = \frac{5 \times 2 + 1}{2} = \frac{11}{2}$

3. Cancel and multiply the fractions: $\quad \frac{\cancel{14}^7}{3} \times \frac{11}{\cancel{2}_1} = \frac{77}{3}$

4. Optional: Convert the improper fraction to a mixed number: $\quad \frac{77}{3} = 25\frac{2}{3}$

Now try these multiplication problems with mixed numbers and whole numbers. Answers are at the end of the lesson.

_____ **26.** $4\frac{1}{3} \times \frac{2}{5}$

_____ **27.** $2\frac{1}{2} \times 6$

_____ **28.** $3\frac{3}{4} \times 4\frac{2}{5}$

Here are a few more real-life problems to test your skills:

_____ **29.** After driving $\frac{2}{3}$ of the 15 miles to work, Dr. Stone received an emergency call from the hospital. How many miles had he driven when he got the call?
a. 5 miles
b. $7\frac{1}{2}$ miles
c. 10 miles
d. 12 miles
e. $15\frac{2}{3}$ miles

_____ **30.** Henry spent $\frac{3}{4}$ of a 40-hour week learning to use new graphic design software. How many hours did he spend in training?
a. $7\frac{1}{2}$ hours
b. 10 hours
c. 20 hours
d. 25 hours
e. 30 hours

_____ **31.** Luke's paycheck was $360, and he deposited $\frac{2}{3}$ of it into his savings account. He gave $\frac{1}{5}$ of it to charity and kept the rest in cash. How much cash did Luke end up with?
a. $26
b. $37
c. $48
d. $52
e. $63

Dividing Fractions

To divide one fraction by a second fraction, invert the second fraction (that is, flip the top and bottom numbers) and then multiply. That's all there is to it!

Example: $\frac{1}{2} \div \frac{3}{5}$

1. Invert the second fraction ($\frac{3}{5}$): $\qquad$ $\frac{5}{3}$
2. Change the division sign ($\div$) to a multiplication sign ($\times$):
3. Multiply the first fraction by the new second fraction: $\qquad$ $\frac{1}{2} \times \frac{5}{3} = \frac{1 \times 5}{2 \times 3} = \frac{5}{6}$

To divide a fraction by a whole number, first change the whole number to a fraction by putting it over 1. Then follow the previous division steps.

Example: $\frac{3}{5} \div 2 = \frac{3}{5} \div \frac{2}{1} = \frac{3}{5} \times \frac{1}{2} = \frac{3 \times 1}{5 \times 2} = \frac{3}{10}$

When the division problem has a mixed number, convert it to an improper fraction and then divide as usual.

Example: $2\frac{3}{4} \div \frac{1}{6}$

1. Convert $2\frac{3}{4}$ to an improper fraction: $\qquad$ $2\frac{3}{4} = \frac{2 \times 4 + 3}{4} = \frac{11}{4}$
2. Divide $\frac{11}{4}$ by $\frac{1}{6}$: $\qquad$ $\frac{11}{4} \div \frac{1}{6}$
3. Flip $\frac{1}{6}$ to $\frac{6}{1}$, change $\div$ to $\times$, cancel and multiply: $\qquad$ $\frac{11}{\underset{2}{4}} \times \frac{\overset{3}{6}}{1} = \frac{11 \times 3}{2 \times 1} = \frac{33}{2}$

Here are a few division problems to try:

_____ **32.** $\frac{3}{8} \div \frac{5}{8}$

_____ **33.** $2\frac{3}{4} \div \frac{1}{2}$

_____ **34.** $\frac{1}{3} \div 5$

_____ **35.** $3\frac{3}{4} \div 2\frac{1}{3}$

Let's wrap this up with some real-life problems.

_____ **36.** Dr. McCarthy's four assistants evenly divided $6\frac{1}{2}$ pounds of candy. How many pounds of candy did each assistant get?
a. $\frac{8}{13}$ pounds
b. $1\frac{5}{8}$ pounds
c. $1\frac{1}{2}$ pounds
d. $1\frac{5}{13}$ pounds
e. 4 pounds

_____ **37.** How many $2\frac{1}{2}$-pound chunks of cheese can be cut from a single 20-pound piece of cheese?
a. 2
b. 4
c. 6
d. 8
e. 10

_____ **38.** Holly's boss paid her $154.40 for working 16 hours. How much was she paid per hour?
a. $9.42
b. $9.65
c. $10.13
d. $10.48
e. $11.25

Comparing Fractions

It's likely that the math test will include a question or two on comparing fractions. When the denominators or numerators of the fractions are the same, comparing is fairly easy. When neither is the same, there's an extra step involved.

Same Denominators

It is easy to see which of two fractions is larger if they have the same denominator.

Example: Which is larger, $\frac{2}{5}$ or $\frac{3}{5}$?

In other words, if you had a pie that was divided into five pieces (the bottom number tells how many pieces the pie is divided into), would you have more pie if you had two of the five pieces or three of the five pieces?

$\frac{3}{5}$ is larger than $\frac{2}{5}$

Same Numerators

Likewise, it is easy to determine which fraction is larger if the numerators are the same.

Example: Which is smaller, $\frac{3}{5}$ or $\frac{3}{7}$?

In other words, would you rather have three pieces from a pie that was divided into five pieces or from a pie that was divided into seven pieces? The pie with seven pieces would have smaller pieces than the pie divided into 5 pieces.

$\frac{3}{7}$ is smaller than $\frac{3}{5}$

Different Denominators and Numerators

If the two fractions being compared do not have the same denominator or the same numerator, it is more difficult to tell which is larger. In this case, it is best to change the original fractions to equivalent fractions with the same denominators.

Example: Which is larger, $\frac{2}{5}$ or $\frac{3}{7}$?

1. Find a common multiple of 5 and 7:　　　　　35
2. Raise both fractions so that they have a bottom number of 35:

$$\frac{2}{5} = \frac{2 \times 7}{5 \times 7} = \frac{14}{35}$$
$$\frac{3}{7} = \frac{3 \times 5}{7 \times 5} = \frac{15}{35}$$

3. Now you can compare the size of the fractions by looking at the numerators. Since 15 is larger than 14, $\frac{3}{7}$ is larger than $\frac{2}{5}$.

Here are a couple problems for you to try. Answers are at the end of the lesson.

39. Which of the following fractions is the smallest?
　a. $\frac{1}{4}$
　b. $\frac{2}{9}$
　c. $\frac{3}{8}$
　d. $\frac{3}{16}$
　e. $\frac{4}{16}$

40. Which of the following fractions is the largest?
　a. $\frac{7}{12}$
　b. $\frac{7}{10}$
　c. $\frac{8}{10}$
　d. $\frac{3}{6}$
　e. $\frac{3}{4}$

Decimals

What Is a Decimal?

A decimal is a special kind of fraction. You use decimals every day when you deal with money—$10.35 is a decimal that represents 10 dollars and 35 cents. The decimal point separates the dollars from the cents. Because there are 100 cents in one dollar, 1¢ is $\frac{1}{100}$ of a dollar, or $.01.

Each decimal digit to the right of the decimal point has a name:

Example: 　.1　　$= 1$ tenth $= \frac{1}{10}$
　　.02　$= 2$ hundredths $= \frac{2}{100}$
　　.003　$= 3$ thousandths $= \frac{3}{1,000}$
　　.0004 $= 4$ ten-thousandths $= \frac{4}{10,000}$

When you add zeros to the right of the final numeral, you don't change the value of the decimal. For example, 6.17 is the same as all of these:

6.170
6.1700
6.17000000000000000

If there are digits on both sides of the decimal point (like 10.35), the number is called a *mixed decimal*. If there are digits only to the right of the decimal point (like .53), the number is called a *decimal*. A *whole number* (like 15) is understood to have a decimal point at its right (15.). Thus, 15 is the same as 15.0, 15.00, 15.000, and so on.

Changing Fractions to Decimals

To change a fraction to a decimal, divide the bottom number into the top number after you put a decimal point and a few zeros on the right of the top number. When you divide, bring the decimal point up into your answer.

Example: Change $\frac{3}{4}$ to a decimal.

1. Add a decimal point and two zeros to the top number (3): 3.00

2. Divide the bottom number (4) into 3.00: Bring the decimal point up into the answer:

$$\begin{array}{r} .75 \\ 4\overline{)3.00} \\ \underline{2\ 8} \\ 20 \\ \underline{20} \\ 0 \end{array}$$

3. The quotient (result of the division) is the answer: .75

Some fractions may require you to add many decimal zeros in order for the division to come out evenly. In fact, when you convert a fraction like $\frac{2}{3}$ to a decimal, you can keep adding decimal zeros to the top number forever because the division will never come out evenly! As you divide 3 into 2, you'll keep getting 6's:

$$2 \div 3 = .6666666666 \text{ etc.}$$

This is called a *repeating decimal* and can be written as $.66\overline{6}$ or as $.66\frac{2}{3}$. You can approximate it as .67, .667, .6667, and so on.

Changing Decimals to Fractions

To change a decimal to a fraction, write the digits of the decimal as the top number of a fraction and write the decimal's name as the bottom number of the fraction. Then reduce the fraction, if possible.

Example: .018

1. Write 18 as the top of the fraction: $\frac{18}{}$

2. Three places to the right of the decimal means *thousandths*, so write 1,000 as the bottom number: $\frac{18}{1,000}$

3. Reduce by dividing 2 into the top and bottom numbers: $\frac{18 \div 2}{1,000 \div 2} = \frac{9}{500}$

Change these decimals or mixed decimals to fractions. Answers are at the end of the lesson.

_____ **41.** 0.15

_____ **42.** 2.25

_____ **43.** 123.456

Comparing Decimals

Decimals are easier to compare when they have the same number of digits after the decimal point. Tack zeros onto the end of the shorter decimals; then all you have to do is compare the numbers as if the decimal points weren't there:

Example: Compare .08 and .1.

1. Tack one zero at the end of .1 to get .10.
2. To compare .10 to .08, just compare 10 to 8.
3. Since 10 is larger than 8, .1 is larger than .08.

Adding and Subtracting Decimals

To add or subtract decimals, line them up so their decimal points are even. You may want to tack on zeros at the end of shorter decimals so you can keep all your digits lined up evenly. Remember, if a number doesn't have a decimal point, then put one at the right end of the number.

Example: 1.23 + 57 + .038

1. Line up the numbers
   like this: 1.230
                                57.000
                              +   .038
2. Add: 58.268

Example: 1.23 − .038

1. Line up the numbers
   like this: 1.230
                              −   .038
2. Subtract: 1.192

Try these addition and subtraction problems.

_____ **44.** 0.905 + 0.02 + 3.075

_____ **45.** 0.005 + 8 + 0.3

_____ **46.** 3.48 − 2.573

_____ **47.** 1.12 + 3.06 − 2.02

_____ **48.** James Peterson drove 3.7 miles to his local sports club. He then walked 1.6 miles on the treadmill to strengthen his legs. He got back into the car, drove 2.75 miles to his favorite juice bar, and then drove 2 miles back home. How many miles did he drive in total?
   a. 8.05 miles
   b. 8.45 miles
   c. 8.8 miles
   d. 10 miles
   e. 10.05 miles

_____ **49.** The soccer field is 12.4 miles from Dave's house. Mike lives halfway between Dave and the soccer field. How many miles away from Dave does Mike live?
   a. 3.75 miles
   b. 4.6 miles
   c. 5.8 miles
   d. 6.2 miles
   e. 7.4 miles

Multiplying Decimals

To multiply decimals, ignore the decimal points and just multiply the numbers. Then count the total number of decimal digits (the digits to the *right* of the decimal point) in the numbers you're multiplying. Count off that number of digits in your answer beginning at the right side and put the decimal point to the *left* of those digits.

Example: 215.7×2.4

1. Multiply 2157 times 24:

   2157
   × 24
   8628
   4314
   51768

2. There are a total of two decimal digits in 215.7 and 2.4. Count off two places from the right in 51768, placing the decimal point to the *left* of the last two digits: 517.68

If your answer doesn't have enough digits, tack zeros on to the left of the answer.

Example: $.03 \times .006$

1. Multiply 3 times 6: $3 \times 6 = 18$
2. You need five decimal digits in your answer, so tack on three zeros: 00018
3. Put the decimal point at the front of the number (which is five digits in from the right): .00018

You can practice multiplying decimals with these. Answers are at the end of the lesson.

_____ **50.** 0.12×0.05

_____ **51.** 0.053×6.4

_____ **52.** 38.1×0.0184

_____ **53.** Joe earns $14.50 per hour as a painting instructor. Last week, he worked 37.5 hours. How much money did he earn that week?
a. $518.00
b. $518.50
c. $525.00
d. $536.50
e. $543.75

_____ **54.** Coffee costs $2.80 a pound, and Diane has just enough money to buy $3\frac{1}{2}$ pounds. How much money does Diane have?
a. $7.75
b. $8.50
c. $8.63
d. $9.00
e. $9.80

Dividing Decimals

To divide a decimal by a whole number, set up the division ($8\overline{)\,.256}$) and immediately bring the decimal point straight up into the answer ($8\overline{)\,.256}$). Then divide as you would normally divide whole numbers:

Example:
$$
\begin{array}{r}
.032 \\
8\overline{)\,.256} \\
\underline{0} \\
25 \\
\underline{24} \\
16 \\
\underline{16} \\
0
\end{array}
$$

To divide any number by a decimal, there is an extra step to perform before you can divide. Move the decimal point to the very right of the number you're dividing by, counting the number of places you're moving it. Then move the decimal point the same number of places to the right in the number you're dividing into. In other words, first change the problem to one in which you're dividing by a whole number.

Example: $.06\overline{)\,1.218}$

1. There are two decimal digits in .06. Move the decimal point two places to the right in both numbers and move the decimal point straight up into the answer: $.06\overline{)\,1.21\,8}$

2. Divide using the new numbers:
$$
\begin{array}{r}
20.3 \\
6\overline{)\,121.8} \\
\underline{12} \\
01 \\
\underline{00} \\
18 \\
\underline{18} \\
0
\end{array}
$$

Under certain conditions, you have to tack on zeros to the right of the last decimal digit in the number you're dividing into:

- if there aren't enough digits for you to move the decimal point to the right, or
- if the answer doesn't come out evenly when you do the division, or
- if you're dividing a whole number by a decimal, then you'll have to tack on the decimal point as well as some zeros

Try your skills on these division problems. Answers are at the end of the lesson.

_____ **55.** $7\overline{)9.8}$

_____ **56.** $0.2\overline{)1.01}$

_____ **57.** $0.05\overline{)28.6}$

_____ **58.** $0.14\overline{)196}$

_____ **59.** If James Worthington drove his new motorcycle 92.4 miles in 2.1 hours, what was his average speed in miles per hour?
  a. 41 mph
  b. 44 mph
  c. 90.3 mph
  d. 94.5 mph
  e. 194.04 mph

_____ **60.** Mary Sanders walked a total of 18.6 miles in four days. On average, how many miles did she walk each day?
  a. 4.15 miles
  b. 4.60 miles
  c. 4.65 miles
  d. 22.60 miles
  e. 74.40 miles

Percents

What Is a Percent?

A percent is a *special kind of fraction* or *part of something*. The bottom number (the *denominator*) is always 100. For example, 17% is the same as $\frac{17}{100}$. Literally, the word *percent* means *per 100 parts*. The root *cent* means 100: A *century* is 100 years and there are 100 *cents* in a dollar. Thus, 17% means 17 parts out of 100. Fractions can also be expressed as decimals—17% is also equivalent to .17, which is 17 hundredths.

You come into contact with percents every day. Sales tax, interest, and discounts are just a few common examples. If you're shaky on fractions, you may want to review the fraction section before reading further.

Changing a Decimal to a Percent and Vice Versa

To change a decimal to a percent, move the decimal point two places to the **right** and tack on a percent sign (%) at the end. If the decimal point moves to the very right of the number, you don't have to write the decimal point. If there aren't enough places to move the decimal point, add zeros on the **right** before moving the decimal point.

To change a percent to a decimal, drop off the percent sign and move the decimal point two places to the **left**. If there aren't enough places to move the decimal point, add zeros on the **left** before moving the decimal point.

Try changing these decimals to percents. Answers are at the end of the lesson.

_____ **61.** 0.45

_____ **62.** 0.035

_____ **63.** $0.16\frac{2}{3}$

Now change these percents to decimals.

_____ **64.** 18%

_____ **65.** $87\frac{1}{2}$%

_____ **66.** 250%

Changing a Fraction to a Percent and Vice Versa

There are two techniques to change a fraction to a percent. Each is illustrated by changing the fraction $\frac{1}{4}$ to a percent:

Technique 1: Multiply the fraction by 100%.
Multiply $\frac{1}{4}$ by 100%:

$$\frac{1}{\underset{1}{4}} \times \frac{\overset{25}{\cancel{100\%}}}{1} = 25\%$$

Technique 2: Divide the fraction's bottom number into the top number; then move the decimal point two places to the **right** and tack on a percent sign (%).
Divide 4 into 1 and move the decimal point two places to the right:

$$4\overline{)1.00} \quad .25 = 25\%$$
$$\quad .25$$

To change a percent to a fraction, remove the percent sign and write the number over 100. Then reduce if possible.

Example: Change 4% to a fraction.

1. Remove the % and write the fraction 4 over 100: $\frac{4}{100}$

2. Reduce: $\frac{4 \div 4}{100 \div 4} = \frac{1}{25}$

Example: Change $16\frac{2}{3}$% to a fraction.

1. Remove the % and write the fraction $16\frac{2}{3}$ over 100: $\frac{16\frac{2}{3}}{100}$

2. Since a fraction means "top number divided by bottom number," rewrite the fraction as a division problem: $16\frac{2}{3} \div 100$

3. Change the mixed number $(16\frac{2}{3})$ to an improper fraction $(\frac{50}{3})$: $\frac{50}{3} \div \frac{100}{1}$

4. Flip the second fraction $(\frac{100}{1})$ and multiply: $\frac{\overset{1}{\cancel{50}}}{3} \times \frac{1}{\underset{2}{\cancel{100}}} = \frac{1}{6}$

Try changing these fractions to percents. Answers are at the end of the lesson.

_____ **67.** $\frac{1}{8}$

_____ **68.** $\frac{13}{25}$

_____ **69.** $\frac{7}{12}$

Now change these percents to fractions.

_____ **70.** 95%

_____ **71.** $37\frac{1}{2}$%

_____ **72.** 125%

Sometimes, it is more convenient to work with a percentage as a fraction or a decimal. Rather than have to *calculate* the equivalent fraction or decimal, consider memorizing the following conversion table. This will increase your efficiency on the math test, and it will also be practical for real-life situations.

Percent Word Problems

Word problems involving percents come in three main varieties:

- Find a percent of a whole.
  Example: What is 30% of 40?
- Find what percent one number is of another number.
  Example: 12 is what percent of 40?
- Find the whole when the percent of it is given.
  Example: 12 is 30% of what number?

Each variety has its own approach, but there is a single shortcut formula you can use to solve each of these:

$$\frac{is}{of} = \frac{\%}{100}$$

The **is** is the number that usually follows or is just before the word **is** in the question.

The **of** is the number that usually follows the word **of** in the question.

The **%** is the number that is in front of the **%** or **percent** in the question.

Or you may think of the shortcut formula as:

$$\frac{part}{whole} = \frac{\%}{100}$$

CONVERSION TABLE		
DECIMAL	**%**	**FRACTION**
.25	25%	$\frac{1}{4}$
.50	50%	$\frac{1}{2}$
.75	75%	$\frac{3}{4}$
.10	10%	$\frac{1}{10}$
.20	20%	$\frac{1}{15}$
.40	40%	$\frac{2}{5}$
.60	60%	$\frac{3}{5}$
.80	80%	$\frac{4}{5}$
$.33\overline{3}$	$33\frac{1}{3}\%$	$\frac{1}{3}$
$.66\overline{6}$	$66\frac{2}{3}\%$	$\frac{2}{3}$

To solve each of the three varieties, we're going to use the fact that the **cross-products** are equal. The cross-products are the products of the numbers diagonally across from each other. Remembering that *product* means *multiply*, here's how to create the cross-products for the percent shortcut:

$$\frac{part}{whole} = \frac{\%}{100}$$
$$part \times 100 = whole \times \%$$

Here's how to use the shortcut with cross-products.

■ Find a percent of a whole.
What is 30% of 40?
30 is the % and 40 is the *of* number: $\frac{is}{40} = \frac{30}{100}$
Cross multiply and solve for *is*:

$$is \times 100 = 40 \times 30$$
$$is \times 100 = 1{,}200$$
$$\mathbf{12} \times 100 = 1{,}200$$

Thus, **12** *is* 30% of 40.

■ Find what percent one number is of another number.
12 is what percent of 40?
12 is the *is* number and 40 is the *of* number: $\frac{12}{40} = \frac{\%}{100}$
Cross multiply and solve for %:

$$12 \times 100 =$$
$$40 \times \%$$
$$1{,}200 = 40 \times \%$$
$$1{,}200 = 40 \times \mathbf{30}$$

Thus, 12 is **30%** of 40.

■ Find the whole when the percent of it is given.
12 is 30% of what number?
12 is the *is* number and 30 is the %: $\frac{12}{of} = \frac{30}{100}$
Cross multiply and solve for the *of* number:

$$12 \times 100 =$$
$$of \times 30$$
$$1{,}200 = of \times 30$$
$$1{,}200 = \mathbf{40} \times 30$$

Thus, 12 is 30% *of* **40**.

You can use the same technique to find the percent increase or decrease. The *is* number is the amount of increase or decrease, and the *of* number is the original amount.

Example: If a merchant puts his $20 hats on sale for $15, by what percent does he decrease the selling price?

1. Calculate the decrease, the *is* number: $20 - $15 = $5
2. The *of* number is the original amount, $20.
3. Set up the equation and solve for *of* by cross multiplying: $\frac{5}{20} = \frac{\%}{100}$
$$5 \times 100 = 20 \times \%$$
$$500 = 20 \times \%$$
$$500 = 20 \times \mathbf{25}$$

4. Thus, the selling price is decreased by **25%**.
If the merchant later raises the price of the hats from $15 back to $20, don't be fooled into thinking that the percent increase is also 25%! It's actually more, because the increase amount of $5 is now based on a lower original price of only $15:

$$\frac{5}{15} = \frac{\%}{100}$$
$$5 \times 100 = 15 \times \%$$
$$500 = 15 \times \%$$
$$500 = 15 \times \mathbf{33\frac{1}{3}}$$

Thus, the selling price is increased by **33%**.

Find a percent of a whole. Answers are at the end of the lesson.

_____ **73.** 3% of 20

_____ **74.** 18.2% of 50

_____ **75.** $37\frac{1}{2}$% of 100

_____ **76.** 125% of 60

Find what percent one number is of another number.

_____ **77.** 10 is what % of 20?

_____ **78.** 6 is what % of 24?

_____ **79.** 12 is what % of 4?

Find the whole when the percent of it is given.

_____ **80.** 15% of what number is 15?

_____ **81.** $37\frac{1}{2}$% of what number is 3?

_____ **82.** 8% of what number is 20?

Now try your percent skills on some real-life problems.

_____ **83.** Peaches were on sale last week for $1.35 a pound—10% off the normal price. What is the normal price?
a. $1.40
b. $1.43
c. $1.50
d. $1.62
e. $1.75

_____ **84.** Thirteen percent of the students at Jennie's high school got A's last semester. There are 300 students. How many got A's?
a. 28 students
b. 32 students
c. 39 students
d. 41 students
e. 56 students

_____ **85.** Ted finished reading seven pages of his homework, which was 28% of the assignment. How many pages had been assigned?
a. 18 pages
b. 23 pages
c. 25 pages
d. 31 pages
e. 36 pages

_____ **86.** Sam's Shoe Store put all its merchandise on sale for 20% off. If Jason saved $10 by purchasing one pair of shoes during the sale, what was the original price of the shoes before the sale?
a. $12
b. $20
c. $40
d. $50
e. $70

Averages

What Is an Average?

An *average*, also called an arithmetic *mean*, is a number that *typifies* a group of numbers, a measure of central tendency. You come into contact with averages on a regular basis: your bowling average, the average grade on a test, the average number of hours you study per week.

To calculate an average, add up the number of items being averaged and divide by the number of items.

Example: What is the average of 6, 10, and 20?
Solution: Add the three numbers together and divide by 3: $\frac{6 + 10 + 20}{3} = 12$

Try these average questions. Answers are at the end of the lesson.

_____ **87.** Bob's bowling scores for the last five games were 180, 182, 184, 186, and 188. What was his average bowling score?

    a. 182

    b. 183

    c. 184

    d. 185

    e. 186

_____ **88.** Chester drove from Easton to Weston, a distance of 28 miles, in 30 minutes. What was his average speed in miles per hour?

    a. 37 mph

    b. 48 mph

    c. 56 mph

    d. 62 mph

    e. 65 mph

_____ **89.** There are 10 females and 20 males in the lifeguarding course. If the females achieved an average score of 85 and the males achieved an average score of 95, what was the class average? (Hint: Don't fall for the trap of taking the average of 85 and 95; there are more 95s being averaged than 85s, so the average is closer to 95.)

    a. $90\frac{2}{3}$

    b. $91\frac{2}{3}$

    c. 92

    d. $92\frac{2}{3}$

    e. 95

Length, Weight, and Time Units

The questions involving length, weight, and time on the math test will ask you either to convert between different measurement units or to add or subtract measurement values.

Converting

You may encounter questions that ask you to convert between units of measurement in length, weight, or time. To convert from a smaller unit (like inches) to a larger unit (like feet), divide the smaller unit by the number of those units necessary to equal the larger unit. To convert from a larger unit to a smaller unit, multiply the larger unit by the conversion number.

    Example: Convert 36 inches to feet.

- Since 1 ft. = 12 in., divide 36 by 12: $36 \div 12 = 3$ ft.

    Example: Convert 4 feet to inches.

- Since 1 ft. = 12 in., multiply 4 by 12: $4 \times 12 = 48$ in.

    Example: Convert 32 ounces to pounds.

- Since 1 lb. = 16 oz., divide 32 by 16: $32 \div 16 = 2$ lb.

    Example: Convert 2 pounds to ounces.

- Since 1 lb. = 16 oz., multiply 2 by 16: $2 \times 16 = 32$ oz.

    Example: Convert 180 minutes to hours.

- Since 1 hr. = 60 min., divide 180 by 60: $180 \div 60 = 3$ hr.

    Example: Convert 4 hours to minutes.

- Since 1 hr. = 60 min., multiply 4 by 60: $4 \times 60 = 240$ min.

Now try some on your own. Convert as indicated. Answers are at the end of the lesson.

_____ **90.** 1 gal. = _____ qts.

_____ **91.** 36 in. = _____ yds.

_____ **92.** 18 in. = _____ ft.

_____ **93.** 3 hr. = _____ min.

Calculating with Length, Weight, and Time Units

You may be asked on the test to add or subtract length, weight, and time units. The only trick to doing this correctly is to remember to convert the smaller units to larger units and vice versa, if need be.

Example: Find the perimeter of the figure shown:

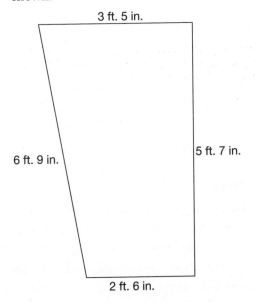

To add the lengths, add each column of length units separately:

$$
\begin{array}{rr}
5 \text{ ft.} & 7 \text{ in.} \\
2 \text{ ft.} & 6 \text{ in.} \\
6 \text{ ft.} & 9 \text{ in.} \\
+ \ 3 \text{ ft.} & 5 \text{ in.} \\
\hline
\mathbf{16 \text{ ft.}} & \mathbf{27 \text{ in.}}
\end{array}
$$

Since 27 inches is more than 1 foot, the total of **16 ft. 27 in.** must be simplified:

- Convert 27 inches to feet and inches:
  $27 \ in. \times \frac{1 \ ft.}{12 \ in.} = \frac{27}{12} \ ft. = 2\frac{3}{12} \ ft. = 2 \ ft. \ 3 \ in.$
- Add: 16 ft.
         $+ \ 2$ ft. 3 in.
         18 ft. 3 in.   Thus, the perimeter is **18 feet 3 inches.**

Finding the length of a line segment may require subtracting lengths of different units. For example, find the length of line segment $\overline{AB}$:

To subtract the lengths, subtract each column of length units separately, starting with the rightmost column.

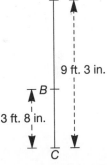

$$
\begin{array}{r}
9 \text{ ft.} \quad 3 \text{ in.} \\
- \ 3 \text{ ft.} \quad 8 \text{ in.} \\
\hline
\end{array}
$$

Warning: You can't subtract 8 inches from 3 inches because 8 is larger than 3! As in regular subtraction, you have to *borrow* 1 from the column on the left. However, borrowing *1 foot* is the same as borrowing *12 inches;* adding the borrowed 12 inches to the 3 inches gives 15 inches. Thus:

$$
\begin{array}{r}
\overset{8}{\cancel{9}} \text{ ft.} \ \overset{\overset{15}{\frown}}{\cancel{3}} \text{ in.} \\
- \ 3 \text{ ft.} \ 8 \text{ in.} \\
\hline
\mathbf{5 \text{ ft.} \ 7 \text{ in.}}
\end{array}
$$

Thus, the length of $\overline{AB}$ is **5 feet 7 inches.**

Add and simplify. Answers are at the end of this lesson.

94.   4 hr. 24 min.
        + 1 hr. 58 min.

95.   3 ft. 11 in.
        + 2 ft. 3 in.

Subtract and simplify.

96.   6 lb. 3 oz.
        − 1 lb. 12 oz.

97. 14 ft. 6 in.
        − 6 ft. 8 in.

Now try these time word problems.

_____ **98.** Betty walked 45 minutes each day, Monday through Friday. She also walked on Saturday, bringing her walking time to $4\frac{1}{2}$ hours for the whole week. How long did Betty walk on Saturday?

a. $\frac{1}{4}$ hour

b. $\frac{2}{3}$ hour

c. $\frac{1}{2}$ hour

d. $\frac{3}{4}$ hour

e. 1 hour

_____ **99.** Rhonda worked a total of 3 hours 30 minutes on an art project, and she spent 50% more time on her biology homework. How much time did she work on biology?

a. 4.75 minutes

b. 5.25 hours

c. 5.5 hours

d. 5.75 hours

e. 6 hours

Algebra

Popular topics for algebra questions on the math test include:

- solving equations
- positive and negative numbers
- algebraic expressions
- equations with two variables

What Is Algebra?

Algebra is a way to express and solve problems using numbers and symbols. These symbols are called *unknowns* or *variables*, letters of the alphabet that are used to represent numbers.

For example, let's say you're asked to find out what number, when added to three, gives you a total of five. Using algebra, you could express the problem as $x + 3 = 5$. The variable x represents the number you're trying to find.

Here's another example, but this one uses only variables. To find the distance traveled, multiply the rate of travel (speed) by the amount of time traveled: $d = r \times t$. The variable d stands for *distance*, r stands for *rate* of travel, and t stands for *time*.

In algebra, the variables may take on different values. In other words, they *vary*, and that's why they're called *variables*.

Operations

Algebra uses the same operations as arithmetic: addition, subtraction, multiplication, and division. In arithmetic, we might say $3 + 4 = 7$, while in algebra, we would talk about two numbers whose values we don't know that add up to 7, or $x + y = 7$. Here's how each operation translates to algebra:

ALGEBRAIC OPERATIONS	
The sum of two numbers	$a + b$
The difference of two numbers	$a - b$
The product of two numbers	$a \times b$ or $a \cdot b$ or ab
The quotient of two numbers	$\frac{a}{b}$

Equations

An *equation* is a mathematical sentence stating that two quantities are equal. Here are some examples:

1. $x + 5 = 8$
2. $2x = 10$

The idea is to find a replacement for the unknown that will make the sentence true. That's called *solving* the equation. Thus, in the first example, $x = 3$ because $3 + 5 = 8$. In the second example, $x = 5$ because $2 \times 5 = 10$.

Sometimes you can solve an equation by inspection, as with the previous examples. Other equations may be more complicated and require a step-by-step solution. Look at these examples:

3. $3x + 4x = 14$
4. $6x = 4x + 8$
5. $4x + 5 = 2x - 3$

The general approach is to consider an equation like a balance scale, with both sides equally balanced. Essentially, whatever you do to one side, you must also do to the other side to maintain the balance. Thus, if you were to add 2 to the left side, you'd also have to add 2 to the right side.

Let's apply this *balance* concept to examples 3, 4, and 5. Remembering that we want to solve for x,

we must somehow rearrange the equation so the x is isolated on one side. Its value will then be on the other side.

Here's how it works:

1. The two terms with x must be added first:

$$3x + 4x = 14$$
$$7x = 14$$

Now, divide by 7:

$$\frac{7x}{7} = \frac{14}{7}$$
$$x = 2$$

2. There are x's on both sides of the equal sign, so move $4x$ to the other side by subtracting:

$$6x = 4x + 8$$
$$\underline{-4x \quad -4x}$$
$$2x = 0 + 8$$
$$2x = 8$$

Now, divide both sides by 2:

$$\frac{2x}{2} = \frac{8}{2}$$
$$x = 4$$

3. Move $2x$ to the left side by subtracting:

$$4x + 5 = 2x - 3$$
$$\underline{-2x \quad -2x}$$
$$2x + 5 = 0 \ -3$$
$$2x + 5 = \quad -3$$

Now, subtract 5 from both sides:

$$\underline{-5 \qquad -5}$$
$$2x + 0 = -8$$
$$2x = -8$$

Divide each side by 2:

$$\frac{2x}{2} = -\frac{8}{2}$$
$$x = -4$$

Notice that each operation in the original equations was undone by using the inverse operation. That is, addition was undone by subtraction, and division was undone by multiplication. In general, each operation can be undone by its *inverse*:

ALGEBRAIC INVERSES			
OPERATION	**INVERSE**	**OPERATION**	**INVERSE**
Addition	Subtraction	Subtraction	Addition
Multiplication	Division	Division	Multiplication
Square	Square Root	Square Root	Square

After you solve an equation, check your work by plugging the answer back into the original equation to make sure it balances. Take example 5 on the previous page. Let's see what happens when we plug -4 in for x:

$$4x + 5 = 2x - 3 \qquad ?$$
$$4(-4) + 5 = 2(-4) - 3 \qquad ?$$
$$-16 + 5 = -8 - 3 \qquad ?$$
$$-11 = -11 \qquad \checkmark$$

Solve each equation. Answers are at the end of this lesson.

_____**100.** $x - 8 = 20$

_____**101.** $6x = 24$

_____**102.** $3x + 6 = 18$

_____**103.** $\frac{1}{4}x = 7$

Positive and Negative Numbers

Positive and negative numbers, also known as *signed* numbers, are best shown as points along the number line:

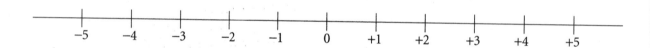

Numbers to the left of zero are *negative* and those to the right are *positive*. Zero is neither negative nor positive. If a number is written without a sign, it is assumed to be *positive*. Notice that when you are on the negative side of the number line, numbers with bigger values are actually smaller. For example, -5 is *less than* -2. You come into contact with negative numbers more often than you might think; for example, very cold temperatures are recorded as negative numbers.

As you move to the right along the number line, the values get larger. Mathematically, to indicate that one number, say 4, is *greater than* another number, say -2, the *greater than* sign ($>$) is used:

$$4 > -2$$

On the other hand, to say that -2 is *less than* 4, we use the *less than* sign ($<$):

$$-2 < 4$$

Arithmetic with Positive and Negative Numbers

The following table illustrates the rules for doing arithmetic with signed numbers. Notice that when a negative number follows an operation (as it does in the second example in the table), it is enclosed in parentheses to avoid confusion.

When more than one arithmetic operation appears, you must know the correct sequence in which to perform the operations. For example, do you know what to do first to calculate $2 + 3 \times 4$? You're right if you said, "Multiply first." The correct answer is 14. If you add first, you'll get the wrong answer of 20! The correct sequence of operations is:

1. Parentheses
2. Exponents
3. Multiplication and Division
4. Addition and Subtraction

If you remember this saying, you'll know the order of operations: **Please Excuse My Dear Aunt Sally.**

Even when signed numbers appear in an equation, the step-by-step solution works exactly as it does for positive numbers. You just have to remember the arithmetic rules for negative numbers. For example, let's solve $-14x + 2 = 5$.

1. Subtract 2 from both sides:

$$-14x + 2 = -5$$
$$\underline{\quad - 2 \quad -2}$$
$$-14x \quad = -7$$

2. Divide both sides by -14:

$$\frac{-14x}{-14} = \frac{-7}{-14}$$
$$x = \frac{1}{2}$$

RULE	EXAMPLE
ADDITION	
If both numbers have the same sign, just add them. The answer has the same sign as the numbers being added.	$3 + 5) = 8$ $-3 + (-5) = -8$
If both numbers have different signs, subtract the smaller number from the larger. The answer has the same sign as the larger number.	$-3 + 5 = 2$ $3 + (-5) = -2$
If both numbers are the same but have opposite signs, the sum is zero.	$3 + (-3) = 0$
SUBTRACTION	
To subtract one number from another, change the sign of the number to be subtracted and then add as described above.	$3 - 5 = 3 + (-5) = -2$ $-3 - 5 = -3 + (-5) = -8$ $-3 - (-5) = -3 + 5 = 2$

RULE	EXAMPLE
MULTIPLICATION	
Multiply the numbers together. If both numbers have the same sign, the answer is positive; otherwise, it is negative.	$3 \times 5 = 15$ $-3 \times (-5) = 15$ $-3 \times 5 = -15$ $3 \times (-5) = -15$
If one number is zero, the answer is zero.	$3 \times 0 = 0$
DIVISION	
Divide the numbers. If both numbers have the same sign, the answer is positive; otherwise, it is negative.	$15 \div 3 = 5$ $-15 \div (-3) = 5$ $15 \div (-3) = -5$ $-15 \div 3 = -5$
If the top number is zero, the answer is zero.	$0 \div 3 = 0$

Now try these problems with signed numbers. Answers are at the end of this lesson.

_____**104.** $(-2)(-4) =$

_____**105.** $-1 - (-4) =$

_____**106.** $1 - 3(-4) =$

_____**107.** $-3x + 6 = -18$

_____**108.** $-\frac{x}{4} + 3 = -7$

Squares and Square Roots

It's not uncommon to see squares and square roots on standardized math tests, especially on questions that involve right triangles.

To find the **square** of a number, multiply that number by itself. For example, the square of 4 is 16, because $4 \times 4 = 16$. Mathematically, this is expressed as:

$$4^2 = 16$$
4 squared equals 16.

To find the **square root** of a number, ask yourself, "What number times itself equals the given number?" For example, the square root of 16 is 4 because $4 \times 4 = 16$. Mathematically, this is expressed as:

$$\sqrt{16} = 4$$
The square root of 16 is 4.

Certain squares and square roots tend to appear more often than others on standardized tests, so the best course is to memorize the most common ones.

COMMON SQUARES AND SQUARE ROOTS					
SQUARES			**SQUARE ROOTS**		
$1^2 = 1$	$7^2 = 49$	$13^2 = 169$	$\sqrt{1} = 1$	$\sqrt{49} = 7$	$\sqrt{169} = 13$
$2^2 = 4$	$8^2 = 64$	$14^2 = 196$	$\sqrt{4} = 2$	$\sqrt{64} = 8$	$\sqrt{196} = 14$
$3^2 = 9$	$9^2 = 81$	$15^2 = 225$	$\sqrt{9} = 3$	$\sqrt{81} = 9$	$\sqrt{225} = 15$
$4^2 = 16$	$10^2 = 100$	$16^2 = 256$	$\sqrt{16} = 4$	$\sqrt{100} = 10$	$\sqrt{256} = 16$
$5^2 = 25$	$11^2 = 121$	$20^2 = 400$	$\sqrt{25} = 5$	$\sqrt{121} = 11$	$\sqrt{400} = 20$
$6^2 = 36$	$12^2 = 144$	$25^2 = 625$	$\sqrt{36} = 6$	$\sqrt{144} = 12$	$\sqrt{625} = 25$

Find the following square roots. Answers are at the end of the lesson.

_____**109.** $\sqrt{64}$

_____**110.** $\sqrt{256}$

_____**111.** $-\sqrt{100}$

Evaluating Algebraic Expressions

An algebraic expression is a group of numbers, unknowns, and arithmetic operations, like: $3x - 2y$. This one may be translated as "three times some number minus two times another number." To *evaluate* an algebraic expression, replace each variable with its value. For example, if $x = 5$ and $y = 4$, we would evaluate $3x - 2y$ as follows:

$$3(5) - 2(4) = 15 - 8 = 7$$

Evaluate these expressions.

_____**112.** $4a + 3b$; $a = 2$ and $b = -1$

_____**113.** $3mn - 4m + 2n$; $m = 3$ and $n = -3$

_____**114.** $-2x - \frac{1}{2}y + 4z$; $x = 5$, $y = -4$, and $z = 6$

_____**115.** The volume of a cylinder is given by the formula $V = \pi r^2 h$, where r is the radius of the base and h is the height of the cylinder. What is the volume of a cylinder with a base radius of 3 and height of 4? (Leave π in your answer.)

Simplifying Algebraic Expressions

If an algebraic expression contains terms with the same variables, the expression can be simplified by combining the like terms. Like terms must have the same variables raised to exactly the same powers. For example:

$3x$ and $4x$ are like terms.
$2ab$ and $7ab$ are like terms.
$3x^2$ and $21x^2$ are like terms.
$3x$ and $4y$ are **not** like terms.
$3x$ and $7y^2$ are **not** like terms.

Example: Simplify $3x + 4y - x + 5y$.

1. Add the x terms: $2x + 4y + 5y$
2. Now add the y terms: $2x + 9y$

Combining Two Algebraic Expressions

Combining algebraic expressions is not hard, as long as you remember to add and subtract the like terms.

Example: Add $(5ab - 7ab^2 + 3a^2b) +$
$(9ab - a^2b)$.

1. Add $5ab$ and $9ab$, since they are like terms:
$(14ab - 7ab^2 + 3a^2b)$
$+ (-a^2b)$

2. Now combine $3a^2b$ and $-a^2b$:
$14ab - 7ab^2 + 2a^2b$
That is all that can be done, since the three remaining terms are **not** like terms.

Example: Subtract $(3x^2 + 4x - 4) - (x^2 - 3x + 7)$. (**Hint:** Subtracting is really adding using opposite signs.)

1. Change the middle minus sign to a plus sign and change all of the signs in the second expression:
$(3x^2 + 4x - 4) +$
$(-x^2 + 3x - 7)$
2. Add $3x^2$ and $-x^2$:
$(2x^2 + 4x - 4) +$
$(3x - 7)$
3. Next, add $4x$ and $3x$:
$(2x^2 + 7x - 4) +$
(-7)
4. Last, combine -4 and -7: $2x^2 + 7x - 11$

Try a few problems on your own. Answers are at the end of the lesson.

_____**116.** $12xy + 9xy$

_____**117.** $4y^2z - 7y^2z + 10$

_____**118.** $(3x^2 - 11y^2) + (-5x^2 + 5y^2)$

_____**119.** $(4a^2 - 6ab + 9b^2) - (3a^2 + 5ab - 7b^2)$

Multiplying Algebraic Expressions

The key to multiplying algebraic expressions correctly is knowing how to treat exponents.

Exponents

An *exponent* is a raised number (superscript) after a number or a variable. It means that the number or variable is multiplied times itself a certain number of times. For example:

$3^2 = 3 \times 3$, or 9
$y^3 = y \times y \times y$, or $(y)(y)(y)$

If two variables with exponents are **multiplied**, the rule is: **Add the exponents.** For example:

$(y^2)(y^3) = (y \times y)(y \times y \times y) = y^{(2+3)} = y^5$

If two variables with exponents are **divided**, the rule is: **Subtract the exponents.** For example:

$y^5 \div y^2 = y^{(5-2)} = y^3$
$x^5 \div x^3 = x^{(5-3)} = x^2$

To multiply terms with a mix of variables and numbers, multiply the numbers and then each variable by itself.

Example: Multiply $(4x^2y^3)(7x^4y^6)$.

1. First multiply the numbers: $28(x^2y^3)(x^4y^6)$
2. Then multiply the x's, adding the exponents:
$28x^{(2+4)}(y^3)(y^6)$
$28x^6(y^3)(y^6)$
3. Now multiply the y's, again adding exponents:
$28x^6y^{(3+6)}$
$28x^6y^9$

Try a few problems on your own. Answers are at the end of the lesson.

_____**120.** $(y^2)(y^5)$

_____**121.** $(3a^3)(5a^2)$

_____**122.** $(7x^2y^2)(5xy^3)$

Multiplying by a Binomial

When multiplying a term such as 6 by a binomial like $x + y$, it is important to remember that you must multiply the 6 by both the x and y, because $6(x + y)$ really means (6 times x + 6 times y) or $6x + 6y$. The 6 must be *distributed* to both the x and the y. **Remember this rule:** An expression must always be multiplied times *everything* inside the parentheses, *one term at a time.*

Example: Multiply $4x(2x^2 + 7x)$.

1. First multiply $4x$ times $2x^2$: $8x^3$
2. Next, multiply $4x$ times $7x$: $28x^2$
3. This leaves you with: $8x^3 + 28x^2$

Example: Multiply $6x^2y^3(4xy + 8xy^2)$.

1. First multiply $6x^2y^3$
   times $4xy$: $24x^3y^4$
2. Next, multiply $6x^2y^3$
   times $8xy^2$: $48x^3y^5$
3. This leaves you with: $24x^3y^4 + 48x^3y^5$

Try a few problems on your own. Answers are at the end of the lesson.

_____**123.** $3x(2x - 7)$

_____**124.** $4a^2(a + 2a^2)$

_____**125.** $5xy^2(2x^2y + 3xy^2)$

Factoring

The opposite operation of multiplication is *factoring*. In the previous example, since:

$$4x(2x^2 + 7x) = 8x^3 + 28x^2 \quad \text{(multiplying)}$$

It is also true that:

$$8x^3 + 28x^2 = 4x(2x^2 + 7x) \quad \text{(factoring)}$$

In order to factor, you need to find two or more quantities that, when multiplied, equal the original quantity. Those quantities are called *common factors*. In the previous example, $4x$ is the common factor. To factor out a common factor:

1. Find the largest common monomial (factor) that will divide into each term.
2. Divide the original polynomial by this factor. The result will be a polynomial.

   Example: In the expression $2x + 4$, 2 divides into both $2x$ and 4; in other words, a 2 can be *factored out.*

   $2x + 4 = 2(x + 2)$ because $2(x + 2) = 2x + 4$

   Example: Factor $7x^2y + 14xy^2$.

   Since $7xy$ is a common factor: $7x^2y + 14xy^2 =$
   $\qquad\qquad\qquad\qquad\qquad\qquad 7xy(x + 2y)$

Try a few factoring problems of your own. Answers are at the end of the lesson.

_____**126.** $3x + 9$

_____**127.** $4y^2 + 6y$

_____**128.** $10a^2b + 15a^3b^2$

Dividing Algebraic Expressions

When dividing algebraic expressions, remember to divide the numbers first and then divide each variable, subtracting the exponents:

Example: $\frac{9x^2}{3x}$

1. First divide the 9 by 3: $\quad \frac{3x^2}{x}$
2. Then divide the variable: $\quad 3x^{(2-1)} = 3x^1 = 3x$

Example: $\frac{18a^2b^5}{6ab^2}$

1. First divide the 18 by 6: $\quad \frac{3a^2b^5}{ab^2}$
2. Then divide a^2 by a: $\quad a^{(2-1)} = a^1 = a$
3. Next, divide b^5 by b^2: $\quad b^{(5-2)} = b^3$
4. Put it together: $\quad \frac{18a^2b^5}{6ab^2} = 3ab^3$

Try a few factoring problems of your own. Answers are at the end of the lesson.

_____**129.** $\frac{3x^2}{3x}$

_____**130.** $\frac{20y^4}{5y^2}$

_____**131.** $\frac{12a^4b^2}{2a^2b}$

Dividing with Binomials

If an expression with more than one term is being divided by another expression, be sure to divide each term in the numerator.

Example: $\frac{4x^2y^2 - 8x^3y^2}{4xy}$

1. First divide $4x^2y^2$ by $4xy$: $\quad 4 \div 4 = 1$
$x^2 \div x = x$
$y^2 \div y = y$
That leaves: $\quad xy$
2. Now divide $-8x^3y^2$ by $4xy$: $\quad -8 \div 4 = -2$
$x^3 \div x = x^2$
$y^2 \div y = y$
That leaves: $\quad -2x^2y$
3. Put it all together: $\quad \frac{4x^2y^2 - 8x^3y^2}{4xy} =$
$xy - 2x^2y$

Try these division problems on your own. Answers are at the end of this lesson.

_____**132.** $\frac{32z - 8}{4}$

_____**133.** $\frac{15x^3y^4 - 9x^2y^2}{3x^2y}$

Equations with Two Variables

An equation with two variables looks like this: $3x + 2y = 6$. There are many values for x and y that will make this equation true. Values for x and y that make an equation *true* will make both sides equal to each other. For example:

- If $x = 4$ and $y = -3$, then $3(4) + 2(-3) = 12 - 6 = 6$
- or, if $x = 2$ and $y = 0$, then $3(2) + 2(0) = 6 + 0 = 6$
- or, if $x = 0$ and $y = 3$, then $3(0) + 2(3) = 0 + 6 = 6$

The values given to x and y in the three previous examples are called *ordered pairs*. An ordered pair is said to be a *solution* to an equation if the values make the equation true. For example, in the first example, $12 - 6$ **does** equal 6, so the ordered pair $(4,-3)$ is a solution. When an ordered pair is written, the x value is always given first and the y value second.

Example: $(1,2)$ is said to be a solution of $3x + y = 5$, since 1 substituted for x and 2 substituted for y gives: $3(1) + 2 = 5$ and $5 = 5$.

Try a few ordered pair questions. Answers are at the end of the lesson.

_____**134.** Is $(2,-5)$ a solution to the equation: $2x + 2y = -6$?

_____**135.** Is $(3,0)$ a solution to the equation: $2x + 4y = 7$?

_____**136.** Is $(0,6)$ a solution to the equation: $2x + 6y = 12$?

Equation of a Line

If you plot all the points that satisfy an equation such as $2x + y = 8$ on a grid with an x- and y-axis, the points will all lie on one line. Therefore, the equation $2x + y = 8$ is actually the *equation of a line*.

When a question asks you whether a graphed line matches a certain equation, see if the points on the line (the x and y values of the points on the line) satisfy the equation (make it true).

> **Example:** In the following line, point A on the line has the coordinates (2,4), which satisfies the equation $2x + y = 8$, since $2(2) + 4 = 8$. Point B, (3,2), also satisfies the equation: $2(3) + 2 = 8$. Therefore, you can say that the line has the equation $2x + y = 8$.

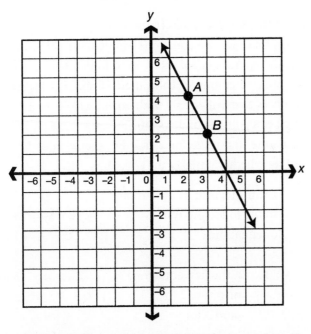

If a question asks you to find the equation of a graphed line, you should use two points on the line and plug them into each equation. The easiest points to use are points that lie on the integer corners of the grid (that fall on the x- and y-axis).

Example: Which of the following is the equation of the line shown in the graph?

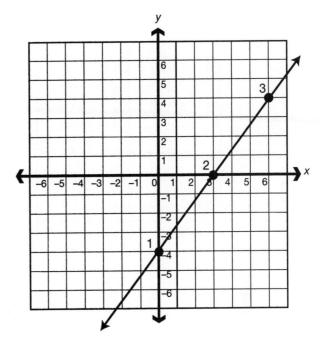

a. $x + y = 8$
b. $2x + y = 4$
c. $4x - 3y = 12$

First, substitute the values for at least two points into each equation to see which one is true. Good points to use are the points labeled 1 and 2. These are called the *intercepts* because they lie on the intersection of the line and the x or y axis. Point 1 has the coordinates (0,–4), and point 2 has the coordinates (3,0). You could also use point 3, which has values (6,4).

a. $x + y = 8; 0 + (-4) \neq 8; 3 + 0 \neq 8$.
   This is not the equation.
b. $2x + y = 4; 2(0) + -4 \neq 4; 2(3) + 0 \neq 4$.
   This is not the equation.
c. $4x - 3y = 12; 4(0) - 3(-4) = 12;$
   $4(3) - 3(0) = 12$.
   This is the correct answer.

Now try some on your own. Find the correct equation for each of the following lines. Answers are at the end of the lesson.

_____ **137.**

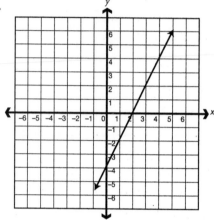

a. $2x + y = 4$
b. $2x - y = 4$
c. $2x + 2y = 4$
d. $y - 2x = 4$
e. $2x - 2y = 4$

_____ **138.**

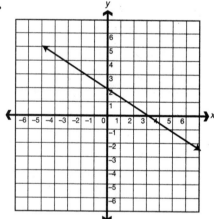

a. $3x + 2y = 6$
b. $2x + 4y = 8$
c. $2x - 3y = 12$
d. $2x + 3y = 3$
e. $2x + 3y = 6$

_____ **139.**

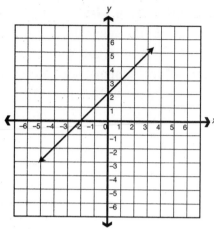

a. $x - y = -2$
b. $x + y = 4$
c. $x - y = 2$
d. $2x - y = -2$
e. $x + y = 2$

Systems of Equations

When there are two equations with two variables, such as x and y, a unique solution can be found that will satisfy both equations. Usually, there is only one pair of numbers that will satisfy both equations. To find out whether a pair of numbers satisfies the equations, substitute the first value for x and the second value for y and see whether it makes the equations true.

Example: Is (2,3) a solution to the following system of equations?

$$2x + 3y = 13$$
$$x - y = -1$$

1. In the first equation, substitute 2 for x and 3 for y:

$$2x + 3y = 13$$
$$2(2) + 3(3) = 13$$
$$4 + 9 = 13$$
$$13 = 13$$

2. Substitute the same numbers in the second equation:

$$x - y = -1$$
$$2 - 3 = -1$$
$$-1 = -1$$

3. Therefore, the answer is yes; (2,3) is a solution to the system of equations, since it makes both of the equations true.

Example: Is (1,2) a solution to the following system of equations?

$$x + 3y = 7$$
$$4x + 3y = 7$$

1. First substitute (1,2) into the first equation:

    $$x + 3y = 7$$
    $$1 + 3(2) = 7$$
    $$1 + 6 = 7$$
    $$7 = 7$$

2. Then check the second equation also:

    $$4x + 3y = 7$$
    $$4(1) + 3(2) \neq 7$$
    $$4 + 6 \neq 7$$
    $$10 \neq 7$$

3. Since (1,2) is a solution for only one equation, the answer is no.

Now try a few on your own. Which of the following is a solution to the system of equations? Answers are at the end of the lesson.

_____**140.** $x + y = 5$
$x - y = 1$
   a. (2,1)
   b. (1,3)
   c. (2,3)
   d. (3,2)
   e. (4,1)

_____**141.** $8x - y = 29$
$2x + y = 11$
   a. (3,4)
   b. (4,3)
   c. (3,5)
   d. (2,5)
   e. (5,3)

_____**142.** $x - y = 6$
$x + y = -2$
   a. (4,2)
   b. (-2,4)
   c. (2,3)
   d. (-2,3)
   e. (2,-4)

Perimeter, Area, and the Pythagorean Theorem

There will be a few questions concerning perimeter and area of quadrilaterals and circles on the math test, as well as a question about the Pythagorean theorem.

Perimeter

Perimeter is the distance around a polygon. The word *perimeter* is derived from *peri*, which means *around* (as in *peri*scope and *peri*pheral vision), and *meter*, which means *measure*. Thus *perimeter* is the *measure around* something. There are many everyday applications of perimeter. For instance, a carpenter measures the perimeter of a room to determine how many feet of ceiling molding she needs. A farmer measures the perimeter of a field to determine how many feet of fencing he needs to surround it.

Perimeter is measured in length units, like feet, yards, inches, and meters.

> To find the perimeter of a polygon, add the lengths of the sides.

Example: Find the perimeter of the following polygon:

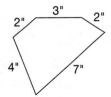

Solution: Write down the length of each side and add:

$$
\begin{array}{r}
3 \text{ inches} \\
2 \text{ inches} \\
7 \text{ inches} \\
4 \text{ inches} \\
+\ 2 \text{ inches} \\
\hline
18 \text{ inches}
\end{array}
$$

The notion of perimeter also applies to a circle; however, the perimeter of a circle is referred to as its *circumference*.

Find the perimeters for these word problems.

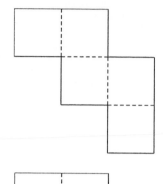

_____**143.** Mark wants to create a wooden frame around his garden using 12-foot pieces of lumber. The garden is 6 feet by 12 feet, so how many pieces of lumber will he need?

_____**144.** Ace Security Company recently installed a security system that uses wiring buried around the perimeter of Pete's home. His yard is 123 feet by 42 feet. How much wiring was installed?

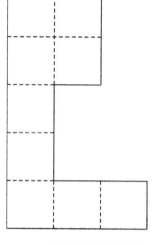

Area

Area is the amount of space taken by a figure's surface. Area is measured in square units. For instance, a square that is 1 unit on all sides covers *1 square unit*. If the unit of measurement for each side is feet, for example, then the area is measured in *square feet*; similarly, other units would be square inches, square miles, square meters, and so on.

You could measure the area of any figure by counting the number of square units the figure occupies. The first two figures that follow are easy to measure because the square units fit into them evenly, while the next two figures are more difficult to measure because the square units don't fit into them evenly.

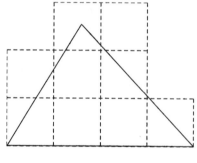

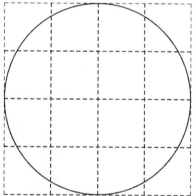

It's not always practical to measure a figure's area by counting the number of square units it occupies. In those cases, an area formula is used. As each figure is discussed, you'll learn its area formula. There are perimeter formulas as well, but you don't really need them (except for circles) if you understand the perimeter concept: It is merely the *sum of the lengths of the sides.*

Quadrilaterals

A quadrilateral is a four-sided polygon. The two quadrilaterals that are most likely to appear on the math test are shown here:

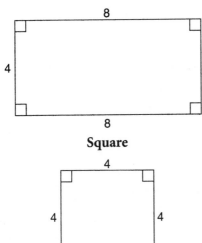

These quadrilaterals have something in common beside having four sides:

- Opposite sides are the same size and parallel.
- Opposite angles are the same size.

Perimeter

Follow this simple rule to find the perimeter of a quadrilateral:

Perimeter = sum of all four sides

Shortcut: Take advantage of the fact that the opposite sides of a rectangle are equal: Add two adjacent sides and double the sum. Similarly, multiply one side of a square by four.

Here are some word problems in perimeters of quadrilaterals. Answers are at the end of the lesson.

_____**145.** What is the length of a side of a square room whose perimeter is 58 feet?
  a. 8 feet
  b. 14 feet
  c. 14.5 feet
  d. 29 feet
  e. 232 feet

_____**146.** What is the perimeter of a rectangle that is 3 feet by 5 feet?
  a. 8 square feet
  b. 12 square feet
  c. 15 square feet
  d. 16 square feet
  e. 24 square feet

Area

To find the **area** of a rectangle or square, use this formula:

Area = base × height

The *base* is the size of the side on the bottom. The *height* (or *altitude*) is the size of a perpendicular line drawn from the base to the opposite side. The height of a rectangle and a square is the same as the size of its vertical side.

Rectangle

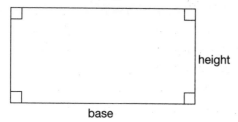

Square

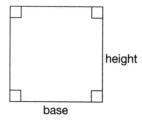

Example: Find the area of a rectangle with a base of 4 meters and a height of 3 meters.

1. Draw the rectangle as close to scale as possible.
2. Label the size of the base and height.
3. Write the area formula; then substitute the base and height numbers into it:

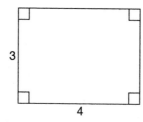

$A = b \times h$

$A = 4 \times 3 = 12$

Thus, the area is **12 square meters.**

Now try some area word problems. Answers are at the end of the lesson.

_____**147.** Quentin wants to fertilize his lawn, which is 38 feet by 62 feet. How much fertilizer does he need?
  a. 650 feet
  b. 1,118 feet
  c. 2,356 feet
  d. 3,008 feet
  e. 4,522 feet

_____**148.** What is the length in feet of a rectangular parking lot that has an area of 8,400 square feet and a width of 70 feet?
  a. 12 feet
  b. 120 feet
  c. 1,200 feet
  d. 4,000 feet
  e. 4,130 feet

Circles

We can all recognize a circle when we see one, but its definition is a bit technical. A *circle* is a set of points that are all the same distance from a given point called the *center*. That distance is called the *radius*. The *diameter* is twice the length of the radius; it passes through the center of the circle.

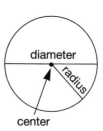

Circumference

The *circumference* of a circle is the distance around the circle (comparable to the concept of the *perimeter* of a polygon). To determine the circumference of a circle, use either of these two equivalent formulas:

> **Circumference = 2πr**
> **or**
> **Circumference = πd**

- *r* is the radius.
- *d* is the diameter.
- π is approximately equal to 3.14 or $\frac{22}{7}$.

Note: Math often uses letters of the Greek alphabet, like π (*pi*). Perhaps that's what makes math seem like Greek to some people! In the case of the circle, you can use π as a hook to recognize a circle question: A *pie* is shaped like a circle.

Example: Find the circumference of a circle whose radius is 7 inches.

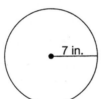

1. Draw this circle and write the radius version of the circumference formula (because you're given the radius): $C = 2\pi r$
2. Substitute 7 for the radius: $C = 2 \times \pi \times 7$
3. On a multiple-choice test, look at the answer choices to determine whether to leave π in your answer or substitute the *value of* π in the formula.
   If the answer choices don't include π,

substitute $\frac{22}{7}$ or 3.14 for π and multiply:

$C = 2 \times \frac{22}{7} \times 7$;
$C = \mathbf{44}$
$C = 2 \times 3.14 \times 7$;
$C = \mathbf{43.96}$

If the answer choices include π, just multiply:

$C = 2 \times \pi \times 7$;
$C = \mathbf{14\pi}$

All the answers—**44 inches, 43.96 inches, and 14π inches**—are considered correct.

Example: What is the diameter of a circle with a circumference of 62.8 centimeters? Use 3.14 for π.

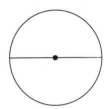

1. Draw a circle with its diameter and write the diameter version of the circumference formula (because you're asked to find the diameter): $C = \pi d$
2. Substitute 62.8 for the circumference, 3.14 for π, and solve the equation.
   The diameter is **20 centimeters.**
   $62.8 = 3.14 \times d$
   $62.8 = 3.14 \times \mathbf{20}$

These word problems require you to find the circumference. Answers are at the end of the lesson.

_____ **149.** What is the circumference of a circular room with a diameter of 15 feet?
  a. 7.5π ft.
  b. 15π ft.
  c. 30π ft.
  d. 45 ft.
  e. 225π ft.

_____ **150.** What is the circumference of a round tower whose radius is $3\frac{2}{11}$ feet?

    a. 10 ft.
    b. 20 ft.
    c. 33 ft.
    d. 40 ft.
    e. 48 ft.

_____ **151.** Find the circumference of a water pipe whose radius is 1.2 inches.

    a. 1.2π in.
    b. 1.44π in.
    c. 2.4π in.
    d. 12π in.
    e. 24π in.

Area

The *area* of a circle is the space its surface occupies. Use this formula to determine the area of a circle:

$$\text{Area} = \pi r^2$$

Hook: To avoid confusing the area and circumference formulas, just remember that *area* is always measured in *square* units, like 12 *square yards* of carpeting. Thus, the *area* formula is the one with the *squared* term in it.

Example: Find the area of the circle at right, rounded to the nearest tenth.

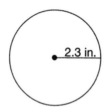

2.3 in.

1. Write the area formula: $A = \pi r^2$
2. Substitute 2.3 for the radius: $A = \pi \times 2.3 \times 2.3$
3. On a multiple-choice test, look at the answer choices to determine whether to use π or the *value of* π (decimal or fraction) in the formula.

If the answers don't include π, use 3.14 for π (because the radius is a decimal):

$A = 3.14 \times 2.3 \times 2.3$;
$\mathbf{A = 16.6}$

If the answers include π, multiply and round off to the nearest tenth:

$A = \pi \times 2.3 \times 2.3$;
$\mathbf{A = 5.3\pi}$

Both answers—**16.6 square inches** and **5.3π square inches**—are correct.

Example: What is the diameter of a circle with an area of 9π square centimeters?

1. Draw a circle with its diameter (to help you remember that the question asks for the diameter); then write the area formula.

$A = \pi r^2$

2. Substitute 9π for the area and solve the equation:

$9\pi = \pi r^2$
$9 = r^2$

Since the radius is 3 centimeters, the diameter is **6 centimeters**.

$3 = r$

Try these word problems on the area of a circle. Answers are at the end of the lesson.

_____ **152.** What is the area in square inches of the bottom of a coffeepot with a diameter of 6 inches?

    a. 6π square inches
    b. 9π square inches
    c. 12π square inches
    d. 18π square inches
    e. 36π square inches

_____**153.** James Band is believed to be hiding within a 5-mile radius of his home. What is the approximate area, in square miles, of the region in which he may be hiding?
- **a.** 15.7 square miles
- **b.** 25 square miles
- **c.** 31.4 square miles
- **d.** 78.5 square miles
- **e.** 157 square miles

_____**154.** If a circular parking lot covers an area of 2,826 square feet, what is the size of its radius? (Use 3.14 for π.)
- **a.** 30 ft.
- **b.** 60 ft.
- **c.** 90 ft.
- **d.** 450 ft.
- **e.** 900 ft.

The Pythagorean Theorem

> To find the missing side of a RIGHT triangle,
> use the Pythagorean theorem:
> $$a^2 + b^2 = c^2$$
> (**c** is the hypotenuse)

Example: What is the length of the missing side of the triangle shown at the right?

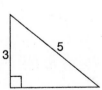

1. Use the Pythagorean theorem: $a^2 + b^2 = c^2$
2. Substitute the given sides for two of the letters. Remember:

Side *c* is always the hypotenuse: $3^2 + b^2 = 5^2$
$9 + b^2 = 25$

3. To solve this equation, subtract 9 from both sides:
$$-9 \qquad -9$$
$$b^2 = 16$$

4. Then take the square root of both sides. Thus, the missing side has a length of **4 units**. $\sqrt{b^2} = \sqrt{16}$

$b = 4$

Find the length of the missing side of each triangle. **Hint:** Use the Pythagorean theorem.

_____**155.**

_____**156.**

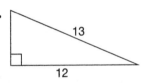

_____**157.** Irene is fishing at the edge of a 40-foot-wide river, directly across from her friend Sam, who is fishing at the edge of the other side. Sam's friend Arthur is fishing 30 feet down the river from Sam. How far is Irene from Arthur?

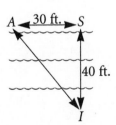

More Help with Math

The review in this lesson was designed to help you pick up more points on the math portions of the test. By getting used to how questions are typically asked and by knowing more about what test makers are actually testing, you're becoming more familiar with the test format and, therefore, more prepared for the test.

However, if there are areas of the math test that continually give you trouble, it's time to ask a teacher or friend for help. Take advantage of the resources available to you, like your school's resource center or extra study periods with your math teacher. When you go the extra mile to improve areas that need work, you're doing yourself a huge favor—you're improving your chances for success.

Answers to Math Problems

Word Problems
1. a.
2. e.
3. d.
4. e.

Number Names
5. 8,755
6. 201
7. seven hundred ten
8. nine thousand one hundred eighty-six

Fractions
9. $\frac{1}{5}$
10. $\frac{1}{3}$
11. $\frac{3}{8}$
12. 10
13. 6
14. 12
15. $1\frac{1}{24}$
16. $\frac{55}{24}$ or $2\frac{7}{24}$
17. $7\frac{1}{4}$
18. $\frac{1}{8}$
19. $\frac{1}{8}$
20. $\frac{19}{12}$ or $1\frac{7}{12}$
21. a.
22. b.
23. $\frac{21}{40}$
24. $\frac{8}{35}$
25. $\frac{2}{3}$
26. $\frac{26}{15}$ or $1\frac{11}{15}$
27. 15
28. $\frac{33}{2}$ or $16\frac{1}{2}$
29. c.
30. e.
31. c.
32. $\frac{3}{5}$

33. $5\frac{1}{2}$

34. $\frac{1}{15}$

35. $\frac{45}{28}$ or $1\frac{17}{28}$

36. b.

37. d.

38. b.

39. d.

40. c.

Decimals

41. $\frac{15}{100}$ or $\frac{3}{20}$

42. $2\frac{1}{4}$

43. $123\frac{456}{1,000}$ or $123\frac{57}{125}$

44. 4

45. 8.305

46. 0.907

47. 2.16

48. b.

49. d.

50. 0.006

51. 0.3392

52. 0.70104

53. e.

54. e.

55. 1.4

56. 5.05

57. 572

58. 1,400

59. b.

60. c.

Percents

61. 45%

62. $3\frac{1}{2}$%

63. $16\frac{2}{3}$% or about 16.67%

64. 0.18

65. 0.875

66. 2.5

67. 12.5% or $12\frac{1}{2}$%

68. 52%

69. $58\frac{1}{3}$% or about 58.33%

70. $\frac{19}{20}$

71. $\frac{3}{8}$

72. $\frac{5}{4}$ or $1\frac{1}{4}$

73. 0.6

74. 9.1

75. $37\frac{1}{2}$ or 37.5

76. 75

77. 50%

78. 25%

79. 300%

80. 100

81. 8

82. 250

83. c.

84. c.

85. c.

86. d.

Averages

87. c.

88. c.

89. b.

Length, Weight, and Time

90. 4

91. 1

92. 1.5

93. 180

94. 6 hr. 22 min.

95. 6 ft. 2 in.

96. 4 lb. 7 oz.

97. 7 ft. 10 in.

98. d.

99. b.

Algebra

100. 28

101. 4

102. 4

103. 28

104. 8

105. 3

106. 13

107. 8

108. 40

109. 8

110. 16

111. −10

112. 5

113. −45

114. 16

115. 36≠

116. $21xy$

117. $-3y^2z + 10$

118. $-2x^2 - 6y^2$

119. $a^2 - 11ab + 16b^2$

120. y^7

121. $15a^5$

122. $35x^3y^5$

123. $6x^2 - 21x$

124. $4a^3 + 8a^4$

125. $10x^3y^3 + 15x^2y^4$

126. $3(x + 3)$

127. $2y(2y + 3)$

128. $5a^2b(2 + 3ab)$

129. x

130. $4y^2$

131. $6a^2b$

132. $8z - 2$

133. $5xy^3 - 3y$

134. yes

135. no

136. no

137. b.

138. e.

139. a.

140. d.

141. b.

142. e.

Area, Perimeter, and Pythagorean Theorem

143. 3

144. 330 feet

145. c.

146. d.

147. c.

148. b.

149. b.

150. b.

151. c.

152. b.

153. d.

154. a.

155. $\sqrt{18}$ or $3\sqrt{2}$

156. 5

157. 50 feet

13▶ PRACTICE HSPT EXAM 2

LESSON SUMMARY

This is the second of the two practice tests in this book based on the HSPT. Use this test to see how much you've improved.

For this exam, simulate the actual test-taking experience as closely as possible. Work in a quiet place, away from interruptions. Tear out the answer sheets on pages 255–257, and use your number 2 pencil to fill in the circles. Use a timer or stopwatch and allow yourself time as follows:

Part 1: Verbal Skills . . . . 16 minutes
Part 2: Quantitative Skills . . . . 30 minutes
Part 3: Reading . . . . 25 minutes
Part 4: Mathematics . . . . 45 minutes
Part 5: Language Skills . . . . 25 minutes

After the exam, again use the answer key that follows it to see your progress on each section and to find out why the correct answers are correct and the incorrect ones incorrect. Then use the scoring section at the end of the exam to see how you did overall.

Part 1: Verbal Skills

	a	b	c	d			a	b	c	d			a	b	c	d
1.		●				21.				●		41.			●	
2.	●					22.	●					42.	●			
3.	●					23.	●					43.				●
4.				●		24.			●			44.	●			
5.		●				25.			●			45.		●		
6.				●		26.				●		46.		●		
7.	●					27.	●					47.			●	
8.			●			28.		●				48.				●
9.	●					29.	●					49.	●		●	
10.			●			30.		●				50.				
11.		●				31.		●				51.	●			
12.	●					32.	●					52.			●	
13.	●					33.	●					53.	●			
14.			●			34.			●			54.				●
15.			●			35.				●		55.	●			
16.			●			36.		●				56.			●	
17.		●				37.			●			✗57.	●			
18.	●					38.	●					58.			●	
19.		●				39.		●				59.		●		
20.				●		40.			●			60.	●			

Part 2: Quantitative Skills

	a	b	c	d			a	b	c	d			a	b	c	d
61.			●			79.			●			97.		●		
62.				●		80.	●					98.			●	
63.	●					81.			●			99.	●			
64.		●				82.				●		100.				●
65.	●					83.		●				101.			●	
66.		●				84.		●				102.	●			
67.	●					85.				●		103.	●			
68.	●					86.				●		104.		●		
69.		●				87.			●			105.				●
70.			●			88.				●		106.				●
71.				●		89.	●					107.		●		
72.		●				90.		●				108.			●	
73.			●			91.	●					109.		●		
74.			●			92.			●			110.		●		
75.	●					93.			●			111.			●	
76.		●				94.				●		112.			●	
77.				●		95.		●								
78.				●		96.			●							

Part 3: Reading Skills

113.	ⓐ	ⓑ	ⓒ	ⓓ
114.	ⓐ	ⓑ	ⓒ	ⓓ
115.	ⓐ	ⓑ	ⓒ	ⓓ
116.	ⓐ	ⓑ	ⓒ	ⓓ
117.	ⓐ	ⓑ	ⓒ	ⓓ
118.	ⓐ	ⓑ	ⓒ	ⓓ
119.	ⓐ	ⓑ	ⓒ	ⓓ
120.	ⓐ	ⓑ	ⓒ	ⓓ
121.	ⓐ	ⓑ	ⓒ	ⓓ
122.	ⓐ	ⓑ	ⓒ	ⓓ
123.	ⓐ	ⓑ	ⓒ	ⓓ
124.	ⓐ	ⓑ	ⓒ	ⓓ
125.	ⓐ	ⓑ	ⓒ	ⓓ
126.	ⓐ	ⓑ	ⓒ	ⓓ
127.	ⓐ	ⓑ	ⓒ	ⓓ
128.	ⓐ	ⓑ	ⓒ	ⓓ
129.	ⓐ	ⓑ	ⓒ	ⓓ
130.	ⓐ	ⓑ	ⓒ	ⓓ
131.	ⓐ	ⓑ	ⓒ	ⓓ
132.	ⓐ	ⓑ	ⓒ	ⓓ
133.	ⓐ	ⓑ	ⓒ	ⓓ

134.	ⓐ	ⓑ	ⓒ	ⓓ
135.	ⓐ	ⓑ	ⓒ	ⓓ
136.	ⓐ	ⓑ	ⓒ	ⓓ
136.	ⓐ	ⓑ	ⓒ	ⓓ
137.	ⓐ	ⓑ	ⓒ	ⓓ
138.	ⓐ	ⓑ	ⓒ	ⓓ
139.	ⓐ	ⓑ	ⓒ	ⓓ
140.	ⓐ	ⓑ	ⓒ	ⓓ
141.	ⓐ	ⓑ	ⓒ	ⓓ
142.	ⓐ	ⓑ	ⓒ	ⓓ
143.	ⓐ	ⓑ	ⓒ	ⓓ
144.	ⓐ	ⓑ	ⓒ	ⓓ
145.	ⓐ	ⓑ	ⓒ	ⓓ
146.	ⓐ	ⓑ	ⓒ	ⓓ
147.	ⓐ	ⓑ	ⓒ	ⓓ
148.	ⓐ	ⓑ	ⓒ	ⓓ
149.	ⓐ	ⓑ	ⓒ	ⓓ
150.	ⓐ	ⓑ	ⓒ	ⓓ
151.	ⓐ	ⓑ	ⓒ	ⓓ
152.	ⓐ	ⓑ	ⓒ	ⓓ
153.	ⓐ	ⓑ	ⓒ	ⓓ

154.	ⓐ	ⓑ	ⓒ	ⓓ
155.	ⓐ	ⓑ	ⓒ	ⓓ
156.	ⓐ	ⓑ	ⓒ	ⓓ
157.	ⓐ	ⓑ	ⓒ	ⓓ
158.	ⓐ	ⓑ	ⓒ	ⓓ
159.	ⓐ	ⓑ	ⓒ	ⓓ
160.	ⓐ	ⓑ	ⓒ	ⓓ
161.	ⓐ	ⓑ	ⓒ	ⓓ
162.	ⓐ	ⓑ	ⓒ	ⓓ
163.	ⓐ	ⓑ	ⓒ	ⓓ
164.	ⓐ	ⓑ	ⓒ	ⓓ
165.	ⓐ	ⓑ	ⓒ	ⓓ
166.	ⓐ	ⓑ	ⓒ	ⓓ
167.	ⓐ	ⓑ	ⓒ	ⓓ
168.	ⓐ	ⓑ	ⓒ	ⓓ
169.	ⓐ	ⓑ	ⓒ	ⓓ
170.	ⓐ	ⓑ	ⓒ	ⓓ
171.	ⓐ	ⓑ	ⓒ	ⓓ
172.	ⓐ	ⓑ	ⓒ	ⓓ
173.	ⓐ	ⓑ	ⓒ	ⓓ
174.	ⓐ	ⓑ	ⓒ	ⓓ

Part 4: Mathematics

175.	ⓐ	ⓑ	ⓒ	ⓓ
176.	ⓐ	ⓑ	ⓒ	ⓓ
177.	ⓐ	ⓑ	ⓒ	ⓓ
178.	ⓐ	ⓑ	ⓒ	ⓓ
179.	ⓐ	ⓑ	ⓒ	ⓓ
180.	ⓐ	ⓑ	ⓒ	ⓓ
181.	ⓐ	ⓑ	ⓒ	ⓓ
182.	ⓐ	ⓑ	ⓒ	ⓓ
183.	ⓐ	ⓑ	ⓒ	ⓓ
184.	ⓐ	ⓑ	ⓒ	ⓓ
185.	ⓐ	ⓑ	ⓒ	ⓓ
186.	ⓐ	ⓑ	ⓒ	ⓓ
187.	ⓐ	ⓑ	ⓒ	ⓓ
188.	ⓐ	ⓑ	ⓒ	ⓓ
189.	ⓐ	ⓑ	ⓒ	ⓓ
190.	ⓐ	ⓑ	ⓒ	ⓓ
191.	ⓐ	ⓑ	ⓒ	ⓓ
192.	ⓐ	ⓑ	ⓒ	ⓓ
193.	ⓐ	ⓑ	ⓒ	ⓓ
194.	ⓐ	ⓑ	ⓒ	ⓓ
195.	ⓐ	ⓑ	ⓒ	ⓓ
196.	ⓐ	ⓑ	ⓒ	ⓓ

197.	ⓐ	ⓑ	ⓒ	ⓓ
198.	ⓐ	ⓑ	ⓒ	ⓓ
199.	ⓐ	ⓑ	ⓒ	ⓓ
200.	ⓐ	ⓑ	ⓒ	ⓓ
201.	ⓐ	ⓑ	ⓒ	ⓓ
202.	ⓐ	ⓑ	ⓒ	ⓓ
203.	ⓐ	ⓑ	ⓒ	ⓓ
204.	ⓐ	ⓑ	ⓒ	ⓓ
205.	ⓐ	ⓑ	ⓒ	ⓓ
206.	ⓐ	ⓑ	ⓒ	ⓓ
207.	ⓐ	ⓑ	ⓒ	ⓓ
208.	ⓐ	ⓑ	ⓒ	ⓓ
209.	ⓐ	ⓑ	ⓒ	ⓓ
210.	ⓐ	ⓑ	ⓒ	ⓓ
211.	ⓐ	ⓑ	ⓒ	ⓓ
212.	ⓐ	ⓑ	ⓒ	ⓓ
213.	ⓐ	ⓑ	ⓒ	ⓓ
214.	ⓐ	ⓑ	ⓒ	ⓓ
215.	ⓐ	ⓑ	ⓒ	ⓓ
216.	ⓐ	ⓑ	ⓒ	ⓓ
217.	ⓐ	ⓑ	ⓒ	ⓓ

218.	ⓐ	ⓑ	ⓒ	ⓓ
219.	ⓐ	ⓑ	ⓒ	ⓓ
220.	ⓐ	ⓑ	ⓒ	ⓓ
221.	ⓐ	ⓑ	ⓒ	ⓓ
222.	ⓐ	ⓑ	ⓒ	ⓓ
223.	ⓐ	ⓑ	ⓒ	ⓓ
224.	ⓐ	ⓑ	ⓒ	ⓓ
225.	ⓐ	ⓑ	ⓒ	ⓓ
226.	ⓐ	ⓑ	ⓒ	ⓓ
227.	ⓐ	ⓑ	ⓒ	ⓓ
228.	ⓐ	ⓑ	ⓒ	ⓓ
229.	ⓐ	ⓑ	ⓒ	ⓓ
230.	ⓐ	ⓑ	ⓒ	ⓓ
231.	ⓐ	ⓑ	ⓒ	ⓓ
232.	ⓐ	ⓑ	ⓒ	ⓓ
233.	ⓐ	ⓑ	ⓒ	ⓓ
234.	ⓐ	ⓑ	ⓒ	ⓓ
235.	ⓐ	ⓑ	ⓒ	ⓓ
236.	ⓐ	ⓑ	ⓒ	ⓓ
237.	ⓐ	ⓑ	ⓒ	ⓓ
238.	ⓐ	ⓑ	ⓒ	ⓓ

Part 5: Language Skills

239.	ⓐ	ⓑ	ⓒ	ⓓ
240.	ⓐ	ⓑ	ⓒ	ⓓ
241.	ⓐ	ⓑ	ⓒ	ⓓ
242.	ⓐ	ⓑ	ⓒ	ⓓ
243.	ⓐ	ⓑ	ⓒ	ⓓ
244.	ⓐ	ⓑ	ⓒ	ⓓ
245.	ⓐ	ⓑ	ⓒ	ⓓ
246.	ⓐ	ⓑ	ⓒ	ⓓ
247.	ⓐ	ⓑ	ⓒ	ⓓ
248.	ⓐ	ⓑ	ⓒ	ⓓ
249.	ⓐ	ⓑ	ⓒ	ⓓ
250.	ⓐ	ⓑ	ⓒ	ⓓ
251.	ⓐ	ⓑ	ⓒ	ⓓ
252.	ⓐ	ⓑ	ⓒ	ⓓ
253.	ⓐ	ⓑ	ⓒ	ⓓ
254.	ⓐ	ⓑ	ⓒ	ⓓ
255.	ⓐ	ⓑ	ⓒ	ⓓ
256.	ⓐ	ⓑ	ⓒ	ⓓ
257.	ⓐ	ⓑ	ⓒ	ⓓ
258.	ⓐ	ⓑ	ⓒ	ⓓ

259.	ⓐ	ⓑ	ⓒ	ⓓ
260.	ⓐ	ⓑ	ⓒ	ⓓ
261.	ⓐ	ⓑ	ⓒ	ⓓ
262.	ⓐ	ⓑ	ⓒ	ⓓ
263.	ⓐ	ⓑ	ⓒ	ⓓ
264.	ⓐ	ⓑ	ⓒ	ⓓ
265.	ⓐ	ⓑ	ⓒ	ⓓ
266.	ⓐ	ⓑ	ⓒ	ⓓ
267.	ⓐ	ⓑ	ⓒ	ⓓ
268.	ⓐ	ⓑ	ⓒ	ⓓ
269.	ⓐ	ⓑ	ⓒ	ⓓ
270.	ⓐ	ⓑ	ⓒ	ⓓ
271.	ⓐ	ⓑ	ⓒ	ⓓ
272.	ⓐ	ⓑ	ⓒ	ⓓ
273.	ⓐ	ⓑ	ⓒ	ⓓ
274.	ⓐ	ⓑ	ⓒ	ⓓ
275.	ⓐ	ⓑ	ⓒ	ⓓ
276.	ⓐ	ⓑ	ⓒ	ⓓ
277.	ⓐ	ⓑ	ⓒ	ⓓ
278.	ⓐ	ⓑ	ⓒ	ⓓ

279.	ⓐ	ⓑ	ⓒ	ⓓ
280.	ⓐ	ⓑ	ⓒ	ⓓ
281.	ⓐ	ⓑ	ⓒ	ⓓ
282.	ⓐ	ⓑ	ⓒ	ⓓ
283.	ⓐ	ⓑ	ⓒ	ⓓ
284.	ⓐ	ⓑ	ⓒ	ⓓ
285.	ⓐ	ⓑ	ⓒ	ⓓ
286.	ⓐ	ⓑ	ⓒ	ⓓ
287.	ⓐ	ⓑ	ⓒ	ⓓ
288.	ⓐ	ⓑ	ⓒ	ⓓ
289.	ⓐ	ⓑ	ⓒ	ⓓ
290.	ⓐ	ⓑ	ⓒ	ⓓ
291.	ⓐ	ⓑ	ⓒ	ⓓ
292.	ⓐ	ⓑ	ⓒ	ⓓ
293.	ⓐ	ⓑ	ⓒ	ⓓ
294.	ⓐ	ⓑ	ⓒ	ⓓ
295.	ⓐ	ⓑ	ⓒ	ⓓ
296.	ⓐ	ⓑ	ⓒ	ⓓ
297.	ⓐ	ⓑ	ⓒ	ⓓ
298.	ⓐ	ⓑ	ⓒ	ⓓ

Part 1: Verbal Skills

Time: 16 minutes

1. Which word does NOT belong with the others?
  a. bed
  b. curtains
  c. dresser
  d. armoire

2. Bird is to hawk as vehicle is to
  a. truck.
  b. eagle.
  c. road.
  d. tree.

3. Walnuts cost more than peanuts. Walnuts cost less than pistachios. Pistachios cost more than both peanuts and walnuts. If the first two statements are true, the third is
  a. true.
  b. false.
  c. uncertain.
  d. repetitive.

4. Window is to pane as book is to
  a. novel.
  b. glass.
  c. cover.
  d. page.

5. Cup is to gallon as centimeter is to
  a. yard.
  b. meter.
  c. pint.
  d. inch.

6. Mutable most nearly means
  a. intangible.
  b. secluded.
  c. impalpable.
  d. inconstant.

7. A perceptible change is
  a. recognizable.
  b. grandiose.
  c. strange.
  d. small.

8. Which word does NOT belong with the others?
  a. unfortunate
  b. sorrowful
  c. unlucky
  d. regrettable

9. Imaginary is the opposite of
  a. reality.
  b. wisdom.
  c. vice.
  d. fact.

10. Rudimentary most nearly means
  a. edible.
  b. unreadable.
  c. basic.
  d. young.

11. Elated is to despondent as enlightened is to
  a. aware.
  b. ignorant.
  c. miserable.
  d. tolerant.

12. Which word does NOT belong with the others?
  a. bowl
  b. flour
  c. sugar
  d. garlic

13. A rigorous schedule is
  a. demanding.
  b. tolerable.
  c. dangerous.
  d. orderly.

14. All of Joshua's white socks are 100% cotton. Joshua's blue socks are not 100% cotton. All of Joshua's socks are either white or blue. If the first two statements are true, the third is
   a. true.
   b. false.
   c. uncertain.
   d. repetitive.

15. Meticulous is the opposite of
   a. untouchable.
   b. graduate.
   c. sloppy.
   d. happy.

16. Which word does NOT belong with the others?
   a. isosceles
   b. equilateral
   c. quadrilateral
   d. scalene

17. The Shop-and-Save Grocery is south of Greenwood Pharmacy. Rebecca's house is northeast of Greenwood Pharmacy. Rebecca's house is west of the Shop-and-Save Grocery. If the first two statements are true, the third is
   a. true.
   b. false.
   c. uncertain.
   d. repetitive.

18. Embarrassed is to humiliated as frightened is to
   a. terrified.
   b. agitated.
   c. courageous.
   d. reckless.

19. Exhaustive is the opposite of
   a. thorough.
   b. cursory.
   c. tired.
   d. energetic.

20. Chastise most nearly means
   a. drink.
   b. race.
   c. engrave.
   d. punish.

21. Domain most nearly means
   a. entrance.
   b. rebellion.
   c. formation.
   d. territory.

22. Which word does NOT belong with the others?
   a. movie
   b. magazine
   c. newspaper
   d. book

23. Whiskers weighs less than Paws. Whiskers weighs more than Tabby. Of the three cats, Tabby weighs the least. If the first two statements are true, the third is
   a. true.
   b. false.
   c. uncertain.
   d. repetitive.

24. All of Harriet's plants are flowering plants. Some of Harriet's plants are succulents. All succulents are flowering plants. If the first two statements are true, the third is
   a. true.
   b. false.
   c. uncertain.
   d. repetitive.

25. Which word does NOT belong with the others?
   a. pecan
   b. walnut
   c. kernel
   d. cashew

26. Which word does NOT belong with the others?
  a. instruct
  b. teach
  c. educate
  d. discipline

27. Innocuous means the opposite of
  a. harmful.
  b. inoffensive.
  c. incubate.
  d. passive.

28. A covert operation is
  a. closed.
  b. secret.
  c. dangerous.
  d. completed.

29. Optimist is to cheerful as pessimist is to
  a. gloomy.
  b. malicious.
  c. petty.
  d. benevolent.

30. Which word does NOT belong with the others?
  a. roof
  b. sidewalk
  c. door
  d. window

31. A detrimental activity is
  a. decisive.
  b. harmful.
  c. worthless.
  d. advantageous.

32. Which word does NOT belong with the others?
  a. basin
  b. water
  c. ice
  d. steam

33. All Lamels are Signots with buttons. No yellow Signots have buttons. No Lamels are yellow. If the first two statements are true, the third statement is
  a. true.
  b. false.
  c. uncertain.
  d. repetitive.

34. Demolish means the opposite of
  a. attend.
  b. consider.
  c. create.
  d. stifle.

35. Notable means the opposite of
  a. oral.
  b. graceful.
  c. legal.
  d. ordinary.

36. City A has a higher population than City B. City C has a lower population than City B. City A has a lower population than City C. If the first two statements are true, the third statement is
  a. true.
  b. false.
  c. uncertain.
  d. repetitive.

37. Jovial means the opposite of
  a. tall.
  b. fast.
  c. grouchy.
  d. plenty.

38. Synopsis most nearly means
  a. summary.
  b. abundance.
  c. stereotype.
  d. verification.

39. Methodical most nearly means
  a. erratic.
  b. deliberate.
  c. humble.
  d. deformed.

40. Which word does NOT belong with the others?
  a. scythe
  b. knife
  c. pliers
  d. saw

41. Scarcity is the opposite of
  a. boredom.
  b. frightening.
  c. abundance.
  d. absence.

42. Candid is to indirect as honest is to
  a. frank.
  b. wicked.
  c. truthful.
  d. devious.

43. Recluse most nearly means
  a. prophet.
  b. fool.
  c. intellectual.
  d. hermit.

44. A novel idea is
  a. new.
  b. ideal.
  c. opinionated.
  d. believable.

45. Martina is sitting at the desk behind Jerome. Jerome is sitting at the desk behind Bryant. Bryant is sitting at the desk behind Martina. If the first two statements are true, the third is
  a. true.
  b. false.
  c. uncertain.
  d. repetitive.

46. A dubious statement is
  a. humorous.
  b. questionable.
  c. true.
  d. sad.

47. Optimum is the opposite of
  a. mediocre.
  b. victorious.
  c. worst.
  d. rational.

48. Harmony is the opposite of
  a. noise.
  b. brevity.
  c. safety.
  d. conflict.

49. Which word does NOT belong with the others?
  a. fork
  b. spoon
  c. plate
  d. knife

50. Pen is to poet as needle is to
  a. thread.
  b. button.
  c. sewing.
  d. tailor.

51. Rationale most nearly means
   a. explanation.
   b. regret.
   c. denial.
   d. anticipation.

52. Chaotic means the opposite of
   a. quickly.
   b. uncertain.
   c. orderly.
   d. ordinary.

53. Which word does NOT belong with the others?
   a. seat
   b. rung
   c. wood
   d. leg

54. A cryptic message is
   a. dead.
   b. dark.
   c. long.
   d. mysterious.

55. Oat cereal has more fiber than corn cereal but less fiber than bran cereal. Corn cereal has more fiber than rice cereal but less fiber than wheat cereal. Rice cereal has the least amount of fiber. If the first two statements are true, the third statement is
   a. true.
   b. false.
   c. uncertain.
   d. repetitive.

56. On the day the Barton triplets were born, Jenna weighed more than Jason. Jason weighed less than Jasmine. Of the three babies, Jasmine weighed the most. If the first two statements are true, the third statement is
   a. true.
   b. false.
   c. uncertain.
   d. repetitive.

57. A malicious act is
   a. spiteful.
   b. changeable.
   c. fearful.
   d. dangerous.

58. Which word does NOT belong with the others?
   a. defendant
   b. prosecutor
   c. trial
   d. judge

59. Which word does NOT belong with the others?
   a. shingle
   b. nail
   c. wood
   d. brick

60. Disperse means the opposite of
   a. gather.
   b. agree.
   c. praise.
   d. satisfy.

Part 2: Quantitative Skills

Time: 30 minutes

61. What number is 50% of 6×4?
  a. 6
  b. 8
  c. 12
  d. 16

62. Examine (A), (B), and (C) and find the best answer.

    (A)   (B)   (C)

  a. (A) is more shaded than (C).
  b. (B) is less shaded than (C).
  c. (A) is more shaded than (B) but less shaded than (C).
  d. (A), (B), and (C) are equally shaded.

63. Examine (A), (B), and (C) and find the best answer.
    (A) $3 \times (3 + 1)$ 12
    (B) $1 \times (4 + 6)$ 10
    (C) $2 \times (9 + 3)$ 24
  a. (C) is two times greater than (A).
  b. (A) plus 2 is equal to (B).
  c. (A) minus (B) is equal to (C).
  d. (C) minus (B) is equal to (A).

64. What number is 6 more than $\frac{1}{2}$ of 22?
  a. 15
  b. 17
  c. 28
  d. 50

65. What number is 10% of 60 divided by 2?
  a. 3
  b. 12
  c. 15
  d. 32

66. Examine (A), (B), and (C) and find the best answer.

    (A)   (B)   (C)

  a. (A) has the same number of diamonds as (C) but more diamonds than (B).
  b. (B) has more diamonds than (A) or (C).
  c. (A) and (B) have the same number of diamonds.
  d. (B) and (C) have the same number of diamonds.

67. Look at this series: 30, 29, 27, 24, . . .
  What number should come next?
  a. 20
  b. 19
  c. 17
  d. 15

68. Examine (A), (B), and (C) and find the best answer.
    (A) 0.5   50%
    (B) 5%
    (C) $\frac{1}{5}$ 20%
  a. (A) is greater than (B).
  b. (B) is greater than (A).
  c. (C) is greater than (A).
  d. (A) and (B) are equal.

69. Look at this series: 66, 59, 52, 45, 38, ...
What number should come next?
   a. 29
   b. 31
   c. 32
   d. 35

70. What number doubled is $\frac{1}{3}$ of 12?
   a. 4
   b. 3
   c. 2
   d. 1

71. What number is 10 more than 25% of 8?
   a. 42
   b. 22
   c. 18
   d. 12

72. Look at this series: 102, 112, 123, 135, ...
What number should come next?
   a. 146
   b. 148
   c. 150
   d. 152

73. Look at this series: $\frac{1}{6}, \frac{1}{3}, \frac{1}{2}, \frac{2}{3}, \ldots$
What number should come next?
   a. 1
   b. $\frac{4}{6}$
   c. $\frac{5}{6}$
   d. $\frac{8}{9}$

74. Examine the rectangle and find the best answer.

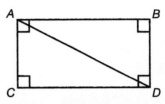

   a. AD is greater than AB.
   b. AD is equal to CD.
   c. AD minus BD is equal to CD.
   d. AB is less than AC.

75. What number is half of $\frac{1}{5}$ of 100?
   a. 10
   b. 12
   c. 15
   d. 21

76. Examine (A), (B), and (C) and find the best answer.
   (A) $\frac{2}{5}$ of 100   40
   (B) $\frac{1}{2}$ of 80   40
   (C) $\frac{1}{8}$ of 160   20
   a. (A) is less than (B) or (C).
   b. (A) and (B) are equal.
   c. (B) and (C) are equal.
   d. (B) is greater than (A) but less than (C).

77. Look at this series: V, VIII, XI, XIV, ...
What number should come next?
   a. IX
   b. XX
   c. XV
   d. XVII

   v = 5
   x = 10
   5 8 11 14

78. Examine the graph and find the best answer.

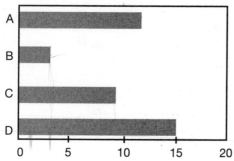

0   5   10   15   20

a. (A) plus (C) is less than (D).
b. (A) is greater than (D).
c. (D) minus (B) is equal to (C).
d. (D) is greater than (B) plus (C).

79. What number is 6 less than $\frac{2}{5}$ of 25?
a. −4
b. 1
c. 4
d. 9

80. What number is 3 times 4% of 20?
a. 2.4
b. 5.4
c. 24
d. 27

81. Look at this series: $\frac{1}{9}, \frac{1}{3}, 1, 3, \ldots$
What number should come next?
a. $\frac{2}{3}$
b. 6
c. 9
d. 12

82. Examine (A), (B), and (C) and find the best answer.
(A) $n \times n$
(B) n^2
(C) $n(n)$
a. (A) plus (C) equals (B).
b. (B) is greater than (C) but less than (A).
c. (A) is less than (C).
d. (A), (B), and (C) are all equal.

83. Look at this series: 12, 15, 20, 23, . . .
What number should come next?
a. 25
b. 28
c. 30
d. 32

84. What number would be doubled to equal 6 × 5?
a. 12
b. 15
c. 18
d. 21

85. Examine (A), (B), and (C) and find the best answer.

a. (A) plus (B) equals (C).
b. (C) minus (A) equals (B).
c. (C) is greater than (A) plus (B).
d. (C) is less than (A) plus (B).

86. Examine (A), (B), and (C) and find the best answer.
(A) 3% of 100
(B) 6% of 50
(C) 12% of 25
a. (A) is less than (B) or (C).
b. (C) is greater than (A) or (B).
c. (B) is less than (C) but greater than (A).
d. (A), (B), and (C) are all equal.

87. What number is three times half of 10?
   a. 8
   b. 12
   c. 15
   d. 17

88. Look at this series: 34, 31, 28, 25, . . .
   What number should come next?
   a. 17
   b. 19
   c. 21
   d. 22

89. What number divided by 5 is $\frac{1}{10}$ of 300?
   a. 150
   b. 100
   c. 50
   d. 30

90. Look at this series: 2, 5, 28, 8, 11, 20, 14, . . .
   What number should come next?
   a. 12
   b. 17
   c. 23
   d. 28

91. Examine the figure and find the best answer.

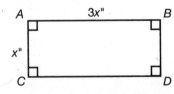

   a. *AC* plus *BD* is less than *AB*.
   b. *AB* minus *CD* is equal to *AC*.
   c. *AB* minus *AC* is equal to *BD*.
   d. *AC* plus *BD* is greater than *CD*.

92. Examine (A), (B), and (C) and find the best answer.
   (A) 7^2 49
   (B) 4^3 32
   (C) $3^2 + 6$ 15
   a. (A) and (B) are equal.
   b. (A) is greater than (B).
   c. (B) minus (A) is equal to (C).
   d. (B) and (C) are equal to (A).

93. Look at this series: 7, 10, 8, 11, 9, ___, 10, . . .
   What number should fill the blank?
   a. 7
   b. 11
   c. 12
   d. 13

94. What number added to 15% of 30 equals 20?
   a. −25
   b. 4.5
   c. 12
   d. 15.5

95. Examine (A), (B), and (C) and find the best answer.

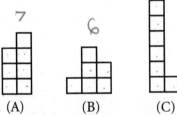

   a. Only (A) and (B) are equal.
   b. Only (A) and (C) are equal.
   c. Only (B) and (C) are equal.
   d. (A), (B), and (C) are all equal.

96. Look at this series: 2, 6, 18, 54, . . .
What number should come next?
   a. 108
   b. 148
   c. 162
   d. 216

97. What number plus 2 times the same number equals 99?
   a. 16
   b. 33
   c. 66
   d. 297

98. What number is 16 more than 12% of 1,000?
   a. 1.36
   b. 13.6
   c. 136
   d. 1,360

$$\frac{12}{100} = \frac{120}{1000}$$

99. Look at this series: 1,000, 200, 40, . . .
What number should come next?
   a. 8
   b. 10
   c. 15
   d. 20

100. Examine (A), (B), and (C) and find the best answer.
   (A) 18
   (B) 6(4 + 1) 30
   (C) 3(4) 12 =
   a. (B) is greater than (C) but less than (A).
   b. (B) divided by (C) is equal to (A).
   c. (C) is greater than (A).
   d. (A) plus (C) is equal to (B).

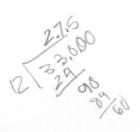

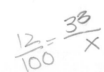

101. Examine (A), (B), and (C) and find the best answer.

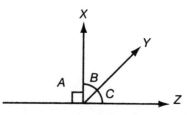

   a. Angle (A) plus angle (B) equals a right angle.
   b. Angle (A) plus angle (B) plus angle (C) equals a right angle.
   c. Angle (B) plus angle (C) equals angle (A).
   d. Angle (A) plus angle (B) equals angle (C).

102. Look at this series: U32, V29, W26, X23, . . .
What should come next?
   a. Y20
   b. Y17
   c. Z20
   d. Z26

Y20

103. Look at this series: 664, 332, 340, 170, 178, . . .
What number should come next?
   a. 89
   b. 94
   c. 109
   d. 184

$\div 2, +8, \div 2, +8$

104. Seven times what number equals 60% of 770 divided by 6?
   a. 7
   b. 11
   c. 12
   d. 110

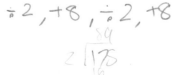

105. 33 is 12% of what number?
   a. 27.5
   b. 39.6
   c. 185
   d. 275

106. Look at this series: 2, IV, 8, XVI, . . .
What number should come next?
a. XXXII
b. XIX
c. 16 $2\ 6\ 8\ 10\ 12$
d. 32

107. Examine the circle graph and find the best answer.

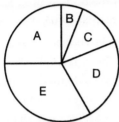

a. B and C are equal to A.
b. E minus A is less than D.
c. B plus C plus D is equal to A plus E.
d. A plus B plus C is equal to D plus E.

108. What number is 42 less than $\frac{1}{5}$ of 820?
a. 98
b. 112
c. 122 $\begin{array}{r} 164 \\ 42 \\ \hline 122 \end{array}$
d. 210

109. Look at this series: 17, __, 28, 28, 39, 39, . . .
What number should fill the blank?
a. 6
b. 17
c. 28
d. 50

110. Examine (A), (B), and (C) and find the best answer.
(A) 52 inches $52\ in$
(B) 1 foot 3 inches $15\ in$
(C) 1 yard 1 inch $37\ in$
a. (A) is three times greater than (B).
b. (A) minus (B) is equal to (C).
c. (A) and (B) are equal.
d. (A) is less than (C).

111. Look at this series: 12, 6, 10, 5, 9, . . .
What number should come next?
a. 3
b. 4.5 $-6,\ +4,\ -5,\ +4$
c. 5
d. 6.2

112. What number divided by 4 is equal to 20% of 10?
a. 5
b. 6 2
c. 8
d. 9

Part 3: Reading

Time: 25 minutes

For questions 113 through 152, read each passage carefully. Answer the questions that follow only on the basis of the preceding passage.

What's Good about Snakes?

About two weeks ago, on a warm summer day, I visited one of my favorite swimming spots in the mountains near my home. After my swim, I sat on a rock, resting and drying myself off. Suddenly I heard a scream, and when I turned toward the sound, I caught a glimpse of a beautiful five-foot-long copperhead snake slithering under the very same rock I'd been sitting on.

Now it's true that copperheads are poisonous, although their bites are rarely fatal. But the scream of surprise made me think—what is it about snakes that makes them so very horrifying to humans? After all, children grow up cuddling teddy bears and adore cartoon dinosaurs they see on television—both animals that are (or were) capable of inflicting tremendous damage to any human who crossed their paths.

In the United States, between 1,000 and 2,000 people are bitten by snakes each year, and about ten of these bites result in death. Snakes can be found all over the world except in the coldest regions, such as the South Pole. They live in deserts, in the mountains, in rain forests, and in the sea; there are over 2,500 different species of snakes. Some are only a few inches long, and others—like the anaconda—can grow to over 20 feet long.

Snakes are cold-blooded, which means they must rely on the heat of the sun to give them energy for movement, although prolonged exposure to extreme heat can be fatal to even a desert-dwelling serpent. Snakes that live in places where winters are cold must stay in a protected area with very little movement until warm weather returns. This is called hibernation.

Most snakes have poor vision, which is replaced by a keen sense of smell. They take in odors through their tongues, not their noses. Snakes can also detect the body heat of another animal even if it is several feet away.

We have much to learn from snakes. Their venom, or poison, can be amazingly powerful. One Australian snake, the *taipan,* can inject enough poison in one bite to kill 200,000 mice! The chemicals in these poisons may hold secrets that can help scientists solve problems in treating some diseases. Snakes are helpful to farmers because they prey on rats and mice, which could destroy food crops if their numbers increased.

Many people—like the screaming park visitor I heard—are afraid of snakes. Others find their brilliant colors and unusual movements fascinating. Some even keep them as pets. Snakes share the earth with humans, and we can find a lot to learn through studying them instead of merely trying to destroy them.

113. Which statement would the author of this article probably agree with?
   a. People should not keep snakes as pets.
   b. People should be afraid of snakes.
   c. Some snakes are dangerous, but snakes can also be helpful.
   d. Snakes should never be killed.

114. Which word in the story describes the way a snake moves?
   a. cold-blooded
   b. slithering
   c. beautiful
   d. predators

115. According to the story, what could happen if too many snakes in a farming area were killed?
- **a.** More snakes would reproduce and replace them.
- **b.** Rats and mice would eat the crops the farmers grew.
- **c.** People would no longer be afraid of snakes.
- **d.** Other animals would start eating rats and mice.

116. Because a snake is cold-blooded, it might
- **a.** lie in the sun on a cool day.
- **b.** spend a lot of time hunting when the weather is cold.
- **c.** hide under a rock when people are near.
- **d.** use its tongue to find something to eat.

117. Which statement is NOT true?
- **a.** There are no snakes at the South Pole.
- **b.** Scientists study the chemicals in snake venom.
- **c.** Snakes smell through their tongues.
- **d.** All snakes are poisonous.

118. Which would be another title for this article?
- **a.** "Watch Out for Snakes"
- **b.** "Copperheads Are Cool"
- **c.** "Let's Learn About Snakes"
- **d.** "How Snakes Use Their Tongues"

The Venus Flytrap

In the damp, swampy bogs of coastal North Carolina grows one of nature's most interesting creations. It is a plant with a one-foot-high stalk topped by a pair of oddly shaped leaves with spiny bristles on its edges.

Insects are attracted by the shiny leaves, but when they land on this plant, they get a most unpleasant surprise: The leaves snap shut, trapping the insect and providing the Venus flytrap with its next meal. After about two weeks, the insect has been completely digested, and the leaves open up to await another victim.

Only a few plants behave in this unusual manner. Most plants get all their food and energy by combining sunlight and carbon dioxide through the process called *photosynthesis*. Animals cannot do this because they lack a substance called *chlorophyll*—but animals make up for this by moving around to find their food.

The Venus flytrap uses two methods to feed itself. These plants will remain healthy without their insect meals, but they will grow really well only when they can trap and digest the insects that are unlucky enough to choose the wrong place to land. Scientists believe that the flytrap has developed this insect-eating diet to get nitrogen that it can't find in the soil where it grows.

You can buy a Venus flytrap and keep it at home, but you must remember that it has very special habits. It needs some sunlight (but not too much), warmth, moisture, and feedings of small amounts of raw meat or boiled egg. There's no need to worry about the plant hurting anyone who touches it—a Venus flytrap isn't strong enough to capture anything much larger than a fly.

119. What is the main idea of the passage?
- **a.** how animals get their food
- **b.** an unusual plant
- **c.** how to grow plants
- **d.** chlorophyll

120. Which word would be most similar to the word "bogs" in the first sentence?
- **a.** fields
- **b.** swamps
- **c.** mountains
- **d.** forests

121. Which statement is NOT true?
   a. Most plants do not eat insects.
   b. Animals do not have chlorophyll.
   c. A Venus flytrap will die if it does not catch any insects.
   d. Venus flytraps can be kept in people's homes.

122. Information in the article leads you to believe that
   a. the Venus flytrap is easy to find.
   b. the Venus flytrap is a dangerous plant.
   c. the Venus flytrap can live almost anywhere.
   d. some other plants may also eat insects.

The Mercury Delivery Company
Mercury Delivery Company was established by Mark Greenwold to <u>address</u> a problem with local mail delivery. Packages and letters mailed from one side of the city to the other side would arrive in one day, while mail sent to addresses in the same part of the city might take three or four days to arrive. This meant that a letter sent two streets away might arrive four days later, while a package could cross the city in a day.

Greenwold applied himself to solve this <u>conundrum</u> and discovered that the local mail union required its employees to deliver mail across town first, leaving other mail to be delivered if time permitted. Greenwold started a company using nonunion employees, which freed him from restrictive red tape. Thus, the city's mail system was transformed beginning in 1987.

123. According to the passage, what did Mark Greenwold's company do differently from the competition?
   a. lowered costs of mail delivery
   b. delivered the mail consistently
   c. changed the address system for the city
   d. fired unproductive employees

124. As used in the passage, the underlined word <u>address</u> most nearly means
   a. pay attention to.
   b. the location of Mercury Delivery Company.
   c. deliver mail.
   d. a woman's garment.

125. The concluding paragraph of this passage implies which of the following?
   a. The other mail companies were on strike.
   b. Mail delivery is complicated.
   c. Greenwold's company was more efficient than the competition.
   d. Zip codes are important.

126. When did Mercury Delivery Company begin delivering mail?
   a. 2005
   b. 2001
   c. 1992
   d. 1987

127. As used in the passage, the underlined word <u>conundrum</u> most nearly means
   a. canal.
   b. deficit.
   c. riddle.
   d. delay.

128. A good title for this passage might be
   a. "The Problems with Unions."
   b. "Origins of the Mercury Delivery Company."
   c. "How to Deliver the Mail."
   d. "The Biography of Mark Greenwold."

Paul Revere

Paul Revere was a patriot who served his country during the time of the American Revolution. He is best remembered for riding his horse from Boston to Lexington to warn other Americans that British troops were about to descend on them. Henry Wadsworth Longfellow wrote the poem "The Midnight Ride of Paul Revere" to commemorate Revere's daring deed. Paul Revere began his career working for his father as a silversmith. He took over the business after his father died, but the silver trade gradually waned in New England during the 1770s. He eventually took another job as a courier for the City of Boston, carrying messages by horseback to cities as far removed as Philadelphia. This new job may have seemed less appealing to him than silver work, but the experience prepared him well for the role that he was to play in the Revolutionary War.

The British army was stationed in Boston and had plans to round up Americans who were trying to gain independence from Britain. In April 1775, they made their move, heading toward Lexington in force to arrest John Hancock, Samuel Adams, and other patriots.

Paul Revere was watching the British army to learn their plans, and he had arranged for a signal to be placed in Boston's Old North Church to indicate their route of attack: one lantern in the steeple if they should move out by land, and two lanterns if they went by water.

On the night of April 18, the army set out toward Lexington, using boats to cross the Charles River. Two lanterns appeared in the tower of the Old North Church, and Paul Revere set off on his horse at breakneck speed to warn the people of Lexington.

129. What did Paul Revere do for a living?
    a. delivered mail
    b. served in the army
    c. trained horses
    d. made things from silver

130. As it is used in this passage, the word commemorate most nearly means
    a. remember.
    b. paint.
    c. repurchase.
    d. rebuke.

131. How did Paul Revere's experiences as a courier for the City of Boston prepare him for his role in the Revolutionary War?
    a. He learned his way around Boston.
    b. He made important friends in many cities.
    c. He learned to carry messages by horseback.
    d. He was able to make saddle parts from silver.

132. Why did two lanterns appear in the church tower?
    a. because Paul Revere didn't know which way to ride
    b. because the British army was crossing the Charles River
    c. to tell the redcoats to move out
    d. because it was a dark night

133. As it is used in the passage, the word waned most nearly means
    a. increased.
    b. decreased.
    c. waxed.
    d. precipitated.

134. A good title for this passage might be
    a. "An Important Warning."
    b. "Famous Silversmiths of Boston."
    c. "The History of the American Revolution."
    d. "The Role of the Church in Wartime."

Acupuncture

Who would think that sticking needles into your skin could bring pain relief? That's what more Americans believe each year. In the past two decades, acupuncture has grown in popularity in the United States and is now widely practiced—by thousands of physicians, dentists, acupuncturists, and other practitioners—for relief or prevention of pain and for various other health conditions.

One of the oldest, most commonly used medical procedures in the world, acupuncture originated in China more than 2,000 years ago. Acupuncture became better known in the United States in 1971, when *New York Times* reporter James Reston wrote about how doctors in China used needles to ease his pain after surgery. American acupuncture practices incorporate medical traditions from China, Japan, and Korea.

People experience acupuncture differently, but most feel no or minimal pain as the needles are inserted. Some people are energized by treatment, while others feel relaxed. The acupuncture technique that has been most studied scientifically involves penetrating the skin with thin, solid, metallic needles that are manipulated by hands or by electrical stimulation. Improper needle placement, movement of the patient, or a defect in the needle can cause soreness and pain during treatment. If you decide to try acupuncture, be sure to seek treatment from a qualified acupuncture practitioner. As more Americans try acupuncture, more trained practitioners can be found.

135. What is the main idea of the passage?
a. Acupuncture is painless.
b. Acupuncture is a much older and more common practice than you might think.
c. Be sure to use a qualified acupuncture practitioner.
d. More Americans are using acupuncture than ever.

136. Which of the following is the best definition of the underlined word incorporate in the second paragraph?
a. include something as part of the whole
b. legally become part of a business
c. to have a bodily form
d. having no material existence

137. American acupuncture practices do NOT incorporate techniques from
a. China.
b. Thailand.
c. Korea.
d. Japan.

138. Acupuncture makes some people feel
a. relaxed.
b. uptight.
c. sleepy.
d. happy.

139. Which of the following is the best definition of the underlined word defect in the third paragraph?
a. having been beaten in a contest
b. not having all the inflections normal for the part of speech
c. to abandon one's country for another one
d. a shortcoming or imperfection

140. Which of the following will NOT cause soreness or pain with the treatment?
a. electrical stimulation
b. improper needle placement
c. movement of the patient
d. a defect in the needle

141. How did acupuncture become better known in the United States?
  a. Physicians, dentists, acupuncturists, and other practitioners used acupuncture.
  b. It was the most common medical procedure in the world.
  c. It was reported in the newspaper.
  d. The word spread because acupuncture relieves pain.

142. Of the following, which would be the best title for this passage?
  a. "Getting the Most Out of Acupuncture"
  b. "Fighting Pain the Old-Fashioned Way"
  c. "Acupuncture: The Human Pin Cushion"
  d. "Acupuncture: The New 'Old' Treatment for Pain"

Fire Safety

During class, students in Mr. Sherman's room listened to an important speaker from the local fire department. He spoke about the importance of fire safety, particularly fire prevention and detection. Because smoke detectors cut a person's risk of dying in a fire in half, he told the class how to install these protective devices in their homes.

A smoke detector should be placed on each floor-level of a home and outside each sleeping area. A good site for a detector would be a hallway that runs between living spaces and bedrooms.

Because of the dead-air space that might be missed by turbulent hot air bouncing around above a fire, smoke detectors should be installed either on the ceiling at least four inches from the nearest wall, or high on a wall at least four but no farther than 12 inches from the ceiling. Detectors should not be mounted near windows, exterior doors, or other places where drafts might direct the smoke away from the unit. Nor should they be placed in kitchens and garages, where cooking and gas fumes are likely to set off false alarms.

This very important information can help all students.

143. What is the main focus of this passage?
  a. how firefighters carry out their responsibilities
  b. the proper installation of home smoke detectors
  c. the detection of dead-air space on walls and ceilings
  d. how smoke detectors prevent fires in homes

144. The passage implies that dead-air space is most likely to be found
  a. on a ceiling, between four and 12 inches from a wall.
  b. close to where a wall meets a ceiling.
  c. near an open window.
  d. in kitchens and garages.

145. The passage states that, when compared with people who do not have smoke detectors, people who live in homes with smoke detectors have a
  a. 50% better chance of surviving a fire.
  b. 50% better chance of preventing a fire.
  c. 100% better chance of detecting a hidden fire.
  d. 200% better chance of not being injured in a fire.

146. A smoke detector should NOT be installed near a window because
  a. outside fumes may trigger a false alarm.
  b. a wind draft may create a dead-air space.
  c. a wind draft may pull smoke away from the detector.
  d. outside noises may muffle the sound of the detector.

147. The passage indicates that one responsibility of a firefighter is to
  a. install smoke detectors in the homes of residents in the community.
  b. check homes to see if smoke detectors have been properly installed.
  c. develop fire safety programs for community leaders and school teachers to use.
  d. speak to school children about the importance of preventing fires.

148. If a home has three levels—a basement with living space, a first floor with living space, and a second floor with four bedrooms—a minimum of how many smoke detectors should be installed?
  a. 2
  b. 3
  c. 4
  d. 5

149. The tone of this passage could best be described as
  a. instructive.
  b. lighthearted.
  c. terrifying.
  d. emotional.

150. Of the following, the best title for this passage would be
  a. "The New Smoke Detector."
  b. "Becoming Aware of Dead-Air."
  c. "A Firefighter's Worst Nightmare."
  d. "Smoke Detectors: Lifesavers for Your Home."

151. Which of the following is the best place to install a smoke detector?
  a. a kitchen
  b. a garage
  c. near a bedroom window
  d. in a hall outside a bedroom

152. Which of the following statements most likely expresses the author's opinion?
  a. Smoke detectors are costly and should be purchased with care.
  b. Firefighters should spend more of their time speaking in their communities.
  c. It is irresponsible not to have a smoke detector in your home.
  d. You should spend time visiting your local fire department.

For questions 153 through 174, choose the word or phrase that most nearly means the same as the underlined word.

153. a <u>furtive</u> glance
  a. secretive
  b. nasty
  c. sudden
  d. unplanned

154. an <u>adroit</u> person
  a. small
  b. sarcastic
  c. overweight
  d. dexterous

155. a <u>sardonic</u> remark
  a. cynical
  b. fishy
  c. serious
  d. unnecessary

156. a <u>bucolic</u> landscape
  a. cow-filled
  b. rustic
  c. happy
  d. urban

157. to <u>recuperate</u> fully
  a. recover
  b. endorse
  c. persist
  d. approve

158. a <u>translucent</u> gem
  a. slow to heat up
  b. very valuable
  c. hard and thick
  d. allows light to pass through

159. regain your <u>composure</u>
  a. status
  b. poise
  c. liveliness
  d. voice

160. her <u>commendable</u> action
  a. admirable
  b. accountable
  c. irresponsible
  d. noticeable

161. a <u>fraudulent</u> statement
  a. lighthearted
  b. suave
  c. gambling
  d. illegal

162. the <u>expansive</u> facility
  a. obsolete
  b. meager
  c. spacious
  d. costly

163. the beautiful <u>mesa</u>
  a. woman
  b. plateau
  c. valley
  d. dwelling

164. a <u>pensive</u> mood
  a. handwritten
  b. thoughtful
  c. angry
  d. loud

165. his <u>animosity</u> toward us
  a. readiness
  b. compassion
  c. hostility
  d. impatience

166. a <u>spurious</u> statement
  a. prevalent
  b. false
  c. melancholy
  d. actual

167. he is <u>boisterous</u>
  a. noisy
  b. stupid
  c. overheated
  d. late

168. the <u>meager</u> supply
  a. sincere
  b. abundant
  c. scant
  d. precise

169. to <u>dissuade</u> a person
  a. persuade
  b. walk beside
  c. discourage
  d. cling to

170. to have <u>equity</u>
  a. justice
  b. certainty
  c. wealth
  d. dread

171. to <u>condone</u> an activity
  a. cover
  b. endorse
  c. make safe
  d. prohibit

172. our neighbor's <u>affluence</u>
  a. disregard
  b. wealth
  c. greed
  d. shame

173. a <u>haggard</u> appearance
  a. ugly
  b. old
  c. frightening
  d. exhausted

174. to <u>defray</u> the cost
  a. pay
  b. defend
  c. delay
  d. reduce

Part 4: Mathematics

Time: 45 minutes

175. Write *ten thousand four hundred forty-seven* in numerals.
  a. 10,499,047
  b. 104,447
  c. 10,447
  d. 1,047

176. In algebra, a *variable* is
  a. the known quantity in the equation.
  b. a symbol that stands for a number.
  c. an inequality.
  d. the solution for the equation.

177. In the following decimal, which digit is in the hundredths place?
0.9402
  a. 9
  b. 0
  c. 2
  d. 4

178. Which of the following numbers is the smallest?
  a. $\frac{6}{10}$
  b. $\frac{8}{15}$
  c. $\frac{33}{60}$
  d. $\frac{11}{20}$

179. 62.5% is equal to
  a. $\frac{1}{16}$
  b. $\frac{5}{8}$
  c. $6\frac{1}{4}$
  d. $6\frac{2}{5}$

180. A straight angle is
  a. exactly 180°.
  b. between 90° and 180°.
  c. 90°.
  d. less than 90°.

181. $(-6)^2 =$
  a. −36
  b. 36
  c. −12
  d. 12

182. What is the result of multiplying 11 by 0.032?
  a. 0.032
  b. 0.0352
  c. 0.32
  d. 0.352

183. Write *fourteen hundred eighty-two* in numerals.
- **a.** 14,822.00
- **b.** 1,482.20
- **c.** 1,480.22
- **d.** 1,482.00

184. The ratio of 2 ounces to 1 pound is
- **a.** 2:1.
- **b.** 1:16.
- **c.** 1:8.
- **d.** 2:8.

185. Which of the following is the best simplification of the following sentence? Salwa is ten years older than Roland.
- **a.** $10 + S = R$
- **b.** $S + R = 10$
- **c.** $R - 10 = S$
- **d.** $S = R + 10$

186. In the following number, which digit is in the thousandths place?
1,248.735
- **a.** 5
- **b.** 7
- **c.** 2
- **d.** 1

187. What is another way to write 2.75×100^2?
- **a.** 275
- **b.** 2,750
- **c.** 27,500
- **d.** 270,000

188. What is the complementary angle to 36°?
- **a.** 324°
- **b.** 144°
- **c.** 54°
- **d.** 36°

189. Which of the following number sentences is true?
- **a.** 4 feet > 3 feet
- **b.** 7 feet < 6 feet
- **c.** 5 feet > 6 feet
- **d.** 3 feet < 2 feet

190. Which of the following is true?
- **a.** 0.008 > 0.08
- **b.** 1.5 > 1.455
- **c.** 3.662 > 3.7
- **d.** 0.5 < 0.09

191. The greatest common factor of 16 and 38 is
- **a.** 2.
- **b.** 4.
- **c.** 8.
- **d.** 16.

192. 2 hours 28 minutes − 1 hour 17 minutes =
- **a.** 1 hour 51 minutes
- **b.** 1 hour 42 minutes
- **c.** 1 hour 23 minutes
- **d.** 1 hour 11 minutes

193. In 1995, the number of insects on earth was estimated at 10^{18}. How many insects were there?
- **a.** 10×10 eighteen times
- **b.** $10 + 18$ ten times
- **c.** 10 million × 18 million
- **d.** 18×18 ten times

194. What is the greatest area possible enclosed by a quadrilateral with a perimeter of 24 feet?
- **a.** 6 square feet
- **b.** 24 square feet
- **c.** 36 square feet
- **d.** 48 square feet

195. What is 0.3642 rounded to the nearest hundredth?
  a. 0.4
  b. 0.37
  c. 0.364
  d. 0.36

196. Which symbol belongs in the box?
  $0.05 \; \boxed{} \; \frac{1}{25}$
  a. <
  b. >
  c. =
  d. ≤

197. Which is the greatest amount?
  a. 6 pints
  b. 3 quarts
  c. 1 gallon
  d. 10 cups

198. What is the difference in perimeter/circumference between a square with a base of 4 feet and a circle with a diameter of 4 feet?
  a. $8 - 2\pi$ feet
  b. $16 - 2\pi$ feet
  c. $16 - 4\pi$ feet
  d. $16 - 8\pi$ feet

199. Mike worked 12 hours and received $102 in pay (before taxes). How much did Mike earn per hour?
  a. $8.00
  b. $8.50
  c. $8.75
  d. $9.25

200. Six friends agree to evenly split the cost of gasoline on a trip. Each friend paid $37.27. What was the total cost of gas?
  a. $370.27
  b. $223.62
  c. $314.78
  d. $262.78

201. Fabio made quiche for dinner last night. He and his family ate $\frac{2}{3}$ of it and saved the rest. The next day, Fabio ate $\frac{1}{2}$ of the remainder for lunch. What fraction of the original quiche is left?
  a. $\frac{1}{5}$
  b. $\frac{1}{6}$
  c. $\frac{1}{7}$
  d. $\frac{1}{8}$

202. Pete earns only $\frac{1}{8}$ what José does. José makes $19.50 an hour. For an eight-hour day, how much does Pete earn?
  a. $18.50
  b. $18.75
  c. $19.50
  d. $19.75

203. Carla has 20 math problems for homework. It takes her between five and seven minutes to do each problem. Which is a reasonable estimate of the total number of minutes it will take her to do her math homework?
  a. 20 minutes
  b. 80 minutes
  c. 120 minutes
  d. 240 minutes

204. $(14 \times 7) + 12 =$
   a. 98
   b. 266
   c. 110
   d. 100

205. 2 feet 4 inches + 4 feet 8 inches =
   a. 6 feet 8 inches
   b. 7 feet
   c. 7 feet 12 inches
   d. 8 feet

206. $17^2 =$
   a. 34
   b. 68
   c. 136
   d. 289

207. $3.16 \div 0.079 =$
   a. 0.025
   b. 2.5
   c. 4.0
   d. 40.0

208. 300% of 20 =
   a. 7
   b. 20
   c. 30
   d. 60

209. Solve for x in the following equation:
   $\frac{1}{3}x + 3 = 8$
   a. 33
   b. 15
   c. 11
   d. 3

210. Change this mixed number to an improper fraction: $5\frac{1}{2}$
   a. $\frac{11}{2}$
   b. $\frac{10}{2}$
   c. $\frac{7}{2}$
   d. $\frac{5}{2}$

211. What is the perimeter of the following polygon?

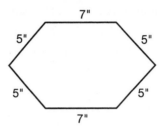

   a. 20 inches
   b. 27 inches
   c. 30 inches
   d. 34 inches

212. Mark's temperature at 9:00 A.M. was 97.2°F. At 4:00 P.M., his temperature was 99°F. By how many degrees did his temperature rise?
   a. 0.8°F
   b. 1.8°F
   c. 2.2°F
   d. 2.8°F

213. For the company's third anniversary, the caterer provided three 1-pound chunks of cheese. At the end of the party, there were $\frac{3}{5}$ pound of Swiss, $\frac{4}{7}$ pound of Vermont cheddar, and $\frac{5}{8}$ pound of feta cheese left. What fraction of the original three pounds was left after the party?
   a. $1\frac{123}{280}$ pounds of cheese
   b. $1\frac{223}{280}$ pounds of cheese
   c. $1\frac{283}{270}$ pounds of cheese
   d. $1\frac{393}{290}$ pounds of cheese

214. Yetta just got a raise of $3\frac{1}{4}$%. Her original salary was $30,600. How much does she make now?
  a. $30,594.50
  b. $31,594.50
  c. $32,094.50
  d. $32,940.50

215. The number of red blood corpuscles in 1 cubic millimeter is about 5,000,000, and the number of white blood corpuscles in 1 cubic millimeter is about 8,000. What is the ratio of white blood corpuscles to red blood corpuscles?
  a. 1:625
  b. 1:40
  c. 4:10
  d. 5:1,250

216. If $\frac{2x}{16} = \frac{12}{48}$, what is x?
  a. 2
  b. 3
  c. 4
  d. 5

217. $7 \div \frac{3}{8} =$
  a. $18\frac{2}{3}$
  b. $12\frac{3}{8}$
  c. $14\frac{5}{6}$
  d. $10\frac{4}{5}$

218. $s = t(3 + 5) - (11 - t)$
  $t = 2$
  $s =$
  a. −7
  b. −5
  c. 5
  d. 7

219. $0.31 + 0.673 =$
  a. 0.0983
  b. 0.983
  c. 0.967
  d. 9.83

220. In order to protect her new VW Bug, Maria needs to build a new garage. The concrete floor needs to be 64.125 square feet and $9\frac{1}{2}$ feet long. How wide does it need to be?
  a. 7.25 feet
  b. 5.5 feet
  c. 6.75 feet
  d. 8.25 feet

221. The price of cheddar cheese is $2.12 per pound. The price of Monterey Jack cheese is $2.34 per pound. If Harrison buys 1.5 pounds of cheddar and 1 pound of Monterey Jack, how much will he spend in all?
  a. $3.18
  b. $4.46
  c. $5.41
  d. $5.52

222. After paying a commission to his broker of 7% of the sale price, a seller receives $103,000 for his house. How much did the house sell for?
  a. $95,790
  b. $110,000
  c. $110,420
  d. $110,753

223. This month, attendance at the baseball park was 150% of what it had been last month. If attendance this month was 280,000, what was the attendance last month, rounded to the nearest whole number?
  a. 140,000
  b. 176,670
  c. 186,667
  d. 205,556

224. Triangles *RST* and *MNO* are similar. What is the length of line segment *MO*?

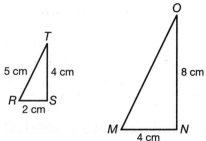

  a. 5 cm
  b. 10 cm
  c. 20 cm
  d. 32 cm

225. The sum of a number and its double is 69. What is the number?
  a. 46.6
  b. 34.5
  c. 23
  d. 20

226. If $10x - 3y = 40$, and $x = 1$, what does y equal?
  a. −10
  b. −4
  c. 4
  d. 10

227. What is the median of the following group of numbers?
  6 8 10 12 14 16 18
  a. 11
  b. 12
  c. 13
  d. 14

228. 35% of what number is equal to 14?
  a. 4
  b. 40
  c. 49
  d. 400

229. Which side is the longest of the following triangles, if triangle *A* is similar to triangle *B*?

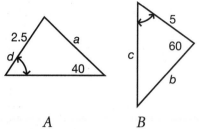

  a. *a*
  b. *b*
  c. *c*
  d. *d*

230. Of the 1,200 videos available for rent at a certain video store, 420 are comedies. What percent of the videos are comedies?
  a. $28\frac{1}{2}\%$
  b. 30%
  c. 32%
  d. 35%

231. One colony of bats consumes 36 tons of mosquitoes per year. At that rate, how many pounds of mosquitoes does the same colony consume in a month?
  a. 36,000 pounds
  b. 12,000 pounds
  c. 6,000 pounds
  d. 3,000 pounds

232. A helicopter flies over a river at 6:02 A.M. and arrives at a heliport 20 miles away at 6:17 A.M. How many miles per hour was the helicopter traveling?
  a. 120 mph
  b. 300 mph
  c. 30 mph
  d. 80 mph

233. Jared and Linda are both salespeople at a certain electronics store. If they made 36 sales one day, and Linda sold three less than twice Jared's sales total, how many units did Jared sell?
   a. 19
   b. 15
   c. 12
   d. 13

234. Karl is four times as old as Pam, who is one-third as old as Jackie. If Jackie is 18, what is the sum of their ages?
   a. 64
   b. 54
   c. 48
   d. 24

235. Solve for x in the following equation:
   $1.5x - 7 = 12.5$
   a. 29.25
   b. 19.5
   c. 13
   d. 5.5

236. What is the area of the rectangle?

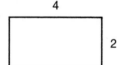

4

2

   a. 6 square feet
   b. 8 square feet
   c. 12 square feet
   d. 16 square feet

237. Gilda is making a quilt. She wants a quilt that is 30 square feet. She has collected fabric squares that are 6 inches by 6 inches. How many squares will she need?
   a. 60 squares
   b. 90 squares
   c. 100 squares
   d. 120 squares

238. 19 more than a certain number is 63. What is the number?
   a. 14
   b. 44
   c. 58
   d. 82

Part 5: Language Skills

Time: 25 minutes

*For questions 239 through 278, find the sentence that has a mistake in capitalization, punctuation, or usage. If you find no mistakes, mark choice **d**.*

239. a. Where is the car?
   b. Mike told me to go home.
   c. That Doctor made me better.
   d. No mistakes.

240. a. If you can, please join us.
   b. Polly turned 14 yesterday.
   c. When will we be finished?
   d. No mistakes.

241. a. I wish that I could go.
   b. I arrived here, today.
   c. I wonder when George will get here.
   d. No mistakes.

242. a. Why is Bob late?
   b. All the time.
   c. Can you spell her name?
   d. No mistakes.

243. a. Naomi should learn better manners.
   b. Whats up with that?
   c. The cat fell asleep in my lap.
   d. No mistakes.

244. a. You're supper is on the table.
  b. Today is my birthday.
  c. There are two ways to get there.
  d. No mistakes.

245. a. Montana is a large state.
  b. The fireplace is made of brick.
  c. Will you be home by Tuesday?
  d. No mistakes.

246. a. "Shut the window. You're letting the heat out!" said Connor.
  b. A thesaurus will help you find another word that means the same thing.
  c. He didn't take no prisoners.
  d. No mistakes.

247. a. They weren't the only ones who didn't like the movie.
  b. "Please come back another time," Aunt Julie begged.
  c. "Threes a crowd," he always says.
  d. No mistakes.

248. a. Anne will head out first, and Nick will follow her.
  b. Maya Angelou, a famous poet, has recently directed a movie.
  c. The clerk asked for my address and phone number.
  d. No mistakes.

249. a. My cousin Randall is an artist and a musician.
  b. I would love to live in Florida during the winter.
  c. Margie wants to become a history professor.
  d. No mistakes.

250. a. Does Judge Parker live on your street?
  b. Twenty government officials met to deal with Wednesday's crisis.
  c. The Mayor spoke at a news conference this morning.
  d. No mistakes.

251. a. John Glenn was a senator from Ohio.
  b. Is Dad going to join us for dinner?
  c. Elizabeth I was one of England's most famous queens.
  d. No mistakes.

252. a. Indira sometimes wears her beautiful sari.
  b. Lyle went shopping, and that he forgot his wallet.
  c. His shoes are just like mine.
  d. No mistakes.

253. a. My brother Isaac is the best player on the team.
  b. Because of the high cost; we decided not to go.
  c. Where's your new puppy?
  d. No mistakes.

254. a. I have learned to appreciate Mozart's music.
  b. My cousin Veronica is studying to be a Veterinarian.
  c. Mr. Shanahan is taller than Professor Martin.
  d. No mistakes.

255. a. We sold less cookies this year than we did last year.
  b. That parrot doesn't talk.
  c. Don't spend too much money.
  d. No mistakes.

256. **a.** My cat's name is Ruggles.
  b. I love you!
  c. I'll see you soon.
  d. No mistakes.

257. **a.** They're logic is faulty.
  b. Stay as long as you can.
  c. What is that smell?
  d. No mistakes.

258. **a.** A penny saved is a penny earned.
  b. Tomorrow is another day.
  c. The two dog's were fighting.
  d. No mistakes.

259. **a.** I think I'll lay down for a nap.
  b. That blanket needs to be washed.
  c. Who said that?
  d. No mistakes.

260. **a.** Graceland is the name of Elvis Presley's mansion.
  b. We set up the tent, but it soon fell over.
  c. Give me a break!
  d. No mistakes.

261. **a.** It has not rained since last April.
  b. The jurors walked solemnly into the room.
  c. Had we known, we would not have come.
  d. No mistakes.

262. **a.** The dog's barking woke us.
  b. Ursula has broke one of your plates.
  c. The sun rose from behind the mountain.
  d. No mistakes.

263. **a.** Do you prefer root beer over orange soda?
  b. In which year did world war II end?
  c. I like to study the geography of the Everglades.
  d. No mistakes.

264. **a.** After we sat down to eat dinner, the phone rung.
  b. "Keep a positive attitude," he always says.
  c. Sign here.
  d. No mistakes.

265. **a.** Colds like many other viruses are highly contagious.
  b. Call me when you feel better.
  c. Did you wash your hands, Michael?
  d. No mistakes.

266. **a.** The Adirondacks are mountains in New York.
  b. President Carter gave the Panama Canal back to Panama.
  c. That river is terribly polluted.
  d. No mistakes.

267. **a.** The children's books are over there.
  b. She missed the bus and arrives late.
  c. There is hardly enough food for a mouse.
  d. No mistakes.

268. **a.** It's not my fault that you and him got caught.
  b. "Do you brush twice a day?" Dr. Evans asked.
  c. What's the weather report?
  d. No mistakes.

269. **a.** Couldn't you arrive fashionably late?
  b. You're assumption is correct.
  c. I know that Bowser will be well treated.
  d. No mistakes.

270. **a.** The industrial revolution began in Europe.
  b. Is Labor Day a national holiday?
  c. General Patton was a four-star general.
  d. No mistakes.

271. **a.** We invited Mayor Chen to speak at our school.
   b. The alarm sounded, and the firefighters jumped into the truck.
   c. The volunteers work as hard as one can.
   d. No mistakes.

272. **a.** The winners were announced yesterday.
   b. Liam is one of the boys who were chosen.
   c. Although Nick was not selected, he was happy for the others.
   d. No mistakes.

273. **a.** I should of gone to school more.
   b. Can you lend me a dime?
   c. In those days, things were different.
   d. No mistakes.

274. **a.** Pam is in the store.
   b. Go sit down!
   c. She sneezes alot.
   d. No mistakes.

275. **a.** Please be quiet.
   b. The library has many books on the subject.
   c. They're going to be late.
   d. No mistakes.

276. **a.** The dog's collar broke.
   b. His price is too high.
   c. Their home is in Canada.
   d. No mistakes.

277. **a.** My aunt Georgia loves to read Eighteenth-Century novels.
   b. Eli's sister's cousin lives in Alaska.
   c. Is that a German shepherd?
   d. No mistakes.

278. **a.** Those shoes are too expensive.
   b. Michael's best friend is Patrick.
   c. Did you hear that Inez got a new puppy.
   d. No mistakes.

For questions 279 through 288, find the sentence that has a mistake in spelling. If you find no mistakes, mark choice **d.**

279. **a.** All employees will be eligible for three weeks of vacation.
   b. The managment team promised to look into the situation.
   c. We saw an enormous animal running toward us.
   d. No mistakes.

280. **a.** The commissioner has assumed responsibility.
   b. Kate likes to visit with her nieghbor.
   c. This is not a commonly held viewpoint.
   d. No mistakes.

281. **a.** Edith and her sister closely resemble each other.
   b. Her handwriting was barely legible.
   c. There are two paring knifes in the drawer.
   d. No mistakes.

282. **a.** The kitchen is being redecorated.
   b. Tomorrow is Wednesday
   c. Two women were talking loudly.
   d. No mistakes.

283. **a.** All the musicians were well trained.
   b. Thank you for your assistance.
   c. You are required to follow standard proceedures.
   d. No mistakes.

284. **a.** I knew she was bored because she wriggled in her seat.
   b. If you want to succeed, please report to work imediately.
   c. He was conscious of his surroundings.
   d. No mistakes.

285. a. My mother will soon celebrate her fortieth birthday.
   b. Autumn is my favorite time of year.
   c. My cousin is going skiing in Feburary.
   d. No mistakes.

286. a. William is the most sensable person I know.
   b. The festival is held at a different time each year.
   c. It is not customary for the members to arrive late.
   d. No mistakes.

287. a. As vice president of the student government, Judith is supposed to help the president.
   b. I recieved a passing grade in history.
   c. What a mess that toddler made!
   d. No mistakes.

288. a. Rachel remembered to ask the author a question.
   b. I vote in the election every November.
   c. Please pick up my perscription at the pharmacy.
   d. No mistakes.

For questions 289 through 298, follow the directions for each question.

289. Choose the word that best joins the sentences.
   Everyone thought the game was lost. _____, at the last minute, the forward threw the ball into the basket and scored a victory.
   a. Consequently
   b. Thus
   c. However
   d. While

290. Choose the word that best joins the thoughts together.
   It's best if you take the highway _____ there are fewer potholes, which is better for your car.
   a. because
   b. nevertheless
   c. and
   d. but

291. Which of these expresses the idea most clearly?
   a. For three weeks, the Linden family was able to stick to their clothing and entertainment budgets.
   b. The Linden family, for three weeks, was able to stick to its clothing and entertainment budgets.
   c. The Linden family knew what their clothing and entertainment allowance was, but for three weeks, they did not know how to follow it.
   d. A clothing and entertainment allowance, for three weeks, was agreed upon by all members of the Linden family.

292. Which of these expresses the idea most clearly?
   a. There is no true relationship between ethics and the law.
   b. Ethics and the law having no true relationship.
   c. Between ethics and the law, no true relationship.
   d. Ethics and the law is no true relationship.

293. Which of these expresses the idea most clearly?
   a. Some students think walking to school is a waste of time and there should be a bus service.
   b. Bus service would save many students a long walk to school.
   c. A waste of time is walking to school is what many students would say.
   d. Having bus service, for many students, would be a good idea.

294. Choose the group of words that best completes this sentence.

My neighbor, Mr. Christiansen, was such a skilled craftsman and woodworker that

   a. he received many awards at local craft shows and in magazines.

   b. he received many awards at local craft shows, and his work was featured in many magazines.

   c. he entered many local craft shows and awards, and then he had his work in many magazines.

   d. he entered his work in magazines and when he received awards at local craft shows.

295. Which of the following topics is best for a one-page essay?

   a. Computers in the Classroom

   b. Computer Projects Designed by Students

   c. How to Use Computers in the Classroom

   d. A Student-Designed Computer Project

296. Which of these best fits under the topic "High Altitudes Increase Risks from the Sun"?

   a. Mountain athletes have always known that the thinner air at high altitudes means less oxygen.

   b. Researchers have found that ultraviolet radiation levels from the sun were 60% higher at 8,500 feet than they were at sea level.

   c. Fourteen minutes of noontime sun exposure in Orlando, Florida, is equal to 25 minutes in upstate New York.

   d. Dr. Darren, a dermatologist at the University Medical Center, is perfecting methods to heal skin that has been severely damaged by the sun.

297. Which sentence does NOT belong in the paragraph?

1) Barbara Miller stumbled on her new business purely by accident. 2) While she was visiting friends in Arizona, she happened to walk past a dog bakery that sold all-natural dog biscuits, beaded collars, and canine gifts. 3) Veterinarians warn dog owners not to feed their pets people food. 4) Now, Miller is about to open her own dog bakery in New York.

   a. sentence 1

   b. sentence 2

   c. sentence 3

   d. sentence 4

298. Where should the sentence "Because of these oxides and minerals, agates can be found in a multitude of colors" be placed in the following paragraph?

1) The stones known as *beach agates* are a form of quartz. 2) Thousands of years before the Ice Age, these agates formed in gravel beds along the coastal plains. 3) They were formed by water-borne silicones, oxides, and metals that were deposited in basalt and other earth forms. 4) No two agates are exactly alike.

   a. before sentence 1

   b. between sentences 1 and 2

   c. between sentences 2 and 3

   d. between sentences 3 and 4

Answers

Part 1: Verbal Skills

1. b. A *bed*, *dresser*, and *armoire* are pieces of furniture. Curtains are not.

2. a. A *hawk* is a type of *bird*, and a *truck* is a type of *vehicle*. A vehicle might drive *on* a road (choice **c**), but it is not a type of vehicle.

3. a. Because the first two statements are true, pistachios are the most expensive of the three.

4. d. A *window* is made up of *panes*, and a *book* is made up of *pages*. The answer is not choice **a**, because a novel is a type of book. The answer is not choice **b**, because glass has no relationship to book. Choice **c** is incorrect because a cover is only one part of a book; a book is not made up of covers.

5. b. A *cup* is a smaller measure than a gallon. A *centimeter* is a smaller measure than meter. Yard, pint, and inch are not metric measurements. A pint is also a liquid measurement.

6. d. *Mutable* and *inconstant* both mean liable to change.

7. a. *Perceptible* and *recognizable* both mean able to be seen or noticed.

8. c. *Unfortunate, sorrowful,* and *regrettable* are all synonyms.

9. a. *Reality* means actually existing; *imaginary* means existing only in the mind.

10. c. *Rudimentary* means *basic* or undeveloped.

11. b. *Elated* is the opposite of *despondent*; *enlightened* is the opposite of *ignorant*. The answer is not choice **a** because aware is a synonym for enlightened. The answer is not choice **c** or **d** because neither of these is the opposite of enlightened.

12. a. *Flour, sugar,* and *garlic* are all ingredients in cooking, but a bowl is used to mix the ingredients.

13. a. A *rigorous* schedule is challenging, difficult, or *demanding*.

14. c. The first two statements give information about Joshua's white socks and blue socks. Information about socks of any other color cannot be determined.

15. c. *Meticulous* means careful and painstaking, which is the opposite of *sloppy*.

16. c. *Quadrilateral* means four-sided. Choices **a**, **b**, and **d** are all types of triangles.

17. b. Because the first two statements are true, Rebecca's house is also northeast of the Shop-and-Save Grocery, which means that the third statement is false.

18. a. If someone has been *humiliated*, he or she has been greatly *embarrassed*. If someone is *terrified*, he or she is extremely *frightened*. The answer is not choice **b** because an agitated person is not necessarily frightened. Choices **c** and **d** are incorrect because neither word expresses a state of being frightened.

19. b. *Exhaustive* means thorough. *Cursory* means hasty and not detailed.

20. d. To *chastise* means to rebuke or *punish*.

21. d. A *domain* is an area governed by a ruler; a *territory* is an area for which someone is responsible.

22. a. *Magazines, newspapers,* and *books* are all forms of printed material, while a movie is not.

23. a. According to the first two statements, Paws weighs the most and Tabby weighs the least.

24. c. Although all of Harriet's succulents are flowering plants, it cannot be determined by the information given whether all succulents are flowering plants.

25. c. *Pecans, walnuts,* and *cashews* are all types of nuts. A kernel is not a type of nut.

26. d. *Instruct, teach,* and *educate* are all synonyms.

27. a. *Innocuous* means not harmful or offensive.

28. b. Something that is *covert* is hidden or *secret*.

29. a. An *optimist* is a person whose outlook is *cheerful*. A *pessimist* is a person whose outlook is *gloomy*. The answer is not choice **b** because a pessimist does not have to be malicious. Choices **c** and **d** are incorrect because neither of these adjectives describes the outlook of a pessimist.

30. b. The *roof*, *door*, and *window* are parts of a house. The sidewalk is in front of the house, but it is not part of the building.

31. b. *Detrimental* means obviously *harmful* or damaging.

32. a. *Water*, *ice*, and *steam* are all forms of water—liquid, solid, and gas. A basin may be used to hold water, but it is not related.

33. a. We know that there are Signots with buttons, or Lamels, and that there are yellow Signots, which have no buttons. Therefore, Lamels do not have buttons and cannot be yellow.

34. c. To *demolish* means to tear apart; to *create* means to build.

35. d. *Notable* means unusual; *ordinary* means usual.

36. b. From the first two statements, we know that of the three cities, City A has the highest population, so the third statement must be false.

37. c. *Jovial* means cheerful or jolly, so the opposite would be *grouchy*.

38. a. A *synopsis* is an abbreviated version; a *summary* is a brief statement of facts or points.

39. b. *Methodical* means careful or in a planned manner; *deliberate* means careful or slow.

40. c. The *scythe*, the *knife*, and the *saw* are all cutting tools. Pliers are tools, but they are not used for cutting.

41. c. *Scarcity* means that something is lacking—a scarcity of food means that there isn't enough to eat. The opposite is *abundance*.

42. d. *Candid* and *indirect* are opposing traits. *Honest* and *devious* are opposing traits. The answer is not choice **a**, because frank means the same thing as candid. Wicked, choice **b**, is incorrect because even though it is a negative trait, it does not mean the opposite of honest. Choice **c** is incorrect because truthful and honest mean the same thing.

43. d. A *recluse* is a person who lives withdrawn or shut away from the world, a *hermit*.

44. a. The adjective *novel* means *new* or not representing something formerly known.

45. b. Given the information in the first two statements, Bryant is sitting in front of both Jerome and Martina, so the third statement must be false.

46. b. A *dubious* statement is doubtful or *questionable*.

47. c. *Optimum* means the most desirable; *worst* means the least desirable.

48. d. *Harmony* means agreement; *conflict* implies a disagreement.

49. c. *Fork*, *knife*, and *spoon* are all types of silverware, while a plate is a type of china.

50. d. A *pen* is a tool used by a *poet*. A *needle* is a tool used by a *tailor*. The answer is not choice **a**, **b**, or **c** because none are people and therefore cannot complete the analogy.

51. a. A *rationale* is a reason for something; an *explanation* is a clarification or definition of something.

52. c. Something that is *chaotic* is filled with chaos—disorder, wildness, lack of control. The opposite is *orderly*.

53. c. *Seat*, *rung*, and *leg* are all parts of a chair. Not all chairs are made of wood.

54. d. A *cryptic* message is literally written in a secret code, so it would be *mysterious*.

55. a. From the first statement, we know that bran cereal has more fiber than both oat cereal and corn cereal. From the second statement, we know that rice cereal has less fiber than both corn and wheat cereals. Therefore, rice cereal has the least amount of fiber.

56. c. We know only that Jasmine weighs more than Jason. There is no way to tell whether Jasmine also weighs more than Jenna.

57. a. A *malicious* action and a *spiteful* action are both intended to harm.

58. c. *Defendant, prosecutor,* and *judge* are all people involved in a trial. The trial is not a person.

59. b. *Shingles, wood,* and *bricks* are all used to cover a house, but a nail fastens them.

60. a. To *disperse* means to scatter; to *gather* means to collect in one place.

Part 2: Quantitative Skills

61. c. $6 \times 4 = 24; 24 \div 2 = 12$.

62. d. The rectangles are all the same size and all are one-half shaded.

63. a. First, solve for (A), (B), and (C): $3 \times (3 + 1) = 12; 1 \times (4 + 6) = 10; 2 \times (9 + 3) = 24$. Then find out which choice is true.

64. b. $\frac{1}{2}$ of $22 = 11; 6 + 11 = 17$.

65. a. 10% of $60 = 6$; 6 divided by $2 = 3$.

66. b. Count the number of diamonds in (A), (B), and (C), and then test each choice to find out whether it is true.

67. a. In this sequence, 1 is subtracted from the first number, 2 from the second number, 3 from the third, and so forth.

68. a. First, change (B) and (C) to decimals: 5% = $0.05; \frac{1}{5} = 0.2$. Then find out which choice is true.

69. b. This is a simple subtraction series; each number is 7 less than the previous number.

70. c. First, set up the equation: $n \times 2 = \frac{1}{3} \times 12$. Then solve: $n \times 2 = 4; n = 2$.

71. d. 25% of $8 = 2; 2 + 10 = 12$.

72. b. In this addition series, 10 is added to the first number, 11 is added to the second number, 12 is added to the third number, and so forth.

73. c. This is a simple addition series. Each number increases by $\frac{1}{6}$.

74. a. The figure forms two right triangles. Line *AD* is the hypotenuse and must be longer than either *AB* or *CD*.

75. a. $100 \div 5 = 20; 20 \div 2 = 10$.

76. b. First, solve for (A), (B), and (C): (A) = 40, (B) = 40, (C) = 20. Then find out which choice is true.

77. d. This is a simple addition series; each number is three more than the previous number.

78. d. First, determine the value of each letter: A = 12, B = 3, C = 9, D = 15. Then test each choice to find out whether it is true.

79. c. $\frac{2}{5}$ of $25 = 10; 10 - 6 = 4$.

80. a. 4% of $20 = 0.8; 3 \times 0.8 = 2.4$.

81. c. This is a multiplication series; each number is three times the previous number.

82. d. (B) and (C) are equal to $n \times n$.

83. b. This is an alternating series using addition. Three is added to the first number, then 5, then 3, and so on.

84. b. First, set up the equation: $n \times 2 = 6 \times 5$. Then solve: $n = 6 \times 5 \div 2; n = 15$.

85. d. First, determine the amounts shown in (A), (B), and (C), and then test each statement to find out whether it is true.

86. d. Of (A), (B), and (C), each is equal to 3.

87. c. First, set up the equation: $n \times 3 = 10 \div 2$. Then solve: $n = (10 \div 2) \times 3; n = 15$.

88. d. In this simple subtraction series, each number decreases by 3.

89. a. First, set up the equation: $n \div 5 = \frac{1}{10} \times 300$. Then solve: $n \div 5 = 30; n = 150$.

90. b. There are two series here, with every third term following the second pattern. The main series begins with 2, and 3 is added to each number to arrive at the next. The second series begins with 28, and 8 is subtracted from each number to arrive at the next.

91. a. *AC* plus *BD* is equal to $2x$ and is therefore less than *AB*, which is $3x$.

92. c. First, solve for (A), (B), and (C): (A) = 49, (B) = 64, (C) = 15. Then find out which choice is true.

93. c. This is a simple alternating addition and subtraction series. In the first pattern, 3 is added; in the second, 2 is subtracted.

94. d. First, set up the equation: $(0.15 \times 30) + n = 20$. Then solve: $4.5 + n = 20; n = 15.5$.

95. b. Count the number of blocks in (A), (B), and (C), and then test each choice to find out which one is true.

96. c. This is a simple multiplication series. Each number is three times more than the previous number.

97. b. First, set up the equation: $n + 2n = 99$. Then solve: $3n = 99; n = 33$.

98. c. 12% of 1,000 = 120; 120 + 16 = 136.

99. a. This is a simple division series. Each number is divided by 5.

100. d. First, solve for (B) and (C): (B) = 30, (C) = 12. Then find out which choice is true.

101. c. Angle (A) is a right triangle. Angle (B) plus angle (C) equals another right triangle.

102. a. In this series, the letters progress by 1; the numbers decrease by 3.

103. a. This is an alternating multiplication and addition series: First, divide by 2, and then add 8.

104. b. First, set up the equation: $7n = (0.6 \times 770) \div 6$. Then solve: $7n = 77; n = 11$.

105. d. First, set up the equation: $33 = 0.12 \times n$. Then solve: $33 \div 0.12 = 275$.

106. d. This is an alternating multiplication series. Each number is two times more than the previous number. Roman numbers alternate with Arabic numbers.

107. b. First, determine an approximate percentage for each letter: A = 25%, B = 5%, C = 15%, D = 22%, E = 33%. Then, test each statement to find out whether it is true.

108. c. $\frac{1}{5}$ of 820 = 164; 164 − 42 = 122.

109. b. In this simple addition with repetition series, each number in the series repeats itself, and then increases by 11 to arrive at the next number.

110. b. First, convert (B) and (C) to inches: (B) = 15 inches and (C) = 37 inches. Then, find out which choice is true.

111. b. In this alternating sequence, the first number is divided by 2, then 4 is added, and so on.

112. c. First, set up the equation: $n \div 4 = 20\% \times 10$. Then solve: $20\% \times 10 = 2; 2 \times 4 = 8; n = 8$.

Part 3: Reading

113. c. Choice **c** reflects the author's point of view. Support material for this answer can be found throughout the passage, especially in the first and fifth paragraphs. Choice **b** is plausible, but ignores the author's view. Choices **a** and **d** are unsupported by the passage.

114. b. Choice **b** is the word the author uses to describe the snake's movement in the first paragraph. Choice **a** describes the biological makeup of the snake. Choices **c** and **d** do not describe the snake's movement.

115. b. Choice **b** describes what would happen if snakes were destroyed. Support for this answer can be found in the sixth paragraph. Choices **a**, **c**, and **d** are not supported by the information from this passage.

116. a. Support for answer choice **a** can be found in the fourth paragraph. The paragraph begins by explaining why a snake needs the sun's heat. Choices **b** and **c** are not supported by the passage; choice **d** is not connected to cold-bloodedness.

117. d. Choices **a**, **b**, and **c** are supported by information in the third, fifth, and sixth paragraphs. Choice **d** is the only false statement.

118. c. Choice **c** correctly expresses the main idea of the passage. Choice **a** contradicts one of the main ideas of the article; choice **b** is not supported anywhere in the passage. Choice **d** describes only a small section in the passage, not the overall idea.

119. b. Choice **b** is the only choice that describes the main subject of the passage. Choices **a**, **c**, and **d** discuss points made in the passage, but they do not reflect the main idea.

120. b. The word *swampy* in the first paragraph gives a context clue in support of choice **b**. Choices **a**, **c**, and **d** are not associated with damp, coastal areas.

121. c. Choice **a** is stated in the third paragraph, as is choice **b**. Choice **d** is stated in the last paragraph. Therefore, choice **c** would be the only statement that is NOT true.

122. d. The third paragraph states, "Only a few plants behave in this unusual manner . . . ," and it refers to eating insects. Therefore, choice **d** is the correct inference. Choices **a** and **c** are not supported by any information in the article and may be untrue. Choice **b** is contradicted by information in the last paragraph.

123. b. The passage highlights a problem with the city's mail delivery: Mail was not delivered in a consistent time frame. None of the other choices is mentioned.

124. a. The word *address* can refer to a location, but it is used in the first sentence to mean *pay attention to.*

125. c. The passage implies that Greenwold's company was able to deliver the mail more efficiently by avoiding complications created by the competition's union.

126. d. The final sentence states that mail delivery was transformed in 1987, which suggests that Mercury Delivery Company began then.

127. c. The word *conundrum* means riddle or difficult problem.

128. b. The passage does speak about Mark Greenwold, but it does not tell the reader anything about his life—nor does it tell us how to deliver the mail. The best answer is choice **b**.

129. d. The passage tells us that Paul Revere was a silversmith, a person who makes things out of silver.

130. a. The word *commemorate* means to do something that will help people remember a person or event.

131. c. Paul Revere worked for a time carrying messages by horseback between Boston and other cities. This taught him how to deliver urgent messages very quickly.

132. b. The Old North Church in Boston placed two lanterns in the steeple because it was a prearranged signal, telling the people of Boston that the British were crossing the river to attack the patriots in Lexington.

133. b. The word *wane* means to decrease or grow smaller.

134. a. The passage tells the history of Paul Revere's famous ride, when he delivered an important message, warning the people of Lexington that the enemy was approaching.

135. b. While all four statements are true, choice **b** is the most accurate about the passage.

136. a. Choices **b** and **c** are other definitions of incorporate, but they do not fit with this passage. Choice **d** is not a meaning of incorporate.

137. b. This is a detail question. The countries from which American acupuncturists draw techniques are listed in the second paragraph.

138. a. The third paragraph states: *Some people are energized by treatment, while others feel relaxed.*

139. d. If the needles have an imperfection, they will cause problems in the treatment.

140. a. This is a detail question. The causes of soreness or pain are listed in the third paragraph.

141. c. James Reston reported his experiences with acupuncture in the *New York Times*.

142. d. Choice **d** is the title that most fully describes the passage. Choice **a** is not accurate because the passage is not about getting the most out of the experience. Choice **b** is not accurate because though acupuncture is an ancient technique, the author does not describe it as "old-fashioned." Choice **c** is too lighthearted in tone.

143. b. Although the passage mentions firefighters' responsibilities (choice **a**), the main focus of the passage is the installation of smoke detectors. Choice **c** is only a detail. Choice **d** is not mentioned.

144. b. The answer can be found in the first sentence of the third paragraph.

145. a. The answer is found in the first paragraph (*smoke detectors cut a person's risk of dying in a fire in half*).

146. c. The answer can be found in the third paragraph.

147. d. The answer is implied by the first sentence of the passage. There is no information in the passage to indicate that the other choices are a firefighter's responsibility.

148. b. The answer is drawn from the second paragraph. The house has three floors and the sleeping areas are all on one of these floors; therefore, the house should have *three* detectors.

149. a. The passage informs and instructs, so this is the best choice. It is clearly not lighthearted (choice **b**). Although the information may be a little frightening, the tone is not terrifying (choice **c**), nor is it presented in an emotional way (choice **d**).

150. d. Of the choices, this is the only workable title. The others are misleading and can be ruled out. The passage does not mention *new* smoke detectors (choice **a**). The passage is not about dead-air, so choice **b** is incorrect. Nor is it about the problems of firefighters, so choice **c**, too, can be ruled out.

151. d. This answer can be found in the second paragraph. The others are ruled out in the third paragraph.

152. c. This is the most likely opinion of the author. Based on the passage, the author believes that all homes should have smoke detectors. There is nothing in the passage to indicate choice **a**. Choices **b** and **d** are attractive, but the passage offers much more support for choice **c**.

153. a. secretive

154. d. dexterous

155. a. cynical

156. b. rustic

157. a. *Recuperate* means to *recover* health or strength.

158. d. Something that is *translucent allows light to pass through.*

159. b. *Composure* means a calmness of mind or appearance; *poise*.

160. a. *Commendable* means praiseworthy or *admirable*.

161. d. illegal

162. c. *Expansive* means having a great expanse; sizable, *spacious*.

163. b. A *mesa* and a *plateau* are both hills with flat tops.

164. b. thoughtful

165. c. *Animosity* is a strong resentment or *hostility* toward something.

166. b. Something that is *spurious* is not genuine.

167. a. noisy

168. c. *Meager* means deficient in quality or quantity; thin; *scant*.

169. c. To *dissuade* someone is to talk him or her out of something; to *discourage* plans.

170. a. *Equity* means *justice* or impartiality.

171. b. endorse

172. b. *Affluence* means having great *wealth*.

173. d. exhausted

174. a. To *defray* means to provide for the payment of something, to *pay*.

Part 4: Mathematics

175. c. The correct answer here is 10,447. It helps, if you are in a place where you can do so, to read the answer aloud; that way, you'll likely catch any mistake. When writing numbers with more than four digits, begin at the right and separate the digits into groups of threes with commas.

176. b. The variable is a symbol that stands for any number under discussion.

177. d. The hundredths place is two digits to the right of the decimal point. The 9 is in the tenths place; the 0 is in the thousandths place; the 2 is in the ten-thousandths place.

178. b. Fractions must be converted to the lowest common denominator, which is 60. $\frac{6}{10} = \frac{36}{60}$; $\frac{11}{20} = \frac{33}{60}$; $\frac{8}{15} = \frac{32}{60}$, which is the smallest fraction.

179. b. $62.5\% = \frac{62.5}{100}$. You should multiply both the numerator and denominator by 10 to move the decimal point, resulting in $\frac{625}{1,000}$, and then factor both the numerator and denominator to find out how far you can reduce the fraction. $\frac{625}{1,000} = \frac{(5)(5)(5)(5)}{(5)(5)(5)(8)}$. If you cancel the three 5s that are in both the numerator and denominator, you will get $\frac{5}{8}$.

180. a. A straight angle is exactly 180°.

181. b. We multiply –6 by itself and get $(-6) \times (-6)$. When multiplying two negative numbers, the answer is always positive: 36.

182. d. To find the answer, do the following equation: $11 \times 0.032 = 0.352$.

183. d. Fourteen hundred is the same as one thousand four hundred, or 1,400. Add in the eighty-two for 1,482.

184. c. There are 16 ounces in one pound, so the ratio of 2 ounces to 1 pound 2:16; reduced, this becomes 1:8.

185. d. First, change the names to letters; remember that the letters then represent, not the people, but their *ages*. S (*Salwa's age*) equals R (*Roland's age*) plus 10 (*years*).

186. a. The thousandths place is three digits to the right of the decimal point. Note that the 1 is in the *thousands* place, not the *thousandths* place.

187. c. The solution to this problem lies in knowing that 100^2 is equal to 100×100, or 10,000. Next, you must multiply $10,000 \times 2.75$ to arrive at 27,500.

188. c. Complementary angles add to 90°. Therefore, the complementary angle is 90° – 36° = 54°.

189. a. The symbol > means "greater than," and the symbol < means "less than." The only sentence that is correct is choice **a**: 4 feet is greater than 3 feet. The other choices are untrue.

190. b. The other choices are all untrue.

191. a. This is the only common factor.

192. d. 2 hours 28 minutes = 148 minutes − 77 minutes = 71 minutes, or 1 hour 11 minutes.

193. a. 10^{18} means 10 to the 18th power, or 10 times itself 18 times.

194. c. The greatest area from a quadrilateral will always be a square. Therefore, a side will be $24 \div 4 = 6$ feet. The area is $6^2 = 36$ square feet.

195. d. The hundredths place is two decimals over from the decimal point. If the digit to the right of it is less than 5, do not round up.

196. b. Since $0.05 = \frac{1}{20}$, 0.05 is greater than $\frac{1}{25}$.

197. c. There are 4 quarts to 1 gallon; 2 pints to a quart; 2 cups to 1 pint.

198. c. The perimeter is 4×4 for the square, and the circumference is $d\pi$ for the circle. This is a difference of $16 - 4\pi$.

199. b. $102 \div 12 = 8.5$.

200. b. $\$37.27 \times 6 = \$223.62$.

201. b. There is $\frac{1}{3}$ of the quiche left after the first day. $\frac{1}{2}$ of $\frac{1}{3} = \frac{1}{2} \times \frac{1}{3} = \frac{1}{6}$.

202. c. First, change the fraction to a decimal: $\frac{1}{8} = 1 \div 8 = 0.125$. Now multiply that by José's hourly wage in order to get Pete's hourly wage: $0.125 \times \$19.50 = \$2.4375$ (rounded). Now multiply Pete's hourly wage by 8 hours: $\$2.4375 \times 8 = 19.50$.

203. c. On average, it takes Carla about 6 minutes to do each math problem. Multiplying 6 minutes by 20 problems gives an answer of about 120 minutes to do her math homework.

204. c. Perform the operation in parentheses first: $14 \times 7 = 98$, and then add 12 to get the answer, which is 110.

205. b. Add the feet first, then the inches: 2 feet + 4 feet = 6 feet. Then, 4 inches + 8 inches = 12 inches. Convert 12 inches into 1 foot to get the correct answer 6 feet + 1 foot = 7 feet.

206. d. 17^2 means 17 squared and is equivalent to 17×17, which equals 289.

207. d. This is a simple division problem with decimals.

208. d. Convert the percent to a decimal, so that it becomes 3.0. Now multiply: $20 \times 3.0 = 60$.

209. b. $\frac{1}{3}x + 3 = 8$. In order to solve the equation, all numbers need to be on one side and all x values on the other. Therefore, $\frac{1}{3}x = 5$; $x = 15$.

210. a. Multiply the whole number by the fraction's denominator. $5 \times 2 = 10$. Add the fraction's numerator to the answer: $1 + 10 = 11$. Now place that answer over the fraction's denominator: $\frac{11}{2}$.

211. d. The sum of the measurements is the perimeter. This is 4×5 inches + 2×7 inches.

212. b. This is a simple subtraction problem. Be sure to align the decimal points: $99.0 - 97.2 = 1.8$.

213. b. The common denominator of the fractions is 280. The sum of the fractions is $\frac{503}{280}$, or $1\frac{223}{280}$. This unwieldy fraction cannot be reduced further.

214. b. First, change the percent to a decimal: $3\frac{1}{4}\% = 3.25\% = 0.0325$. Now multiply: $30,600 \times 0.0325 = 994.5$. Finally, add: $\$30,600 + 994.50 = \$31,594.50$ for Yetta's current salary.

215. a. The unreduced ratio is 8,000:5,000,000; reduced, the ratio is 8:5,000. Now divide: $5,000 \div 8 = 625$, for a ratio of 1:625.

216. a. Cross multiplying: $(2x)(48) = (16)(12)$; $96x = 192$. Thus, $x = 2$.

217. a. The correct answer is $18\frac{2}{3}$.

218. d. $s = (2 \times 8) - (11 - 2)$; $s = 16 - (11 - 2)$; $s = 16 - 9$; $s = 7$.

219. b. The last digit has to be a 3, which rules out choice **c**. You can rule out choices **a** and **d** because of their place values.

220. c. The formula for area is *area = length × width*; in this case, $64.125 = 9.5 \times width$, or 6.75.

221. d. This problem requires both multiplication and addition. First, multiply 2.12 by 1.5 to find the price of the cheddar cheese: $2.12 \times 1.5 = 3.18$. Then add: $3.18 + 2.34 = 5.52$.

222. d. The seller's $103,000 represents only 93% of the sale price (100% − 7%). The broker's commission is NOT 7% of $103,000, but rather 7% of the whole sale price. The question is: $103,000 is 93% of what figure? So, let $x = \frac{103,000}{93} = 110,752.68$, rounded to $110,753.

223. c. This percent problem involves finding the whole when the percent is given. 280,000 is 150% of last month's attendance. Convert 150% to a decimal. 150% = 1.5. 280,000 = 1.5 × LMA. Next, divide: 280,000 ÷ 1.5 = 186,666.6666 Round up to the nearest whole number: 186,667.

224. b. The dimensions of triangle *MNO* are double those of triangle *RST*. Line segment *RT* is 5 cm; therefore, line segment *MO* is 10 cm.

225. c. If the number is represented by *n*, its double is 2*n*. Therefore, $n + 2n = 69$; $3n = 69$; $n = 23$.

226. a. $10 − 3y = 40$; $−3y = 30$; $y = −10$.

227. b. The *median* is merely the number in the *middle of the series* when the numbers are arranged in order, which, in this case, is 12.

228. b. Change the percent to a decimal: 0.35; then, to find the answer, divide: 14 ÷ 0.35 = 40.

229. b. Since the 5-inch side and the 2.5-inch side are similar, the second triangle must be larger than the first. The two angles without congruent marks add up to 100°, so 180° − 100° = 80°. This is the largest angle, so the choice opposite it must be largest, in this case, choice **b.**

230. d. To find what percent one number is of another, first write out an equation. Since $x\% = \frac{x}{100}$ the equation is: $\frac{x}{100} = \frac{420}{1,200}$. Cross multiply: $1,200x = (420)(100)$. Simplify: $x = \frac{42,000}{1,200}$. Thus $x = 35$, which means 35% of the videos are comedies.

231. c. First, convert tons to pounds: 1 ton = 2,000 pounds; 36 tons (per year) = 72,000 pounds (per year); 1 year = 12 months, so the average number of pounds of mosquitoes the colony of bats can consume in a month is: 72,000 ÷ 12, or 6,000 pounds.

232. d. We want to know *R* = helicopter's speed in miles per hour. To solve this problem recall that *rate* × *time* = *distance*. It is given that *T* = 6:17 − 6:02 = 15 minutes = 0.25 hour and *D* = 20 miles. Substituting: *R* × 0.25 = 20. Simplifying: *R* = 20 ÷ 0.25. Thus, *R* = 80 mph.

233. d. The total sales equal the sum of Linda and Jared's sales or *L* + *J* = 36. Since Linda sold three less than twice Jared's total, *L* = 2*J* − 3. The equation (2*J* − 3) + *J* = 36 models this situation. This gives 3*J* = 39; *J* = 13.

234. c. Karl is four times as old as Pam means *K* = 4*P*, Pam is one-third as old as Jackie means $P = \frac{1}{3}J$. We are given *J* = 18. Working backward, $P = \frac{1}{3}(18) = 6$; *K* = 4(6) = 24. The sum of their ages = *K* + *P* + *J* = 24 + 6 + 18 = 48.

235. c. Seven is added to both sides of the equation, giving 1.5*x* = 19.5. 19.5 ÷ 1.5 = 13.

236. b. Area is equal to base times height: 2 × 4 = 8.

237. d. Each quilt square is $\frac{1}{4}$ of a square foot; 6 inches is $\frac{1}{2}$ of a foot, 0.5 × 0.5 = 0.25 of a square foot. Therefore, each square foot of the quilt requires 4 quilt squares. 30 square feet × 4 = 120 quilt squares.

238. b. Let *x* equal the number sought. Nineteen more than a certain number is 63 means: *x* + 19 = 63 or *x* = 63 − 19. Thus, *x* = 44.

Part 5: Language Skills

239. c. The word *Doctor* should not be capitalized.

240. d. All the answers are correct.

241. b. There should not be a comma before *today*.

242. b. This is a fragment, not a complete sentence.

243. b. There should be an apostrophe in *what's*.

244. a. *You're* should be *your*.

245. d. All the answers are correct.

246. c. This sentence contains a double negative.

247. c. The contraction *Three's*, which means *Three is*, is the correct usage.

248. d. All the answer choices are correct.

249. d. All the answer choices are correct.

250. c. *Mayor* should not be capitalized because it does not refer to a particular mayor.

251. d. All the answer choices are correct.

252. b. This sentence has a faulty shift in construction; the word *that* should be omitted from the sentence.

253. b. A semicolon is not used between a dependent and an independent clause. Use a comma or no punctuation.

254. b. *Veterinarian* is not a proper noun and should not be capitalized.

255. a. This sentence has a usage error: *fewer* cookies, not *less* cookies.

256. d. All the answer choices are correct.

257. a. *They're* is a contraction of *they are*. It should be *Their*.

258. c. There should be no apostrophe in *dogs*.

259. a. The verb *lay* should be *lie*.

260. d. All the answer choices are correct.

261. d. All the answer choices are correct.

262. b. The correct verb form is *has broken*.

263. b. *World War* is a proper noun and should be capitalized.

264. a. The correct verb form is *rang*.

265. a. The phrase *like many other viruses* should be set off by commas because it is a nonessential element in the sentence.

266. d. All the answer choices are correct.

267. b. There is an illogical shift in tense. Both verbs should be in the past tense.

268. a. The pronoun *him* is incorrect. *He* should be used because *you* and *he* are the subjects of the dependent clause.

269. b. The contraction *You're* should be replaced with the possessive *Your*.

270. a. *Industrial Revolution* should be capitalized.

271. c. This sentence makes a shift in person. It should read: The volunteers work as hard as *they* can.

272. b. The verb should agree with *one*, not *boys*; so the singular verb *was* should be used.

273. a. *I should have gone.*

274. c. There is no such word as *alot*. She sneezes *a lot*.

275. d. All the answer choices are correct.

276. d. All the answer choices are correct.

277. a. The names of centuries are not capitalized.

278. c. This sentence asks a question and should end with a question mark.

279. b. management

280. b. neighbor

281. c. knives

282. d. All the words are spelled correctly.

283. c. procedures

284. b. immediately

285. c. February

286. a. sensible

287. b. received

288. c. prescription

289. c. This is the only choice that is logical. The other choices imply a cause and effect that does not exist.

290. a. This is the only choice that shows a cause and effect between the two parts of the sentence.

291. a. The other choices are awkwardly constructed and difficult to read.

292. a. Choices **b** and **c** are sentence fragments. Choice **d** represents confused sentence structure as well as lack of agreement between subject and verb.

293. b. This choice most clearly states the advantage of having bus service.

294. b. This is the only choice that states the information clearly.

295. d. The other choices are much too broad to be adequately covered in a short essay.

296. b. This is the best choice because it is the only one that refers to risks from the sun at high altitudes. Choice **a** has nothing to do with risks from the sun; choice **c** gives no reference to high altitudes; choice **d** is about healing, not sun risk.

297. c. This sentence shifts the topic away from Barbara Miller and her dog bakery.

298. d. This is the only logical choice. This new sentence could not logically appear before sentence 3 because sentence 3 introduces the oxides and minerals.

Scoring

Find out how you did on this practice exam by counting the number of questions you got right in each part. Remember, questions you skipped or got wrong don't count against your score—only the number of correct answers is important. Then divide the number you got right by the number of questions in the section:

Part 1: Verbal Skills

_____ correct divided by 60 = _____ %

Part 2: Quantitative Skills

_____ correct divided by 52 = _____%

Part 3: Reading

_____ correct divided by 62 = _____%

Part 4: Mathematics

_____ correct divided by 64 = _____%

Part 5: Language Skills

_____ correct divided by 60 = _____%

This percentage score is not the same kind of score you will receive when you take the real HSPT. But you can use your percentage score to:

- compare with your score on the first practice exam and see where you've improved
- find out where you still have areas of weakness, so you can study those areas more thoroughly

The key to success in almost any pursuit is to prepare for all you're worth. By taking the practice exams in this book, you've made yourself better prepared than many of the other students taking the exam with you. You've diagnosed where your strengths and weaknesses lie and learned how to deal with the various kinds of questions that will appear on the test. So go into the exam with confidence, knowing that you're ready and equipped to do your best.

14 ▶ PRACTICE COOP EXAM 2

LESSON SUMMARY

This is the second of the two practice tests in this book based on the COOP exam. Use this test to see how much you've improved.

As you take this practice test, imitate the actual test-taking situation as closely as possible. Find a quiet place where you won't be interrupted. Tear out the answer sheets on pages 303–304, and gather your number 2 pencils to fill in the circles. Use a timer or stopwatch and allow yourself time as follows:

SUBTESTS	NUMBER OF QUESTIONS (APPROXIMATE)	TIME ALLOTTED (APPROXIMATE)
1. Sequences	20	15 minutes
2. Analogies	20	7 minutes
3. Quantitative Reasoning	20	15 minutes
4. Verbal Reasoning—Words	20	15 minutes
5. Verbal Reasoning—Context	20	15 minutes
15-MINUTE BREAK		

SUBTESTS	NUMBER OF QUESTIONS (APPROXIMATE)	TIME ALLOTTED (APPROXIMATE)
6. Reading and Language Arts	40	40 minutes
7. Mathematics	40	35 minutes

After the exam, again use the answer key that follows it to see your progress and to find out why the correct answers are correct and the incorrect ones incorrect. Then use the scoring section at the end of the exam to see your progress and judge how you did overall.

LEARNINGEXPRESS ANSWER SHEET

Test 1: Sequences

1. (a) (b) (c) (d)
2. (a) (b) (c) (d)
3. (a) (b) (c) (d)
4. (a) (b) (c) (d)
5. (a) (b) (c) (d)
6. (a) (b) (c) (d)
7. (a) (b) (c) (d)
8. (a) (b) (c) (d)
9. (a) (b) (c) (d)
10. (a) (b) (c) (d)
11. (a) (b) (c) (d)
12. (a) (b) (c) (d)
13. (a) (b) (c) (d)
14. (a) (b) (c) (d)
15. (a) (b) (c) (d)
16. (a) (b) (c) (d)
17. (a) (b) (c) (d)
19. (a) (b) (c) (d)
20. (a) (b) (c) (d)

Test 2: Analogies

1. (a) (b) (c) (d)
2. (a) (b) (c) (d)
3. (a) (b) (c) (d)
4. (a) (b) (c) (d)
5. (a) (b) (c) (d)
6. (a) (b) (c) (d)
7. (a) (b) (c) (d)
8. (a) (b) (c) (d)
9. (a) (b) (c) (d)
10. (a) (b) (c) (d)
11. (a) (b) (c) (d)
12. (a) (b) (c) (d)
13. (a) (b) (c) (d)
14. (a) (b) (c) (d)
15. (a) (b) (c) (d)
16. (a) (b) (c) (d)
17. (a) (b) (c) (d)
19. (a) (b) (c) (d)
20. (a) (b) (c) (d)

Test 3: Quantitative Reasoning

1. (a) (b) (c) (d)
2. (a) (b) (c) (d)
3. (a) (b) (c) (d)
4. (a) (b) (c) (d)
5. (a) (b) (c) (d)
6. (a) (b) (c) (d)
7. (a) (b) (c) (d)
8. (a) (b) (c) (d)
9. (a) (b) (c) (d)
10. (a) (b) (c) (d)
11. (a) (b) (c) (d)
12. (a) (b) (c) (d)
13. (a) (b) (c) (d)
14. (a) (b) (c) (d)
15. (a) (b) (c) (d)
16. (a) (b) (c) (d)
17. (a) (b) (c) (d)
19. (a) (b) (c) (d)
20. (a) (b) (c) (d)

Test 4: Verbal Reasoning—Words

1. (a) (b) (c) (d)
2. (a) (b) (c) (d)
3. (a) (b) (c) (d)
4. (a) (b) (c) (d)
5. (a) (b) (c) (d)
6. (a) (b) (c) (d)
7. (a) (b) (c) (d)
8. (a) (b) (c) (d)
9. (a) (b) (c) (d)
10. (a) (b) (c) (d)
11. (a) (b) (c) (d)
12. (a) (b) (c) (d)
13. (a) (b) (c) (d)
14. (a) (b) (c) (d)
15. (a) (b) (c) (d)
16. (a) (b) (c) (d)
17. (a) (b) (c) (d)
19. (a) (b) (c) (d)
20. (a) (b) (c) (d)

Test 5: Verbal Reasoning—Context

1. (a) (b) (c) (d)
2. (a) (b) (c) (d)
3. (a) (b) (c) (d)
4. (a) (b) (c) (d)
5. (a) (b) (c) (d)
6. (a) (b) (c) (d)
7. (a) (b) (c) (d)

8. (a) (b) (c) (d)
9. (a) (b) (c) (d)
10. (a) (b) (c) (d)
11. (a) (b) (c) (d)
12. (a) (b) (c) (d)
13. (a) (b) (c) (d)
14. (a) (b) (c) (d)

15. (a) (b) (c) (d)
16. (a) (b) (c) (d)
17. (a) (b) (c) (d)
19. (a) (b) (c) (d)
20. (a) (b) (c) (d)

Test 6: Reading and Language Arts

1. (a) (b) (c) (d)
2. (a) (b) (c) (d)
3. (a) (b) (c) (d)
4. (a) (b) (c) (d)
5. (a) (b) (c) (d)
6. (a) (b) (c) (d)
7. (a) (b) (c) (d)
8. (a) (b) (c) (d)
9. (a) (b) (c) (d)
10. (a) (b) (c) (d)
11. (a) (b) (c) (d)
12. (a) (b) (c) (d)
13. (a) (b) (c) (d)
14. (a) (b) (c) (d)

15. (a) (b) (c) (d)
16. (a) (b) (c) (d)
17. (a) (b) (c) (d)
18. (a) (b) (c) (d)
19. (a) (b) (c) (d)
20. (a) (b) (c) (d)
21. (a) (b) (c) (d)
22. (a) (b) (c) (d)
23. (a) (b) (c) (d)
24. (a) (b) (c) (d)
25. (a) (b) (c) (d)
26. (a) (b) (c) (d)
27. (a) (b) (c) (d)
28. (a) (b) (c) (d)

29. (a) (b) (c) (d)
30. (a) (b) (c) (d)
31. (a) (b) (c) (d)
32. (a) (b) (c) (d)
33. (a) (b) (c) (d)
34. (a) (b) (c) (d)
35. (a) (b) (c) (d)
36. (a) (b) (c) (d)
37. (a) (b) (c) (d)
38. (a) (b) (c) (d)
39. (a) (b) (c) (d)
40. (a) (b) (c) (d)

Test 7: Mathematics

1. (a) (b) (c) (d)
2. (a) (b) (c) (d)
3. (a) (b) (c) (d)
4. (a) (b) (c) (d)
5. (a) (b) (c) (d)
6. (a) (b) (c) (d)
7. (a) (b) (c) (d)
8. (a) (b) (c) (d)
9. (a) (b) (c) (d)
10. (a) (b) (c) (d)
11. (a) (b) (c) (d)
12. (a) (b) (c) (d)
13. (a) (b) (c) (d)
14. (a) (b) (c) (d)

15. (a) (b) (c) (d)
16. (a) (b) (c) (d)
17. (a) (b) (c) (d)
18. (a) (b) (c) (d)
19. (a) (b) (c) (d)
20. (a) (b) (c) (d)
21. (a) (b) (c) (d)
22. (a) (b) (c) (d)
23. (a) (b) (c) (d)
24. (a) (b) (c) (d)
25. (a) (b) (c) (d)
26. (a) (b) (c) (d)
27. (a) (b) (c) (d)
28. (a) (b) (c) (d)

29. (a) (b) (c) (d)
30. (a) (b) (c) (d)
31. (a) (b) (c) (d)
32. (a) (b) (c) (d)
33. (a) (b) (c) (d)
34. (a) (b) (c) (d)
35. (a) (b) (c) (d)
36. (a) (b) (c) (d)
37. (a) (b) (c) (d)
38. (a) (b) (c) (d)
39. (a) (b) (c) (d)
40. (a) (b) (c) (d)

Test 1: Sequences

You have 15 minutes for this section. Select the answer choice that best completes the sequence given.

1. △ □ △ | □ ○ □ | ○ ◇ ○ | ◇ □ —

   ◇   □   ○   △

  a.   **b.**   **c.**   **d.**

2. ↑ ↗ → ↘ ↓ ↙ —

   ↖   ←   ↑   ↔

  a.   **b.**   **c.**   **d.**

3. BBꙄB | ᗺBBB | BᗺᗺB | BB —

  ᗺB   BB   BB   BᗺB

  a.   **b.**   **c.**   **d.**

4. ⌐ ⌐⌐ | ▢ ⬠ ▢ | ⊔ —

  ▢⬠   ⌐▢   ⌐⌐   ⌐⌐

  a.   **b.**   **c.**   **d.**

5. ◼◪ | ◼⊠ | ◪◪ | ◀◼ —

  ⊠◪   ◼◪   ◪◪   ◪⊠

  a.   **b.**   **c.**   **d.**

6. Ô Ö Ø Q̊ | Q̇ Q̣ Ø Ø | Ô _ Ø

  ØQ̣   ÖQ̇   QÖ   ÖØ

  a.   **b.**   **c.**   **d.**

7. ◓ ⊕ ◒ | ▭ ▭ ▭ | ▤ —

  ▥   ▨   ◪   ▧

  a.   **b.**   **c.**   **d.**

8. 20 11 2 | 32 23 14 | 76 __ 58
- **a.** 58
- **b.** 60
- **c.** 66
- **d.** 67

9. 3 8 13 | 12 17 22 | __ 24 29
- **a.** 19
- **b.** 18
- **c.** 17
- **d.** 16

10. 8 16 11 | 12 20 15 | 3 11 __
- **a.** 5
- **b.** 6
- **c.** 7
- **d.** 8

11. 0.2 0.04 0.0016 | 0.3 0.09 0.0081 | 0.1 0.01 __
- **a.** 0.0001
- **b.** 000.1
- **c.** 0.02
- **d.** 0.2

12. 13 14 17 | 21 22 11 | 51 __ 26
- **a.** 24
- **b.** 53
- **c.** 52
- **d.** 2

13. 90 30 27 | 12 4 1 | 27 9 __
- **a.** 1
- **b.** 3
- **c.** 6
- **d.** 16

14. 5 7 21 | 10 12 36 | 8 10 __
   a. 12
   b. 24
   c. 28
   d. 30

15. LKJ CDE IHG ____
   a. FGH
   b. KJL
   c. ABC
   d. EDC

16. AAB ABB BBC ____
   a. CBA
   b. ABC
   c. BBC
   d. BCC

17. B1C C2D D3E ____
   a. F4G
   b. E4E
   c. E4F
   d. E5F

18. BOC COB DOE EOD __
   a. FOG
   b. DOG
   c. DOF
   d. FOE

19. LML NON PQP RSR __
   a. TUT
   b. RTR
   c. STS
   d. TRT

20. ZA_5 Y_4B XC_6 W_3D ___
   a. E_7V
   b. V_2E
   c. VE_5
   d. VE_7

Test 2: Analogies

You have 7 minutes for this section. Choose the picture that would go in the empty box so that the two bottom pictures are related in the same way as the top two are related.

1.

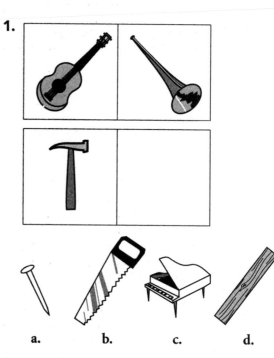

a.   b.   c.   d.

2.

a.   b.   c.   d.

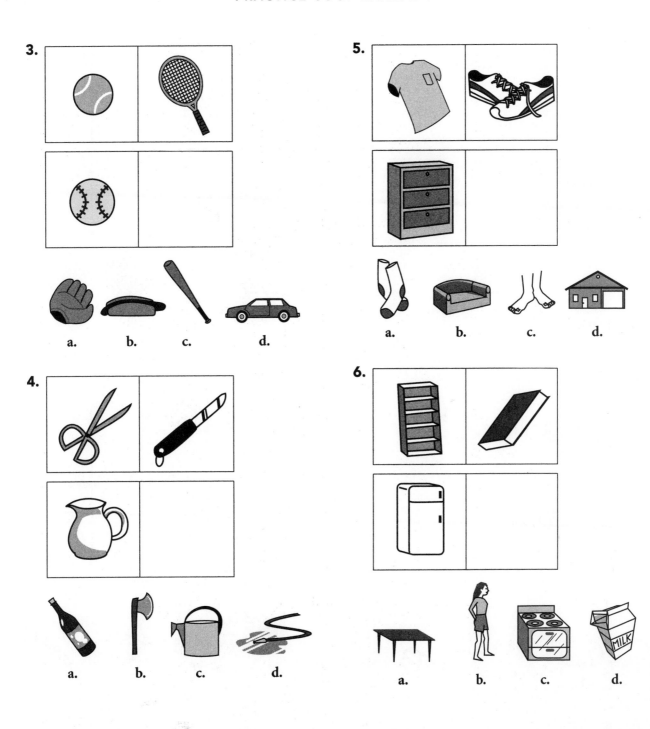

3.

a.   b.   c.   d.

4.

a.   b.   c.   d.

5.

a.   b.   c.   d.

6.

a.   b.   c.   d.

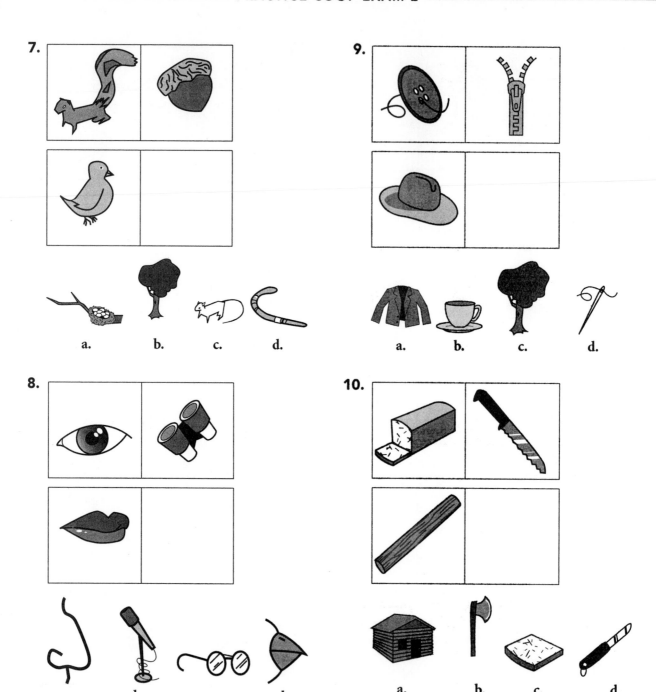

7.

a.   b.   c.   d.

8.

a.   b.   c.   d.

9.

a.   b.   c.   d.

10.

a.   b.   c.   d.

11.

a.   b.   c.   d.

13.

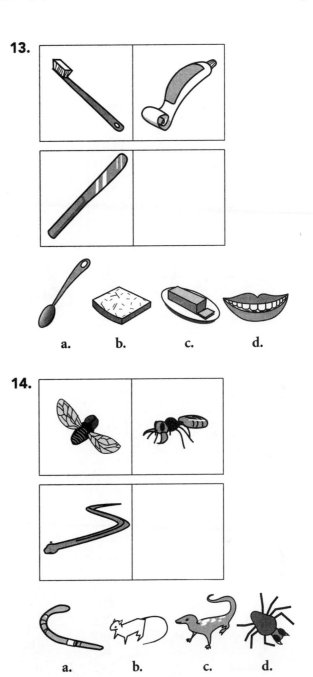

a.   b.   c.   d.

12.

a.   b.   c.   d.

14.

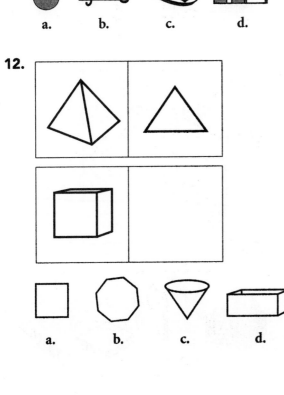

a.   b.   c.   d.

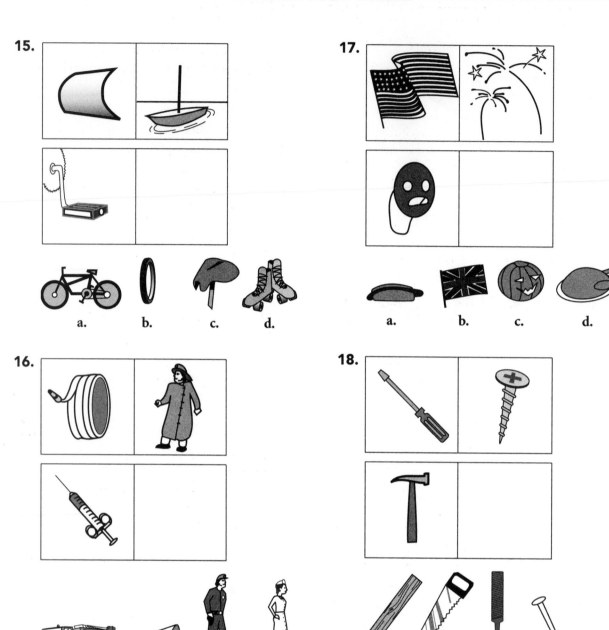

15.

a.   b.   c.   d.

16.

a.   b.   c.   d.

17.

a.   b.   c.   d.

18.

a.   b.   c.   d.

19.

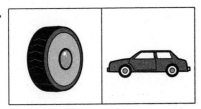

a.　b.　c.　d.

20.

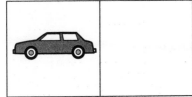

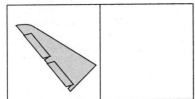

a.　b.　c.　d.

Test 3:
Quantitative Reasoning

For questions 1 through 7, find the relationship of the numbers in one column to the numbers in the other column. Then find the missing number.

1. 21 → ▌ → 7
　　33 → ▌ → 11
　　48 → ▌ → 16
　　9 → ▌ →
　　a. 7
　　b. 3
　　c. 12
　　d. 19

2. 9 → ▌ → 16
　　17 → ▌ → 24
　　3 → ▌ → 10
　　8.3 → ▌ →
　　a. 15.3
　　b. 9.7
　　c. 18
　　d. 10.7

3. 3 → ▌ → 18
　　6 → ▌ → 36
　　5 → ▌ → 30
　　4 → ▌ →
　　a. 20
　　b. 24
　　c. 18
　　d. 15

4. 10 → ▌ → −1
　　14 → ▌ → 3
　　8 → ▌ → −3
　　5 → ▌ →
　　a. −8
　　b. −4
　　c. −6
　　d. −8

5. 12 → ▋ → 6
8 → ▋ → 4
10 → ▋ → 5
4 → ▋ →
   a. 1
   b. 2
   c. 0.2
   d. 0.1

6. −3 → ▋ → 0
3 → ▋ → 6
0 → ▋ → 3
1 → ▋ →
   a. −3
   b. 3
   c. −4
   d. 4

7. 7 → ▋ → 21
12 → ▋ → 36
6 → ▋ → 18
4 → ▋ →
   a. 12
   b. 18
   c. 14
   d. 16

For questions 8 through 14, find the shaded fraction of the grid.

8.

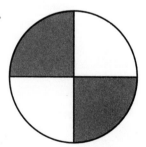

   a. $\frac{1}{2}$
   b. $\frac{1}{4}$
   c. $\frac{2}{3}$
   d. $\frac{2}{4}$

9.

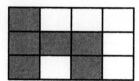

   a. $\frac{1}{2}$
   b. $\frac{1}{6}$
   c. $\frac{6}{9}$
   d. $\frac{2}{8}$

10.

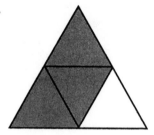

   a. $\frac{2}{3}$
   b. $\frac{1}{4}$
   c. $\frac{4}{3}$
   d. $\frac{3}{4}$

11.

   a. $\frac{1}{6}$
   b. $\frac{3}{8}$
   c. $\frac{1}{3}$
   d. $\frac{3}{4}$

12.

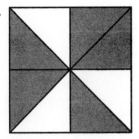

a. $\frac{5}{8}$

b. $\frac{8}{5}$

c. $\frac{3}{8}$

d. $\frac{1}{3}$

13.

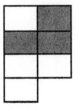

a. $\frac{1}{3}$

b. $\frac{3}{7}$

c. $\frac{1}{7}$

d. $\frac{7}{3}$

14.

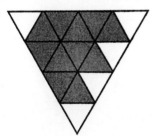

a. $\frac{16}{7}$

b. $\frac{7}{16}$

c. $\frac{3}{8}$

d. $\frac{11}{16}$

For questions 15 through 20, look at the scale showing sets of shapes of equal weight. Find an equivalent pair of sets that would also balance the scale.

15.

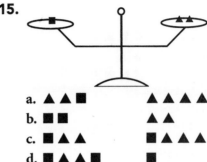

a. ▲ ▲ ■   ▲ ▲ ▲ ▲

b. ■ ■   ▲ ▲

c. ■ ▲ ▲   ■ ▲ ▲ ▲

d. ■ ▲ ▲ ■   ■

16.

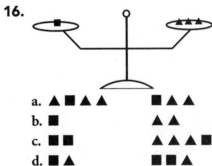

a. ▲ ■ ▲ ▲   ■ ▲ ▲

b. ■   ▲ ▲

c. ■ ■   ▲ ▲ ▲ ■

d. ■ ▲   ■ ■ ▲

17.

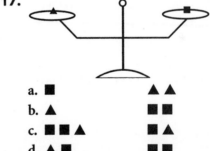

a. ■   ▲ ▲

b. ▲   ■ ■

c. ■ ■ ▲   ■ ■ ▲

d. ▲ ■   ■ ■

18.

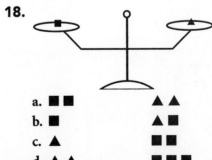

a. ■ ■   ▲ ▲

b. ■   ▲ ■

c. ▲   ■ ■

d. ▲ ▲   ■ ■ ■

19.

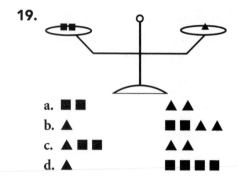

   a. ■■   ▲▲
   b. ▲   ■■▲▲
   c. ▲■■   ▲▲
   d. ▲   ■■■■

20.

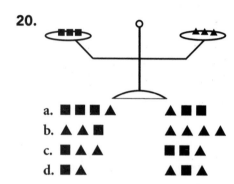

   a. ■■■▲   ▲■■
   b. ▲▲■   ▲▲▲▲▲
   c. ■▲▲   ■■▲
   d. ■▲   ▲■▲

Test 4:
Verbal Reasoning—Words

You have 15 minutes for this section. For questions 1 through 7, find the word that names a necessary part of the underlined word.

1. swimming
   a. kicking
   b. arms
   c. water
   d. nose plug

2. television
   a. electricity
   b. program
   c. advertisement
   d. remote

3. book
   a. words
   b. paper
   c. ink
   d. store

4. beach
   a. shells
   b. sunshine
   c. ocean
   d. shore

5. lightning
   a. electricity
   b. thunder
   c. brightness
   d. rain

6. monopoly
   a. corrupt
   b. exclusive
   c. rich
   d. gigantic

7. tide
   a. river
   b. flood
   c. gravity
   d. current

For questions 8 through 13, the words in the top row are related in some way. The words in the bottom row are related in the same way. For each item, find the word that completes the bottom row of words.

8.

ant	fly	bee
hamster	squirrel	____

   a. spider
   b. mouse
   c. rodent
   d. cat

9.

firefighter	ladder	hose
veterinarian	thermometer	____

   a. stethoscope
   b. kitten
   c. doctor
   d. injury

10. table   wood   oak

shirt   cloth   ____

   a. sewing

   b. dress

   c. cotton

   d. tree

11. rule   command   dictate

doze   sleep   _____

   a. snore

   b. govern

   c. awaken

   d. hibernate

12. meal   banquet   feast

shelter   palace   ____

   a. mansion

   b. hallway

   c. protection

   d. haven

13. fence   wall   boundary

path   alley   _____

   a. passageway

   b. ramp

   c. airfield

   d. pedestrian

For questions 14 through 17, three of the words in the group belong together. Find the word that does NOT belong.

14. Which word does NOT belong with the others?

   a. noun

   b. preposition

   c. punctuation

   d. adverb

15. Which word does NOT belong with the others?

   a. quarter

   b. dime

   c. nickel

   d. wallet

16. Which word does NOT belong with the others?

   a. cherry

   b. apple

   c. banana

   d. potato

17. Which word does NOT belong with the others?

   a. fender

   b. car

   c. tire

   d. door

For questions 18 through 20, find the word that is most like the underlined words.

18. cool   chilly   cold

   a. boiling

   b. frigid

   c. desert

   d. breezy

19. wing   beak   feather

   a. nest

   b. talon

   c. fly

   d. egg

20. happy   sad   cheerful

   a. outgoing

   b. large

   c. stupid

   d. joyful

Test 5:
Verbal Reasoning—Context

For questions 1 through 20, find the statement that is true according to the given information.

1. Mike's dog, Rover, eats 10 pounds of dog food a week. Pete's dog, Fido, eats 8 pounds of dog food a week. Rover is bigger than Fido.
   a. Rover is overweight.
   b. Rover eats more than Fido.
   c. Big dogs eat more than small dogs.
   d. Mike and Pete are friends.

2. Tom's Kitchen serves breakfast daily from 6 A.M. until noon, lunch from noon until 6 P.M., and dinner from 6 P.M. until midnight. Between the hours of midnight and 6 A.M., Tom's Kitchen is closed. Jeff came to Tom's Kitchen hoping to get a serving of blueberry pancakes breakfast special, but, not without disappointment, ended up ordering chicken pot pie lunch special instead.
   a. Jeff came into Tom's Kitchen between the hours of 6 P.M. and midnight.
   b. Jeff came into Tom's Kitchen between the hours of midnight and 6 A.M.
   c. Jeff came into Tom's Kitchen after noon.
   d. When Jeff sat down to order, he realized that he was not hungry.

3. Dave earned $48 for three hours' work. Mark earned $52 for the work that he did. Donna earned $76 at her job.
   a. Donna makes more per hour than Mark.
   b. Mark earned more than Dave.
   c. Women earn more than men.
   d. Dave's work is inferior.

4. According to the recent Princeton Review research, a student must receive a verbal score of approximately 700 on his or her SAT to be considered for acceptance to Brown University. Laura is a second-year student at Brown University, majoring in comparative literature.
   a. Laura did not spend very much time studying for the SAT.
   b. Laura's verbal SAT score was approximately 550.
   c. Laura's verbal SAT score was approximately 700.
   d. Laura does not like her major.

5. Gina and John Scaronni go out for a cup of coffee every Saturday morning. While they drink coffee, Gina likes to read her book, which she carries everywhere with her, and John likes to listen to his CD player, which he also carries everywhere with him.
   a. Gina and John Scaronni are a couple.
   b. Gina and John Scaronni always go out together.
   c. Gina owns a pair of reading glasses.
   d. John owns a pair of headphones.

6. Jamie found a "buy a dozen, get half a dozen free" sale on long-stem roses. She walked out of the store carrying 36 long-stem roses.
   a. Jamie paid for two dozen roses.
   b. Jamie paid for three dozen roses.
   c. Roses are Jamie's favorite flowers.
   d. Jamie always buys roses by the dozen.

7. Occasionally, Jonathan and Alberto go to used vinyl stores together to search for rare, out-of-print albums. Today was a great day for both of them—Jonathan found three albums and Alberto found two.

   a. Jonathan and Alberto are very knowledge-able about rare, out-of-print albums.

   b. Alberto found fewer albums than Jonathan.

   c. Jonathan usually finds better deals then Alberto.

   d. One of the albums that Jonathan found was much too expensive.

8. Before going on an out-of-town business trip, Natasha took her cats over to her friend Amy's house. Shortly after Natasha's departure, Amy got ill and had to be taken to a hospital, where she stayed for the next two days.

   a. Natasha's cats spent two days unattended.

   b. When Natasha learned that Amy was in a hospital, she canceled her trip.

   c. Natasha picked up her cats after two days.

   d. Amy felt bad about leaving Natasha's cats unattended.

9. During the week, Leo studies for his MCAT exam. On Mondays and Wednesdays, he studies biological and physical sciences. On Thursdays, he practices the verbal reasoning assignments. On Tuesdays and Fridays, he volunteers at a hospital. During the weekends, Leo takes a break from his studies and enjoys spending time with his friends.

   a. Leo volunteers at a hospital because he believes it will help him pass his exam.

   b. Leo studies for the MCAT at least four days a week.

   c. Leo prefers volunteering over studying.

   d. Leo does not study during the weekends.

10. Over summer vacation, Mark and Consuela took their car on a road trip to Mexico City. Mark spent 48 hours behind the wheel, and Consuela spent 36 hours driving.

   a. Mark and Consuela are excellent drivers.

   b. Consuela spent less time driving the car than Mark.

   c. Mark drove below the speed limit.

   d. Mark is a more experienced driver than Consuela.

11. By the time Roma approached his building, he remembered that he had forgotten his apartment keys at the office. Through the windows of his apartment, he saw that the lights were on in the kitchen, but when he rang the doorbell, no one answered.

   a. Roma could not get into his apartment.

   b. Somebody was in the kitchen.

   c. Roma has a spare set of keys at his office.

   d. Whoever was in the kitchen did not want to open the door for Roma.

12. When Steve's dog needs medical assistance, Steve always takes him to his favorite veterinarian, Dr. Katz. In Steve's opinion, to become a great vet, a person must, first and foremost, love animals.

   a. These days, veterinarians are very expensive.

   b. In Steve's opinion, everybody must take their pets to Dr. Katz.

   c. Steve's dog does not need medical assistance very often.

   d. In Steve's opinion, Dr. Katz must love animals.

13. The Petersens have three children—one-year-old Pete, three-year-old Jim, and five-year-old Michele. Linda is six years old.
   a. Linda is younger than Michele.
   b. Linda is Michele's friend.
   c. Linda is the Petersens' neighbors' daughter.
   d. Linda is not one of the Petersens' children.

14. Jenny is flying nonstop from New York City to Vancouver, BC via the Cathay Pacific airline. The nonstop flight from New York City to Vancouver, BC takes approximately six hours.
   a. Jenny prefers flights between the cities where she can fly nonstop.
   b. It takes approximately six hours by plane to get to Vancouver, BC from New York City.
   c. Jenny will arrive to Vancouver, BC in approximately six hours.
   d. The Cathay Pacific airline serves better food than all other airlines known to Jenny.

15. Phil lives 14 hours from New York City. He drove eight hours on Monday, and six hours on Tuesday.
   a. Phil drove 14 hours over two days.
   b. Phil arrived in New York City on Tuesday.
   c. Phil drives fast.
   d. Phil spent Monday night at a hotel.

16. Gasoline costs $3.25 a gallon at Redstone Citgo, and $3.28 a gallon at Bluebell Sunoco. White's Mobil, however, charges only $3.23 per gallon.
   a. White's gas costs less than Redstone's.
   b. Citgo's gas costs more than Mobil's.
   c. These three stations are in different towns.
   d. The oil companies charge too much for gasoline.

17. Megan never drinks her coffee black. Sometimes she has sugar in it, but she always has cream. She had three cups of coffee today.
   a. Megan had sugar today.
   b. Megan does not like black coffee.
   c. Megan had cream today.
   d. Megan drinks too much coffee.

18. Depending on the type of orchid, some bloom once a year; others bloom several times a year; some bloom continuously. A beautiful orchid in Sasha's greenhouse has recently bloomed again for the second time this year.
   a. Sasha wishes her orchid bloomed more than twice a year.
   b. Sasha owns a number of species of the orchid family in her greenhouse.
   c. Orchids bloom continuously in areas where there is a steady breeze.
   d. Sasha owns a greenhouse.

19. When it rains, the high school soccer team cancels field practice after school, unless they have a match the following day. Igor, a high school senior, came home today covered in mud.
   a. Igor is on the high school soccer team.
   b. Igor's team has a match tomorrow.
   c. Igor is a high school student.
   d. It rained today.

20. In order to receive a scholarship, an applicant must first fill out all the necessary paperwork, which is then followed by two rounds of interviews, each three hours long. Kerry received a phone call this morning from her counselor, who invited her to come in for the second round of interviews.
   a. Kerry has already completed her paperwork.
   b. Kerry did not pass her first round of interviews.
   c. Kerry's counselor is certain that Kerry will receive a scholarship.
   d. Kerry is certain she will receive a scholarship.

Test 6:
Reading and Language Arts

You have 40 minutes for this section. For questions 1 through 7, read the passage carefully. Then read each item and choose the correct answer.

The Tryout

A lark—that's what Alexander's family called him because he sang all the time. Personally, Alexander believed he sounded more like a crow, but it didn't concern him. He simply liked singing. He sang in the shower, he sang while he did his homework, and he sang while he walked to school. He couldn't have cared less what he sounded like, until Kevin started talking about the tryouts for the City Boys' Choir.

"Yeah, I'm attending the tryouts this weekend," he heard Kevin bragging one day in class. "I'm not nervous at all. I mean, with my voice, I'm pretty much guaranteed a spot. I imagine that they'll want me to perform lots of solos, too."

Everyone at school knew that Kevin, who had been taking lessons for years and was always talking about the competitions he had won, had a fantastic singing voice. Normally, Alexander just ignored him, but while he was walking home from school (singing as usual), he kept imagining himself as a member of the City Boys' Choir. Wouldn't it be exciting, he thought, to sing competitively with other kids? Wouldn't it be challenging to rehearse complicated pieces and have someone actually teach him about singing?

"Mom?" he hollered as he opened the door, "Can I try out for the City Boys' Choir this weekend? If the other boys have voices like Kevin's, I won't have much of a chance, but I'd like to give it a try."

"Of course you can try out, Alexander. I'm sure they'd be delighted to have you as part of their choir."

Bright and early Saturday morning, Alexander's mom dropped him off at the auditorium where the tryouts were being held. She gently encouraged him, saying, "Now just stay calm, honey, and show them how much you love to sing. I'll be back later to pick you up."

Alexander took a deep breath, walked into the building, registered at a large table, and then joined the other boys who were all chattering nervously in the hallway. The only one who didn't look nervous was Kevin. He was holding court at one end of the hallway, explaining how to use proper breathing techniques to a few other boys. Proper breathing? Alexander didn't know anything about breathing techniques. What on earth was he doing here?

Luckily, the choir director, Mr. Robeson, walked in and immediately got things started. He had each boy stand up on the auditorium stage, announce himself, and sing a song. When Alexander's turn came, he pretended he was singing in the shower and did his best to ignore the people sitting in the front row, who were taking detailed notes on his performance. He felt satisfied when he was done, at least until Kevin's turn came. As Kevin's confident voice filled the room, Alexander realized that he would never sound that good.

After the boys had finished their individual performances, Mr. Robeson put them into groups of four or five and asked them to sing again, this time as a group. Alexander thoroughly enjoyed singing with the other boys. He did his best to blend his voice with theirs. Kevin's group sang right after Alexander's, and even with four other boys singing, Kevin's voice was clear, distinct, and completely unmistakable; it seemed to reach the farthest corners of the auditorium.

When the groups finished singing, Mr. Robeson began the interview process. When he asked Alexander about his performance experience, any music lessons he'd had, any training he'd received, all Alexander could think of saying was, "I just really enjoy singing. I sing all the time, and I want to learn more." He kept imagining the lengthy and detailed answers Kevin would give to each of Mr. Robeson's questions.

Afterward, Alexander slunk miserably out of the building and climbed into his mother's car.

"How did it go, honey? Were they impressed with you?" his mother cheerfully inquired.

"I'd rather not discuss it right now. I don't think it went very well."

Although Alexander was convinced that he hadn't earned a position in the choir, he began to feel curious about who had made it. The next afternoon, he pedaled his bicycle over to the auditorium where a list of new members was supposed to be posted. Quickly, he scanned the list, and then he read it again more deliberately. There must have been some mistake. His name was on the list, and Kevin's name was not.

Just then, the door opened and Mr. Robeson strolled out. "Um, excuse me, Mr. Robeson," stammered Alexander. "What happened? How did *I* make the choir?"

"You love singing, and what better quality could a choir member have? Your voice isn't the best I've ever heard, but with training, I think it will improve quite a bit. That improvement will take a lot of practice, however. You *are* willing to practice, aren't you?"

"Of course I am. But what about Kevin? Why didn't he make it? He has such a good voice."

"Talent alone is not enough," said Mr. Robeson. "We need boys who are willing to work hard. Even the best singers in the world must continue to practice. Just think about it, Alexander. This is a choir where all the members are equal. We weren't looking for soloists. We were looking for boys who seemed to have the right voice and attitude to be part of a choir. Enough about tryouts, though. Will we see you at choir practice this week?"

"Absolutely, Mr. Robeson!" Alexander said. He climbed back onto his bicycle and rode home, singing the whole way.

1. This story is told mainly from the point of view of
   a. Mr. Robeson.
   b. Alexander.
   c. Alexander's mother.
   d. Kevin.

2. The author's purpose in writing this story is to
   a. encourage the reader to participate in a choir.
   b. demonstrate to the reader how to sing properly.
   c. entertain the reader with a story about a tryout.
   d. prove to the reader that singing is hard work.

3. Why does Alexander want to be in the choir?
   a. He needs something to do each day after school.
   b. He thinks it will be exciting and challenging.
   c. He wants to be a professional singer someday.
   d. He is tired of people saying that he sings like a crow.

4. In addition to a good voice, what did Mr. Robeson want the boys in the choir to have?
   a. the ability to sing loudly enough to reach the back of a room
   b. an interest in becoming a lead singer
   c. the talent to win many musical competitions
   d. the ability to sing with others in a group

5. Which statement best characterizes Kevin's attitude toward his own singing ability?
   a. I am one of many great singers at school.
   b. I strive to be a singer who is a team player.
   c. I know all there is to know about singing.
   d. I am a talented soloist with a lot to learn.

6. Alexander reads the new members list a second time because he
   a. thinks there has been a mistake.
   b. does not see his name anywhere.
   c. is not a particularly good reader.
   d. wants to remember all the names.

7. The author wants the reader to think that Alexander will
   a. become a world-famous solo performer.
   b. gradually lose his enthusiasm for singing.
   c. tell Kevin why he didn't make the choir.
   d. learn a lot and improve his singing voice.

For questions 8 through 12, read the passage carefully. Then read each item and choose the correct answer.

Subways

Issues of overcrowding and congestion have plagued U.S. cities since the 1940s, and the total U.S. population has increased by more than 20 million each decade since. Even 200 years ago, large population increases caused problems. From 1810 through the mid-1800s, for example, New York City's population increased, on average, 58% each decade. Amid this dramatic population increase, it was jokingly said that one could travel halfway from New York to Philadelphia quicker than one could travel the length of Broadway. This Manhattan boulevard was often in such a state of chaos that it required the forceful presence of police officers to maintain order.

The dire situation of New York's streets prompted publisher Alfred Ely Beach to search for an alternative mode of transportation. In February 1870, Beach opened a below-ground transportation system that set a precedent in subterranean travel. "Pneumatic transit," as the system was known, consisted of a 312-foot wind tunnel and a 22-passenger car propelled over the tracks by a 100-horsepower fan. While this curious solution to urban transport was not the wave of the future, it paved the way for the American subway.

However, the first subway was not built in New York. Toward the end of the nineteenth century, Boston found itself in a similar situation as New York City. Rapid population growth caused an enormous strain on traffic in the downtown area, and many commuters began to rely extensively on the street-level trolley system. Owned and operated by the West End Company, these electric-powered trolleys contended with the large number of cars and pedestrians also crowding Boston's streets. Under increasing public pressure, West End partnered with the Boston Transit Commission to fund the excavation and construction of America's first subway. This underground system, nicknamed the "T," opened on September 1, 1897.

Other American cities soon followed suit. New York opened its first subway—merely nine miles long—in October 1904. Philadelphia constructed a system combining subway lines with above-ground and elevated trolley lines, much like the one in Boston, between 1905 and

1908. Although there have been ups and downs in the popularity of subways, today, most major cities, including San Francisco, Los Angeles, Baltimore, Washington, DC, and Atlanta, all have subway systems.

8. Why were subways built?
   a. Every city needs a subway system.
   b. Cities were too congested and overcrowded.
   c. People preferred underground trains.
   d. People rely on trains to go to work.

9. According to the passage, Boston built a subway system because
   a. New York City had one.
   b. the street-level trolleys could not contend with the other traffic.
   c. the West End Company partnered with the Boston Transit Commission to fund the excavation and construction.
   d. they wanted to be the first.

10. Which of these best describes "pneumatic transit"?
   a. electric-powered trolleys
   b. street-level passenger cars
   c. subterranean trolleys
   d. wind-powered passenger cars

11. This article is mainly about
   a. the history of train travel.
   b. which cities have subway systems.
   c. Boston's subway system.
   d. why subways came to be.

12. Which of the following cities do NOT have a subway system?
   a. Baltimore
   b. Atlanta
   c. Cleveland
   d. San Francisco

For questions 13 through 17, read the passage carefully. Then read each item and choose the correct answer.

Champs-Élysées

The Champs-Élysées is a broad avenue in the French capital, Paris. With its cinemas, cafés, and luxury specialty shops, the Champs-Élysées is one of the most famous streets in the world. Its name refers to the Elysian Fields, the kingdom of the dead in Greek mythology. This grand avenue runs nearly two miles through northwestern Paris, from the Place de la Concorde in the east with its obelisk to the Place Charles de Gaulle in the west, where the Arc de Triomphe is located.

Queen Marie Antoinette drove with her friends and took music lessons at the grand Hôtel de Crillon on the Place Louis XV. The avenue from the Rond Point to the Etoile was built up during the Empire. The Champs-Élysées itself became city property in 1828, and footpaths, fountains, and gas lighting were added. Over the years, the avenue has undergone numerous transitions, most recently in 1993, when the sidewalks were widened.

Every year on Bastille Day, the largest military parade in France passes down the Champs-Élysées, overseen by the president of the republic. The Champs-Élysées is also the traditional end of the last stage of the <u>prestigious</u> bike race, the Tour de France. Although this avenue was named for the dead, it remains a vital—and very much alive—part of Paris.

13. Which of the following would be the best title for this passage?
   a. "A Little Bit about the Champs-Élysées"
   b. "Biking the Champs-Élysées"
   c. "An Extensive History of the Most Famous Boulevard in the World"
   d. "Champs-Élysées: The Boulevard of the Dead"

14. What is the best definition of the underlined word <u>prestigious</u> as it is used in the last paragraph of the passage?
  a. challenging
  b. famous
  c. hilly
  d. inspiring respect

15. According to the passage, the Champs-Élysées runs from
  a. the Elysian Fields to the Place de la Concorde.
  b. the Arc de Triomphe to the Tour de France.
  c. the Place de la Concorde in the east with its obelisk to the Place Charles de Gaulle in the west.
  d. the Place Charle de Gaulle to the Bastille.

16. With which of the following statements about the Champs-Élysées would the author of the passage most likely agree?
  a. The Champs-Élysées is probably the most important boulevard in France.
  b. The Champs-Élysées is famous because of Marie Antoinette.
  c. The meaning of the name of the boulevard is appropriate.
  d. The improvements to the Champs-Élysées have been good.

17. Which of these changes were NOT made to the Champs-Élysées?
  a. The sidewalks were widened.
  b. Gaslights were added.
  c. Trees were planted.
  d. Fountains were added.

For questions 18 through 23, read the passage carefully. Then read each item and choose the correct answer.

Journey to a New Life

For hundreds of years, people have come to the United States from other countries seeking a better life. One of the first sights to greet many immigrants is the Statue of Liberty. Tatiana remembered the first time she saw the symbol of her new life and told the story to her children many times.

In 1909, when Tatiana was just 11 years old, her parents and older brother traveled to the United States. Because the family could not afford to buy her a ticket, she had to remain in Russia. She had lived with her uncle and cousins for almost a year in a small and crowded house before the special letter arrived from her father. "Dear Tatiana," he wrote. "At last, we have earned enough money to pay for your ticket. After you join us in New York, we will travel by train to a place called South Dakota, where we have bought a farm."

A week later, Tatiana's uncle took her into the city of St. Petersburg and, using the money her father had sent, bought her a ticket for the *Louisa Jane*, a steamship that was leaving for America. Tatiana clutched her bag nervously and walked up the ramp onto the steamship that would be her home until she reached America. She listened to the ship's whistle give a piercing blast and then leaned over the railing to wave good-bye to her uncle.

Although she was lonely and missed her family, Tatiana quickly made friends with the other children aboard the *Louisa Jane*. They invented games that could be played on the ship and ran around the decks. One afternoon, tired of being pestered with questions, the ship's engineer gave them a tour of the engines.

The next day, as Tatiana was walking along the deck, she heard some of the passengers talking about the Statue of Liberty. This conversation confused her because she knew that liberty was an idea; it was intangible. No one could see or touch it, so how could you make a statue of liberty? When she asked her friend's father, Mr. Dimitrivitch, he explained that the statue looked like a woman, but it represented freedom. This explanation just made Tatiana more curious to see the statue for herself.

One morning, Tatiana woke up to the sound of wild shouting. Convinced that the ship must be sinking, she grabbed her life-jacket and ran upstairs. All of the passengers were crowded onto the deck, but the ship wasn't sinking. The shouts were really cries of excitement because the *Louisa Jane* had finally reached the United States. When Tatiana realized that she would soon see her family again, she joined in with shouts of her own.

As the *Louisa Jane* came closer to shore, the tall figure of a woman holding a torch became visible on the horizon. The cries died away, and the passengers stared in awed silence at the Statue of Liberty. Tatiana gazed at the woman's solemn face as the ship steamed past. Mr. Dimitrivitch had told her that the statue represented freedom, and she finally understood what he meant. At that moment, Tatiana knew that she was free to start her new life.

18. For Tatiana, the Statue of Liberty was a symbol of
    a. a new beginning.
    b. interesting ideas.
    c. the excitement of traveling.
    d. the ability to earn money.

19. Which words in the story tell the reader that these events took place long ago?
    a. "... stared in awed silence at the Statue of Liberty."
    b. "... a steamship that was leaving for the United States."
    c. "... she was lonely and missed her family ..."
    d. "... Tatiana's uncle took her into the city ..."

20. The engineer showed the children the ship's engines because
    a. he was tired of answering their many questions.
    b. the parents asked him to amuse their children.
    c. Tatiana had asked him to do so.
    d. the tour was included in the price of the tickets.

21. Tatiana stayed behind when her family traveled to the United States because
    a. she was too young to travel on a ship.
    b. her uncle wanted her to stay with him in Russia.
    c. they did not have enough money for her ticket.
    d. she was not willing to live in a new country.

22. The best way to learn more about the kind of ship described in this story would be to
    a. ask someone who builds sailboats.
    b. read a book about the immigrants in New York.
    c. visit a port where large ships dock.
    d. look in an encyclopedia under "steamships."

23. Why did the author write this story?
    a. to describe a particular statue
    b. to express the author's opinion
    c. to persuade the reader to take an action
    d. to describe one person's experience

For questions 24 through 29, read the passage carefully. Then read each item and choose the correct answer.

The Gateway Arch

The skyline of St. Louis, Missouri, is fairly unremarkable, with one huge exception—the Gateway Arch that stands on the banks of the Mississippi as part of the Jefferson National Expansion Memorial. The arch is an amazing structure built to honor St. Louis's role as the gateway to the West.

The Design

In 1947, a group of interested citizens known as the Jefferson National Expansion Memorial Association held a nationwide competition to select a design for a new monument that would celebrate the growth of the United States. Other U.S. monuments are spires, statues, or imposing buildings, but the winner of this contest was a plan for a completely different type of structure. The man who submitted the winning design, Eero Saarinen, later became a famous architect. In designing the arch, Saarinen wanted to "create a monument which would have lasting significance and would be a landmark of our time."

The Gateway Arch is a masterpiece of engineering, a monument even taller than the Great Pyramid in Egypt. In its own way, the arch is at least as majestic as the Great Pyramid. The shape of the Gateway Arch is that of an inverted catenary curve, the same shape that a heavy chain will form if it is suspended between two points. The arch is covered with a sleek skin of stainless steel that often reflects dazzling bursts of sunlight. In a beautiful display of symmetry, the height of the arch is the same as the distance between the legs at ground level. The legs of the arch are equilateral triangles that decrease gracefully as the height increases.

Inside the arch, there are structural reinforcements and a complex tram system to take visitors to the top.

The Construction

Construction of the arch on the St. Louis waterfront finally began in February 1964. First, excavators dug 60 feet into the ground to lay the foundations for the arch. Then, using derricks, cranes, and other equipment, each section of the arch was hoisted into place and carefully welded together. Although the project was very dangerous, no one was killed during the construction. When the arch was finished in October 1965, more than 5,000 tons of steel and 38,000 tons of concrete had been used in the structure. The overall cost of the project was $13 million.

Visiting the Arch

Today, the arch stands high over the surrounding community, an architectural masterpiece and a beautiful tribute to the explorers and pioneers who passed through St. Louis on their journeys westward. It is administered by the National Park Service and staffed with park rangers. In a single day, 6,400 visitors can travel to the top of the arch by means of the special tram system that operates inside the structure. Although the windows at the top are small because of structural pressures, the view is magnificent. On a clear day, people can see the horizon 30 miles away or gaze at closer landmarks from a unique perspective.

24. This article is mainly about
   a. how and why a special monument was built.
   b. why a city needs a monument for its skyline.
   c. how monuments serve to inspire mankind.
   d. why people build monuments to their past.

25. The author compares the arch to the Great Pyramid in Egypt in order to
a. show readers that the arch was more difficult to construct.
b. convince readers that the arch is more beautiful than the Great Pyramid.
c. make readers aware of how much time it took to build the arch.
d. give readers some idea of the height of the arch.

26. The author would probably agree with which of the following statements?
a. The St. Louis skyline is more interesting because of the Gateway Arch.
b. St. Louis should build more monuments along the Mississippi River.
c. Eero Saarinen is the greatest architect who ever lived.
d. The Gateway Arch is the greatest monument ever built.

27. Which of these statements could best be included in the paragraph labeled "Visiting the Arch"?
a. At the base, each side of the legs of the arch is 54 feet long.
b. Below the arch stands the Museum of Westward Expansion.
c. Eero Saarinen is known for designing large institutional structures.
d. The arch would have cost more than $13 million if it were built today.

28. You can tell that the author probably considers the arch to be
a. amusing.
b. old-fashioned.
c. impressive.
d. terrifying.

29. Who chose Saarinen's design for the arch?
a. a team of St. Louis architects
b. the Jefferson National Expansion Memorial Association
c. Eero Saarinen's engineering partners
d. the National Park Service

For questions 30 through 34, read the passage carefully. Then read each item and choose the correct answer.

First Aid
One of the most common injuries teenagers and adults experience is a sprained ankle. A sprain occurs when the ligaments of a joint are twisted and, possibly, torn. Ligaments are bands of stringy fibers that hold the bones of a joint in position. A sprain can occur from a sudden wrenching at the joint, or a stretching or tearing of the fibers of the ligaments. The injured area usually swells and becomes black and blue. Stepping down off the sidewalk at the wrong angle or having one foot land in a hole while jogging can leave you rolling on the ground in agony, with an ankle on fire! If you can't walk without experiencing intense pain, you must seek medical help. If the pain is manageable and you can walk, here are three words to help you remember how to treat yourself when you get home:

- elevate
- cool
- bandage

As soon as there is injury to that ligament, there will be a certain amount of bleeding under the skin. Once the blood pools around the damaged blood vessels, inflammation and swelling occur. The pressure from the swell results in additional stress and tenderness to the region. In order to minimize the degree of swell, lie down as soon as possible and keep the ankle elevated so that it is actually higher than your heart. Next, to shrink the blood vessels and keep bleeding and bruising to a minimum, apply a cold pack. After 20 minutes, take the pack off, wait half an hour, and then reapply. This can be done several times a day for a total of three days.

Never leave a cold pack on for more than 20 minutes at a time. Reducing the temperature in that area for an extended period of time signals the body to *increase* blood flow to raise the body temperature! Therefore, one inadvertently triggers more blood distribution to the affected area by leaving a cold pack on too long! Finally, bandage the ankle. Be careful not to wind it too tightly around the ankle; doing so can restrict blood flow and cause harm to the entire foot.

30. The main idea of the passage is to
a. describe sprains to the ligaments.
b. explain how to bandage injuries.
c. explain how to treat your own sprained ankle.
d. explain how the temperature of a wound is important.

31. According to the passage, a sprain is caused by
a. enlarged blood vessels in the foot.
b. fluctuating temperature signaling the elevation of body temperature.
c. torn tissue in the ball of the foot.
d. torn or twisted ligament fibers that hold the joint in position.

32. Which of the following is NOT mentioned as a warning?
a. If there is intense pain, seek medical attention.
b. Do not wind the bandage too tightly.
c. Do not put your ankle near the fire.
d. Do not keep the cold pack on for more than 20 minutes at a time.

33. According to the directions, once the initial cold pack is removed, what is to be done?
a. Begin wrapping the bandage.
b. Begin wrapping by encircling the ball of the foot twice.
c. Wait 20 minutes and then reapply the ice pack for 30 minutes.
d. Wait 30 minutes and then reapply the ice pack for 20 minutes.

34. It can be inferred that the "black and blue" symptom of the sprain is due to
a. torn fibers of ligaments.
b. too tight a bandage.
c. bleeding under the skin.
d. dirt ground into the wound from the fall.

For questions 35 through 40, read the passage carefully. Then read each item and choose the correct answer.

Little Rhody

Rhode Island is the smallest state in the union, yet its history is as large as any other's. It was the first state to declare independence from British rule prior to the Revolutionary War, and it was the first state to send soldiers to defend the nation's capital at the onset of the Civil War. The American Industrial Revolution began in Rhode Island, which led the way in producing textiles and jewelry.

The state itself actually began as two separate colonies, each established as a refuge for people with independent religious convictions. Roger Williams established a colony at the head of a river and was soon joined by many others who shared his religious views. Williams considered the colony to be blessed by God, and so he named it Providence Plantations—guided by the hand of Providence.

Soon after, another group <u>emigrated</u> from the Massachusetts colonies to establish a haven for their own religious views. This group was strongly influenced by a woman named Anne

Hutchinson. These people established themselves on several islands situated at the mouth of the Providence River, the largest of which was called Aquidneck Island. Some thought that Aquidneck resembled the Isle of Rhodes off the coast of Greece, so the community came to be known as Rhode Island.

The early years of these little colonies were filled with trouble, as the colonists tried to establish their own rights of self-<u>governance</u>. The colonies in Connecticut and Massachusetts tried repeatedly to establish their authority over both groups, while political battles in England used the little colonies like a tug-of-war rope.

In the end, however, the two groups—one at each end of the Providence River—joined together to become the State of Rhode Island and Providence Plantations. This is still the official name of the state today, but most of us know it simply as Rhode Island—or, more affectionately, as Little Rhody.

35. As it is used in this passage, the word <u>emigrated</u> most nearly means
   a. evolved.
   b. moved.
   c. resisted.
   d. developed.

36. Which of these events happened first?
   a. the Industrial Revolution
   b. Roger Williams established Providence Plantations.
   c. the Revolutionary War
   d. Anne Hutchinson moved to Aquidneck Island.

37. According to the passage, Rhode Island was settled because
   a. there was good whale hunting there.
   b. the colonies in Connecticut and Massachusetts wanted more land.
   c. people wanted independence from England.
   d. people wanted greater religious freedom.

38. What does the author mean that the Rhode Island colonies were used "like a tug-of-war rope"?
   a. Rhode Island was establishing a growing trade in rope.
   b. British politicians fought for control of Rhode Island.
   c. Religious freedom created trouble in Rhode Island.
   d. Politics had people tied up in knots.

39. As used in this passage, the word <u>governance</u> most nearly means
   a. babysitter.
   b. capitalism.
   c. authority.
   d. taxation.

40. Which of the following best states the main idea of the passage?
   a. Religious freedom has a long history in America.
   b. People should not allow others to tell them what to do.
   c. Rhode Island was named for the Isle of Rhodes.
   d. Rhode Island may be small, but its history is important.

Test 7: Mathematics

You have 35 minutes for this section. For questions 1 through 40, read each problem and find the answer.

1. Which of these values is not equal to the others?
   a. 120%
   b. $\frac{6}{5}$
   c. 1.2
   d. $1\frac{1}{20}$

2. The graph shows the Johnson family budget for one month.

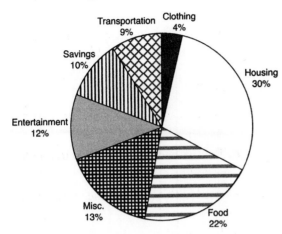

In percent of overall expenses, how much more money is spent on food than on transportation and clothing combined?

a. 9%
b. 11%
c. 13%
d. 22%

3. Which of the following is a simplification of $(x^2 + 4x + 4) \div (x + 2)$?

a. $x - 2$
b. $x + 4$
c. $x^2 + 3x + 2$
d. $x + 2$

4. What is the estimated product when 157 and 817 are rounded to the nearest hundred and multiplied?

a. 160,000
b. 180,000
c. 16,000
d. 80,000

5. What number is marked by the P on the following number line?

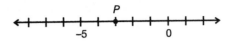

a. -7
b. 7
c. -3
d. 3

6. Ms. Carrillo wants to take the students in her band class to the City Pops concert. To get the group rate of $6 per ticket, a $7 service charge must be paid. Which equation should Ms. Carrillo use to find the total cost *(C)* for taking her students to the concert? Let n represent the number of people.

a. $C = 7n + 6$
b. $C = 6n - 7$
c. $C = 6n + 7$
d. $C = 13n$

7. Hans has $5\frac{1}{2}$ pounds of sugar. He wants to make cookies for his son's kindergarten class. The cookie recipe calls for $\frac{2}{3}$ pound of sugar per dozen cookies. How many dozen cookies can he make?

a. $6\frac{1}{3}$ dozen cookies
b. $7\frac{1}{5}$ dozen cookies
c. $8\frac{1}{4}$ dozen cookies
d. $9\frac{1}{2}$ dozen cookies

8. Felipe is planning to get Internet service. Two service providers, A and B, offer different rates as shown on the table. If Felipe plans on using 25 hours of Internet service per month, which of the following statements is true?

INTERNET SERVICE RATES			
Provider	Free Hours	Base Charge	Hourly Charge
A	17.5	$20.00	$1.00
B	20	$20.00	$1.50

a. Provider A will be cheaper.
b. Provider B will be cheaper.
c. The providers will cost the same per month.
d. The answer cannot be determined from the information given.

9. A supermarket offers 25% off all pumpkins one day, just before Halloween. If a certain pumpkin is sale-priced at $4.20, what was the original price?
a. $5.62
b. $5.60
c. $5.58
d. $5.56

10. A 600-page book is 1.5 inches thick. What is the thickness of each page?
a. 0.0010 inch
b. 0.0030 inch
c. 0.0025 inch
d. 0.0600 inch

11. The graph shows how many pounds of dog food seven dogs of different breeds ate in one month.

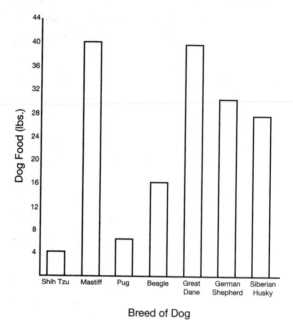

How many pounds of dog food did the two largest eaters eat in the month?
a. 40 lbs.
b. 66 lbs.
c. 71 lbs.
d. 79 lbs.

12. Which is an equation of line q?

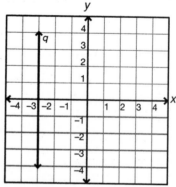

a. $y = 3$
b. $y = -3$
c. $x = 3$
d. $x = -3$

13. Yuri works in the school library. He needs to put away books with these call numbers: 513.26, 513.59, 513.7, and 513.514. In which order should Yuri place these books on the shelf?

a. 513.514, 513.59, 513.26, 513.7
b. 513.7, 513.26, 513.59, 513.514
c. 513.7, 513.26, 513.514, 513.59
d. 513.26, 513.514, 513.59, 513.7

14. For her summer job, Tennille operates a drink stand at the zoo. The following graph shows the types of drinks she sells on a typical day.

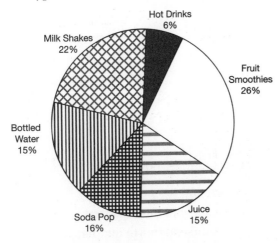

If Tennille sells 325 drinks one day, how many fruit smoothies does she sell?

a. 11
b. 85
c. 253
d. 8,624

15. A pool is surrounded by a tile border that measures 21 meters by 11 meters. The pool itself is 17 meters by 9 meters. Which expression represents the area of the tile border in square meters?

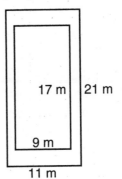

a. $(21 - 17) \times (11 - 9)$
b. $(21 - 9) \times (17 - 11)$
c. $(21 \times 11) - (17 \times 9)$
d. $(21 - 17)^2 \times (11 - 9)^2$

16. This is a picture of Albert under a palm tree. Albert is really 68 inches tall, but on the picture, he is only $\frac{3}{4}$ inch tall. The tree is $5\frac{1}{4}$ inches tall in the picture. How many inches tall is the actual palm tree?

a. 544 inches
b. 476 inches
c. 9.7 inches
d. 0.06 inch

17. If $x = 6$, $y = -2$, and $z = 3$, what is the value of the following expression?

$$\frac{xz - xy}{z^2}$$

    a. $-\frac{2}{3}$

    b. $\frac{2}{3}$

    c. $3\frac{1}{3}$

    d. 5

18. When the product of three and a number is taken away from the sum of that number and six, the result is zero. What is the number?

    a. 3

    b. 7

    c. 9

    d. 14

19. If a school buys three computers at a, b, and c dollars each, and the school gets a discount of 10%, which expression would determine the average price paid by the school?

    a. $0.9 \times \frac{a+b+c}{3}$

    b. $\frac{(a+b+c)}{0.9}$

    c. $(a+b+c) \times 0.9$

    d. $\frac{a+b+c}{3}$

20. The dimensions of the floor of Sophia's rectangular doghouse are 3 feet by 2 feet. If Sophia's master buys a doghouse with twice the length and width of her original doghouse, what will be the change in the area of the doghouse's floor?

 2 ft.

    3 ft.

    a. 4 times as large

    b. 2 times as large

    c. $\frac{1}{2}$ as large

    d. $\frac{1}{4}$ as large

21. How many of the following figures are regular polygons?

    a. 0

    b. 1

    c. 2

    d. 3

22. What is the perimeter of the shaded area if the shape is a quarter circle with a radius of 8?

    a. 2π

    b. 4π

    c. $2\pi + 8$

    d. $4\pi + 16$

23. The chart shows quarterly sales for Cool-Air's air-conditioning units. Which of the following combinations contributed 70% to the total?

Sales for 2007

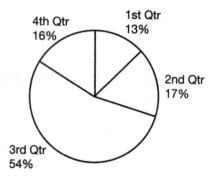

    a. first and second quarters

    b. second and third quarters

    c. second and fourth quarters

    d. third and fourth quarters

24. Which of the following expressions can be used to calculate 14% of 232?

    a. 14×232

    b. 0.14×232

    c. $\frac{14}{100} \times 232$

    d. b and c

25. According to the following table, what was Lubbock's production in the month of April?

PRODUCTION OF FARM-IT TRACTORS FOR THE MONTH OF APRIL	
FACTORY	**APRIL OUTPUT**
Dallas	450
Houston	425
Lubbock	
Amarillo	345
TOTAL	**1,780**

a. 345
b. 415
c. 540
d. 560

26. Use the following table to answer this question. A train moving at a constant speed leaves Chicago for Los Angeles at time $t = 0$. If Los Angeles is 2,000 miles from Chicago, which of the following equations describes the distance from Los Angeles at any time?

DISTANCE TRAVELED FROM CHICAGO WITH RESPECT TO TIME	
TIME (HOURS)	**DISTANCE FROM CHICAGO (MILES)**
1	60
2	120
3	180
4	240

a. Distance = $60t - 2{,}000$
b. Distance = $60t$
c. Distance = $2{,}000 - 60t$
d. Distance = $-2{,}000 - 60t$

27. Joline gave $\frac{1}{2}$ of her sandwich to Eddie at lunchtime and ate $\frac{1}{3}$ of it herself. How much of the sandwich did she have left?

a. $\frac{1}{6}$
b. $\frac{3}{5}$
c. $\frac{4}{5}$
d. $\frac{5}{6}$

28. $\frac{x}{4} + \frac{3x}{4} =$

a. $\frac{1}{2}x$
b. $\frac{x^3}{4}$
c. 1
d. x

29. A line intersects two parallel lines in the following figure. If angle P measures 40°, what is the measure of angle Q?

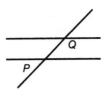

a. 50°
b. 60°
c. 80°
d. 140°

30. Convert $\frac{7}{40}$ to a percentage.

a. 0.0175%
b. 0.175%
c. 1.75%
d. 17.5%

31. Wanda is designing a label for a can that is 7 centimeters tall and has a 14-centimeter diameter. The label wraps around the can, and there must be one centimeter for overlap. What should be the label dimensions? Use $\frac{22}{7}$ for π.

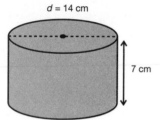

d = 14 cm

7 cm

   a. 7 cm × 45 cm

   b. 7 cm × 89 cm

   c. 8 cm × 44 cm

   d. 14 cm × 23 cm

32. A group of volunteers is searching for a lost camper within a 45-mile radius of the forest ranger's station. Which formula can be used to calculate the total search area, T, in square miles?

   a. $T = 902\pi$

   b. $T = 45^2\pi$

   c. $T = 90\pi$

   d. $T = 45\pi$

33. Generic oatmeal costs $\frac{2}{3}$ the price of the leading name brand. If the generic brand is $1.50, how much does the name brand cost?

   a. $1.00

   b. $1.75

   c. $2.00

   d. $2.25

34. Mr. Tate is building a deck along two sides of his rectangular pool as shown. What is the area of the deck?

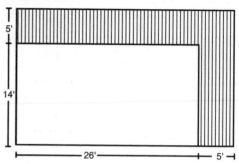

5'

14'

26'   5'

   a. 200 ft.^{2}

   b. 225 ft.^{2}

   c. 250 ft.^{2}

   d. 364 ft.^{2}

35. Which of the following is between $\frac{1}{3}$ and $\frac{1}{4}$?

   a. $\frac{1}{5}$

   b. $\frac{2}{3}$

   c. $\frac{2}{5}$

   d. $\frac{2}{7}$

36. What is the perimeter of the following parallelogram shown?

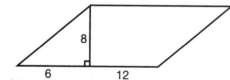

8

6   12

   a. 26

   b. 32

   c. 48

   d. 56

37. What is the perimeter of the following right triangle?

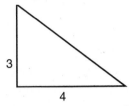

    a. 12
    b. 9
    c. 8
    d. 7

38. You can quickly figure a 20% tip on a restaurant bill of $18 by
    a. multiplying 18×20, then rounding down.
    b. multiplying 18×20.
    c. multiplying 18×2, then moving the decimal over one space to the left.
    d. multiplying $18 \times \frac{1}{2}$ and rounding up.

39. Which value of x will make the following inequality true?

$3x - 14 \leq 3$

    a. 4
    b. 6
    c. 8
    d. 10

40. If the radius of circle Z is doubled, what will be the change in the area of the circle?

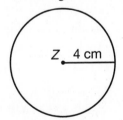

    a. $\frac{1}{4}$ as large
    b. $\frac{1}{8}$ as large
    c. 2 times as large
    d. 4 times as large

Answers

Test 1: Sequences

1. a. Look at each segment. You will notice that in each, the figure on the right and the figure on the left are the same; the figure in between is different. To continue this pattern in the last segment, the diamond on the left will be repeated on the right. Choice **a** is the only possible answer.

2. b. Each arrow in this continuing series moves a few degrees in a clockwise direction. Think of these arrows as the big hand on a clock. The first arrow is at noon. The last arrow before the blank would be 12:40. Choice **b**, the correct answer, is at 12:45.

3. c. Study the pattern carefully. In the first segment, two letters face right and the next two face left. The first letter in the second segment repeats the last letter of the previous segment. The same is true for the third segment. But the fourth segment changes again; it is the opposite of the first segment, so the last two letters must face right.

4. d. This sequence concerns the number of sides on each figure. In the first segment, the three figures have one side, and then two sides, and then three sides. In the second segment, the number of sides increases and then decreases. In the third segment, the number of sides continues to decrease.

5. a. In this series, the figures increase the amount of shading by one-fourth and later decrease the amount of shading by the same amount. In the second segment, you will notice that the figure goes from completely shaded to completely unshaded. This is why choice **a** is the correct choice.

6. d. This is an alternating series. The first and third segments are repeated. The second segment is simply a reverse of the other two.

7. d. In each of the segments, the figures alternate between one-fourth and one-half shaded.

8. d. In this simple subtraction series, each number in each set of three segments is 9 less than the previous number.

9. a. In this simple addition series, each number in each set of three segments is 5 more than the previous number.

10. b. In each sequence, 8 is added to the first number, and then 5 is subtracted from the second number.

11. a. This is a simple multiplication series. In each segment, the numbers are multiplied by themselves. The last segment is $0.1 \times 0.1 = 0.01$; $0.01 \times 0.01 = 0.0001$.

12. c. In each set of three numbers, 1 is added to the first number and then the second number is divided by 2.

13. c. This is an alternating division and subtraction series, in which the first number is divided by 3 and the third number is 3 less than the second number.

14. d. Here is an addition and multiplication series. Two is added to the first number. The second number is then multiplied by 3.

15. a. The first and third series are reverse alphabetical, while the second and fourth series are alphabetical.

16. d. Each sequence moves sequentially through the alphabet, using double letters.

17. c. The numbers are counting up by one, and the last letter in each sequence becomes the first letter in the next sequence.

18. a. The middle letters are the same, so concentrate on the first and third letters. The series involves an alphabetical order with a reversal of the letters. The first letters are in alphabetical order: B, C, D, E, F. The second and fourth segments are reversals of the first and third segments. The missing segment begins with a new letter.

19. a. This series consists of a simple alphabetical order with the first two letters of all segments: L, M, N, O, P, Q, R, S, T, U. The third letter of each segment is a repetition of the first letter.

20. d. There are three series to look for here. The first letters are alphabetical in reverse: Z, Y, X, W, V. The second letters are in alphabetical order, beginning with A. The number series is as follows: 5, 4, 6, 3, 7.

Test 2: Analogies

1. b. Guitar is to horn as hammer is to saw. This relationship is about grouping. The *guitar* and *horn* are musical instruments. The *hammer* and *saw* are carpentry tools.

2. d. Tree is to leaf as bird is to feather. This relationship shows part to whole. The *leaf* is a part of the *tree*; the *feather* is a part of the *bird*.

3. c. A *tennis ball* is hit by a *tennis racket*, just as a *baseball* is hit by a *bat*.

4. c. Scissors is to knife as pitcher is to watering can. This relationship is about function. The *scissors* and *knife* are both used for cutting. The *pitcher* and *watering can* are both used for watering.

5. b. A T-shirt is to a pair of shoes as a chest of drawers is to a couch. The relationship shows to which group something belongs. The *T-shirt* and *shoes* are both articles of clothing; the *chest* and *couch* are both pieces of furniture.

6. d. A bookshelf is to a book as a refrigerator is to a carton of milk. The *book* is placed on a *bookshelf*; the *milk* is placed in a *refrigerator*.

7. d. A squirrel is to an acorn as a bird is to a worm. A *squirrel* eats *acorns*; a *bird* eats *worms*.

8. b. An eye is to a pair of binoculars as a mouth is to a microphone. This relationship shows magnification. The *binoculars* help one to see farther. The *microphone* helps one to speak louder.

9. a. A *button* and a *zipper* are both types of fasteners, just as a *hat* and a *jacket* are both types of clothing.

10. b. Bread is to knife as log is to ax. This relationship shows function. The *knife* cuts the *bread*; the *ax* chops the *log*.

11. b. *Flour* is used to make *bread*, just as a *violin* is used to make *music*.

12. a. Pyramid is to triangle as cube is to square. This relationship shows dimension. The *triangle* shows one dimension of the *pyramid*; the *square* is one dimension of the *cube*.

13. c. Toothbrush is to toothpaste as butter knife is to butter. This relationship shows function. The *toothbrush* is used to apply the *toothpaste* to teeth; the *knife* is used to apply *butter* to bread.

14. c. Fly is to ant as snake is to lizard. The *fly* and *ant* are both insects; the *snake* and *lizard* are both reptiles.

15. a. Sail is to sailboat as pedal is to bicycle. The *sail* makes the *sailboat* move; the *pedal* makes the *bicycle* move.

16. d. Hose is to firefighter as needle is to nurse. This relationship shows the tools of the trade. A *hose* is a tool used by a *firefighter*; a *needle* is a tool used by a *nurse*.

17. c. A U.S. flag is to a fireworks display as a Halloween mask is to a pumpkin. This relationship shows symbols. The *flag* and *fireworks* are symbols for the Fourth of July. The *mask* and *pumpkin* are symbols of Halloween.

18. d. A *screwdriver* drives in a *screw*, just as a *hammer* drives in a *nail*.

19. b. Dishes are to kitchen sink as car is to hose. *Dishes* are cleaned in the *sink*; the *car* is cleaned with the *hose*.

20. a. A *tire* is part of a *car*, and a *wing* is part of an *airplane*.

Test 3: Quantitative Reasoning

1. b. What is done to 21 to get 7? It is divided by 3. Divide 33 by 3 to get 11; divide 9 by 3 to get 3.

2. a. In this set, 7 is added to the first number: $9 + 7 = 16$; $17 + 7 = 24$; etc. Therefore, $8.3 + 7 = 15.3$.

3. b. In this set, the first number is multiplied by 6: $3 \times 6 = 18$; $6 \times 6 = 36$; etc. Therefore, $4 \times 6 = 24$.

4. c. First, figure out what action is being performed. In the first set of numbers, 11 is subtracted from 10 to make -1. Similarly, $14 - 11 = 3$, and $8 - 11 = -3$. Thus, $5 - 11 = -6$.

5. b. What is done to 12 to make it 6? It is divided by 2. 8 divided by 2 gives 4; 10 divided by 2 gives 5, and 4 divided by 2 is 2.

6. d. In this set, 3 is being added to all first numbers. Three is added to -3 to make zero. Three is added to 3 to make 6. Three is added to 0 to make 3. So, $1 + 3$ gives us 4.

7. a. What is done to 7 to make it 21? It is multiplied by 3. Twelve multiplied by 3 gives 36, and 6 multiplied by 3 gives 18. Thus, 4 multiplied by 3 gives 12.

8. a. There are 4 parts total, of which 2 are shaded. That is 2 parts out of 4, or $\frac{2}{4}$, which reduces to $\frac{1}{2}$.

9. a. There are 12 parts total, of which 6 are shaded. That is 6 parts out of 12, or $\frac{6}{12}$, which reduces to $\frac{1}{2}$.

10. d. There are 4 parts total, of which 3 are shaded. That is 3 parts out of 4, or $\frac{3}{4}$.

11. c. There are 6 parts total, of which 2 are shaded. That is 2 parts out of 6, or $\frac{2}{6}$, which reduces to $\frac{1}{3}$.

12. a. There are 8 parts total, of which 5 are shaded. That is 5 parts out of 8, or $\frac{5}{8}$.

13. b. There are 7 parts total, of which 3 are shaded. That is 3 parts out of 7, or $\frac{3}{7}$.

14. d. There are 16 parts total, of which 11 are shaded. That is 11 parts out of 16, or $\frac{11}{16}$.

15. a. The scales indicate that 1 cube = 2 cones. To make it easier for you to see the answers, convert all shapes to cones as follows:
   a. 2 cones + 2 cones (1 cube) = 4 cones. That's the correct answer.
   b. 4 cones (2 cubes) ≠ 2 cones
   c. 2 cones (1 cube) + 2 cones ≠ 2 cones (1 cube) + 3 cones
   d. 2 cones (1 cube) + 2 cones + 2 cones (1 cube) ≠ 2 cones (1 cube)

16. c. The scales indicate that 1 cube = 3 cones. Convert all shapes to cones as follows:
   a. 1 cone + 3 cones (1 cube) + 2 cones ≠ 3 cones + 2 cones
   b. 3 cones (1 cube) ≠ 2 cones
   c. 6 cones (2 cubes) = 3 cones + 3 cones (1 cube). That's the correct answer.
   d. 3 cones + 1 cone ≠ 6 cones (2 cubes) + 1 cone

17. d. The scale shows that 1 cone = 1 cube. Therefore:
   a. 1 cube ≠ 2 cones
   b. 1 cone ≠ 2 cubes
   c. 2 cubes + 1 cone ≠ 1 cube 1 cone
   d. 1 cone + 1 cube = 2 cubes. Since 1 cube = 1 cone, that's the correct answer.

18. a. The scale shows that 1 cube = 1 cone. Therefore:
   a. 2 cubes = 2 cones. Since 1 cube = 1 cone, that's the correct answer.
   b. 1 cube ≠ 1 cone + 1 cube
   c. 1 cone ≠ 2 cubes
   d. 2 cones ≠ 3 cubes

19. c. The scales indicate that 2 cubes = 1 cone. Convert all shapes to cones as follows:
   a. 1 cone (2 cubes) ≠ 2 cones
   b. 1 cone ≠ 1 cone (2 cubes) + 2 cones
   c. 1 cone + 1 cone (2 cubes) = 2 cones. That's the correct answer.
   d. 1 cone ≠ 2 cones (4 cubes)

20. c. The scale shows that 3 cubes = 3 cones. Therefore:
   a. 3 cubes + 1 cone ≠ 1 cone + 2 cubes
   b. 2 cones + 1 cube ≠ 4 cones
   c. 1 cube + 2 cones = 2 cubes + 1 cone. Since 1 cube = 1 cone, that's the correct answer.
   d. 1 cube + 1 cone ≠ 1 cone + 1 cube + 1 cone

Test 4: Verbal Reasoning—Words

1. c. Water is necessary for swimming. The other choices are elements that may or may not be present.

2. a. Electricity is necessary for a television to operate. The other choices are elements that may or may not be a part of a television.

3. a. Words are necessary for a book. A book does not have to be written with ink or paper. Books may or may not be sold in a store.

4. d. A beach must have a shore. The other choices are elements that may or may not be present.

5. a. Lightning is produced from a discharge of electricity, so electricity is essential. Thunder and rain are not essential to the production of lightning. Brightness may be a by-product.

6. b. The essential part of a monopoly is that it involves exclusive ownership or control.

7. c. The gravitational pull of the sun and moon are essential to the tide. Rivers, floods, and currents may be associated with tides, but they are not essential.

8. b. The three above the line are all insects. The hamster and squirrel are rodents, so the correct answer is choice **b** because the mouse is the only choice that represents a rodent.

9. a. In the relationship above the line, the ladder and hose are tools used by the firefighter. In the relationship below the line, the stethoscope and thermometer are tools used by the veterinarian.

10. c. A table made of wood could come from an oak tree. A shirt made of cloth could come from a cotton plant.

11. d. The words above the line show a continuum: Command is more extreme than rule, and dictate is more extreme than command. Below the line, the continuum is as follows: Sleep is more than doze, and hibernate is more than sleep.

12. a. A banquet and a feast are both *large meals;* a palace and a mansion are both *large* places of shelter.

13. a. A fence and a wall *mark* a boundary. A path and an alley *mark* a passageway.

14. c. The noun, preposition, and adverb are classes of words that make up a sentence. Punctuation belongs in a sentence, but punctuation is not a class of a word.

15. d. A quarter, dime, and nickel are coins, while a wallet holds money.

16. d. A cherry, apple, and banana are types of fruit, but a potato is a vegetable.

17. b. A car has fenders, tires, and doors—which are all *parts* of the car.

18. b. The three adjectives all describe cold, as does *frigid.*

19. b. A bird has wings, feathers, a beak, and also talons. The other choices may be associated with birds, but they are not parts of a bird.

20. d. These three adjectives describe emotions, and so does *joyful.* The other choices are not emotions.

Test 5: Verbal Reasoning—Context

1. b. The only conclusion that we can draw from the information given is that Rover eats more than Fido. The other choices are not addressed.

2. c. Let us consider the information available to us. We know the hours Tom's Kitchen serves breakfast, lunch, and dinner. We are also told that Jeff came into Tom's Kitchen wishing to get a breakfast special, but ended up ordering a lunch special instead. Now, let's look at the available options. Jeff could not have come in between the hours of 6 P.M. and midnight (choice **a**), because these are the hours when Tom's Kitchen serves dinner (and Jeff ordered lunch). It is not possible that Jeff came in between the hours of midnight and 6 A.M. (choice **b**), because Tom's Kitchen is closed during that time. In the third statement, we are told that Jeff ordered the lunch special "not without disappointment," which suggests that the blueberry pancakes were not available. If Jeff came in around noon (choice **c**), Tom's Kitchen would already be serving lunch. This is the likeliest reason why Jeff ordered a lunch special instead. Had Jeff realized that he was not hungry (choice **d**), he would not have ordered one special instead of another.

3. b. Notice that we only know how many hours Dave worked—we are not told how long it took Mark and Donna to earn their money. The only thing that we can conclude for certain is that Mark made more than Dave.

4. c. Based only on the information given, we do not know whether Laura does not like her major (choice **d**) or how much time she spent studying for the SAT (choice **a**). We do know that Laura's score could not have been approximately 550 (choice **b**), because the first statement says that a student must receive a verbal score of approximately 700 in order to be considered for acceptance to Brown University, and we are also told that Laura is a student at the university. Therefore, the only answer that is correct is choice **c**.

5. d. The only thing we can be sure of is that John owns a pair of headphones (choice **d**), because we are told that he likes to listen to his CD player, which he carries everywhere with him. Just because Gina always carries her book with her does not mean that she owns a pair of reading glasses (choice **c**). Gina and John Scaronni are not necessarily a couple (choice **a**)—they could be brother and sister or parent and child. The Scaronnis may or may not always go out together (choice **b**)—there is no evidence in the statements given to us to support this choice.

6. a. Based on the information available, we can conclude that Jamie paid for two dozen roses (choice **a**), because she walked out carrying 36 roses (3 dozen), and we know that the "buy a dozen, get half a dozen free" deal would allow her to have a dozen roses (two half dozens) for free, since she bought two dozen. Jamie would not have paid for three dozen (choice **b**), because she walked out with 3 dozen (36 roses), and we know that she received some of them for free. Choices **c** and **d** may be true, but we do not have enough information to make these conclusions.

7. b. Consider the facts available to us. The only thing we can conclude for certain is that Alberto found fewer albums than Jonathan (choice **b**) since we are told that Alberto found two, while Jonathan found three. Choices **c** and **d** may be true, but we cannot determine their validity based on the information provided to us. Similarly, there is no way to measure the level of Jonathan and Alberto's knowledge (choice **a**).

8. a. The only thing we can conclude for certain is that Natasha's cats spent two days unattended (choice **a**). We have no way of knowing whether Natasha canceled her trip (choice **b**) or how soon she returned to pick up her cats (choice **c**). Amy may have felt bad about leaving Natasha's cats unattended (choice **d**), but we have no way of verifying this.

9. d. Leo definitely does not study during the weekends (choice **d**), because we are told that he takes a break from his studies on the weekends to enjoy spending time with his friends. Leo does not study at least four days a week (choice **b**), because we are told that he studies on Mondays, Wednesdays, and Thursdays. Leo may prefer volunteering to studying (choice **c**), or he may believe that volunteering will help him pass his exam (choice **a**), but we do not have enough evidence in the information given to us to support these options.

10. b. Based on the statements given, we can conclude that Consuela spent less time driving than Mark (choice **b**), because we are told that she spent 36 hours behind the wheel, while Mark spent 48 hours. We do not know (based only on the statements) what kind of drivers Mark and Consuela are (choice **a**) or who is a more experienced driver (choice **d**). Just because Mark spent more time behind the wheel does **not** mean that he drove below the speed limit (choice **c**).

11. a. The statements tell us only that Roma could not get into his apartment (choice **a**). The fact that the lights in the kitchen were on does not mean that somebody was in the kitchen (choices **b** and **d**). Someone who lives in the apartment (including Roma) could have forgotten to turn the lights off when he or she left. Roma may have a spare set of keys at his office (choice **c**), but there is no evidence to support this fact.

12. d. Since we are told that Dr. Katz is Steve's favorite, we can conclude that Steve thinks Dr. Katz is a great veterinarian. Because we are told that Steve believes that a great vet must love animals, in Steve's opinion, Dr. Katz must love animals (choice **d**). In the statements provided to us, we do not know how often Steve's dog needs medical assistance (choice **c**). Veterinarians may be very expensive (choice **a**), or Steve may believe everybody should take their pets to Dr. Katz (choice **b**), but we do not have enough evidence to support these options.

13. d. The only thing we can conclude for certain is that Linda is not one of the Petersens' children (choice **d**). Linda cannot be younger than Michele (choice **a**) because we are told that Linda is 6 and Michele is 5. Linda does not have to be a daughter of the Petersens' neighbors (choice **c**)—she could be a relative. Linda may certainly be Michele's friend (choice **b**), but we do not have enough evidence to support this option.

14. b. Based on the available information, the only thing we can conclude for certain is that it takes approximately six hours by plane to get to Vancouver, BC from New York City (choice **b**). We do not know how soon Jenny will arrive to Vancouver, BC (choice **c**), because we do not know how long she has been on the plane. Choices **a** and **d** may be true, but we do not have enough evidence to support them.

15. a. Notice that we are not told in what direction Phil is driving—he might not be heading toward New York City at all. The only conclusion that we can draw is that he drove 14 hours over two days.

16. a. We are not told where these gas stations are located, nor are we told what the various brands cost at other stations. We can only conclude that gas costs less at White's than at Redstone.

17. c. We are told that Megan never drinks black coffee, but we are *not* told why. Therefore, we cannot conclude that she doesn't like coffee black. She may or may not have put sugar in her three cups, but we know that she did use cream.

18. d. Based on the information available to us, the only fact we know for certain is that Sasha owns a greenhouse (choice **d**), since we are told an orchid at her greenhouse has just bloomed. We are not told how Sasha feels about her orchid blooming only twice a year (choice **a**). Sasha may or may not own a number of species of the orchid family (choice **b**)—we cannot make this assumption, because we are only notified of one orchid. Similarly, orchids may bloom continuously in areas with a steady breeze (choice **c**), but we do not possess enough information to arrive at this conclusion.

19. c. Based on the information available to us, the only thing we can be certain of is that Igor is a high school student (choice **c**), since we are told in the second statement that he is a senior in high school. We cannot pick choices **a** or **b**, because nothing in the given statements tells us that Igor is on the school's soccer team. Choice **d** is also wrong because there could have been a number of reasons (besides the rain) why Igor came home covered in mud.

20. a. Had Kerry not passed her first round of interviews (choice **b**), she would not have been invited to come in for the second round. Nothing in the statements provided tells us how Kerry and her counselor feel about Kerry's chances of receiving a scholarship (choices **c** and **d**). Since Kerry was invited for the second round of interviews, we can be certain that she has already completed her paperwork (choice **a**).

Test 6: Reading and Language Arts

1. b. The story is told mainly from Alexander's point of view. The reader is told how Alexander reacts, what his feelings are, and what he is thinking. Although there are details about the other characters, the story does not show how they are thinking and feeling. The reader gets only Alexander's interpretation of the events.

2. c. The purpose of the story is to entertain, so this is the best choice. There is no encouragement by the author to get readers to join a choir (choice **a**). The author's intent is not to demonstrate proper singing techniques (choice **b**). And although Mr. Robeson warns Alexander that improvement will require practice and hard work, it is not the author's purpose to prove this (choice **d**).

3. b. In the third paragraph, Alexander imagines what it would be like to be in the choir— "Wouldn't it be exciting? . . . Wouldn't it be challenging?" There is no mention of needing something to do (choice **a**) or wanting to be a professional singer (choice **c**). No one says he sings like a crow (choice **d**), except Alexander himself.

4. d. Mr. Robeson tells Kevin, "This is a choir where all the members are equal. We weren't looking for soloists." This implies the need for teamwork. The other choices are not supported by the passage.

5. c. Throughout the story, Kevin goes on and on about his accomplishments. This implies that Kevin thinks that he has "made it" as a singer and does not need to learn anything. There is no support for choices **a**, **b**, or **d**.

6. a. Support for this choice is in the following sentence: "Alexander scanned quickly down the list, then he read it again more deliberately. There must have been some mistake. His name was on the list."

7. d. Alexander thinks it would be great to learn, and Mr. Robeson emphasizes the need to practice, work, and thereby improve, so choice **d** is the best answer. There is no evidence to support the other choices.

8. b. The first paragraph describes the over-crowding conditions that led to the construction of subways. Choices **a** and **c** are not necessarily true. Choice **d** is not discussed in the passage.

9. b. The third paragraph describes the crowding of Boston's streets. Choice **a** is not true. Choice **c** does not describe why the system was built. We do not know whether choice **d** is true from the passage.

10. d. Pneumatic transit was subterranean, but more important, it was powered by wind.

11. d. The passage states that overcrowding and population increases were the reasons subways were built. Choice **a** is not accurate because trains are not necessarily only subways. Choices **b** and **c** are true, but they are only part of the passage's topic.

12. c. This is a detail question. The answer is located in the last paragraph.

13. a. The passage gives a little bit of information about the Champs-Élysées; thus, choice **c** is not a good title. Choices **b** and **d** are only part of the information given in the passage.

14. d. When something is prestigious, it inspires respect and admiration.

15. c. The first paragraph gives this information.

16. a. Because of the various pieces of information that the author gives us in the passage about the Champs-Élysées, we can assume that the author thinks the boulevard is very important. We do not know whether the author agrees with the statements in choices **b** and **d**. The author probably does not agree that "kingdom of the dead" is an appropriate name for the boulevard.

17. c. Although trees were probably planted at some point in the history of the Champs-Élysées, the passage does not include this information.

18. a. The introduction refers to the Statue of Liberty as "the symbol of her new life." Also, the last sentence states that when Tatiana saw the statue, she "knew that she was free to start her new life." There is no evidence to support the other choices.

19. b. The clue that these events occurred long ago is the steamship. Today, people would not travel across the ocean on a steamship. The other choices are incorrect because any of those statements could be made today.

20. a. The children had been pestering the engineer with questions, so he gave them a tour of the engine room. There is no evidence in the story to support the other choices.

21. c. The story clearly states that the family could not afford Tatiana's ticket, so her father sent for her as soon the family had the money. Choice **a** is incorrect because even though she was young when her family left, she wasn't much older when she traveled all the way by herself. Choice **b** is incorrect because she stayed with her uncle only until her family could afford her ticket. Choice **d** is incorrect because she was willing to move to America.

22. d. An encyclopedia entry would most likely provide detailed information about steamships. Choice **a** is incorrect because sailboats are different from steamships. Choice **b** is incorrect because a book on the immigrants in New York would not give many details about steamships. Choice **c** is incorrect because looking at modern ships would not provide much information about steamships.

23. d. The story describes Tatiana's experience of coming to America. Choice **a** is incorrect because there are only a few details about the setting of the story. Choices **b** and **c** are incorrect because few opinions are presented in the story, and there is no attempt to persuade the reader to any particular view.

24. a. The main point of the passage is to explain why the arch was built and to describe the actual construction of the monument. The other choices are too vague or too narrow to be the main idea.

25. d. See the second paragraph under the heading "The Design." The phrase "a monument even taller than the Great Pyramid in Egypt" is evidence that the author wanted readers to understand how tall the arch was. There is no evidence in the article to support choices **a** or **c**. Choice **b** can be ruled out because the article says, "the arch is *at least* as majestic as the Great Pyramid," not *more* majestic.

26. a. Support for this answer can be found in the first sentence. There is no support for choices **b** or **c**. Although the author probably believes the arch is a great monument, the article never says that it is "the greatest monument ever built."

27. b. This is the best choice because it is the only one that provides information about what a visitor to the arch might see. Choice **a** is incorrect because details about the arch's structure belong in the section labeled "The Design." Choice **c** is incorrect because details about the architect also belong in the section labeled "The Design." Choice **d** is incorrect because details about the cost of construction belong in the section labeled "The Construction."

28. c. This is the best choice because the author consistently refers to the arch as "magnificent," "amazing," and "a masterpiece."

29. b. The second paragraph states that the Jefferson National Expansion Memorial Association held the contest to choose a design for the monument.

30. c. The specific focus of this passage is stated in the first sentence. It introduces the topic of the sprained ankle. Choice **a** is only one detail of the passage; the entire passage does not deal with describing sprains. Choice **b** is incorrect since there are only two sentences that deal with bandaging, and they only mention ankle sprains. Choice **d** also focuses only on one detail of the passage.

31. d. This is explicitly stated in the fourth sentence of the first paragraph. Choice **a** is not supported by the passage; enlarged blood vessels are not discussed. Choice **b** is not the cause of a sprain. This was an explanation of the danger of keeping an ice pack on the wound for too long. Choice **c** confuses two details: The ball of the foot is used as the starting point for wrapping the bandage; tissue is not mentioned, while *torn* describes damage to the ligament.

32. c. Choices **a**, **b**, and **d** are all clearly stated in the passage as warnings. Only choice **c** is not supported by the passage. "Ankle" and "fire" appear in the same sentence, but only to describe the pain of the injury.

33. d. The passage explicitly states that, once the first cold pack is removed, one should wait 30 minutes and then reapply it for another 20 minutes. Choice **a** is incorrect since it is not the next step, but the third. Both choices **a** and **b** bypass the reapplication of the cold pack. Choice **c** has the timing of the packs reversed.

34. c. This is implied in the sentence, "bleeding, hence bruising . . ." demonstrating a clear relationship between bleeding and the "black and blue" of the question. Choice **a** is not a direct cause of the bruising; again, blood is. Choice **b** is incorrect since the passage states that wrapping the bandage too tightly will interfere with circulation to the foot, the opposite of the condition needed for bruising. Choice **d** is irrelevant to the passage.

35. b. The word *emigrate* means to move or to relocate. People relocated from the Massachusetts Bay Colonies to the Rhode Island area.

36. b. Roger Williams was the first to colonize the Providence area. Anne Hutchinson and others followed later, and this all occurred long before the Revolutionary War.

37. d. Each of the choices is actually true in Rhode Island's history, but the reason that it was originally settled was for religious freedom, as stated in the passage.

38. b. The author uses a tug-of-war rope to picture two political groups fighting, with Rhode Island caught in the middle. Each group was trying to pull Rhode Island away from the other group.

39. c. The word *governance* means *authority* or *government*.

40. d. The passage does address religious freedom, but it does not trace its history in America. The main idea of the passage is that Rhode Island has an important history, despite its small size.

Test 7: Mathematics

1. d. $1\frac{1}{20} = 1.05 = 105\%$. The other choices are all the same: $\frac{6}{5} = 1\frac{1}{5} = 1.2 = 120\%$.

2. a. To find the difference between food and the combined total of transportation and clothing expenses, look at the numbers for the graph. Food is 22%, transportation is 9%, and clothing is 4%. $22 - (9 + 4) = 9\%$.

3. d. $(x^2 + 4x + 4)$ factors into $(x + 2)(x + 2)$. Therefore, one of the $(x + 2)$ terms can be canceled with the denominator. This leaves $x + 2$.

4. a. Here, 157 is rounded to 200; 817 is rounded to 800. 200×800 equals 160,000.

5. c. The number marked is -3.

6. c. The cost (C) is found by multiplying the number of people (n) by the price per ticket ($6) and adding the service charge ($7): $C = 6n + 7$.

7. c. To find out how many dozen cookies Hans can make, divide $5\frac{1}{2}$ by $\frac{2}{3}$. First, convert $5\frac{1}{2}$ to $\frac{11}{2}$, then multiply by $\frac{3}{2}$, which is the same as dividing by $\frac{2}{3}$. $\frac{11}{2} \times \frac{3}{2} = \frac{33}{4}$, or $8\frac{1}{4}$ dozen.

8. c. The cost for 25 hours for both providers must be found. For A, the base charge is $20, plus 7.5 hours at $1 per hour. This is $27.50. For B, the base charge is $20, plus 5 hours at $1.50. This is also $27.50. Therefore, they will cost the same.

9. b. Here, $4.20 = 75% of full price. Divide $4.20 by 0.75 to get the full price of $5.60.

10. c. This problem is done by dividing: $1.5 \div 600 = 0.0025$ inch.

11. d. The two largest eaters in the group are the Mastiff, which eats 40 pounds of food, and the Great Dane, which eats 39 pounds of food. Adding these two numbers together gives a total of 79 pounds of dog food.

12. d. Line q runs through the point $x = -3$. For every point on the y-axis, line q is at $x = -3$. The equation of line q is $x = -3$.

13. d. When comparing and ordering decimals, it may help to imagine these numbers with additional zeros: 513.260, 513.514, 513.590, 513.700.

14. b. The graph shows that 26% of the drinks sold (325) are smoothies. $0.26 \times 325 = 84.5$.

15. c. To find the area of the tile border, find the total area of the pool and border (21×11) and subtract the area of the pool (17×9).

16. b. To find the height of the tree, begin by converting the fractions to decimals: $\frac{3}{4} = 0.75$ and $5\frac{1}{4} = 5.25$. You can then set up a proportion: $\frac{0.75}{68} = \frac{5.25}{x}$. Cross multiply: $(68)(5.25) = (0.75)(x)$; then, $357 = 0.75x$; $476 = x$.

17. c. The solution is as follows: $[6(3) - 6(-2)] \div 9$. The equation then becomes $[18 - (-12)] \div 9$, and then, because two minuses become a plus, $30 \div 9 = 3\frac{1}{3}$.

18. a. Let x equal the number sought. Working in reverse order, we have: The sum of that number and six becomes $(x + 6)$, the product of three and a number becomes $3x$. Combining terms: $(x + 6) - 3x = 0$. Simplifying: $2x = 6$ or $x = 3$.

19. a. The 10% discount is over all three items; therefore, the total price is $(a + b + c) \times 0.9$. The average is the total price divided by the number of computers: $0.9 \times \frac{a+b+c}{3}$.

20. a. Doubling the length and width of Sophia's original doghouse floor gives new dimensions of 6 feet by 4 feet. The area of the new doghouse is 24 square feet. The original doghouse floor had an area of 6 square feet (24 divided by 6 equals 4). The new doghouse has four times the area of the original doghouse floor.

21. b. A polygon is a closed figure made of line segments. A regular polygon has all sides and all angles congruent. Thus, the only regular polygon shown is the triangle.

22. d. The perimeter is the distance around the figure. The straight edges must be 8 because they are radii, thus, so far we have $8 + 8$. Now we have to add in that curved part. Notice that the curved part is a portion of a circumference, and circumference = $2\pi r$. We are interested in only $\frac{1}{4}$ of the circumference, so we will add in $\frac{1}{4}(2\pi r)$, or $\frac{1}{2}\pi(8)$, which is 4π. Therefore, the perimeter is $4\pi + 8 + 8$, or $4\pi + 16$.

23. d. The third and fourth quarters are 54% and 16%, respectively. This adds to 70%.

24. d. To express 14% mathematically, you just put the 14 over 100, which gives you $\frac{14}{100}$. You can divide this out to yield 0.14. If you need 14% of 232, remember that "of" means *times*. This means 14% of $232 = 14\% \times 232 = \frac{14}{100} \times 232 = 0.14 \times 232$. Thus, choices **b** and **c** are correct.

25. d. The production for Lubbock is equal to the total minus the other productions: $1{,}780 - 450 - 425 - 345 = 560$.

26. c. The speed of the train is 60 miles per hour, obtained from the table. Therefore, the distance from Chicago would be equal to $60t$. However, as the train moves on, the distance decreases from Los Angeles, so there must be a function of $-60t$ in the equation. At $t = 0$, the distance is 2,000 miles, so the function is $2{,}000 - 60t$.

27. a. First, find the least common denominator of the two fractions, which is 6. Then add the fractions of the sandwich Joline gave away: $\frac{3}{6}$ (which she gave to Eddie) $+ \frac{2}{6}$ (which she ate) $= \frac{5}{6}$. Now subtract the fraction from one whole sandwich $(1 = \frac{6}{6})$: $\frac{6}{6} - \frac{5}{6} = \frac{1}{6}$.

28. d. The first step in solving this problem is to add the fractions to get the sum of $\frac{4x}{4}$. This fraction reduces to x.

29. d. A line that intersects two parallel lines forms complementary angles on either side of it. Complementary angles are angles whose measures add up to 180°. $180° − 40° = 140°$.

30. d. Begin by converting $\frac{7}{40}$ into a decimal: $\frac{7}{40} = 0.175$. Next, multiply by 1 in the form of $\frac{100}{100}$ to convert from decimal form to percent form: $(0.175)(\frac{100}{100}) = \frac{17.5}{100}$ or 17.5%.

31. a. The circumference of the can corresponds to the length of the label. Since the diameter is 14 cm, the circumference is: $C = \pi d$; $C = \frac{22}{7}$; $C = 44$. Add 1 cm for the overlap for a length of 45 cm. The height of the can equals the height of the label, 7 cm.

32. b. When describing the search area, this question tells you that it encompasses a 45-mile radius. When you see the term *radius*, you know that you are dealing with a circle. You also know that you need to come up with a formula for T, which is an area in square miles. The area of a circle is πr^2. Thus, $A = \pi r^2$ becomes $T = \pi r^2$. Substituting 45 in for r, your formula becomes $T = \pi(45)^2$. Rearranging, you get choice **b**, $T = 45^2\pi$.

33. d. Let G stand for the generic oatmeal and N for the name brand: $G = \frac{2}{3}N$; $G = \$1.50$. $\$1.50 \div \frac{2}{3} = \$2.25$.

34. b. One way to find the area of the deck is to find the area of the pool and deck, and then subtract the area of the pool. (Area of pool + deck) − (area of pool) = area of deck. $A = (14 + 5)(26 + 5) − (14 \times 26)$. Then, $A = (19 \times 31) − (14 \times 26)$; $A = 589 − 364$; $A = 225$.

35. d. Find the answer by changing the fractions to decimals: $\frac{1}{3} = 0.333$; $\frac{1}{4} = 0.25$; $\frac{2}{7} = 0.286$. 0.286, or $\frac{2}{7}$, is between the other two.

36. d. The slant height is found with the Pythagorean theorem to be 10. The perimeter is therefore $(2 \times 18) + (2 \times 10) = 56$.

37. a. By using the Pythagorean theorem, the hypotenuse is found to be 5. The sum of the sides is the perimeter, giving a perimeter of 12.

38. c. In your head, you can quickly multiply this figure by 2 to get 36. Then move the decimal point over one space to the left to get 3.60.

39. a. If the inequality is solved as an equation, the largest value that fulfills the inequality is found. Therefore, $3x − 14 = 3$; $3x = 17$; $x = 5\frac{2}{3}$. Any number smaller than this will fulfill the inequality. The only number less than $5\frac{2}{3}$ is 4.

40. d. The area of a circle is equal to πr^2, so doubling the radius causes the area to increase by four times the original size.
$\pi \times (4)^2 = 16\pi$
$\pi \times (8)^2 = 64\pi$
$\frac{64\pi}{16\pi} = 4$

Scoring

Find out how you did on this practice exam by counting the number of questions you got right in each part. Remember, questions you skipped or got wrong don't count against your score—only the number of correct answers is important. Then divide the number you got right by the number of questions in the section (see the first page of this lesson). If you need to check your math, use the tables at the end of Lesson 6.

Note which parts of the exam gave you the most trouble, and for the time you have left, concentrate your study on those parts.

The key to success in almost any pursuit is preparation. If you have worked through this book and faithfully done the practice exams, you're better prepared than many of the other students who will be taking the exam with you. You've looked carefully to see where your strengths and weaknesses lie and learned how to deal with the various kinds of questions that will appear on the test. So you can relax and go into the exam with the confidence that comes from knowing you're ready and armed with the tools to do your best.

15 ▶ PRACTICE TACHS EXAM 2

LESSON SUMMARY
This is the second of the two practice tests in this book based on the Test for Admission into Catholic High Schools (TACHS). Use this test to see how much you have improved.

For this exam, simulate the actual test-taking experience as closely as possible. Work in a quiet place, away from interruptions. Tear out the answer sheets on pages 351–352, and use your number 2 pencil to fill in the circles. Use a timer or stopwatch and allow yourself time as follows:

Reading: Part 1 . . . . 10 minutes
Reading: Part 2 . . . . 25 minutes
Language . . . . 30 minutes
Math . . . . 40 minutes
Ability . . . . 32 minutes

After the exam, again use the answer key that follows it to see your progress on each section and to find out why the correct answers are correct and the incorrect ones incorrect. Then use the scoring section at the end of the exam to see how you did overall.

Reading: Part 1

1. (a) (b) (c) (d)
2. (a) (b) (c) (d)
3. (a) (b) (c) (d)
4. (a) (b) (c) (d)
5. (a) (b) (c) (d)
6. (a) (b) (c) (d)
7. (a) (b) (c) (d)

8. (a) (b) (c) (d)
9. (a) (b) (c) (d)
10. (a) (b) (c) (d)
11. (a) (b) (c) (d)
12. (a) (b) (c) (d)
13. (a) (b) (c) (d)
14. (a) (b) (c) (d)

15. (a) (b) (c) (d)
16. (a) (b) (c) (d)
17. (a) (b) (c) (d)
19. (a) (b) (c) (d)
20. (a) (b) (c) (d)

Reading: Part 2

1. (a) (b) (c) (d)
2. (a) (b) (c) (d)
3. (a) (b) (c) (d)
4. (a) (b) (c) (d)
5. (a) (b) (c) (d)
6. (a) (b) (c) (d)
7. (a) (b) (c) (d)
8. (a) (b) (c) (d)
9. (a) (b) (c) (d)
10. (a) (b) (c) (d)

11. (a) (b) (c) (d)
12. (a) (b) (c) (d)
13. (a) (b) (c) (d)
14. (a) (b) (c) (d)
15. (a) (b) (c) (d)
16. (a) (b) (c) (d)
17. (a) (b) (c) (d)
18. (a) (b) (c) (d)
19. (a) (b) (c) (d)
20. (a) (b) (c) (d)

21. (a) (b) (c) (d)
22. (a) (b) (c) (d)
23. (a) (b) (c) (d)
24. (a) (b) (c) (d)
25. (a) (b) (c) (d)
26. (a) (b) (c) (d)
27. (a) (b) (c) (d)
28. (a) (b) (c) (d)
29. (a) (b) (c) (d)
30. (a) (b) (c) (d)

Language

1. (a) (b) (c) (d)
2. (a) (b) (c) (d)
3. (a) (b) (c) (d)
4. (a) (b) (c) (d)
5. (a) (b) (c) (d)
6. (a) (b) (c) (d)
7. (a) (b) (c) (d)
8. (a) (b) (c) (d)
9. (a) (b) (c) (d)
10. (a) (b) (c) (d)
11. (a) (b) (c) (d)
12. (a) (b) (c) (d)
13. (a) (b) (c) (d)
14. (a) (b) (c) (d)
15. (a) (b) (c) (d)
16. (a) (b) (c) (d)
17. (a) (b) (c) (d)

18. (a) (b) (c) (d)
19. (a) (b) (c) (d)
20. (a) (b) (c) (d)
21. (a) (b) (c) (d)
22. (a) (b) (c) (d)
23. (a) (b) (c) (d)
24. (a) (b) (c) (d)
25. (a) (b) (c) (d)
26. (a) (b) (c) (d)
27. (a) (b) (c) (d)
28. (a) (b) (c) (d)
29. (a) (b) (c) (d)
30. (a) (b) (c) (d)
31. (a) (b) (c) (d)
32. (a) (b) (c) (d)
33. (a) (b) (c) (d)
34. (a) (b) (c) (d)

35. (a) (b) (c) (d)
36. (a) (b) (c) (d)
37. (a) (b) (c) (d)
38. (a) (b) (c) (d)
39. (a) (b) (c) (d)
40. (a) (b) (c) (d)
41. (a) (b) (c) (d)
42. (a) (b) (c) (d)
43. (a) (b) (c) (d)
44. (a) (b) (c) (d)
45. (a) (b) (c) (d)
46. (a) (b) (c) (d)
47. (a) (b) (c) (d)
48. (a) (b) (c) (d)
49. (a) (b) (c) (d)
50. (a) (b) (c) (d)

Math

1.	ⓐ	ⓑ	ⓒ	ⓓ	18.	ⓐ	ⓑ	ⓒ	ⓓ	35.	ⓐ	ⓑ	ⓒ	ⓓ
2.	ⓐ	ⓑ	ⓒ	ⓓ	19.	ⓐ	ⓑ	ⓒ	ⓓ	36.	ⓐ	ⓑ	ⓒ	ⓓ
3.	ⓐ	ⓑ	ⓒ	ⓓ	20.	ⓐ	ⓑ	ⓒ	ⓓ	37.	ⓐ	ⓑ	ⓒ	ⓓ
4.	ⓐ	ⓑ	ⓒ	ⓓ	21.	ⓐ	ⓑ	ⓒ	ⓓ	38.	ⓐ	ⓑ	ⓒ	ⓓ
5.	ⓐ	ⓑ	ⓒ	ⓓ	22.	ⓐ	ⓑ	ⓒ	ⓓ	39.	ⓐ	ⓑ	ⓒ	ⓓ
6.	ⓐ	ⓑ	ⓒ	ⓓ	23.	ⓐ	ⓑ	ⓒ	ⓓ	40.	ⓐ	ⓑ	ⓒ	ⓓ
7.	ⓐ	ⓑ	ⓒ	ⓓ	24.	ⓐ	ⓑ	ⓒ	ⓓ	41.	ⓐ	ⓑ	ⓒ	ⓓ
8.	ⓐ	ⓑ	ⓒ	ⓓ	25.	ⓐ	ⓑ	ⓒ	ⓓ	42.	ⓐ	ⓑ	ⓒ	ⓓ
9.	ⓐ	ⓑ	ⓒ	ⓓ	26.	ⓐ	ⓑ	ⓒ	ⓓ	43.	ⓐ	ⓑ	ⓒ	ⓓ
10.	ⓐ	ⓑ	ⓒ	ⓓ	27.	ⓐ	ⓑ	ⓒ	ⓓ	44.	ⓐ	ⓑ	ⓒ	ⓓ
11.	ⓐ	ⓑ	ⓒ	ⓓ	28.	ⓐ	ⓑ	ⓒ	ⓓ	45.	ⓐ	ⓑ	ⓒ	ⓓ
12.	ⓐ	ⓑ	ⓒ	ⓓ	29.	ⓐ	ⓑ	ⓒ	ⓓ	46.	ⓐ	ⓑ	ⓒ	ⓓ
13.	ⓐ	ⓑ	ⓒ	ⓓ	30.	ⓐ	ⓑ	ⓒ	ⓓ	47.	ⓐ	ⓑ	ⓒ	ⓓ
14.	ⓐ	ⓑ	ⓒ	ⓓ	31.	ⓐ	ⓑ	ⓒ	ⓓ	48.	ⓐ	ⓑ	ⓒ	ⓓ
15.	ⓐ	ⓑ	ⓒ	ⓓ	32.	ⓐ	ⓑ	ⓒ	ⓓ	49.	ⓐ	ⓑ	ⓒ	ⓓ
16.	ⓐ	ⓑ	ⓒ	ⓓ	33.	ⓐ	ⓑ	ⓒ	ⓓ	50.	ⓐ	ⓑ	ⓒ	ⓓ
17.	ⓐ	ⓑ	ⓒ	ⓓ	34.	ⓐ	ⓑ	ⓒ	ⓓ					

Ability

1.	ⓐ	ⓑ	ⓒ	ⓓ		18.	ⓐ	ⓑ	ⓒ	ⓓ	ⓔ	35.	ⓐ	ⓑ	ⓒ	ⓓ	ⓔ
2.	ⓐ	ⓑ	ⓒ	ⓓ		19.	ⓐ	ⓑ	ⓒ	ⓓ	ⓔ	36.	ⓐ	ⓑ	ⓒ	ⓓ	ⓔ
3.	ⓐ	ⓑ	ⓒ	ⓓ		20.	ⓐ	ⓑ	ⓒ	ⓓ	ⓔ	37.	ⓐ	ⓑ	ⓒ	ⓓ	ⓔ
4.	ⓐ	ⓑ	ⓒ	ⓓ		21.	ⓐ	ⓑ	ⓒ	ⓓ	ⓔ	38.	ⓐ	ⓑ	ⓒ	ⓓ	ⓔ
5.	ⓐ	ⓑ	ⓒ	ⓓ		22.	ⓐ	ⓑ	ⓒ	ⓓ	ⓔ	39.	ⓐ	ⓑ	ⓒ	ⓓ	ⓔ
6.	ⓐ	ⓑ	ⓒ	ⓓ		23.	ⓐ	ⓑ	ⓒ	ⓓ	ⓔ	40.	ⓐ	ⓑ	ⓒ	ⓓ	ⓔ
7.	ⓐ	ⓑ	ⓒ	ⓓ		24.	ⓐ	ⓑ	ⓒ	ⓓ	ⓔ	41.	ⓐ	ⓑ	ⓒ	ⓓ	ⓔ
8.	ⓐ	ⓑ	ⓒ	ⓓ		25.	ⓐ	ⓑ	ⓒ	ⓓ	ⓔ	42.	ⓐ	ⓑ	ⓒ	ⓓ	ⓔ
9.	ⓐ	ⓑ	ⓒ	ⓓ		26.	ⓐ	ⓑ	ⓒ	ⓓ	ⓔ	43.	ⓐ	ⓑ	ⓒ	ⓓ	ⓔ
10.	ⓐ	ⓑ	ⓒ	ⓓ		27.	ⓐ	ⓑ	ⓒ	ⓓ	ⓔ	44.	ⓐ	ⓑ	ⓒ	ⓓ	ⓔ
11.	ⓐ	ⓑ	ⓒ	ⓓ		28.	ⓐ	ⓑ	ⓒ	ⓓ	ⓔ	45.	ⓐ	ⓑ	ⓒ	ⓓ	ⓔ
12.	ⓐ	ⓑ	ⓒ	ⓓ		29.	ⓐ	ⓑ	ⓒ	ⓓ	ⓔ	46.	ⓐ	ⓑ	ⓒ	ⓓ	ⓔ
13.	ⓐ	ⓑ	ⓒ	ⓓ		30.	ⓐ	ⓑ	ⓒ	ⓓ	ⓔ	47.	ⓐ	ⓑ	ⓒ	ⓓ	ⓔ
14.	ⓐ	ⓑ	ⓒ	ⓓ		31.	ⓐ	ⓑ	ⓒ	ⓓ	ⓔ	48.	ⓐ	ⓑ	ⓒ	ⓓ	ⓔ
15.	ⓐ	ⓑ	ⓒ	ⓓ	ⓔ	32.	ⓐ	ⓑ	ⓒ	ⓓ	ⓔ	49.	ⓐ	ⓑ	ⓒ	ⓓ	ⓔ
16.	ⓐ	ⓑ	ⓒ	ⓓ	ⓔ	33.	ⓐ	ⓑ	ⓒ	ⓓ	ⓔ	50.	ⓐ	ⓑ	ⓒ	ⓓ	ⓔ
17.	ⓐ	ⓑ	ⓒ	ⓓ	ⓔ	34.	ⓐ	ⓑ	ⓒ	ⓓ	ⓔ						

Reading: Part 1

For questions 1 through 5, choose the word or phrase that most nearly means the same as the underlined word.

1. an <u>impulsive</u> decision
  a. hasty
  b. jolly
  c. brilliant
  d. small

2. an <u>ornate</u> design
  a. simple
  b. complicated
  c. ordinary
  d. furious

3. a <u>devout</u> friend
  a. funny
  b. difficult
  c. fancy
  d. dedicated

4. a vehicle in <u>transit</u>
  a. style
  b. trouble
  c. motion
  d. use

5. a harsh <u>reprimand</u>
  a. praise
  b. concern
  c. idea
  d. warning

For questions 6 through 10, choose the word or phrase that most nearly means the opposite of the underlined word.

6. a <u>superb</u> choice
  a. wonderful
  b. misunderstood
  c. colorful
  d. terrible

7. an <u>optimistic</u> woman
  a. sure
  b. negative
  c. intelligent
  d. positive

8. a <u>gruesome</u> monster
  a. pleasant
  b. frightful
  c. tall
  d. imaginary

9. a <u>jovial</u> personality
  a. fierce
  b. gloomy
  c. happy
  d. unlikely

10. <u>glorify</u> heroes
  a. select
  b. copy
  c. condemn
  d. praise

For questions 11 through 15, choose the word or phrase that most nearly means the same as the underlined word.

11. I have decided to <u>forgo</u> desserts and eat only healthy foods.
    a. eat
    b. take in
    c. create
    d. give up

12. The old, neglected cottage was extremely <u>dingy</u>.
    a. dirty
    b. distant
    c. disgusting
    d. distinct

13. Vitamin c is <u>beneficial</u> to your health.
    a. unimportant
    b. helpful
    c. significant
    d. damaging

14. Hester is always <u>famished</u> right before dinnertime.
    a. hungry
    b. busy
    c. satisfied
    d. anxious

15. Trevor's mistakes were too <u>insignificant</u> to cause him to lose the game.
    a. interesting
    b. sincere
    c. minor
    d. important

For questions 16 through 20, choose the word that best completes the sentence.

16. If you pick up the baby and sing to her, you will _____ her.
    a. pacify
    b. enrage
    c. confuse
    d. teach

17. Patrick is a real _____; he never holds onto his money for very long.
    a. genius
    b. leader
    c. supervisor
    d. spendthrift

18. My friend Rochelle may be _____, but she's still a good person.
    a. incredible
    b. fast
    c. imperfect
    d. sturdy

19. If you practice _____, you may become an excellent violinist.
    a. occasionally
    b. persistently
    c. complicatedly
    d. absurdly

20. Always _____ any mistakes you find in your essay before you hand it to your teacher.
    a. examine
    b. discover
    c. ignore
    d. revise

Reading: Part 2

For questions 1 through 30, read each passage carefully. Answer the questions that follow only on the basis of the preceding passage.

Waiting for Godot

The English language premiere of Samuel Beckett's play *Waiting for Godot* took place in London in August 1955. *Godot* is an avant-garde play with only five characters (not including Mr. Godot, who never arrives) and a minimal setting: one rock and one bare tree. The play has two acts; the second act repeats what little action occurs in the first with few changes: The tree, for instance, acquires one leaf. In a statement that was to become famous, the critic Vivian Mercier has described *Godot* as "a play in which nothing happens twice."

On opening night, critics and playgoers greeted the play with <u>bafflement</u> and derision. The line, "Nothing happens, nobody comes, nobody goes. It's awful," was met by a loud rejoinder of "Hear! Hear!" from an audience member. *Waiting for Godot* was in danger of closing the first week of its run and of becoming nothing more than a footnote in the annals of the English stage. However, Harold Hobson's review in *The Sunday Times* managed to recognize the play for what history has proven it to be, a revolutionary moment in theater.

1. With which statement would the author probably agree?
   a. *Waiting for Godot* is an important play.
   b. Mr. Godot is the most interesting character in *Waiting for Godot*.
   c. *Waiting for Godot* is a play in which nothing happens twice.
   d. It is a good thing that *Waiting for Godot* has been forgotten.

2. Which word in the passage describes the setting of the play?
   a. awful
   b. famous
   c. minimal
   d. dangerous

3. As it is used in the passage, the underlined word <u>bafflement</u> most nearly means
   a. enthusiasm
   b. confusion
   c. understanding
   d. joy

4. Information in the passage leads you to believe
   a. Samuel Beckett is still thought of as a phony.
   b. Vivian Mercer was open to new ideas.
   c. Godot was originally supposed to appear in the play.
   d. Harold Hobson was very forward-thinking.

5. Which statement is NOT true?
   a. *Waiting for Godot* was not well liked when it debuted.
   b. A tree is part of the setting of *Waiting for Godot*.
   c. Act 2 of *Waiting for Godot* is very different from Act 1.
   d. There are five characters in *Waiting for Godot*.

6. Which would be another title for this passage?
   a. "A Forgotten Play"
   b. "A Play ahead of Its Time"
   c. "A Rock and a Leaf"
   d. "The Most Hated Play in History"

Healthy Hearts

In her lecture, Dr. Miranda Woodhouse challenged Americans to join her in the fight to reduce the risks of heart disease. Her plan includes four basic strategies meant to increase public awareness and prevent heart disease. Eating a healthy diet that contains nine full servings of fruits and vegetables each day can help lower cholesterol levels. More fruits and vegetables mean less dairy and meat, which, in turn, means less cholesterol-boosting saturated fat. Be aware of your blood pressure and cholesterol levels at all times. Because there are often no symptoms, many people don't even know that they have high blood pressure. This is extremely dangerous since uncontrolled high blood pressure can lead to heart attack, kidney failure, and stroke. Finally, relax and be happy. Studies show that being constantly angry and depressed can increase your risk of heart disease, so take a deep breath, smile, and focus on the good things in life.

7. A good title for this passage might be
   a. "Keeping Your Heart Healthy"
   b. "Dr. Miranda Woodhouse: An American Hero"
   c. "Eating More Fruits and Vegetables"
   d. "The Most Dangerous Diseases"

8. According to the passage, what will happen if you eat more fruits and vegetables?
   a. You will get all the pleasure of eating cake.
   b. You may lower your cholesterol level.
   c. You will prevent heart disease.
   d. You will be aware of your cholesterol level.

9. Because high blood pressure often doesn't have any symptoms,
   a. it isn't a very serious condition.
   b. it can be treated quickly and easily.
   c. a person may only think they have it.
   d. a person might not know whether they have it.

10. The passage implies which of the following?
   a. If you are too relaxed, you can get sick.
   b. Health and happiness are connected.
   c. Deep breathing can cure all illnesses.
   d. Listening to music is a great way to relax.

11. How did Dr. Woodhouse pass along her information?
   a. in a book
   b. in a lecture
   c. in a nationwide study
   d. in a newspaper article

12. What might be unhealthy about meat?
   a. It can cause depression.
   b. Gristle is hard to swallow.
   c. Fat can increase cholesterol.
   d. Meat is very expensive.

A History of the Bicycle

Today, bicycles are <u>elegantly</u> simple machines that are common around the world. Many people ride bicycles for recreation, whereas others use them as a means of transportation. The first bicycle, called a *draisienne*, was invented in Germany in 1818 by Baron Karl de Drais de Sauerbrun. Because it was made of wood, the *draisienne* wasn't very durable nor did it have pedals. Riders moved it by pushing their feet against the ground.

In 1839, Kirkpatrick Macmillan, a Scottish blacksmith, invented a much better bicycle. Macmillan's machine had tires with iron rims to keep them from getting <u>worn</u> down. He also used foot-operated cranks, similar to pedals, so his bicycle could be ridden at a quick pace. It didn't look much like the modern bicycle, though, because its back wheel was substantially larger than its front wheel. Although Macmillan's bicycles could be ridden easily, they were never produced in large numbers.

It wasn't until 1874 that the first truly modern bicycle appeared on the scene. Invented by an Englishman, H.J. Lawson, the safety bicycle would look familiar to today's cyclists. The safety bicycle had equal-sized wheels, which made it much less prone to toppling over. Lawson also attached a chain to the pedals to drive the rear wheel. By 1893, the safety bicycle had been further improved with air-filled rubber tires, a diamond-shaped frame, and easy braking. With the improvements provided by Lawson, bicycles became extremely popular and useful for transportation. Today, they are built, used, and enjoyed all over the world.

13. What is the main idea of this passage?
   a. The bicycle has undergone many changes throughout the years.
   b. The first bicycle was called a *draisienne*.
   c. Macmillan's bicycle had tires with iron rims.
   d. Bicycles are popular all over the world.

14. Which word would be most similar to the word <u>elegantly</u> in the first sentence?
   a. popularly
   b. clumsily
   c. stupendously
   d. gracefully

15. Which statement is NOT true?
   a. The safety bicycle was easy to brake.
   b. An early bicycle did not have pedals.
   c. H.J. Lawson invented the bicycle we still use today.
   d. The first bicycle was made in Germany.

16. When did the bicycle first have a diamond-shaped frame?
   a. 1818
   b. 1839
   c. 1874
   d. 1893

17. According to the passage, what did H.J. Lawson do differently from Kirkpatrick Macmillan?
   a. He invented a bicycle with foot-operated cranks.
   b. He created a bicycle with equal-sized wheels.
   c. His bicycle was intended for transportation.
   d. His bicycle had a soft, cushioned seat.

18. As it is used in the passage, the word <u>worn</u> most nearly means
   a. drained.
   b. put on.
   c. ruined.
   d. annoyed.

School Schedules

Both year-round school and regular school schedules are found throughout the United States. With year-round school schedules, students attend classes for nine weeks, and then have three weeks' vacation. This continues all year long. The regular school schedule requires that students attend classes from September to June, with a three-month summer vacation at the end of the year. This schedule began because farmers needed their children at home to help with crops during the summer. Today, most people work in businesses and offices. Year-round school is easier for parents who work in businesses and don't have the summer to be with their children. The regular school schedule is <u>ideal</u> for kids who like to have a long summer vacation. While some educational systems have changed their schedules to keep up with their population, others still use the old agrarian calendar. Both systems have disadvantages and advantages, which is why schools use different systems.

19. What is the main idea of the passage?
   a. Year-round school schedules are better than regular ones.
   b. Farmers need their children to help with the crops.
   c. Most people work in offices today.
   d. There are two ways to schedule school.

20. Which of the following is the best definition of the word underlined ideal in the paragraph?
   a. perfect
   b. incorrect
   c. basic
   d. problematic

21. Which of the following will students NOT do on a regular schedule?
   a. be happy
   b. attend school in July
   c. attend school in February
   d. be well-educated

22. Who most affected the creation of the regular school schedule?
   a. teachers
   b. students
   c. farmers
   d. office workers

23. The passage implies that schools will
   a. all agree to use regular school schedules.
   b. all convert to year-round schedules.
   c. develop a stronger focus on farming and business skills.
   d. continue to use both regular and year-round schedules.

24. Of the following, which would be the best title for this passage?
   a. "The Benefits of Different Schedules"
   b. "Keeping up with the Population"
   c. "The Old Agrarian Calendar"
   d. "Spending Time with Your Kids in the Summer"

Making a Scrapbook

A scrapbook is an easy craft that can reflect the style, format, and contents of its creator's unique personality. All it takes is initiative. Interest and inspiration help, too. Begin by choosing a cover style for your scrapbook. You can purchase one premade in a store or create your own. You might want to use a plastic binder with a clear front cover and decorate it. Next, choose what theme you want for your scrapbook. Is it for your entire family or just you? Do you want it to focus on school activities alone or your life in general? Perhaps you would like it to only be about spring break or summer vacation.

Do you know what to include in your scrapbook? The more variety you use, the better. How about some ticket stubs and postcards? You might want to include personal letters, drawings, report cards, or greeting cards. Other possibilities include newspaper clippings, pressed flowers, concert programs, and certificates. I have all those in mine and it looks fantastic!

25. As it is used in the passage, the word unique most nearly means
   a. mature.
   b. special.
   c. artistic.
   d. attractive.

26. Why is variety important for a scrapbook?
    a. Variety will help people understand your scrapbook better.
    b. Variety will keep your scrapbook from looking like anything else.
    c. Variety makes a scrapbook look better.
    d. Variety makes a scrapbook more informative.

27. As it is used in the passage, the word <u>focus</u> most nearly means
    a. concentrate.
    b. gather.
    c. balance.
    d. sharpness.

28. A good title for this passage might be
    a. "Pressed Flowers"
    b. "A Summer Vacation Scrapbook"
    c. "Choosing a Cover Style"
    d. "So Many Options!"

29. Which of the following possible scrapbook items does the author NOT mention?
    a. photographs
    b. postcards
    c. clippings
    d. programs

30. Which of the following is something a scrapbook should have?
    a. initiative
    b. a theme
    c. professional quality
    d. a report card

Language

For questions 1 through 30, find the sentence that has a mistake in capitalization, punctuation, or usage. If you find no mistakes, mark choice d.

1. a. When is Aunt Ruth going to respond to my letter?
   b. How was the Statue of Liberty shipped to America?
   c. Have you seen a movie called the *Wizard of Oz*?
   d. No mistakes.

2. a. Remember to return that book to the library this week.
   b. Your magazine arrived today.
   c. At six o'clock, I will let the cat in.
   d. No mistakes.

3. a. These potato chips are making me thirsty.
   b. I wrote my schedule on a dry-erase board.
   c. I borrowed his pen because mine ran out of ink.
   d. No mistakes.

4. a. Mark is bringing the sandwiches, and Elise is bringing the juice.
   b. Be sure to turn off the faucet you don't want to waste water.
   c. Leave your passport on the nightstand so you don't forget to bring it tomorrow.
   d. No mistakes.

5. a. May I ask you something!
   b. You're my best friend!
   c. Be careful; you're walking on ice!
   d. No mistakes.

6. a. My sister is going to the University of Colorado.
   b. Next year we are moving to Richmond, Virginia.
   c. We are going to meet in front of the Empire State building.
   d. No mistakes.

7. a. I used to live on that street; now I live on Beekman Place.
   b. The box was full of old things: trophies, photos, and letters.
   c. Someone I know—I won't mention his name—thinks you're funny.
   d. No mistakes.

8. a. We can hang the poster in your bedroom, or we can hang it in the den.
   b. I need another bookcase, there isn't enough room in this one to store all my books.
   c. Please mark this on your calendar: On February 15, we are taking a day trip up the coast.
   d. No mistakes.

9. a. Who is on my baseball team, my friend, is coming to the movies with us.
   b. That sweater, which is my favorite, was a gift from Cousin Ethel.
   c. This table, which is made of oak, has been in my family for generations.
   d. No mistakes.

10. a. The cabinet is full of supplies: a flashlight, a medical kit, and empty bottles for water.
   b. The music room had so many instruments: trumpets, trombones, violins, a tuba, and a piano.
   c. The supermarket is having a sale on several essential items: cereal, milk, eggs, and cheese.
   d. No mistakes.

11. a. If you don't like that book: you can return it to the bookstore.
   b. When I woke up this morning, I had a sore throat.
   c. We spent two hours cleaning the backyard after the party.
   d. No mistakes.

12. a. My mother works for the Hartford Corporation.
   b. Shakespeare wrote the play *The Merchant of Venice*.
   c. "You," Tara began, "Are welcome here anytime."
   d. No mistakes.

13. a. When the snow started falling.
   b. Hello, John.
   c. Is that your coat?
   d. No mistakes.

14. a. The tide washed over the shore.
   b. The sun is shining in the sky.
   c. The moon rise over the horizon.
   d. No mistakes.

15. a. Miriam played beautifully the piano.
   b. Should you choose to call me, I'll be home all day.
   c. Be careful not to break that glass.
   d. No mistakes.

16. a. Next, I'm going to do my famous card trick.
   b. We're going to meet again on Tuesday.
   c. She can't make it to the game; she has other plans.
   d. No mistakes.

17. a. I have been playing basketball since I was nine years old.
   b. This weekend, the yankees are going to play the red sox.
   c. We need to bring bats, balls, and baseball helmets to the park.
   d. No mistakes.

18. a. Is that his favorite television show?
   b. This is your ballpoint pen.
   c. The car is missing it's front tires.
   d. No mistakes.

19. a. The teacher is writing with white chalk.
   b. That lesson was a real eye-opener.
   c. Patches is such a friendly looking dog.
   d. No mistakes.

20. a. The picture has falled off the wall.
   b. Louie leapt over the puddle.
   c. The track team ran 20 miles.
   d. No mistakes.

21. a. He and I are lab partners.
   b. Will you invite me and she to the party?
   c. That is not her house.
   d. No mistakes.

22. a. The scientist created a new invention.
   b. Those kids are extremely helpful.
   c. Without thinking, I caught the ball.
   d. No mistakes.

23. a. My math Professor, Theresa Allen, is very intelligent.
   b. Are you going to Mr. Rodriguez's class now?
   c. Sergeant Drake wants to talk to Private Murray.
   d. No mistakes.

24. a. The birds sang in the trees.
   b. The mirror cracked when I dropped it.
   c. The phone ringed at noon.
   d. No mistakes.

25. a. Bea wondered how long she would have to wait.
   b. May I have a peanut, Veronica asked.
   c. A sign reading "Stop" was at the end of the street.
   d. No mistakes.

26. a. This program, which I just learned to use, is very helpful.
   b. That blanket is not very warm, so you might want to use this one instead.
   c. If you're going to stop by tomorrow, please call me first.
   d. No mistakes.

27.
  a. I am now going to listened to my favorite album.
  b. Rita played chess while Rocky read a book.
  c. The grass is getting long, so I am going to mow it.
  d. No mistakes.

28.
  a. The lightbulb burned out, so I replaced it.
  b. Do you like to play table tennis?
  c. The chef served pancakes.
  d. No mistakes.

29.
  a. Can I have your phone number?
  b. Your the best musician in the band.
  c. I know you are a serious student.
  d. No mistakes.

30.
  a. This avenue is being repaved.
  b. Wales is a country in the United Kingdom.
  c. That was a great production of *Romeo And Juliet*.
  d. No mistakes.

For questions 31 through 40, find the sentence that has a mistake in spelling. If you find no mistakes, mark choice **d**.

31.
  a. The kitten loves to cuddel.
  b. The supply is going to increase.
  c. We rested on the plateau.
  d. No mistakes.

32.
  a. The triangle has sharp angles.
  b. I saw that sculpsher at the museum.
  c. Please inflate the balloon.
  d. No mistakes.

33.
  a. I didn't get hurt, but my bicycle was recked in the fall.
  b. My brother can impersonate any celebrity!
  c. There were subtraction and addition questions on the math test.
  d. No mistakes.

34.
  a. The cowboy wrangled the animals into the corral.
  b. Please write a summary of the book you just read.
  c. I am planning to modifey the painting to make it better.
  d. No mistakes.

35.
  a. That was a very humorous story!
  b. There is much activity around the beehive.
  c. We are going swimming in the lake.
  d. No mistakes.

36.
  a. The flourist arranged the roses into a bouquet.
  b. The substitute teacher was very kind to the class.
  c. Can you detect your reflection in the window?
  d. No mistakes.

37.
  a. Mrs. Ling is a prominent member of the community.
  b. I generaly find sports to be uninteresting.
  c. The clerk stocked the merchandise onto the shelves.
  d. No mistakes.

38. **a.** That town is experiencing an increase in population.
   b. We skated along the surface of the ice rink.
   c. I loaded the lumber into the wheelbarrow.
   d. No mistakes.

39. **a.** The two opponents decided to compromize.
   b. The acrobats swung on the trapeze.
   c. You can use the encyclopedia as a reference.
   d. No mistakes.

40. **a.** The authorities will emprison the criminal.
   b. We enjoyed a nutritious snack.
   c. My birthday is in February.
   d. No mistakes.

For questions 41 through 50, follow the directions for each question.

41. Choose the word that best joins the sentences.
   I do not consider myself to be afraid of heights. _____, I felt uncomfortable at the top of the 50-story building.
   a. And
   b. Nevertheless
   c. Therefore
   d. Because

42. Choose the word that best joins the thoughts together.
   My daughter loves to go to the amusement park, _____ my son prefers to stay at home.
   a. thus
   b. consequently
   c. and
   d. so

43. Which of these expresses the idea most clearly?
   a. We should call Hector and Cletus if the weather, and go biking, is sunny on Saturday.
   b. If the weather is sunny on Saturday, we should call Hector and Cletus and go biking.
   c. If the weather is sunny on Saturday, we should call Hector and Cletus go biking.
   d. If the weather is sunny we should call, on Saturday, Hector and Cletus and go biking.

44. Which of these expresses the idea most clearly?
   a. The deer ambled through the forest, ate some grass, and took a nap in the shade of a tree.
   b. The deer ambled through the forest, and ate some grass, took a nap in the shade of a tree.
   c. Eating some grass, the deer ambled through the forest and took a nap in the shade of a tree.
   d. Ambling through the forest, ate some grass, and took a nap in the shade of a tree, the deer.

45. Which of these expresses the idea most clearly?
   a. If you eat spicy food you may get an upset stomach and have unpleasant dreams shortly before bedtime.
   b. If you eat spicy food shortly before bedtime, get an upset stomach, and have unpleasant dreams.
   c. If you eat spicy food shortly before bedtime, you may get an upset stomach and have unpleasant dreams.
   d. If you eat spicy food shortly before bedtime, and you may get an upset stomach and have unpleasant dreams.

46. Choose the group of words that best completes the sentence.

History may not be my best subject,
a. I am determined to study hard and get a good grade on tomorrow's exam.
b. but I am determined to study hard. I am determined to get a good grade on tomorrow's exam.
c. but I am determined to study hard and get a good grade on tomorrow's exam.
d. but I am determined, and get a good grade, to study hard on tomorrow's exam.

47. Which of the following topics is best for a one-page essay?
a. a history of European music
b. my favorite song of 2013
c. how to play the piano
d. the twenty best musicians of the twentieth century

48. Which of these best fits under the topic "The Moon: Our Planet's Closest Neighbor"?
a. Scientists believe there is iron in the core of the moon.
b. The moon is Earth's only natural satellite.
c. There has never been a manned mission to Mars.
d. If I could go anywhere in the universe, I'd go to the moon.

49. Which sentence does NOT belong in the paragraph?
(1) Theodore Roosevelt was born with asthma and poor eyesight. (2) Charles Warren Fairbanks was Roosevelt's vice president. (3) Yet this sickly child later won fame as a political leader and hero of the people. (4) To conquer his disabilities, Teddy trained in a gym and became a lightweight boxer at Harvard.
a. sentence 1
b. sentence 2
c. sentence 3
d. sentence 4

50. Where should the sentence "It was a humble beginning that did not foretell his later popularity" be placed in the following paragraph?
(1) Milton Hershey was born near the small village of Derry Church, Pennsylvania, in 1857. (2) Milton only attended school through the fourth grade; at that point, he was apprenticed to a printer in a nearby town. (3) Fortunately for all chocolate lovers, Milton did not excel as a printer. (4) After a while, he left the printing business to take a position for which he was better suited: he apprenticed to a Lancaster, Pennsylvania, candymaker.
a. before sentence 1
b. between sentences 1 and 2
c. between sentences 2 and 3
d. between sentences 3 and 4

Math

1. Compute 390 − 285.
  a. 205
  b. 95
  c. 105
  d. 115

2. Compute 24 + 58 + 36.
  a. 218
  b. 98
  c. 118
  d. 108

3. Compute 4,020 ÷ 20.
  a. 2,001
  b. 210
  c. 21
  d. 201

4. Compute the product of 20 and 40.
  a. 2,040
  b. 60
  c. 80
  d. 800

5. Compute the sum of 6.73 and 18.07.
  a. 11.34
  b. 24.80
  c. 24.70
  d. 23.80

6. Compute 0.01 ÷ 0.001.
  a. 1
  b. 10
  c. 100
  d. 0.00001

7. Compute 3.178 × 2.
  a. 6.356
  b. 6.246
  c. 6.346
  d. 6.256

8. Compute $(5.86 − 1.86)^3$.
  a. 81
  b. 16
  c. 64
  d. 12

9. Compute $5 + \frac{5}{4}$.
  a. $\frac{9}{4}$
  b. 5
  c. $\frac{11}{4}$
  d. $\frac{21}{4}$

10. Compute $\frac{31}{8} − 2$.
  a. $\frac{29}{8}$
  b. $\frac{47}{8}$
  c. $\frac{15}{8}$
  d. $\frac{25}{8}$

11. Compute 20% of 51.5.
  a. 13
  b. 1,030
  c. 11.3
  d. 10.3

12. Compute $3 ÷ \frac{2}{9}$.
  a. $12\frac{1}{2}$
  b. $13\frac{1}{2}$
  c. $\frac{2}{3}$
  d. $\frac{2}{27}$

13. Compute $\frac{90}{17} × \frac{51}{100}$.
  a. $\frac{27}{10}$
  b. $\frac{27}{100}$
  c. $\frac{10}{27}$
  d. $\frac{36}{10}$

14. Compute 300% of $\frac{2}{9}$.
 a. $\frac{600}{9}$
 b. $\frac{2}{27}$
 c. $\frac{2}{3}$
 d. $\frac{1}{2}$

For questions 15 through 20, an exact answer is not expected. Give the best estimate and complete these problems mentally. Write nothing down when solving these problems.

15. What is the best estimate of $(1.809 + 3.221)^3$?
 a. 15
 b. 64
 c. 12
 d. 125

16. Determine which of the following is the closest estimate of 896 + 588 + 391.
 a. 1,900
 b. 1,600
 c. 2,100
 d. 2,300

17. Which of the following is the closest estimate of $(2.91 + 3.16) - (0.87 + 1.16)$?
 a. 3
 b. 4
 c. 5
 d. 6

18. Which is the best estimate of $(16\frac{1}{8} + 9\frac{8}{9}) - 7\frac{1}{10}$?
 a. 17
 b. 18
 c. 19
 d. 20

19. Determine the closest estimate of 302.3% of 16.85.
 a. 600
 b. 51
 c. 60
 d. 510

20. Determine the best estimate of 6.1 ÷ 0.003.
 a. 20
 b. 200
 c. 6,000
 d. 2,000

21. You make $420 per week and pay 11% in taxes. What is your take-home pay?
 a. $373.80
 b. $415.38
 c. $466.20
 d. $46.20

22. A manufacturer finds that 3% of its batteries are defective. In a shipment of 15,000 batteries, how many would you expect to be defective?
 a. 750
 b. 4,500
 c. 450
 d. 5,000

23. You can harvest 3 dozen strawberries per minute. How many minutes does it take to harvest 500 strawberries? Round your answer to the nearest minute.
 a. 167 minutes
 b. 14 minutes
 c. 17 minutes
 d. 42 minutes

24. A carnival game has 400 stuffed Angry Birds of three varieties. If $\frac{3}{10}$ are red birds and $\frac{1}{4}$ are yellow birds, how many are blue Angry Birds?

    a. 220

    b. 45

    c. 180

    d. 55

Use the following bar graph to solve questions 25 and 26.

This bar graph illustrates the average number of texts that that three people send during school hours and after school hours.

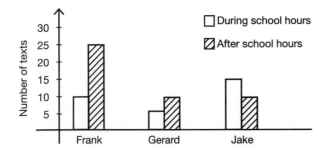

25. How many texts, all told, are sent on a typical weekday by all three students?

    a. 75

    b. 35

    c. 50

    d. 25

26. What is the difference between the total number of texts sent after school hours and the number of texts sent during school hours by these individuals on a typical day?

    a. 75

    b. 45

    c. 30

    d. 15

27. Compute $8 \times 7 - 7 \times 6$.

    a. 0

    b. 14

    c. 294

    d. 98

28. Which of the following whole numbers is prime?

    a. 113

    b. 108

    c. 111

    d. 105

29. Which of the following is a complete list of factors of 56?

    a. 2,4,6,7,8,14,28,56

    b. 1,2,3,4,5,6,7,8,14,28,56

    c. 1,2,4,7,8,14,28,56

    d. 1,4,7,8,14,56

30. A local TV station gives your school 300 T-shirts to give away. If there are 20 different homerooms at your school, and you wish to distribute them evenly among them, how many T-shirts should each homeroom get?

    a. 15

    b. 14

    c. 150

    d. 30

31. Which of the following is a multiple of 40?

    a. 8

    b. 20

    c. 380

    d. 120

32. Convert $\frac{13}{22}$ to a decimal and round to the nearest ten-thousandth.

    a. 0.6000

    b. 0.5900

    c. 0.5910

    d. 0.5909

33. Determine the value of x such that $15x = 480$.
  a. 465
  b. 495
  c. 32
  d. 7,200

34. Compute 3^4.
  a. 64
  b. 81
  c. 12
  d. 27

35. Joel earns a monthly salary of $1,500, plus $55 per new contract that he secures beyond 30. If he secures 46 new contracts in a month, what would his salary be for that month?
  a. $1,500
  b. $2,380
  c. $3,150
  d. $1,516

36. Keith started reading in the evening at 8:30 P.M. and stopped the next morning at 4:15 A.M. If he read 130 pages, approximately how many pages did he read per hour, on average? Round your answer to the nearest hundredth of a page.
  a. 37.14
  b. 27.37
  c. 15.75
  d. 8.25

37. Mike completes a 1-mile run in $\frac{3}{4}$ the time it takes Susan, and it takes Bob $1\frac{1}{4}$ times as long as Susan to do so. If the sum of the times it takes the three of them to complete a 1-mile run is 21 minutes, how long does it take Bob to complete such a run?
  a. 21 minutes
  b. 5 minutes 25 seconds
  c. 7 minutes
  d. 8 minutes 45 seconds

38. The distance between town A and town B on a map is 4 inches. If the actual distance is 200 miles, what is the ratio of the map to the actual distance?
  a. 200:4
  b. 1:15,840
  c. 15,840:1
  d. 4:200

39. Nolan spends $650 on sporting equipment, and Ken spent 18% more than Nolan. What is the difference in the amounts they spent?
  a. $117
  b. $18
  c. $585
  d. $767

40. The price of a hot item on eBay started at $75 at noon. The price had increased by 230% by 9 P.M. that evening, at which time the auction ended. What was the final selling price of the item?
  a. $150
  b. $305
  c. $172.50
  d. $247.50

41. During the holidays, Penny spends $3\frac{1}{2}$ hours baking on Monday, 4 hours baking on Tuesday, and $2\frac{3}{4}$ hours baking on Wednesday. What is the average amount of time she spends baking on these three days?
  a. $5\frac{1}{8}$ hours
  b. $10\frac{1}{4}$ hours
  c. $3\frac{5}{12}$ hours
  d. 3 hours

42. Tanya intends to buy 4 concert tickets this summer for her friend's birthday. The tickets cost $360, and she currently has $190. She earns $15 per week babysitting. How many weeks will it take Tanya to save enough money to buy these tickets? Round your answer to the nearest week.

a. 11
b. 12
c. 24
d. 13

Use the following circle graph to answer questions 43 and 44.

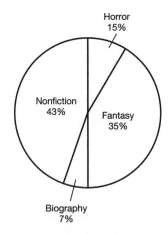

43. The circle graph shows the percentage of a local college freshman class who favor certain genres of literature. If 800 freshmen were asked this question, how many of them prefer horror?

a. 56
b. 280
c. 12
d. 120

44. What is the ratio of the freshmen who prefer fantasy novels to those who prefer horror novels?

a. 1:1
b. 7:10
c. 3:7
d. 7:3

Use the following bar chart to answer questions 45 and 46. It depicts the cost to rent a moped per hour at a beach resort from May to August.

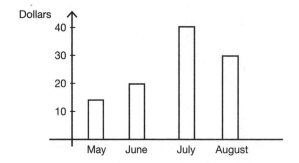

45. What is the average cost per hour for renting a moped during these months?

a. $40
b. $25
c. $26.25
d. $30

46. By what percentage did the cost per hour increase from June to July?

a. 100%
b. 20%
c. 33%
d. 50%

Use the following table to answer questions 47 and 48.

NUMBER OF NATIONAL ATHLETIC AWARDS GIVEN			
	2010	2011	2012
Freshmen	1	0	3
Sophomores	2	3	1
Juniors	5	5	7
Seniors	9	6	10

47. In 2012, approximately what percentage of athletic awards received were by juniors?
   a. 14%
   b. 33%
   c. 48%
   d. 5%

48. How many more awards were given in 2012 than in 2010?
   a. 4
   b. 7
   c. 21
   d. 17

Use the following chart to answer questions 49 and 50.

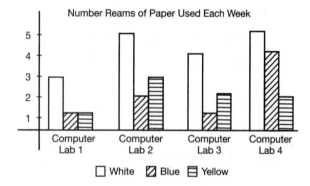

Number Reams of Paper Used Each Week

□ White ▨ Blue ⊟ Yellow

49. Which computer lab uses the most paper all told during a week?
   a. lab 1
   b. lab 2
   c. lab 3
   d. lab 4

50. Which computer lab used the least amount of nonwhite paper?
   a. lab 1
   b. lab 2
   c. lab 3
   d. lab 4

Ability

1. Find the next term in the sequence:
$1\frac{1}{4}, 2\frac{3}{4}, 4\frac{1}{4}, 5\frac{3}{4},$ _____
   a. $7\frac{1}{4}$
   b. $6\frac{1}{4}$
   c. $8\frac{1}{4}$
   d. $7\frac{3}{4}$

2. Find the next term in the sequence:
$\frac{7}{5}, \frac{9}{5}, \frac{13}{5}, \frac{19}{5},$ _____
   a. $\frac{23}{5}$
   b. 5
   c. $\frac{27}{5}$
   d. $\frac{37}{5}$

3. Find the next two terms of the sequence:
$22\frac{3}{8}, 19\frac{3}{4}, 17\frac{1}{8}, 14\frac{1}{2},$ _____, _____
   a. $11\frac{7}{8}, 9\frac{1}{4}$
   b. $12\frac{1}{2}, 10\frac{1}{2}$
   c. $12\frac{7}{8}, 10\frac{1}{4}$
   d. $10\frac{1}{4}, 12\frac{7}{8}$

4. Find the missing term in the sequence:
8, 1.6, 0.32, _____, 0.128
   a. 6.4
   b. 0.64
   c. 0.064
   d. 0.0064

5. Find the missing term in the sequence:
$\frac{3}{8}, \frac{9}{8}, \frac{27}{8}, \frac{81}{8}, $ _____

    a. $\frac{243}{8}$

    b. $\frac{729}{8}$

    c. $\frac{81}{24}$

    d. $\frac{243}{24}$

6. Find the missing terms of the sequence:
9.5, 1.05, 11.3, 0.95, 13.1, 0.85, _____, _____

    a. 0.75, 14.9

    b. 14.9, 0.75

    c. 16.7, 0.75

    d. 14.9, 0.65

7. Find the next two terms of the sequence:
20.2, $8\frac{1}{2}$, 18, 10, 15.8, $11\frac{1}{2}$, _____, _____

    a. 13, 13.6

    b. 13.8, $12\frac{1}{2}$

    c. 13.6, 13

    d. 12.4, $14\frac{1}{2}$

8. Find the next two terms of the sequence:
CI, CLI, CCI, _____, _____

    a. CCILI, CCCI

    b. CCCI, CCL

    c. CCCI, CCCLI

    d. CCLI, CCCI

9. Find the next term of the sequence: 50.25, 61, 71.75, _____

    a. 82.50

    b. 82

    c. 93.25

    d. 81.75

10. Find the next term of the sequence: 86, 70, 80, 64, 74, _____

    a. 58

    b. 48

    c. 84

    d. 68

11. Find the next two terms of the sequence:
43, 38, 40, 35, 37, _____, _____

    a. 32, 30

    b. 30, 32

    c. 34, 32

    d. 32, 34

12. Find the next two terms of the sequence:
C, 2, XC, 1, CLXXX, $\frac{1}{2}$, _____, _____

    a. CLX, $\frac{1}{8}$

    b. CLXX, $\frac{1}{4}$

    c. CLXX, $\frac{1}{8}$

    d. $\frac{1}{4}$, CLXX

13. Find the next term of the sequence:
V, XV, XXX, L, LXXV, _____

    a. XC

    b. CV

    c. XCV

    d. CXL

14. Find the next two terms of the sequence:
1000, 950, 850, 700, _____, _____

    a. 600, 550

    b. 500, 250

    c. 550, 400

    d. 250, 500

Patterns

For questions 15 through 25, the first three figures are alike in some way. Select the choice that goes with these three figures.

15.

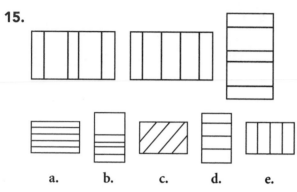

16.

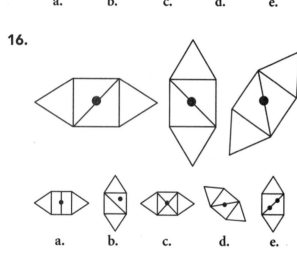

17.

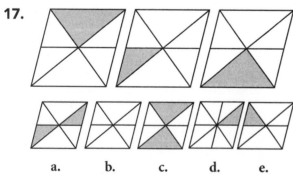

18.

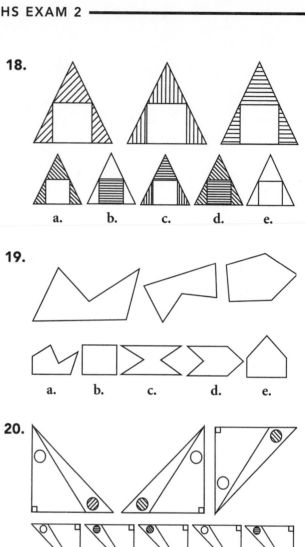

19.

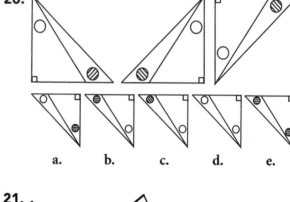

20.

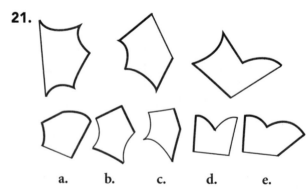

21.

a.   b.   c.   d.   e.

22.

23.

24.

25.

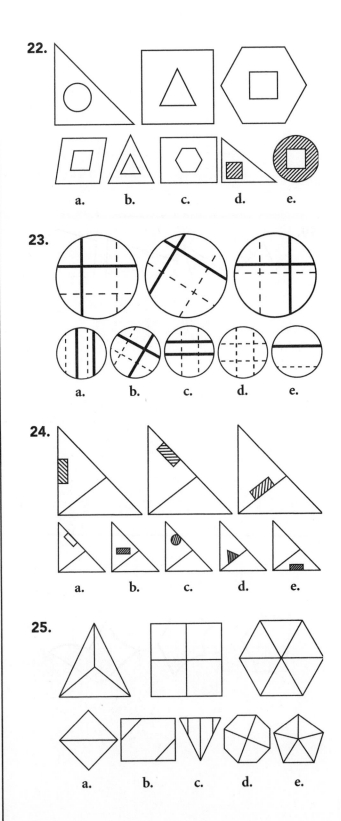

a.   b.   c.   d.   e.

Analogy

For questions 26 through 37, the first figure is changed into the second figure. The third figure is changed in the same way to make one of the answer choices. Choose the answer that goes with the third figure.

26.

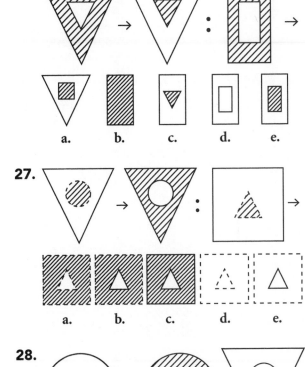

a.   b.   c.   d.   e.

27.

a.   b.   c.   d.   e.

28.

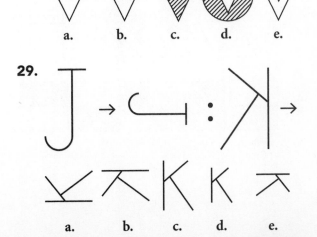

a.   b.   c.   d.   e.

29.

a.   b.   c.   d.   e.

30.

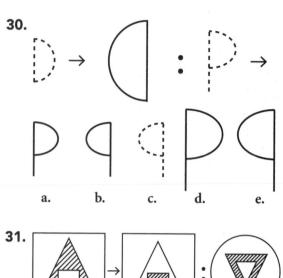

a.   b.   c.   d.   e.

31.

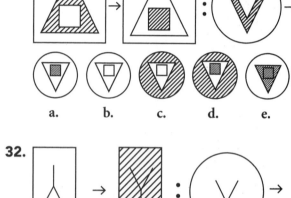

a.   b.   c.   d.   e.

32.

a.   b.   c.   d.   e.

33.

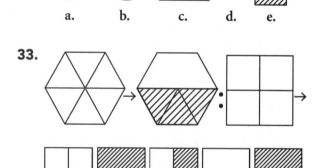

a.   b.   c.   d.   e.

34.

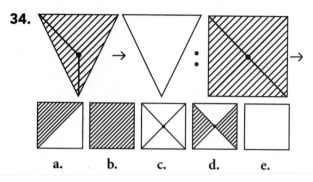

a.   b.   c.   d.   e.

35.

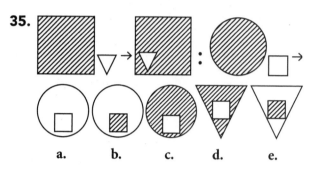

a.   b.   c.   d.   e.

36.

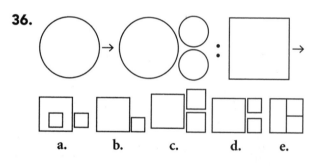

a.   b.   c.   d.   e.

37.

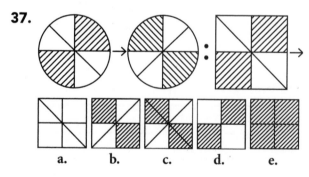

a.   b.   c.   d.   e.

For questions 38 through 50, a piece of paper is folded (as shown in the first diagram) and then holes are punched (as shown in the second diagram). If the paper is then unfolded, choose the answer choice that shows exactly what holes would appear on the entire piece of paper.

38.

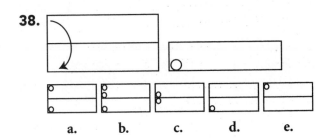

a.   b.   c.   d.   e.

39.

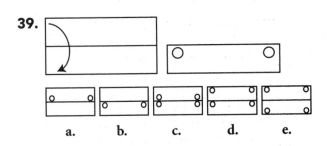

a.   b.   c.   d.   e.

40.

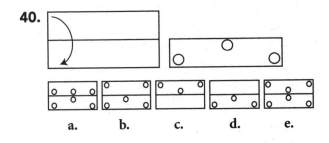

a.   b.   c.   d.   e.

41.

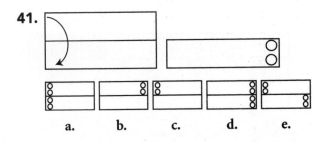

a.   b.   c.   d.   e.

42.

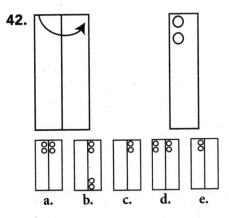

a.   b.   c.   d.   e.

43.

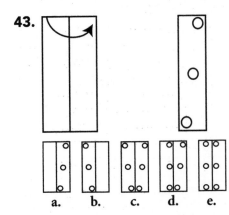

a.   b.   c.   d.   e.

44.

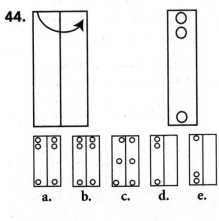

a.   b.   c.   d.   e.

45.

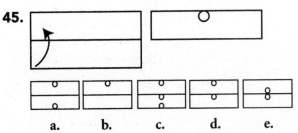

a.   b.   c.   d.   e.

46.

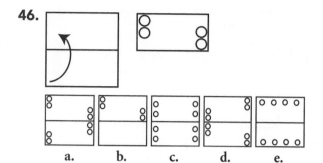

a.　　b.　　c.　　d.　　e.

50.

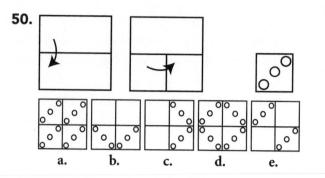

a.　　b.　　c.　　d.　　e.

47.

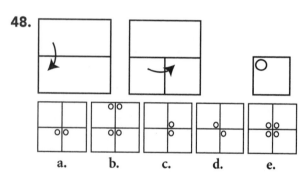

a.　　b.　　c.　　d.　　e.

48.

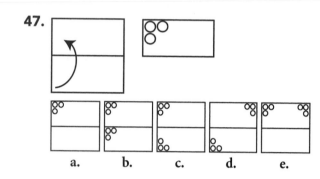

a.　　b.　　c.　　d.　　e.

49.

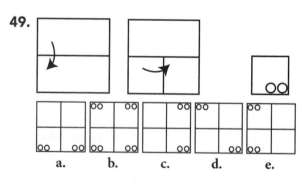

a.　　b.　　c.　　d.　　e.

Answers

Reading: Part 1

1. a. *Impulsive* means *hasty*.

2. b. *Ornate* means elaborate or *complicated*.

3. d. *Devout* means devoted or *dedicated*.

4. c. *Transit* means *motion*. The prefix *trans* means *across*.

5. d. *Reprimand* means *warning*.

6. d. *Superb* means wonderful, and since the opposite of the word is required, *terrible* is the best answer.

7. b. *Optimistic* means positive, and the opposite of *positive* is *negative*.

8. a. *Pleasant* is the opposite of *gruesome*. Frightful has the same meaning as gruesome, so choice **b** can be eliminated.

9. b. *Jovial* means happy, and the opposite of happy is *gloomy*.

10. c. To *glorify* someone is to praise them, and *condemn* means the opposite of praise.

11. d. Someone who has decided to only eat healthy foods would probably *give up* eating desserts, which are usually unhealthy. Take in is the opposite of forgo, so choice **b** can be eliminated.

12. a. Something that is old and neglected will probably be *dirty*. Disgusting is too strong a word, so choice **c** is not the best answer.

13. b. Vitamins are *helpful* for remaining in good health. Damaging means the opposite of *beneficial*, so choice **d** can be eliminated.

14. a. *Famished* means *hungry*, which someone might feel before eating dinner.

15. c. The prefix *in-* means not, so *insignificant* means not significant or *minor*. Important means significant, which is the opposite of insignificant, so choice **d** can be eliminated.

16. a. Picking up a baby and singing to her or him usually calms or *pacifies* the baby. Enrage is the opposite of pacify, so choice **b** can be eliminated.

17. d. A *spendthrift* is someone who wastes his or her money.

18. c. The prefix *im-* means not, so someone who is not perfect is *imperfect*. Incredible is the opposite of imperfect, so choice **a** can be eliminated.

19. b. *Persistently* means steadily, constantly, or tirelessly. Someone who practices the violin in such a way has a better chance of becoming an excellent musician. Choice **a** can be eliminated because occasionally is the opposite of persistently.

20. d. *Revise* means fix or correct. Merely examining (choice **a**) or ignoring (choice **c**) mistakes would not be the best way to handle mistakes in an essay.

Reading: Part 2

1. a. The author ends the passage by calling *Waiting for Godot* "a revolutionary moment in theater," which indicates that the author thinks it is an important play. Since Mr. Godot never actually arrives in the play, it is unlikely the author thinks he is the play's most interesting character, so choice **b** is incorrect. Choice **c** is the opinion of a critic, not the author of this passage. Choice **d** is wrong because *Waiting for Godot* has not been forgotten.

2. c. The author says the play has "a minimal setting." A critic called the play "awful," not the setting, so choice **a** is incorrect.

3. b. *Waiting for Godot* is a highly unusual play that confused people, so *confusion* is the best synonym for *bafflement*. Understanding is the opposite of confusion and bafflement, so choice **c** can be eliminated. Most people disliked the play at first, so they did not greet it with positive feelings of enthusiasm (choice **a**) or joy (choice **d**).

4. d. Harold Hobson was the rare critic who appreciated *Waiting for Godot* when it debuted, and now many people appreciate the play. This shows that he was a forward-thinking man. Many critics thought Samuel Beckett was a phony (choice **a**) when his play debuted, but since it is so widely appreciated these days, this is not how most people see him anymore. *Waiting for Godot* was apparently too revolutionary for Vivian Mercer, so it is unlikely that he was open to new ideas (choice **b**). There is no evidence in the passage that suggests Beckett ever intended Godot to appear in the play (choice **c**).

5. c. The author explains, "the second act repeats what little action occurs in the first with few changes." The other answer choices are all supported by information in the passage.

6. b. A good title should reflect the main idea of a passage, and choice **b** does this well. *Waiting for Godot* has not been forgotten, so choice **a** would be a poor title. Choice **c** merely describes the play's setting and does not reveal anything about the main idea. Since the play is no longer hated, as it was when it debuted, choice **d** is a poor title.

7. a. A good title should reflect the main idea of a passage, and this passage is about various ways to keep your heart healthy. Although Dr. Woodhouse should be admired for her efforts to keep Americans healthy, choice **b** does not reflect the main idea best. Choice **c** only refers to a single detail in the passage and does not sum up the main idea. The passage is only about heart disease, not several diseases, so choice **d** does not make sense.

8. b. The author writes, "Eating a healthy diet that contains nine full servings of fruits and vegetables each day can help lower cholesterol levels." Not everyone may agree that eating fruits and vegetables is as pleasurable as eating cake, so choice **a** is not the best answer. Eating fruits and vegetables is not a guarantee for preventing heart disease, so choice **c** is incorrect. Simply eating something will not tell you your cholesterol level, so choice **d** is incorrect.

9. d. The author writes, "Because there are often no symptoms, many people don't even know that they have high blood pressure." Just because a condition does not have symptoms does not mean it isn't serious (choice **a**) or can be treated quickly and easily (choice **b**). Choice **c** is not the best answer.

10. b. The author writes, "Studies show that being constantly angry and depressed can increase your risk of heart disease," which suggests that a happy person is more likely to be healthy. Choice **a** expresses the opposite idea. Although the author mentions the benefit of deep breathing, the author never suggests it can cure all illnesses, so choice **c** is wrong. Music is never mentioned in the passage, so choice **d** is wrong.

11. b. The passage begins, "In her lecture, Dr. Miranda Woodhouse challenged Americans to join her in the fight to reduce the risks of heart disease."

12. c. The author suggests eating less meat because it contains "cholesterol-boosting saturated fat." Although depression can have a negative effect on one's heart, the passage never suggests that meat causes depression, so choice **a** is incorrect. Choice **b** is wrong because gristle is never mentioned in the passage. Expense has nothing to do with health, nor is the cost of meat ever mentioned in the passage, so choice **d** is incorrect.

13. a. The passage shows the many ways bicycles have changed throughout the years. Choices **b**, **c**, and **d** only describe single details in the passage, not its main idea.

14. d. The words *elegantly* and *gracefully* have the same meaning. Clumsily has the opposite meaning of elegantly, so choice **b** can be eliminated. Stupendously is too strong a word, so choice **c** is not the best answer.

15. c. The author states that further improvements were made on H.J. Lawson's bicycle. The other answer choices are all true.

16. d. The author provides the year that the bicycle first had a diamond-shaped frame in the final paragraph of the passage.

17. b. Macmillan's bicycle had a back wheel that was larger than the front wheel and Lawson's had equal-sized wheels. Choice **a** is incorrect because Macmillan invented the bicycle with foot-operated cranks. All bicycles are intended for transportation, so choice **c** is incorrect. Choice **d** is never mentioned in the passage.

18. c. Each answer choice is a synonym for *worn*, but the word is only used to mean *ruined* in the second paragraph of the passage.

19. d. The passage is mainly about the two ways to schedule school. Choice **a** is incorrect because the author states, "Both systems have disadvantages and advantages." Choices **b** and **c** only refer to single details in the passage, and not the passage's main idea.

20. a. *Ideal* means *perfect*. Choice **d** can be eliminated because problematic is the opposite of ideal.

21. b. July is a vacation month on the regular school schedule. Some students prefer the regular schedule, so choice **a** is incorrect. February is a school month on the regular schedule, so choice **c** is incorrect. There is nothing in the passage that suggests a student won't be well-educated on a regular school schedule, so choice **d** is wrong.

22. c. The regular school schedule started because farmers needed their children to help with the crops at home during the summer.

23. d. The passage ends by stating that there are advantages and disadvantages to the two schedules, which is why different schools decide what works best for them. There is no evidence that this will stop being the case. This eliminates choices **a** and **b**. Information in the passage does not support choice **c**.

24. a. The passage discusses the benefits of both year-round and regular school schedules, and choice **a** best reflects this main idea. The other answer choices refer to relatively unimportant details in the passage.

25. b. As it is used in the passage, *unique* means *special*.

26. c. After discussing the variety of his own scrapbook, the author says it makes his book look "fantastic." The other answer choices are not indicated in the passage.

27. a. All the answer choices are synonyms of *focus*, but the word is only used to mean *concentrate* in this passage.

28. d. The passage is about the many options for making a scrapbook. The other titles only refer to minor details in the passage, and therefore would not make good titles.

29. a. The author never mentions *photographs* in the passage. All the other answer choices are mentioned in the passage.

30. b. The author writes of the importance of choosing a *theme* for a scrapbook. Initiative is something the scrapbook maker should have, not the scrapbook itself, so choice **a** is incorrect. The author never says that a scrapbook should have professional quality, so choice **c** is incorrect. A report card is just one example of something a scrapbook might have, so choice **d** is not the best answer.

Language

1. c. *The* is part of the movie's title, so it should be capitalized.

2. c. *In* is a preposition, and it is incorrect to end a sentence with a preposition.

3. d. All the answer choices are correct.

4. b. This is a run-on sentence since it needs the conjunction *because* between *faucet* and *you* to join the two clauses. Alternatively, you could insert a semicolon.

5. a. This sentence is a question, so it should be punctuated with a question mark.

6. c. *Building* is part of a proper name, so it should be capitalized.

7. d. All the answer choices are correct.

8. b. The two clauses need to be separated by either a semicolon or the conjunction *because*.

9. a. The parts of this sentence are out of order, so it is not clear. The phrase *Who is on my baseball team* should be placed between *friend* and *is*.

10. d. All the answer choices are correct.

11. a. This sentence is punctuated incorrectly. It requires a comma, not a colon.

12. c. "*Are welcome here anytime*" is not a complete sentence; it completes the sentence that began with "*You.*" Therefore, *are* should not be capitalized.

13. a. This sentence is a fragment because it lacks a subject and verb. The other sentences are short, but they are both complete.

14. c. There is no agreement between the subject and the verb, which should either be *rises* or *rose*.

15. a. This sentence has a misplaced modifier; *beautifully* should follow *piano*.

16. d. All the answer choices are correct.

17. b. *Yankees* and *Red Sox* are the names of teams, so they should be capitalized.

18. c. It's is a contraction of it is. This sentence requires the possessive form of it: *its*.

19. d. All the answer choices are correct.

20. a. The correct verb form is *fallen*.

21. b. The correct pronoun is not *she*, it is *her*.

22. d. All the answer choices are correct.

23. a. Professor is not used as a title in this sentence, so it should not be capitalized.

24. c. The proper past-tense form of ring is *rang*, not ringed.

25. b. *May I have a peanut* is something Veronica asked, and therefore, it should end with a question mark and be placed within quotation marks.

26. d. All the answer choices are correct.

27. a. There is an illogical shift in tense; both verbs should be in the present tense.

28. d. All the answer choices are correct.

29. b. *Your* should be replaced with the contraction *you're*.

30. c. *And* should not be capitalized in titles.

31. a. cuddle

32. b. sculpture

33. a. wrecked

34. c. modify

35. d. All the words are spelled correctly.

36. a. florist

37. b. generally

38. d. All the words are spelled correctly.

39. a. compromise

40. c. imprison

41. b. The second sentence presents information that seems to contradict the first one. *Nevertheless* shows such a relationship.

42. c. *And* is the only conjunction that makes sense because the other answer choices indicate a causal relationship that does not exist in this sentence.

43. b. Choice **b** is the only clear and correct sentence. Choices **a** and **d** have confusing syntax. Choice **c** is a run-on sentence.

44. a. Choice **a** is the only clear and correct sentence. The conjunction *and* is misplaced in choice **b**. Choice **c** suggests the deer ate grass *while* it ambled and napped. The subject is misplaced in choice **d**.

45. c. Choice **c** is the only clear and correct sentence. Choice **a** suggests you may have unpleasant dreams *before* bedtime, which does not make sense. Choice **b** is a run-on sentence. The addition of the conjunction *and* between *bedtime* and *you* makes it seem as though there is no direct relationship between the two halves of the sentence, so choice **d** is incorrect.

46. c. Choice **c** is the only one that is clear and correct. Choice **a** is missing a necessary conjunction. Choice **b** is repetitious. Choice **d** is worded confusingly.

47. b. The other answer choices are much too broad to adequately discuss in a short essay.

48. b. The topic refers to the relationship between the moon and Earth, and choice **b** is the only one that addresses this topic directly. Choice **a** does not refer to Earth at all. Choice **c** refers to neither Earth nor the moon. Choice **d** is a personal comment that does not belong in an essay with a scientific topic.

49. b. This passage is about how Theodore Roosevelt overcame his disabilities, and a sentence about his vice president strays from that topic. The other sentences are all relevant to the topic.

50. b. The sentence refers to Hershey's "humble beginning," which is discussed in the first sentence. After that, the passage moves on to his work as an apprentice, so inserting the sentence later than between sentences 1 and 2 would disrupt the topic.

Math

1. c. Choice **a** is incorrect because you did not subtract the hundreds place correctly. Choice **b** is incorrect because you mistakenly borrowed from the hundreds place. Choice **d** is incorrect because you did not borrow from the tens place correctly.

2. c. Choice **c** is correct because $(24 + 36) + 58 = 60 + 58 = 118$. Choice **a** is incorrect because the hundreds place is incorrect. Choice **b** is incorrect because the tens place is incorrect. Choice **d** is incorrect because you did not compute the tens place correctly.

3. d. Choice **a** is incorrect because you have one too many zeros. Choice **b** is incorrect because you transposed the last two digits. Choice **c** is incorrect because you forgot to retain a zero placeholder after the initial division of 20 into 40.

4. d. Choice **d** is correct because $20(40) = 800$. Choice **a** is incorrect because you simply listed the two numbers, one after the other, without actually multiplying them. Choice **b** is incorrect because you computed the sum, not the product. Choice **c** is incorrect because you have one too few zeros.

5. b. Choice **a** is incorrect because you computed the difference, not the sum. Choice **c** is incorrect because you didn't carry correctly. Choice **d** is incorrect because you computed the ones place incorrectly.

6. b. Choice **b** is correct because $0.01 \div 0.001 = 10 \div 1 = 10$. Choice **a** is incorrect because you moved the decimal point one too few places to the right. Choice **c** is incorrect because you moved the decimal point one too many places to the right. Choice **d** is incorrect because you multiplied instead of dividing.

7. a. Choice **b** is incorrect because you didn't carry to the tenths or the hundredths place correctly. Choice **c** is incorrect because you didn't carry to the hundredths place correctly. Choice **d** is incorrect because you didn't carry to the tenths place correctly.

8. c. Choice **c** is correct because $(5.86 - 1.86)^3 = 4^3 = 4 \times 4 \times 4 = 64$. Choice **a** is incorrect because this is 3^4, not 4^3. Choice **b** is incorrect because this is 4^2, not 2^4. Choice **d** is incorrect because you multiplied base times exponent when computing 4^3.

9. d. Choice **d** is correct because $4 + \frac{5}{4} = \frac{16}{4} + \frac{5}{4} = \frac{21}{4}$. Choice **a** is incorrect because you did not first get a least common denominator when adding the fractions. Choice **b** is incorrect because you multiplied instead of adding. Choice **c** is incorrect because you subtracted instead of adding.

10. c. Choice **c** is correct because $\frac{31}{8} - 2 = \frac{31}{8} - \frac{16}{8} = \frac{15}{8}$. Choice **a** is incorrect because you did not first get a least common denominator before subtracting. Choice **b** is incorrect because you added instead of subtracting. Choice **d** is incorrect because you did not borrow correctly when subtracting the numerators, after applying the least common denominator.

11. d. Choice **d** is correct because $0.20(51.5) = \frac{51.5}{5} = 10.3$. Choice **a** is incorrect because you did not divide 51.5 by 5 correctly. Choice **b** is incorrect because you multiplied 20 times 51.5 instead of 0.20 times 51.5. Choice **c** is incorrect because the ones place is incorrect.

12. b. Choice **b** is correct because $3 \div \frac{2}{9} = 3 \times \frac{9}{2} = \frac{27}{2} = 13\frac{1}{2}$. Choice **a** is incorrect because once you took the reciprocal of the fraction following the division sign, you multiplied incorrectly. Choice **c** is incorrect because you multiplied instead of dividing. Choice **d** is incorrect because this is the reciprocal of the answer.

13. a. Choice **d** is correct because $\frac{90}{17} \times \frac{51}{100} = \frac{9 \cdot \cancel{10}}{\cancel{17}} \times \frac{\cancel{17} \cdot 3}{\cancel{10} \cdot 10} = \frac{27}{10}$. Choice **b** is incorrect because you did not cancel a common factor in the denominator. Choice **c** is incorrect because this is the reciprocal of the answer. Choice **d** is incorrect because 51 equals 17(3), not 17(4).

14. c. Choice **c** is correct because $300\% = 3.0$, so that 3 times $\frac{2}{9} = \frac{2}{3}$. Choice **a** is incorrect because you multiplied 300 times $\frac{2}{9}$ rather than 3 times 2.9; remember, $300\% = 3.0$, not 300. Choice **b** is incorrect because you divided $\frac{2}{9}$ by 3 instead of multiplying by 3. Choice **d** is incorrect because this is the reciprocal of the answer.

15. d. Choice **d** is correct because the given expression is close to 5^3, which is 125. Choice **a** is incorrect because you calculated 5^3 (a good estimate) by multiplying exponent times base. Choice **b** is incorrect because you estimated the sum by 4, not 5. Choice **c** is incorrect because you used the estimate 4^3, but then computed it incorrectly by multiplying exponent times base.

16. a. Choice **a** is correct because the sum is close to $900 + 600 + 400 = 1,900$. Choice **b** is incorrect because you truncated each term rather than rounding to get 1,600. Choice **a** is better. Choice **c** is incorrect because, while it is not bad, it is larger than choice **a**, which is larger than the actual sum; so, choice **a** is better. Choice **d** is incorrect because you rounded the first two terms to the nearest thousand, but rounding to the nearest hundred (as in choice **a**) is better.

17. b. Choice **b** is correct because the expression is approximately equal to $6 - 2 = 4$. Choice **a** is incorrect because you approximated the expression by $5 - 2$, but the first term in the expression is actually closer to 6 than 5, so choice **b** is better. Choice **c** is incorrect because you used $6 - 1$, but the second term is closer to 2, so choice **b** is better. Choice **d** is incorrect because this is too large of an estimate in comparison to the others.

18. c. Choice **c** is correct because the given expression is approximately equal to $26 - 7$, which is 19. Choice **a** is incorrect because this is too small. You used $25 - 8$, while the first term is closer to 26 and the second is closer to 7. Choice **b** is incorrect because you used $25 - 7$, but $26 - 7$ (as in choice **c**) is better. Choice **d** is incorrect because you estimated this as $27 - 7 = 20$, but choice **c** is closer.

19. b. Choice **b** is correct because this is close to 300% of 17, which is $3(17) = 51$. Choice **a** is incorrect because you misinterpreted 300% as 30, not 3, and approximated 16.85 as 20, not 17. Choice **c** is incorrect because you used 300% of 20 not 17, so choice **b** is better. Choice **d** is incorrect because you computed 300% as 30, not 3.

20. d. Choice **d** is correct because the given expression is close to $6 \div 0.003 = 6,000 \div 3 = 2,000$. Choice **a** is incorrect because the decimal point is in the wrong location. Choice **b** is incorrect because the decimal point is in the wrong location. Choice **c** is incorrect because you approximated 0.003 by 0.001, but choice **d** is closer.

21. a. Choice **a** is correct because $\$420 - 0.11(\$420) = \$373.80$. Choice **b** is incorrect because $11\% = 0.11$, not 0.011. Choice **c** is incorrect because you added the tax to $420 rather than subtracting it. Choice **d** is incorrect because this is the amount of tax that you pay.

22. c. Choice **c** is correct because $0.03(15,000) = 450$. Choice **a** is incorrect because this is 5% of the shipment, not 3%. Choice **b** is incorrect because 3% is not equal to 0.3; it equals 0.03. Choice **d** is incorrect because you divided 15,000 by 3 when you should have multiplied by 0.03.

23. b. Choice **b** is correct because $\frac{500}{36}$ is approximately 13.889, which we round to 14. Choice **a** is incorrect because you did not convert 3 dozen to 36 strawberries. Choice **c** is incorrect because 1 dozen strawberries = 12 strawberries, not 10. Choice **d** is incorrect because this assumes that it takes 1 minute to harvest 1 dozen strawberries.

24. c. Choice **c** is correct because $\frac{3}{10} + \frac{1}{4} = \frac{55}{100}$. So, 45% of $400 = 180$ Angry Birds. Choice **a** is incorrect because this is not the number of blue Angry Birds. Choice **b** is incorrect because this is the percent of blue Angry Birds, not the number of them. Choice **d** is incorrect because this is the percentage of Angry Birds that are NOT blue.

25. a. Choice **a** is correct because $10 + 25 + 5 + 10 + 15 + 10 = 75$. Choice **b** is incorrect because this is only the number that Frank sent. Choice **c** is incorrect because you forgot to include the number that Jake sent. Choice **d** is incorrect because this is only the number that Jake sent.

26. d. Choice **d** is correct because there are $25 + 10 + 10 = 45$ texts sent after school hours, and $10 + 5 + 15 = 30$ texts sent during school hours. So, the difference is $45 - 30 = 15$. Choice **a** is incorrect because this is the sum of the texts sent during and after school hours, not the difference. Choice **b** is incorrect because this is the number of texts sent after school hours. Choice **c** is incorrect because this is the number of texts sent during school hours.

27. b. Choice **b** is correct because $8 \times 7 - 7 \times 6 = 56 - 42 = 14$. Choice **a** is incorrect because you did the subtraction first; the order of operations requires that you perform multiplication from left to right first. Choice **c** is incorrect because you performed the operations from left to right rather than following the order of operations. Choice **d** is incorrect because while you multiplied correctly from left to right, once you did this you added instead of subtracting.

28. a. Choice **a** is correct because no whole number aside from 1 and 113 divides evenly into 113. Choice **b** is incorrect because 3 divides evenly into 108. Choice **c** is incorrect because 3 divides evenly into 111. Choice **d** is incorrect because 5 divides evenly into 105.

29. c. Choice **c** is correct because all these numbers divide evenly into 56, and no other whole number not included in this list divides evenly into 56. Choice **a** is incorrect because 6 is not a factor of 56, and you forgot to list 1. Choice **b** is incorrect because 3 is not a factor of 56. Choice **d** is incorrect because you forgot to include 2 and 28.

30. a. Choice **a** is correct because $\frac{300}{20} = 15$. Choice **b** is incorrect because this is one too few. Choice **c** is incorrect because you did not divide 300 by 20; you divided by 2. Choice **d** is incorrect because this would be the amount if there had been 10 homerooms, not 20.

31. d. Choice **d** is correct because $40(3) = 120$. Choice **a** is incorrect because 8 is a factor of 40, not a multiple of it. Choice **b** is incorrect because 20 is a factor of 40, not a multiple of it. Choice **c** is incorrect because 40 does not divide evenly into 380, so 380 cannot be a multiple of 40.

32. d. Choice **d** is correct because $\frac{13}{22}$ is approximately equal to 0.590909, which is then rounded to 0.5909. Choice **a** is incorrect because you rounded to the nearest tenth. Choice **b** is incorrect because you rounded to the nearest hundredth. Choice **c** is incorrect because you rounded to the nearest thousandth.

33. c. Choice **c** is correct because dividing both sides by 15 yields $x = \frac{480}{15} = 32$. Choice **a** is incorrect because you subtracted 15 from 480 instead of dividing 480 by 15. Choice **b** is incorrect because you added 15 to both sides of the equation instead of dividing by 15. Choice **d** is incorrect because you multiplied both sides by 15 instead of dividing by it.

34. b. Choice **b** is correct because $3^4 = 3(3)(3)(3) = 81$. Choice **a** is incorrect because this is 4^3, not 3^4. Choice **c** is incorrect because you multiplied base times exponent. Choice **d** is incorrect because this is 3^3, not 3^4.

35. b. Choice **b** is correct because $1,500 + (46 − 30)(\$55) = \$2,380$. Choice **a** is incorrect because you forgot to add the amount earned for the 16 new contracts he secured beyond 30. Choice **c** is incorrect because you used 30, not 16, for the number of contracts secured beyond 30. Choice **d** is incorrect because you did not multiply 16 (the number of contracts secured beyond 30) by $55.

36. c. Choice **c** is correct because he read for $3\frac{1}{2} + 4\frac{3}{4} = 7\frac{5}{4} = 8\frac{1}{4}$ hours. So, divide the total number of pages read (130) by $8\frac{1}{4} = 8.25$ hours to get approximately 15.75 pages per hour. Choice **a** is incorrect because this accounts only for the time period 8:30 A.M. to midnight. Choice **b** is incorrect because this accounts only for the time period midnight to 4:15 A.M. Choice **d** is incorrect because this is the total number of hours that he spent reading.

37. d. Let $x =$ time it takes Susan to complete a 1-mile run. Then, Mike's time is $(\frac{3}{4})x$ and Bob's time is $(\frac{5}{4})x$. The sum of the times yields the following equation:
$$x + (\tfrac{3}{4})x + (\tfrac{5}{4})x = 21$$
$$3x = 21$$
$$x = 7$$
So, it takes Bob $(\frac{5}{4})(7) = \frac{35}{4} = 8.75$ minutes $= 8$ minutes 45 seconds to complete such a run. Choice **a** is incorrect because this is the sum of the times it takes them to complete such a run. Choice **b** is incorrect because this is the time it takes Mike to complete such a run. Choice **c** is incorrect because this is the time it takes Susan to complete such a run.

38. b. Choice **b** is correct because 1 mile = 5,280 feet = 63,360 inches. So, the ratio is 4:63,360 or, equivalently, 1:15,840. Choice **a** is incorrect because the ratio is listed in the wrong order, and you did not convert miles to inches. Choice **c** is incorrect because you reversed the terms in the ratio. Choice **d** is incorrect because you did not use the same units.

39. a. Choice **a** is correct because the difference in the amounts they spent is $0.18(\$650) = \$117$. Choice **b** is incorrect because 18% as a number does not equal the difference; it must be applied to Nolan's amount. Choice **c** is incorrect because this would be true had Ken spent 10% more than Nolan, not 18%. Choice **d** is incorrect because you forgot to subtract Nolan's amount from the amount Ken spent.

40. d. Choice **d** is correct because $\$75 + 2.30(\$75) = \$247.50$. Choice **a** is incorrect because this would account for a 100% increase in price, not a 230% increase. Choice **b** is incorrect because you treated 230% as $230, and added it to $75 as if it was the increase. You need to apply 230% to $75 and add *that* to $75. Choice **c** is incorrect because this is the amount by which the price increased, not the selling price.

41. c. Choice **c** is correct because $\frac{3\frac{1}{2} + 4 + 2\frac{3}{4}}{3} = \frac{10\frac{1}{4}}{3} = \frac{41}{12} = 3\frac{5}{12}$ hours. Choice **a** is incorrect because you divided the sum of the times by 2, not 3. Choice **b** is incorrect because this is the total time spent baking—you did not divide by 3 to get the average time baking on any of these days. Choice **d** is incorrect because you ignored the fractional parts of the times listed.

42. b. Choice **b** is correct because she needs to earn $170. The amount of time it will take her to earn this amount is $\frac{\$170}{15} = 11\frac{1}{3}$ weeks. So, rounding up, she would need to work for 12 weeks. Choice **a** is incorrect because this is not quite enough time. Choice **c** is incorrect because you divided 360 by 15, so that you did not account for the amount of money she already had saved. Choice **d** is incorrect because you divided 190 (the amount already saved) by 15, rather than dividing 170 by 15.

43. d. Choice **d** is correct because $800(0.15) = 120$. Choice **a** is incorrect because this is the number who prefer biographies. Choice **b** is incorrect because this is the number who prefer fantasy novels. Choice **c** is incorrect because $15\% = 0.15$, not 0.015.

44. d. Choice **d** is correct because the ratio is 35:15, which is equivalent to 7:3. Choice **a** is incorrect because this would imply that the same number prefer horror and fantasy novels, which we know not to be the case from the circle graph. Choice **b** is incorrect because this is 35:50, and the second number is incorrect. Choice **c** is incorrect because this ratio is written backward.

45. c. Choice **c** is correct because $\frac{30 + 40 + 20 + 15}{4} = \frac{105}{4} = \$26.25$. Choice **a** is incorrect because this is the maximum cost for the four months shown, not the average cost across the four months. Choice **b** is incorrect because you forgot to include August. Choice **d** is incorrect because you forgot to include May.

46. a. Choice **a** is correct because $\frac{40 - 20}{20} \times 100\% = 100\%$. Choice **b** is incorrect because this is the difference in cost, not the percent increase. Choice **c** is incorrect because this is the percent increase from May to June. Choice **d** is incorrect because this is the percent increase from June to August.

47. b. Choice **b** is correct because $\frac{7}{21} \times 100\%$ is approximately 33%. Choice **a** is incorrect because this is the percentage received by freshmen. Choice **c** is incorrect because this is the percentage received by seniors. Choice **d** is incorrect because this is the percentage received by sophomores.

48. a. Choice **a** is correct because there were 17 given in 2010 and 21 given in 2012, for a difference of 4. Choice **b** is incorrect because this is the change from 2011 to 2012. Choice **c** is incorrect because you did not subtract the number given in 2010 from the number given in 2012. Choice **d** is incorrect because this is the number given in 2010—you need to subtract this from the number given in 2012.

49. d. Choice **d** is correct because lab 4 uses 11 reams of paper, which is the most of any lab. Choice **a** is incorrect because this lab uses the least amount of paper. Choice **b** is incorrect because lab 4 uses 1 ream more than lab 2. Choice **c** is incorrect because both labs 2 and 4 use more paper than lab 3.

50. a. Choice **a** is correct because this lab only used 2 reams of color paper, the least amount of all four labs listed. Choice **b** is incorrect because this lab used 5 reams of color paper, which is more than labs 1 and 3. Choice **c** is incorrect because this lab used 3 reams of color paper, which is more than lab 1. Choice **d** is incorrect because this lab used more color paper than any of the other three labs.

Ability

1. a. Because the pattern is to add $1\frac{1}{2}$ to the previous term. Doing so here yields $5\frac{3}{4} + 1\frac{1}{2} = 7\frac{1}{4}$. Choice **b** is incorrect because you did not add the whole parts. Choice **c** is incorrect because the whole part is incorrect. Choice **d** is incorrect because the fractional part is incorrect.

2. c. Choice **c** is correct because the pattern used to generate the sequence is to add $\frac{2}{5}$ to get the second term, $\frac{4}{5}$ to get the third term, $\frac{6}{5}$ to get the fourth term, and so on. Choice **a** is incorrect because you should have added $\frac{8}{5}$, not $\frac{4}{5}$, to $\frac{19}{5}$ to get the next term. Choice **b** is incorrect because you added $\frac{6}{5}$, not $\frac{8}{5}$, to $\frac{19}{5}$. Choice **d** is incorrect because you skipped a term. This would be the sixth term of the sequence.

3. a. Choice **a** is correct because the pattern is to subtract $2\frac{5}{8}$ from the previous term to get the next one. Choice **b** is incorrect because you subtracted 2, not $2\frac{5}{8}$, from the previous term to get the next one. Choice **c** is incorrect because the terms are each off by 1. Choice **d** is incorrect because the terms are each off by 1, and their order should be switched.

4. c. Choice **c** is correct because the pattern is to multiply the previous term by 0.2 to get the next one. Doing so here yields $0.32(0.2) = 0.064$. Choice **a** is incorrect because the decimal point is in the wrong location. Choice **b** is incorrect because the decimal point is in the wrong location. Choice **d** is incorrect because the decimal point is in the wrong location.

5. a. Choice **a** is correct because the pattern is to multiply the previous term by 3 to get the next one. Choice **b** is incorrect because you skipped a term. Choice **c** is incorrect because you multiplied the wrong number by 3. Choice **d** is incorrect because you multiplied the numerator and the denominator—you should have only multiplied the numerator by 3.

6. b. Choice **b** is correct because the terms of the sequence are interlaced. For the first, third, fifth, . . . terms, you add 1.8 to get the next term; for the second, fourth, sixth, . . . terms, you subtract 0.10. Choice **a** is incorrect because the terms are written in the wrong order. Choice **c** is incorrect because the second term is fine, but the first term listed is incorrect—you skipped over a term in the sequence to get it. Choice **d** is incorrect because the first term is fine, but the second term listed is incorrect—you skipped over a term in the sequence to get it.

7. c. Choice **c** is correct because the terms of the sequence are interlaced. For the first, third, fifth, . . . terms, you subtract 2.2 to get the next term; for the second, fourth, sixth, . . . terms, you add $1\frac{1}{2}$. Choice **a** is incorrect because the terms are written in the wrong order. Choice **b** is incorrect because you did not apply the correct pattern to generate the terms. Choice **d** is incorrect because these are the two terms after those being asked for.

8. d. Choice **d** is correct because the pattern is to add L to the previous term to get the next one. Choice **a** is incorrect because the second term is correct, but the first one is not. Choice **b** is incorrect because the second term is off by I, and the two terms are written in the wrong order. Choice **c** is incorrect because you skipped over a term of the sequence.

9. a. Choice **a** is correct because the pattern is that you add 10.75 to the previous term to get the next one. Choice **b** is incorrect because you added 10.25, not 10.75, to the previous term. Choice **c** is incorrect because you skipped a term; this is the one after the term being asked for. Choice **d** is incorrect because you added 10, not 10.75, to the previous term.

10. a. Choice **a** is correct because the terms of the sequence are interlaced. For the first, third, fifth, . . . terms, you subtract 16 to get the next term; for the second, fourth, sixth, . . . terms, you add 10. Choice **b** is incorrect because you subtracted 16 from the wrong number in the sequence. Choice **c** is incorrect because you added 10, but should have subtracted 16 to get this term. Choice **d** is incorrect because you skipped a term.

11. d. Choice **d** is correct because the terms of the sequence are interlaced. For the first, third, fifth, . . . terms, you subtract 5 to get the next term; for the second, fourth, sixth, . . . terms, you add 2. Choice **a** is incorrect because 30 should be 34. Choice **b** is incorrect because the first term is wrong (you subtracted 5 from 35, not 37). Choice **c** is incorrect because the terms are written in the wrong order.

12. b. Choice **b** is correct because the terms of the sequence are interlaced. For the first, third, fifth, . . . terms, you subtract X to get the next term; for the second, fourth, sixth, . . . terms, you divide by 2. Choice **a** is incorrect because you skipped over two terms of the sequence. Choice **c** is incorrect because the second term is wrong. Choice **d** is incorrect because the order of the terms is incorrect.

13. b. Choice **b** is correct because the pattern is to add X to the first term to get the second, XV to the second to get the third, XX to the third to get the fourth, and so on. To get the missing term, you need to add XXX to the previous term. Choice **a** is incorrect because you added XV, not XXX, to the previous term. Choice **c** is incorrect because you only added XX, not XXX. Choice **d** is incorrect because you skipped a term.

14. b. Choice **b** is correct because the pattern is to subtract 50 to go from the first term to the second, subtract 100 to go from the second to the third, subtract 150 to go from the third to the fourth, and so on. Choice **a** is incorrect because you reversed the pattern. Choice **c** is incorrect because you subtracted 150 each time, but should have subtracted 200 and then 250 to get the two terms, respectively. Choice **d** is incorrect because the terms are written in the wrong order.

15. b. Choice **b** is correct because there are four internal line segments, and they are parallel to the shorter side. Choice **a** is incorrect because the internal line segments are parallel to the wrong side—they should be parallel to the shorter side. Choice **c** is incorrect because the internal line segments should be parallel to the shorter side. Choice **d** is incorrect because the number of internal line segments is too small. Choice **e** is incorrect because the number of internal line segments is too small.

16. d. Choice **d** is correct because this figure is just a rotation of those given, which is correct. Choice **a** is incorrect because the internal line segment should be diagonal, not parallel to one of the sides. Choice **b** is incorrect because the internal dot is misplaced. Choice **c** is incorrect because there are too many internal line segments. Choice **e** is incorrect because there are too many internal dots.

17. e. Choice **e** is correct because the number of parts into which the figure is divided is correct, and one of them is shaded. Choice **a** is incorrect because there are too many shaded portions. Choice **b** is incorrect because there should be one portion shaded. Choice **c** is incorrect because there are too many shaded portions. Choice **d** is incorrect because the figure has been subdivided into too many parts.

18. a. Choice **a** is correct because the correct parts are shaded and in the same direction. Choice **b** is incorrect because the wrong portion is shaded. Choice **c** is incorrect because the correct portions are shaded, but not all in the same direction. Choice **d** is incorrect because the square should not be shaded. Choice **e** is incorrect because the triangles should be shaded and in the same direction.

19. e. Choice **e** is correct because this figure has 5 sides, like the others. Choice **a** is incorrect because this figure has 6 sides, not 5 like the others. Choice **b** is incorrect because this figure has 4 sides, not 5 like the others. Choice **c** is incorrect because this figure has 6 sides, not 5 like the others. Choice **d** is incorrect because this figure has 6 sides, not 5 like the others.

20. c. Choice **c** is correct because the figure has been rotated correctly in the sense that the circle is shaded and in the correct direction. Choice **a** is incorrect because the wrong circle is shaded. Choice **b** is incorrect because the circle is shaded in the wrong direction. Choice **d** is incorrect because the circle needs to be shaded. Choice **e** is incorrect because only one of the circles should have been shaded.

21. a. Choice **a** is correct because the figure is comprised of two bold curves, 2 bold line segments, and 1 non-bold line segment. Choice **b** is incorrect because there are no bold line segments. Choice **c** is incorrect because there are no bold curves. Choice **d** is incorrect because there are too few bold curves and line segments. Choice **e** is incorrect because one of the segments should not be in bold.

22. c. Choice **c** is correct because the shape inside is different from the surrounding shape, and nothing is shaded—just like those listed. Choice **a** is incorrect because the shape inside is the same as the surrounding shape, unlike those listed. Choice **b** is incorrect because the shape inside is the same as the surrounding shape, unlike those listed. Choice **d** is incorrect because while the shape inside is different from the surrounding one, it is shaded, which is not a characteristic in common with those given. Choice **e** is incorrect because while the shape inside is different from the surrounding one, the part outside of it, but within the outer figure, is shaded, which is not a characteristic in common with those given.

23. b. Choice **b** is correct because there are two pairs of parallel dotted and solid lines, and one pair is perpendicular to the other pair. Choice **a** is incorrect because a pair of bold and dotted segments should be perpendicular to the other pair. Choice **c** is incorrect because a pair of bold and dotted segments should be perpendicular to the other pair. Choice **d** is incorrect because there are no bold segments internal to the figure, unlike those given. Choice **e** is incorrect because there are too few internal line segments.

24. e. Choice **e** is correct because the internal shape is a rectangle, it is shaded, and it shares an edge with the triangle, just as in those given. Choice **a** is incorrect because the internal rectangle is not shaded. Choice **b** is incorrect because the rectangle should share an edge with the outer triangle. Choice **c** is incorrect because the shaded shape inside should be a rectangle, not a circle. Choice **d** is incorrect because the shaded shape inside should be a rectangle, not a triangle.

25. e. Choice **e** is correct because the figure is divided into 5 equal-sized parts (and the number of parts equals the number of sides, just as with those figures given). Choice **a** is incorrect because this figure should be divided into 4 parts, not 2. Choice **b** is incorrect because this figure should be divided into 4 parts, not 3. Choice **c** is incorrect because the figure should be divided into 3 parts, not 4 as shown. Choice **d** is incorrect because this figure should be divided into 8 parts, not 4.

26. e. Choice **e** is correct because the inner shape is correct and is shaded. Choice **a** is incorrect because the outer shape is wrong. Choice **b** is incorrect because there is no inner shape, and the shading is wrong. Choice **c** is incorrect because the inner shape is wrong. Choice **d** is incorrect because the inner shape should be shaded.

27. b. Choice **b** is correct because the shapes are both correct and the correct portion is shaded. Choice **a** is incorrect because the inner triangle should be composed of solid lines, not dotted ones. Choice **c** is incorrect because the outer square should be dotted. Choice **d** is incorrect because the inner triangle should be composed of solid lines, not dotted ones, and the region surrounding the triangle is shaded. Choice **e** is incorrect because the region surrounding the triangle should be shaded.

28. c. Choice **c** is correct because the shapes are both correct, and the correct region is shaded. Choice **a** is incorrect because the region surrounding the circle should be shaded. Choice **b** is incorrect because the wrong region is shaded. Choice **d** is incorrect because the two shapes should be swapped. Choice **e** is incorrect because the inner shape is incorrect.

29. a. Choice **a** is correct because the original figure was rotated by a proper amount, and the size of the figure remained the same. Choice **b** is incorrect because the original figure was rotated in the wrong direction. Choice **c** is incorrect because the original figure was rotated by the wrong amount. Choice **d** is incorrect because the original figure was rotated by the wrong amount, and shrunk in size. Choice **e** is incorrect because the original figure was rotated by the wrong amount, and shrunk in size.

30. e. Choice **e** is correct because the figure has increased in size and has been reflected over the long edge (so that it would be written backward). Choice **a** is incorrect because the figure should be larger, and it should have been reflected over the long edge (so that it would be written backward). Choice **b** is incorrect because the figure should be larger. Choice **c** is incorrect because the figure should be larger and comprised of solid lines/curves, not dotted ones. Choice **d** is incorrect because the figure should be reflected over the long edge (so that it would be written backward).

31. a. Choice **a** is correct because all three shapes are correct, and the correct portion is shaded. Choice **b** is incorrect because there is no shading within the figure. Choice **c** is incorrect because the wrong portion is shaded. Choice **d** is incorrect because the outermost portion should not be shaded. Choice **e** is incorrect because the portion outside the square, but within the triangle, should not be shaded.

32. b. Choice **b** is correct because the outer shape is correct, the figure inside the circle has been flipped, and the inside of the circle has been shaded. Choice **a** is incorrect because the inside of the circle has not been shaded. Choice **c** is incorrect because the outer shape should be a circle. Choice **d** is incorrect because the outer shape and corresponding shading are both absent. Choice **e** is incorrect because the outer shape should be a circle and the figure inside should have been flipped.

33. d. Choice **d** is correct because the correct portion is shaded, and the internal line segment from the unshaded portion appropriately removed. Choice **a** is incorrect because the wrong internal line segment was removed; the unshaded portion should not have any internal line segments and the shaded one should have retained them. Choice **b** is incorrect because the partition lines within the figure are missing and there is too much shading. Choice **c** is incorrect because the wrong portion of the figure is shaded and the top partition line hasn't been removed. Choice **e** is incorrect because the wrong portion is shaded.

34. e. Choice **e** is correct because the internal lines and shading have all been removed. Choice **a** is incorrect because both the internal lines and shading should have been removed. Choice **b** is incorrect because there should be no shading. Choice **c** is incorrect because the internal line segments should not be there. Choice **d** is incorrect because both the internal lines and shading should have been removed.

35. c. Choice **c** is correct because the shapes and shading are both correct. Choice **a** is incorrect because the shading is missing. Choice **b** is incorrect because the wrong portion is shaded. Choice **d** is incorrect because the shapes are reversed. Choice **e** is incorrect because the shapes are reversed and the wrong portion has been shaded.

36. d. Choice **d** is correct because the two squares on the right are smaller than the one on the left, and they are both outside the larger one. Choice **a** is incorrect because both smaller squares should be outside the larger one. Choice **b** is incorrect because there should be two smaller squares outside the larger one. Choice **c** is incorrect because the two squares on the right side should be smaller. Choice **e** is incorrect because the smaller squares should both occur outside the larger one.

37. b. Choice **b** is correct because the shading and placement of the internal line segments is correct. Choice **a** is incorrect because the shading is missing, and the diagonal line is misplaced. Choice **c** is incorrect because there should not be two diagonal line segments present. Choice **d** is incorrect because the figure is missing the two diagonal line segments and the shading is misplaced. Choice **e** is incorrect because too much of the figure is shaded.

38. a. Choice **a** is correct because the number and placement of the holes is correct. Choice **b** is incorrect because there should be two holes, not three—the one closest to the fold should not be present. Choice **c** is incorrect because both holes are too close to the fold. Choice **d** is incorrect because the hole above the fold is missing. Choice **e** is incorrect because the hole below the fold is missing.

39. c. Choice **c** is correct because the number and placement of the holes on both sides of the fold is correct. Choice **a** is incorrect because the holes below the fold are missing. Choice **b** is incorrect because the holes above the fold are missing. Choice **d** is incorrect because the holes above the fold are too far from the fold. Choice **e** is incorrect because both sets of holes (above and below the fold) are too far from the fold.

40. e. Choice **e** is correct because the number and placement of the holes on both sides of the fold is correct. Choice **a** is incorrect because the two outermost holes above the fold should be further away from the fold. Choice **b** is incorrect because there is one too few holes—the one closest to the fold below it should have a matching hole above the fold. Choice **c** is incorrect because the holes below the fold are missing. Choice **d** is incorrect because the holes above the fold are missing.

41. d. Choice **d** is correct because the number and placement of all holes on both sides of the fold is correct. Choice **a** is incorrect because the holes all appear along the wrong edge of the paper. Choice **b** is incorrect because the holes below the fold are missing. Choice **c** is incorrect because the holes below the fold are missing, and the holess above the fold appear along the wrong edge. Choice **e** is incorrect because the two holes above the fold occur along the wrong edge.

42. a. Choice **a** is correct because the number and placement of all holes on both sides of the fold is correct. Choice **b** is incorrect because this alignment of holes does not result from this particular fold. Choice **c** is incorrect because the holes on the left side of the fold are missing. Choice **d** is incorrect because the holes on the left side of the fold should be closer to the fold. Choice **e** is incorrect because the holes on the right side of the fold are missing.

43. c. Choice **c** is correct because the number and placement of all holes on both sides of the fold is correct. Choice **a** is incorrect because the holes on the left side of the fold are missing. Choice **b** is incorrect because the holes on the right side of the fold are missing. Choice **d** is incorrect because the holes on the left side should appear diagonally, not in a column. Choice **e** is incorrect because the holes on both sides of the fold should appear diagonally, not in columns.

44. b. Choice **b** is correct because the number and placement of all holes on both sides of the fold is correct. Choice **a** is incorrect because the holes on the left side of the fold are too far from the fold. Choice **c** is incorrect because the holes on the left side of the fold should appear in a column rather than diagonally. Choice **d** is incorrect because the holes on the right side are missing. Choice **e** is incorrect because the holes on the right side are missing.

45. a. Choice **a** is correct because the number and placement of all holes on both sides of the fold is correct. Choice **b** is incorrect because the hole below the fold is missing. Choice **c** is incorrect because there is one hole too many. Choice **d** is incorrect because the hole beneath the fold is too close to the fold. Choice **e** is incorrect because both holes are too close to the fold.

46. a. Choice **a** is correct because the number and placement of all holes on both sides of the fold is correct. Choice **b** is incorrect because the holes beneath the fold are missing. Choice **c** is incorrect because the holes along the right edge should be slightly lower in comparison to each of the pairs along the left edge. Choice **d** is incorrect because this is a mirror image of where the holes ought to be. Choice **e** is incorrect because all the holes are aligned incorrectly and along the wrong edges.

47. c. Choice **c** is correct because the number and placement of all holes on both sides of the fold is correct. Choice **a** is incorrect because the holes beneath the fold are missing. Choice **b** is incorrect because the holes beneath the fold are not oriented correctly. Choice **d** is incorrect because the holes should be along the same edge, not in opposite corners. Choice **e** is incorrect because the holes should not all be on the same side of the fold.

48. e. Choice **e** is correct because the number and placement of all holes on all sides of the folds is correct. Choice **a** is incorrect because the holes above the horizontal fold are missing. Choice **b** is incorrect because the holes above the horizontal fold are too far from the fold. Choice **c** is incorrect because the holes to the left of the vertical fold are missing. Choice **d** is incorrect because the holes along the diagonal near the center of both folds are missing.

49. b. Choice **b** is correct because the number and placement of the holes on all sides of the folds is correct. Choice **a** is incorrect because the holes above the horizontal fold are missing. Choice **c** is incorrect because the holes to the left of the vertical fold are missing. Choice **d** is incorrect because the holes in the other two corners are missing. Choice **e** is incorrect because the holes to the right of the vertical fold are missing.

50. d. Choice **d** is correct because the number and placement of all holes along all folds is correct. Choice **a** is incorrect because the alignment of the holes across both folds is incorrect. Choice **b** is incorrect because the holes above the horizontal fold are missing. Choice **c** is incorrect because the holes to the left of the vertical fold are missing. Choice **e** is incorrect because the holes are missing in the empty squares.

Scoring

Find out how you did on this practice exam by counting the number of questions you got right in each part. Remember, questions you skipped or got wrong don't count against your score—only the number of correct answers is important. Then divide the number you got right by the number of questions in the section:

Reading: Part 1

_____ correct divided by 20 = _____%

Reading: Part 2

_____ correct divided by 30 = _____%

Language

_____ correct divided by 50 = _____%

Math

_____ correct divided by 50 = _____%

Ability

_____ correct divided by 50 = _____%

This percentage score is not the same kind of score you will receive when you take the real TACHS. But you can use your percentage score to:

- compare your score on the first practice exam and see where you've improved
- find out where you still have areas of weakness, so you can study those areas more thoroughly

Note which parts of the exam gave you the most trouble and concentrate your study on those parts.

The key to success in almost any pursuit is to prepare for all you're worth. By taking the practice exams in this book, you've made yourself better prepared than many of the other students taking the exam with you. You've diagnosed where your strengths and weaknesses lie and learned how to deal with the various kinds of questions that will appear on the test. So go into the exam with confidence, knowing that you're ready and equipped to do your best.

ADDITIONAL ONLINE PRACTICE

Whether you need help building basic skills or preparing for an exam, visit the LearningExpress Practice Center! Using the code below, you'll be able to access additional Catholic High School Entrance Exams online practice exams. This online practice will also provide you with:

Immediate Scoring
Detailed answer explanations
Personalized recommendations for further practice and study

Log in to the LearningExpress Practice Center by using the URL: **www.learnatest.com/practice**

This is your Access Code: **9339**

Follow the steps online to redeem your access code. After you've used your access code to register with the site, you will be prompted to create a username and password. For easy reference, record them here:

Username: _____ **Password:** _____

With your username and password, you can log in and access your additional practice materials. If you have any questions or problems, please contact LearningExpress customer service at 1-800-295-9556 ext. 2, or e-mail us at **customerservice@learningexpressllc.com.**